Teaching the Chi...

Psychological and Pedagogical Perspectives

David A. Watkins & John B. Biggs
Editors

First published 2001
First reprint 2009 by

Comparative Education Research Centre
Faculty of Education
The University of Hong Kong
Pokfulam Road
Hong Kong, China

and

The Australian Council for Educational Research Ltd
19 Prospect Hill Road
Private Bag 55
Camberwell, Melbourne
Victoria 3124
Australia

Copyright © CERC and ACER

All rights reserved. No part of this publication may be reproduced, stored in a retrieval system or transmitted in any form or by any means, electronic, mechanical, photocopying, recording or otherwise, without the written permission of the publisher.

ISBN 10: 962 8093 72 X
ISBN 13: 978 962 8093 72 4

Contents

	Page
Setting the Scene	
1. The Paradox of the Chinese Learner and Beyond *David A. Watkins and John B. Biggs*	3
Teacher Thinking	
2. Towards a Model of Teaching Conceptions of Chinese Secondary School Teachers of Physics *Gao Lingbiao and David A. Watkins*	27
3. The Role of Assessment in Student Learning: The Views of Hong Kong and Swedish Lecturers *Bo Dahlin, David A. Watkins and Mats Ekholm*	47
Teacher Practice	
4. Teacher-Student Interaction: Attributional Implications and Effectiveness of Teachers' Evaluative Feedback *Farideh Salili*	77
5. Are Chinese Teachers Authoritarian? *Irene T. Ho*	99
6. Large Classes in China: 'Good' Teachers and Interaction *Martin Cortazzi and Jin Lixian*	115
7. Two Faces of the Reed Relay: Exploring the Effects of the Medium of Instruction *Dorothy F.P. Ng, Amy B.M. Tsui and Ference Marton*	135
8. Solving the Paradox of the Chinese Teacher? *Ida Mok, P.M. Chik, P.Y. Ko, Tammy Kwan, M.L. Lo, Ference Marton, Dorothy F.P. Ng, M.F. Pang, U. Runesson and L.H. Szeto*	161

9. Promoting Learning and Understanding through Constructivist   181
    Approaches for Chinese Learners
    Carol K.K. Chan

10. Problem-Based Learning in a Chinese Context: Faculty Perceptions   205
    Stephanie F. Stokes

Changing Teachers

11. The Influence of Teacher Education on Conceptions of Teaching   221
    and Learning
    Thomas K.W. Tang

12. A Conceptual Change Approach to University Staff Development   239
    Angela S.P. Ho

13. Transforming Teaching through Action Research   255
    David Kember

Overview and Conclusions

14. Insights into Teaching the Chinese Learner   277
    John B. Biggs and David A. Watkins

About the Authors   301

Index   305

Preface

In *The Chinese Learner*, we compiled studies based on a variety of methodologies, quantitative and qualitative, emic and etic. Out of that emerged a picture of students who were learning rather more effectively than they "should" have been, given what Western research predicted to be counter-productive teaching/learning environments. Part of the answer to that paradox we found to lie in global factors in the Confucian heritage culture: beliefs about memorisation and understanding, socialisation practices, attribution for success and failure, high values accorded to education, and so on.

But that answer still leaves unanswered much more specific questions about the context. And it is the context that is the focus of the present book, *Teaching the Chinese Learner*. First, a word about the title. We oscillated between the present title, and *Teaching Chinese Learners*, which some saw as more immediate and concrete. However this is not a handbook on teaching, which the other title might convey, but a distillation from research *about* teaching in some Confucian heritage cultures. We have concentrated on classrooms in Mainland China and in Hong Kong, with some comparative reference to Australians and Swedes in their own classrooms, and a conceptual framework based on student learning research.

We are greatly indebted to Fanny Wong, of the Department of Education at the University of Hong Kong, who has as usual done a magnificent job with the original preparation and formatting of the manuscript and to Emily Mang, for then taking charge of the manuscript on the production side so competently.

David A. Watkins and John B. Biggs

August 2001

SETTING THE SCENE

1

The Paradox of the Chinese Learner and Beyond

David A. Watkins and John B. Biggs

In the concluding chapter of our edited book, *The Chinese Learner* (Watkins & Biggs, 1996), we pointed to a number of accepted principles of Western educational psychology that, according to research reported in that book and elsewhere, did not appear to transfer easily to the Chinese learner. The result is that Chinese learners are commonly misunderstood by Westerners.

At the centre of these Western misconceptions is the so-called "paradox of the Chinese learner". There are two aspects to this paradox:

1. Students from Confucian-heritage cultures (CHC) such as China, Hong Kong, Taiwan, Singapore, Korea and Japan, are taught in classroom conditions that in terms of Western standards cannot be conducive to good learning: large classes, expository methods, relentless norm-referenced assessment, and harsh classroom climate. Yet CHC students out-perform Western students, at least in science and mathematics, and have deeper, meaning-oriented, approaches to learning.
2. A particular aspect of this paradox is the relationship between memorising and understanding. CHC students are perceived as passive rote learners, yet show high levels of understanding.

In *The Chinese Learner* we addressed the paradox from the point of view of the learner and the culture of learning. But we still have to explain how it is that CHC teachers, working with class sizes that would be simply unmanageable in the West, and where drilling for external examinations is the norm, can still produce these very positive results. In this book, we address the paradox from the point of view of the teacher and the culture of teaching. This "paradox of the Chinese teacher" goes something like this:

1. Given that teachers in Confucian-heritage cultures operate under substandard classroom conditions in terms of Western standards, and that CHC students perform so well, how do these teachers do it? How can teachers engage students in productive learning activities when they teach large numbers at a time, in an expository manner, in which the students' role is essentially passive? Do students learn in spite of, or because of, the way teachers operate in their classrooms?

2. A particular aspect of this paradox is "vernacular Confucianism" (Chang, 2000), those common beliefs about the nature of teaching and learning that are held by Chinese teachers, parents, and students. These include beliefs such as the following: "children are spoiled if praised", "scolding builds character", "failure is the result of laziness", and "no pain, no gain", all of which run counter to the sort of optimal learning climate indicated by Western research and theory. We shall be meeting many of these beliefs in forthcoming pages.

In *The Chinese Learner* we saw many examples of differences in perception and interpretation of educational issues between East and West that lay in the culture rather than in the classroom. In the present book, we move from the culture in general to the teaching culture as it is represented inside the classroom, and even inside the heads of the teachers and students. But before embarking on that intimate journey, let us address a geographical problem.

Where is the Chinese Learner to be Found?

Chang (2000) remarks that researching the Chinese people has become "the flavour of the month", amongst Western cross-cultural researchers (p.125). Unfortunately, she says, they "find 'Chineseness' in all the wrong places"; it is defined demographically, as an independent variable, while Western derived instruments provide the dependent variables. Thus, Chineseness is in effect defined in terms of deviance from Western norms, and generally as being interestingly different from the world defined by and constructed within mainstream, that is Western, psychology.

The "right places" are where the Chinese identify themselves as being Chinese in places where they normally exist, in classrooms not in laboratories, and who describe themselves using constructs contextualised within their community. Chang refers to such constructs as involving "vernacular Confucianism", that is Confucianism as it may be relevant and interpreted by ordinary Chinese people today. Thus, there is a sense in which Lee Kuan Yew can call Singapore a "Confucian" society, when many of its values are far indeed from what Confucius would even recognise, let alone endorse. In *The Chinese Learner*, Lee (1996) described many educational Confucian values deriving from the *Analects*, yet these are hard to square with the vernacular Confucianism espoused by many Hong Kong teachers today, as described by Salili and by Ho in Chapters 4 and 5 below. We have noted some of these beliefs already, such as "no pain, no gain", "scolding builds character", "failure is the result of laziness". They stem if anywhere from the grim Xun Zi, rather than from the constructivist Confucius described by Lee. But the point is not to which current beliefs about the raising and educating of children can be attributed to what ancient scholars, but the fact itself that these beliefs are current today, within the focus culture, and that they influence what teachers do in present day classrooms.

All this implies that the study of the Chinese is to be done *in situ*, using constructs deriving from the focus culture (Chang, 2000). Yang (2000) in reacting to Chang's article says that the drive to globalise universities and knowledge, and the methods now of funding departments and appointing and promoting individuals, has meant that young psychologists in places like Hong Kong are forced to do the sort of research that is publishable in mainstream, international journals. They must use constructs familiar to the reviewers of their papers. If they took Chang's admonitions seriously, "we should make our academic careers very short" (p.157).

If Yang is right, it would be the death of indigenous psychology. Possibly this book is a part answer to her, published internationally as it is. Chang also asks who is to do the research. Does it have to be by Chinese themselves? Not necessarily, and in fact there is a case for arguing that outsiders to a culture may better perceive what is figure and what is ground than insiders (Chang, 2000).

The chapters comprising this book score well on these issues. The authors here are looking inside school and university classrooms in Mainland China and in Hong Kong. They are also variously "insiders" to their focus context (Chan, I. Ho, A. Ho, Tang), "outsiders" (Stokes, Salili, Kember), and frequently both (Gao & Watkins, Cortazzi & Jin, Marton and many colleagues). And while it is true that sometimes Western derived instruments have been used, they are triangulated with "bottom up" and qualitative data.

This book is then more focused than its predecessor, and more emic in flavour. Here, we are trying to understand this process of teaching the Chinese learner precisely where that process is taking place, in terms of constructs that work out to be most helpful, whether those constructs are indigenous or prompted from prototypes that might already exist in the literature.

Culture and the Chinese learner

In *The Chinese Learner* (Watkins & Biggs, 1996) we described several positive features in the general culture, outside the classroom, that are conducive to academic learning. These can be grouped into six categories, as follows.

Memorising and understanding

One aspect of the paradox of the Chinese learner is based on the following premises: rote learning (memorising without understanding) is known to lead to poor learning outcomes; most Chinese students are rote learners; therefore Chinese students should perform badly academically. But as we have seen, that is not the case, as shown for example when comparing across countries is the studies of the International Association for the Evaluation of Educational Achievement (IEA) (Beaton et al., 1996a, 1996b; Stevenson & Stigler, 1992), or as international students at Western universities (see also Stevenson & Lee, 1996). An additional question in this paradox is why Chinese students typically appear to Western teachers to be rote learners when their responses to learning strategy questionnaires indicate quite the contrary. Research reported in *The*

Chinese Learner suggested that the explanation lay in cultural differences in the perception of the relationship between memorising and understanding.

While Western education had in the past depended on rote learning, educators today reject such learning. In doing so, many have failed to draw a distinction between *rote* learning, that is, memorising "without thought of understanding" (*Oxford English Dictionary*), and *repetitive* learning, that is learning in order to enhance future recall alongside understanding. Memorising without understanding undoubtedly leads to very limited learning outcomes, but many Western teachers mistakenly assume that when Chinese students memorise, they are rote learning at the expense of understanding. In fact, Chinese students frequently learn repetitively, both to ensure retention *and* to enhance understanding. Various chapters of *The Chinese Learner* and elsewhere reported that, on the basis of both questionnaire and in-depth interview data with teachers and students in Hong Kong and China, many of the teachers and better students do not see memorising and understanding as separate but rather as interlocking processes, and that high quality learning outcomes usually require both processes, as complementary to each other (Biggs, 1996; Kember, 1996; Marton, Tse & Dall'Alba, 1996; Marton, Watkins & Tang, 1997; Watkins, 1996a). This then was the solution to that part of the paradox. Chinese students were observed correctly as making great use of memorisation, but were not necessarily rote learning, as their Western teachers supposed. Many students actually develop their understanding through the process of memorisation.

This theme was taken up by Dahlin & Watkins (2000). Through in-depth interviews with Western international school and Chinese system secondary school students in Hong Kong, they showed that Chinese students, unlike their Western counterparts, used repetition for two different purposes. On the one hand it was associated with creating a "deep impression" and thence with memorisation, but on the other it was used to deepen or develop understanding by discovering new meaning. The Western students on the other hand tended to use repetition only to check that they had really remembered something. This finding was consistent with another cross-cultural difference identified by Dahlin & Watkins (2000). Whereas Western students saw understanding as usually a process of sudden insight, Chinese students typically thought of understanding as a long process that required considerable mental effort.

Effort versus ability attributions

Viewed in the above light, the frequent finding that Chinese students are more likely to attribute academic success primarily to effort, rather than to both effort and ability as do Western students (Salili, 1996), makes more sense. If acquiring understanding is not a sudden, insightful process, but a slow process requiring much hard work, effort attribution for academic success seems logical. Indeed, to many Chinese students, teachers, and parents, intelligence itself is not something innate and relatively fixed but rather something that can be improved by hard work. So to a Chinese, future success is in your own hands. If you believe that effort leads to success, you will achieve more, and be less devastated by failure, than if you believe that ability is the key to success. The downside however is that when the task is perceived as too difficult, pressure to increase effort yet further may lead to the ultimate snapping point. As noted in an editorial of the *South China Morning Post* (5 January 1993):

> In the 1991/92 academic year alone, there were 21 student suicides, aged from 10 to 18.... High academic demands and heavy homework schedules are thought to take their toll not only on the less able, but also on the brighter children expected to do well under all circumstances.

Intrinsic versus extrinsic motivation

Other Western dichotomies that do not seem to travel to the Orient are related to the construct of motivation. Western psychology books typically treat intrinsic and extrinsic motivation as mutually exclusive, with intrinsic considered the more desirable by Western educators: "To offer a prize for doing a deed is tantamount to saying that the deed is not worth doing for its own sake" (Neill, 1960: p.162). Contrast this with the Chinese saying that "there are golden houses and beautiful girls in books" (see Lee, 1996: p.37). For Western students intrinsic motivation is an antecedent of the desired deep learning strategies where the intention is to understand what is being learned (Biggs, 1987), but for Chinese students the adoption of deep strategies may be activated by "a head of mixed motivational steam: personal ambition, family face, peer support, material reward, and, yes, possibly even interest" (Biggs & Watkins, 1996: p.273).

General patterns of socialisation

Then, within Confucian heritage culture itself, "internal dispositions (that) create a sense of diligence and receptiveness" (Hess & Azuma, 1991: p.7) are cultivated, so that children tend to be brought up to be respectful to adults, to spend a long time on essentially uninteresting tasks, to conform to group norms. These things create that "sense of diligence and receptiveness" that is precisely what is required by teachers in schools anywhere. In the West, however, these dispositions to learn are not cultivated so assiduously, hence the reliance in school on intrinsic and extrinsic motivation. In short, Chinese, Korean and Japanese children are groomed for the demands of schooling before they get there, in a way that Western children usually are not.

Achievement motivation: ego versus social

It has long been recognised that another mainstay of Western educational psychology, achievement motivation, also seems to take a different form in Confucian heritage and other non-Western cultures. In Western societies, achievement motivation is highly individualistic and ego-enhancing, characterised by individual competition, where winning is its own reward (Atkinson, 1964). But in East Asian societies the notion of success needs to be reinterpreted in a collectivist framework, which may involve significant others, the family, peers, or even society as a whole (see also Holloway, 1988). In Hong Kong, it may involve individual ambition but it also involves family, so that the pressure to succeed academically is there for all children, irrespective of the parent's educational level, and failure has a high cost, in terms of family face (Ho, 1993; Salili, 1996).

Collective versus individual orientation

The above discussion is linked to the dimension of Individualism-Collectivism which has been widely used in cross-cultural psychology to explain differences between cultural groups if not without controversy (Hofstede, 1980; Kim et al., 1994). Countries of the non-Western world are typically characterised as being collectivist in nature, placing more emphasis on the group rather than the individual good.

The relationships between student and teacher, and student and student, seem to take on a somewhat different character in collectivist East Asia. Thus, peer tutoring works well in Hong Kong schools (Winter, 1995); Hong Kong students spontaneously collaborate to study outside the tertiary classroom more than do Western students (Tang, 1996); classrooms in Japan and China are characterised by high levels of support and lack of teasing of weaker students (Jin & Cortazzi, 1998); and Hong Kong students prefer a more collaborative learning environment which they see as promoting deeper learning strategies (Chan & Watkins, 1994).

These then are some of the learning-related factors we found outside the classroom. Our next step is to move our focus inside, because that is where we shall find some clues as to the paradox of the Chinese teacher. Let us look first at the thinking that drives teaching.

Conceptions of Learning and Teaching

Much of the research in *The Chinese Learner* was based on the theoretical stance which has become known as the Student Approaches to Learning (SAL) paradigm (Biggs, 1987, 1993; Entwistle & Ramsden, 1983). SAL emphasises that to be understood properly, learning needs to be viewed from the perspective of the learner not the researcher. The starting point was the classic study by Marton & Säljö (1976), in which two different ways that Swedish students went about reading an academic article were identified. Some tried to comprehend the message the passage was trying to convey by focusing on the theme or main ideas. Others focused on the reading at the word or sentence level and often tried to memorise details so they could answer subsequent questions. These two qualitatively different ways of approaching reading have been shown to apply to the way students learn in general in numerous studies in many cultures (see Watkins, 2001, for a review of this literature). These two approaches to learning have become known as the deep and the surface approach, respectively.

Quantitative measures have been developed to assess these two approaches to learning, and a third dimension as well, referred to as "achieving" or "strategic", in the Learning Process Questionnaire (LPQ, for secondary school populations), and the Study Process Questionnaire (SPQ) (Biggs, 1987) and the Approaches to Studying Inventory (ASI) (Entwistle & Ramsden, 1983), for tertiary populations. The construct validity of these instruments shows that they are appropriate for use with students in a number of non-Western as well as Western cultures (Watkins, 1996b), and they provide the data for several chapters in this book.

Qualitative studies in the SAL tradition have, until at least the early 1990s, focused primarily on how students conceptualise learning. The approach to research typically adopted is known as phenomenography (Marton, 1981), which can be described as the study of the qualitatively different ways in which people experience or conceptualise various phenomena. Before proceeding further we should define what we mean by the term 'conception'. A definition that seems to be consistent with the phenomenographic tradition was provided by Pratt (1992) as follows:

> Conceptions are specific meanings attached to phenomena which then mediate our response to situations involving these phenomena. We form conceptions of virtually every aspect of our perceived world, and in so doing, use those abstract representations to delimit something from, and relate it to, other aspects of our world. In effect, we view the world through the lenses of our conceptions, interpreting and acting in accordance with our understanding of the world. (p.204)

Conceptions of learning

Marton, Dall'Alba, & Beaty (1993), building on the work of Säljö (1979) & Giorgi (1986), reanalysed interviews with UK Open University students and identified the following six major conceptions of learning as espoused by these students:

A. Increasing one's knowledge;
B. Memorising and reproducing;
C. Applying;
D. Understanding;
E. Seeing things in a different way; and
F. Changing as a person.

According to Marton et al. these six conceptions are ordered in a hierarchy from least to most sophisticated, with A through C taking an essentially *quantitative* view, and D through F focusing on the constitution of meaning, where learning is viewed from a *qualitative* perspective. A similar hierarchy is reported in a number of countries, but often with culturally specific variations (Marton & Booth, 1997). One such variation is that memorising and understanding seem to be intertwined in many transcripts of interviews of Chinese teachers (Marton et al., 1996), a finding that was one important step in solving the paradox of the Chinese learner described earlier.

The nature of the gaps between steps in this hierarchy is however problematic. Marton et al. (1993) suggest a relative continuity between A to C, but a major gap to D and later categories. However, applying is often a sophisticated, meaning-oriented conception. In a later study with Hong Kong Chinese high school students (Marton et al., 1997), a two dimensional representation of the outcome space of conceptions of learning was proposed, with a temporal dimension depending on the stage of learning (from 'acquisition' to 'making use of') and a depth dimension (from 'committing words to memory' to 'understanding phenomena'). The A-F categorisation of Marton et al. (1996) was mapped against this two-dimensional model and it was proposed that there was a continuum in the 'making use of' depth dimension from 'reproducing' to 'being able to do things differently' and 'being able to do different things'.

Logically, one would expect a relationship between conceptions of learning and approaches to learning, with quantitative conceptions of learning being associated with a surface approach, and qualitative conceptions with a deep approach, but attempts to link these supposedly different constructs have not been as clearcut as we might wish. Part of the problem is that it can be difficult to unconfound such variables in phenomenographic interviews, and claims of a relationship may be an artefact of the method adopted, as Kember & Kwan (1999) point out.

Conceptions of teaching

In the teacher education literature over the last 15 years or so there has been a shift from a focus primarily on teaching skills and content knowledge to one on teacher thinking. Indeed, the idea of "teacher as a reflective practitioner" has become emphasised in teacher education around the world. The underlying philosophy behind this approach is the assumption that the way a teacher thinks about the nature of teaching and learning will influence how they teach, and thence how their students learn, and in turn the learning outcomes they achieve.

The term "conception of teaching" implies the overall view that teachers have of the process of teaching (Kember, 1997); or the unit of description used when that teacher wishes to characterise how teaching appears to him/her (Larsson, 1983). Conceptions of teaching are qualitatively different categories of teachers' descriptions about their experience of teaching, that are based on some fundamental elements (dimensions) in the teaching process (Pratt, 1992). Kember (1997) reviewed 13 studies of mainly Western university teachers and concluded that there was much commonality amongst their findings. Two broad orientations seemed to overlay these categories: teacher-centred/content-oriented and student-centred/learning-oriented. Kember further suggested that these orientations in turn had two sub-categories. He labelled these as imparting information and transmitting structured knowledge in the case of the teacher-centred orientation while for the student-centred orientation as facilitating understanding and conceptual change/intellectual development. Kember & Kwan (1999) identified a similar conceptual structure in an interview study with Hong Kong university lecturers.

Kember (1997) proposed five dimensions for studying conceptions of teaching: (a) the essence of learning and teaching, (b) the roles of student and teacher, (c) the aims and expected outcome of teaching, (d) the content of teaching, and (e) the preferred styles and approaches to teaching. He also proposed five first order conceptions (imparting information, transmitting structured knowledge, student teacher interaction/apprenticeship, facilitating understanding, and conceptual change/intellectual development) and two higher-order orientations (teacher-centred/content-oriented, and student-centred/learning-oriented).

Biggs (1999) argues that the link between the conceptions teachers hold and what they do is provided by the dominant focus of their thinking. There is probably a developmental sequence in this. When teachers commence teaching they tend to see teaching as transmitting facts and skills. Their job is to impart information, and the students' job is to receive it accurately and report back as required. It quickly becomes obvious that some students receive better than others; and the reason for that must lie in differences between students. Some are lazier than others, brighter, less motivated, less academically oriented. These student differences thus become the teacher's explanation for differences in learning outcomes. This Level 1 conception of teaching is thus a deficit model, the deficit lying in the student. Where teaching fails, it is the students' fault.

A more sophisticated conception still sees teaching as a transmission process, but of structured knowledge, rather than straight information, so that teaching skill becomes important in helping students learn this more complex information (Prosser & Trigwell, 1998). The focus here in Level 2 is on what teachers do. Good teachers are those who have an array of teaching competencies, they use IT, they plan carefully, they are good classroom managers, they do all those teacherly things that work for the system they are working within. We look at Outstanding Teachers, and reward them, and look at what they do. However Level 2 thinking is still based on a deficit model, the deficit this time lying in the teacher.

Yet focusing on what the teacher does is not the point either. The real point is that students learn, and they do so because the appropriate learning activities have been engaged. At Level 3, then, the focus is on those teaching practices that work within the context, *and that produce the desired learning outcomes*. Here the focus is not on student differences, not on being a good teacher, but on students engaging the learning processes appropriate to their acquiring what it is they are to learn. Level 3, then, coincides with Kember's higher order student-centred/learning-oriented orientation. Good teaching is defined not in terms of what teachers do, but in terms of producing high order outcomes. This is a view of teaching that transcends cultural boundaries (Biggs, 2001).

Researchers have expressed different views of the relationships between different categories of teaching conceptions. Some see conceptions as hierarchical (Biggs, 1999; Dall'Alba 1990; Martin & Balla, 1990), others do not see the more sophisticated conceptions as including the less sophisticated ones (Samuelowicz & Bain, 1992). Most researchers have preferred to organise conceptions into a linear sequence underlying which are two contrasting orientations. This reasoning led to the development of a multiple-level model shown in Figure 1.1 (Kember, 1997), which describes the interrelationships between different categories of teaching conceptions and orientations.

Figure 1.1
A multiple-level categorisation of conceptions of teaching
(After Kember, 1997: p.264)

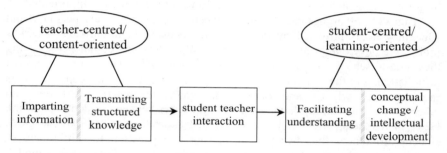

The great majority of the studies on teacher conceptions have been conducted with lecturers at Western universities. One of the aims of this book is to test whether such a model is appropriate for teachers from the Confucian heritage, and for both secondary school and university levels.

Relations of Conceptions and Approaches to Teaching and Learning

On the basis of an interview study with Hong Kong lecturers, Kember & Gow (1994) developed a questionnaire measuring knowledge transmission and learning facilitation orientations to teaching. They administered this questionnaire to university teachers from a number of disciplines, while their students were asked to complete the Study Process Questionnaire. As predicted, analysis at the department level showed substantial correlations between teachers' espoused transmission and facilitation orientations and their students' approaches to learning: transmission orientation being associated with surface, and facilitation with deep, approaches to learning. Using a qualitative approach, Kember & Kwan (1999) established a strong relationship between Hong Kong lecturers who espoused transmission or facilitation views of teaching and utilised content-centred and learning-centred approaches to teaching, respectively.

The programme of Trigwell, Prosser, and their associates has been particularly impressive in the way it has integrated qualitative and quantitative methodologies. As well as phenomenographic studies of conceptions of learning, approaches to learning, perceptions of the teaching environment, conceptions of teaching, and approaches to teaching, these researchers have utilised quantitative measures, mainly self-developed, of the approach and perception constructs. In a series of studies, Prosser & Trigwell (1998) report evidence of relatively close links between these variables. While their evidence and the logic behind it is fairly convincing, some of the measures utilised are newly developed and need further psychometric support, especially to demonstrate that they actually do measure different but conceptually close constructs. Moreover, apart from the work of Kember and his associates, the research is done for the most part in the context of first year science courses at several Australian universities. And although the proposition that conceptions and teaching practice is not meant to be culturally specific, the generalisability for other disciplinary areas, for schools as well as higher university years, and for non-Western students and teachers, needs to be established.

What is particularly interesting to us here is the cultural dimension. Do different conceptions and approaches to teaching prevail in different cultures? If so, might this have something to do with our new paradox of the Chinese teacher?

Current teaching practice in CHC classrooms

If teachers' conceptions influence practice, let us briefly summarise where we are starting from. We actually do not have fine-grained information about what is happening inside Mainland Chinese classrooms. It is a huge country, with a rich legacy of educational thought and practice (Lee, 1996), but a stormy educational history including in recent times the Cultural Revolution, which resulted in the almost total destruction of the then prevailing educational system in a stunning reversal of traditional educational values. What we can say at the present time is that current classes are large in size, up to 60 students, greatly under-resourced by Western standards, and examination-dominated; and that currently, Chinese students perform very well indeed, compared to students from the USA (IEA, 1996; Stevenson & Stigler, 1992). These last authors (Stigler & Stevenson, 1991: 43) compared elementary classrooms in China, Taiwan, and Japan, and the Mid-West of the USA and give us some clues as to what might be happening:

> A common Western stereotype is that the Asian teacher is an authoritarian purveyor of information, one who expects students to listen and memorise correct answers and procedures rather than to construct knowledge themselves. This does not describe the dozens of elementary school teachers that we have observed.

The teachers that Stigler and Stevenson observed, in China, Taiwan, and Japan, saw their task as posing provocative questions, allowing reflective wait time, and varying techniques to suit individual students. Their work did not extend however into secondary school.

Here, then, is some clue as to the "paradox" of the Chinese teacher. As with the Chinese learner, as we saw in Watkins & Biggs (1996), things are not what they seem from the outside. Obviously, we need to find out more, a lot more, but in this book we have to be content largely with one issue: coping with class size. Given the large classes, and the examinations, how do Chinese teachers get these positive results? Chapter 6, by Cortazzi and Jin, examines this issue.

The Hong Kong Context

Hong Kong classrooms have been rather more researched than those in China itself but the results could be seen to be even more puzzling. There is a strong British influence in the structure of schooling and the curriculum, but the language of instruction is Chinese (Cantonese) in primary and most secondary schools, English being used now in a decreasing number of secondary schools. The values of teachers, parents and students, are strongly Chinese as we shall see. In terms of performance, as judged by the recent IEA studies in mathematics and science Hong Kong students perform around the mean of participating countries in lower secondary school, but exceptionally well in senior secondary school (International Association for the Evaluation of Educational Achievement, 1996).

Students in Hong Kong at the end of primary school are segregated into five "bands" of ability and allocated into secondary schools on that basis. The allocation into bands is made by means of a mystifyingly elaborate system that takes into account performance in all school subjects except P.E., with mathematics, Chinese, and English weighted more heavily, teacher's ratings, gender, and the status of the primary school. The latter, until 2000, is determined by the Academic Aptitude Test (AAT), a test designed to be immune from coaching, but that feature only challenged teachers to devote all the more time to coaching for it, because the status of the school was at stake. Children from high status primary schools are given a higher weighting than children from low status primary schools, because actuarially the former subsequently perform better than the latter. A different argument might be that a child from a low status school who performs equally as well as a child from a high status school should be rated more rather than less favourably, because they have overcome a disadvantage. Oddly, when it comes to gender, the disadvantage argument does prevail. Since girls mature earlier than boys, girls are allocated fewer Band 1 places than boys, because of the "disadvantage" nature has imposed upon boys! To be fair, the procedures relating to both AAT and gender are currently under review, and in the long term it is proposed to abolish banding entirely. But until this happens, each student will be allocated according to ability into one of five bands, those in Band 1 having first choice of secondary school, and so on down the line.

Then, when all students have been banded, like young birds from an endangered species, they go to secondary schools that all follow the same curriculum: a Band 1 curriculum. Presumably this bizarre practice exists to allow all students in theory the opportunity of sitting the public examinations at the end of Form 5, and because of the general belief that effort counts, not ability, the Band 5 children will simply have to put in more effort to pass. If this is so, then the logic of banding by ability, in a culture that sees effort as the most important factor in success, is completely opaque. But the cruel consequence is that children in the lower bands are quite unable to handle the academic Band 1 curriculum, and are blamed for putting in insufficient effort.

What may then happen is described by Pauline Bunce, an expatriate teacher, as plumbing the "dreadful depths of dreary teaching" (*South China Morning Post*, 27 October, 1999), where students plod their way through a mountain of abstract meaningless tasks, which teachers for their part duly correct late into the night. In the correspondence following Bunce's article, another teacher (Witham, 1999) said of General English in a Band 5 school:

> students blindly copy sentences of which they have little or no understanding .... (This) is the illusion of learning... forced onto teachers in a futile attempt to prepare them for exams the majority cannot hope to pass.

In the exam referred to, in 1999 over 16,000 Band 5 students sat for the usual six to eight subjects in the public Certificate exams at the end of Form 5, and passed none; that is, of 100,000 student/exams sat, all were failed, and all fully expected to fail!

One cannot the blame the teachers for this. Attempts by teachers to engage in more enlightened practices are frequently stymied by local culture. A primary school teacher reports that some parents at her school checked their children's homework to ensure that all chapters in the textbook had been covered, and all work items in the text had been set. If they were not satisfied, they immediately filed a complaint to the District Education Office, which took their side and put pressure on the headmaster to bring the teachers into line.[1] In the fiercely competitive game of norm-referenced testing, in preparing for secondary selection, parents are determined that no other child might get an edge on their own child. It was in this kind of hothouse atmosphere that the criterion-referenced Target Oriented Curriculum (TOC) was introduced, and was of course seen as worse than irrelevant to what teacher and parents were really concerned about.

What about the top Band schools? Certainly the IEA studies seem to indicate that achievement is high. An interesting pointer is given by Salili et al. (2001) who compared Hong Kong students both to senior secondary Chinese students who had migrated to Canada, and to European Canadian students. The Hong Kong students were more anxious, had lower academic self efficacy, and spent far longer studying (Salili et al., 2001). There is normally a positive relationship between time spent in studying and academic results. But not in Forms 6 and 7 in Hong Kong; the more you study, the worse your performance! This is a sure sign that the limits have been reached. When compared on internal exams, 90% of Chinese Canadians, and 82% of European Canadians received a mark exceeding 70%, while only 35% of Hong Kong students exceeded 70%.

---

[1] Private communication. The teacher concerned wishes to remain anonymous.

On the other hand, 65% of Hong Kong students got less than 60%, and only 2% of all Canadians did. The Hong Kong teachers were extraordinarily mean in their marking, a deliberate strategy for extracting ever more effort from students.

There is a potent mix of factors here. Normally effort attributions are adaptive, but when aiming for top performance, while believing that success is within the student's control, makes students in a collectivist culture feel that others are contemptuous or disapproving of them if they do not attain their highest aspirations. The low marking is designed precisely to tell them that they are in danger of failing, so they experience high anxiety, embarrassment, guilt, and humiliation (Grant & Dweck, 2001). All done, of course, with the very best and most professional of intentions. And to be fair, the results in Band 1 schools are extremely good, and the students are a dream to teach when they go to university. But it is an ordeal by fire.

So this is part at least of what goes on in Hong Kong. It is a system that, whatever the rhetoric, is driven by "vernacular Confucianism". At the top end, we can see why students do so well. It is a recipe made up of the application of heavy pressure induced by relentless norm-referenced assessment. This pressure is intensified by cultural beliefs in relation to ability, effort and relative status, by the respective values of praise and blame, and by structuring assessments so that the work is perceived as more difficult than it really is, so that failure is an ever-present threat. What is going on at the middle and bottom bands is even harder to understand in terms of Western theories of motivation, according to which motivation disappears when expectations of success are next to zero. The Level 3 idea that good teaching must imply that learning occurs has no place in that scheme of things. In fact, Bunce (1999) described the system as Level 1; when the system fails, the students are to blame for not putting in enough effort.

There is obviously much to be criticised in this system, and indeed the Education Commission of the Hong Kong Government has proposed radical changes (Education Commission, 2000). The implementation of reform raises some very interesting issues in terms of the model (Figure 1.1) in which conceptions drive practice. This model explains why so many innovations imported from the West are like organ transplants that are rejected, the most recent being the spectacular failure of Target Oriented Curriculum (TOC) (Morris, Chan, & Lo, 1998). This was an innovation that Western best practice would prescribe as just what Hong Kong needed, a carefully designed criterion-referenced scheme that replaced the rigours of norm-referencing with individually paced learning. But teachers with a theory-in-use deriving from vernacular Confucianism simply would not see what the problem was. Moreover, the innovation was prescribed top-down, with little or no attempt to change teachers' or parents' thinking about the function of assessment. It will be interesting to see how the Education Commission's present parcel of reforms will handle that problem of inducing change. Can the conceptions and practices of teachers be readily changed to accommodate the new ways of thinking about practice that underlie the reforms the Commission wishes to implement? It is to be hoped that by end of this book we may be further along the road to addressing that question.

Overview of this book

This book is divided for convenience into three main sections – teacher's thinking, teaching practices, and changing teachers – but there is an underlying unity linking all three aspects that is represented in Figure 1.2 (see also Trigwell, Prosser & Waterhouse, 1999). Simply, it is suggested that teachers' thinking about learning influences their conceptions of teaching, which are linked to their approaches to teaching. We then see a similar chain from the students' perspective: the teaching context affects students' conceptions and then their approaches to learning, which ultimately determine the learning outcomes. Trigwell et al. are cautious about ascribing causality to that relationship, because the research methods utilised in this area to date are not sufficient for such an ascription, but it seems clear that they consider the predominant causal path to be from left to right in Figure 1.2. This book in Chapters 11 and 12 provides strong evidence, from different research methods appropriate for testing causality, that would support this view. In that case, the viability of any reform measures, including those proposed throughout the Hong Kong system, would depend on how the question of changing teacher thinking was addressed.

Figure 1.2
Linking conceptions and approaches to teaching and learning

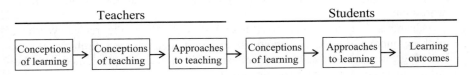

We thus have a set of components in our discussion of the Chinese teacher: teachers' thinking, teachers' practices, and changing teachers.

Teachers' thinking

Chapters 2 and 3 pick up the points about teacher's conceptions of teaching and learning and how they may influence their classroom practice. Chapter 2, by Gao & Watkins, is an exploration of the conceptions of teaching held by Guangzhou physics teachers. It is found that Mainland Chinese teachers do in fact hold different conceptions of teaching from those emerging from the Western literature. This is an important clue to our study of the paradox. Chapter 3, by Dahlin, Watkins and Ekholm, compares Swedish and Hong Kong tertiary teachers on their conceptions of the role of assessment. The issue probed here is whether lecturers perceive a relationship between curriculum and assessment, and if they try to use such a relationship to improve the quality of learning outcomes.

Teachers' practices

We next move to the action in the classroom. Most of this work reports what is going on in Hong Kong classrooms. The studies group themselves into terms of what is already going on in terms of teacher interaction with students, teacher pedagogy, and the efficacy of Western innovative teaching in Chinese contexts.

Chapters 4 (Salili) and 5 (I. Ho) compare how Chinese and Western teachers relate to their students. Basic differences are found in terms of teacher control and the role of feedback, which can only be understood in the cultural contexts involved. Ho's work also supports Gao's findings that Chinese teachers are more likely than Western teachers to emphasise a holistic whole person view of teaching, focusing on the development of students' values, morals, and conduct inside and outside the classroom.

The work on teacher pedagogy in classrooms in China and Hong Kong, reported in Chapter 6 by Cortazzi and Jin, and in Chapter 8 by Mok et al., respectively, reveals fascinating insights into how Chinese teachers are able to create positive learning environments. Their tightly orchestrated teacher centred teaching allows students to be very active in even large classes. This research questions Western educational notions that student-centred teaching is necessary for students to be actively involved in their teaching. Nevertheless, the research described in Chapter 7 by Ng, Tsui, and Marton suggests such active learning is much more likely to occur when mother-tongue is used for the medium of instruction.

Chapters 9 (Chan) and 10 (Stokes) describe how the recent Western teaching innovations of constructivist teaching methods and Problem Based Learning can work well with Chinese learners if carefully implemented with the full involvement of the teachers concerned.

Changing teachers

Can teachers with traditional beliefs about teaching be changed so that they can adopt more learner-centred approaches, with a focus on creative, critical thinking? This is in a sense the way forward for a dynamic system like that in Hong Kong, which is badly in need of change, and with change foreshadowed. Staff development is crucial: Can teachers change their thinking? Can they be per-suaded to adopt different teaching practices? How should innovations be introduced to facilitate such changes?

Chapter 11, by Tang, looks at the effect of teacher education courses on the conceptions of teaching and learning held by teachers and principals undertaking an in-service B.Ed, course run by the Open University of Hong Kong. Tang argues that meaningful changes in teaching thinking are only likely to occur if such teachers encounter learning experiences that differ from those to which they are accustomed, and they are encouraged to reflect on the differences.

Chapters 12, by A. Ho working with tertiary teachers at one Hong Kong university, and 13 by Kember, who reviews a massive series of projects on staff development through action research, paint a very positive picture of future prospects. Both chapters also provide clear blueprints for achieving such positive outcomes.

Finally, in Chapter 14, we review the findings, generalise what we can, and in particular the differences between teaching in Hong Kong and in Mainland China, and integrate them within the model here outlined. There is a message here for reform, and we hope that the stakeholders will listen to it.

REFERENCES

Anon. (1993). Editorial. *South China Morning Post*, 5 January.

Atkinson, J.W. (1964). *An Introduction to Motivation*. New York: Van Nostrand.

Beaton, A.E., Martin, M.O., Mullis, I.V.S., Gonzalez, E.J., Smith, T.A. & Kelly, D.L. (1996a). *Science Achievement in the Middle School Years: IEA Third International Mathematics and Science Study*. Chestnut Hill, MA: Center for the Study of Testing, Evaluation, and Educational Policy, Boston College.

Beaton, A.E., Martin, M.O., Mullis, I.V.S., Gonzalez, E.J., Smith, T.A. & Kelly, D.L. (1996b). *Mathematics Achievement in the Middle School Years: IEA Third International Mathematics and Science Study*. Chestnut Hill, MA: Center for the Study of Testing, Evaluation, and Educational Policy, Boston College.

Biggs, J.B. (1987). *Student Approaches to Learning and Studying*. Melbourne: Australian Council for Educational Research.

Biggs, J.B. (1993). What do Inventories of Students' Learning Processes Really Measure? A Theoretical Review and Clarification. *British Journal of Educational Psychology*, 63, 3-19.

Biggs, J.B. (1996). Western Misperceptions of the Confucian-heritage Learning Culture. In D.A. Watkins & J.B. Biggs (Eds.), *The Chinese Learner: Cultural, Psychological, and Contextual Influences*. Hong Kong / Melbourne: Comparative Education Research Centre, The University of Hong Kong / Australian Council for Educational Research, 45-68.

Biggs, J.B. (1999). *Teaching for Quality Learning at University*. Buckingham: Open University Press.

Biggs, J.B. (2001). Teaching across Cultures. In F. Salili, C.Y. Chiu & Y.Y. Hong (Eds.), *Student Motivation: The Culture and Context of Learning*. New York: Plenum.

Biggs, J.B. & Watkins, D.A. (1996). The Chinese Learner in Retrospect. In D.A. Watkins & J.B. Biggs (Eds.), *The Chinese Learner: Cultural, Psychological, and Contextual Influences*. Hong Kong / Melbourne: Comparative Education Research Centre, The University of Hong Kong / Australian Council for Educational Research, 269-285.

Bunce, P. (1999). The Dreadful Depths of Dreary Teaching. *South China Morning Post*, 27 October.

Chan, Y-Y.G. & Watkins, D.A. (1994). Classroom Environment and Approaches to Learning: An Investigation of the Actual and Preferred Perceptions of Hong Kong Secondary School Students. *Instructional Science*, 22, 233-246.

Chang, W.C. (2000). In Search of the Chinese in all the Wrong Places! *Journal of Psychology in Chinese Societies*, 1(1), 125-142.

Dahlin, B. & Watkins, D.A. (2000). The Role of Repetition in the Processes of Memorising and Understanding. A Comparison of the Views of Western and Chinese Secondary School Students in Hong Kong. *British Journal of Educational Psychology*, 70, 65-84.

Dall'Alba, G. (1990). Foreshadowing Conceptions of Teaching. *Research and Development in Higher Education*, 13, 291-297.

Education Commission (2000). *Review of Education System: Reform Proposals*. Hong Kong: Government Printing Office. http://www.e-c.edu.hk.

Entwistle, N.J. & Ramsden, P. (1983). *Understanding Student Learning*. London: Croom Helm.

Giorgi, A. (1986). A Phenomenological Analysis of Descriptions of Learning obtained from a Phenomenographic Perspective. Report from Department of Education, University of Gothenburg, No.18.

Grant, H. & Dweck, C. (2001). Cross-cultural Response to Failure: Considering Outcome Attributions with Different Goals. In F. Salili, C.Y. Chiu & Y.Y. Hong (Eds.), *Student Motivation: The Culture and Context of Learning*. New York: Plenum.

Hess, R.D. & Azuma, M. (1991). Cultural Support for Schooling: Contrasts between Japan and the United States. *Educational Researcher*, 20(9), 2-8.

Ho, D.Y.F. (1993). Relational Orientation in Asian Social Psychology. In U. Kim & J.W. Berry (Eds.), *Indigenous Psychologies*. Newbury Park, CA: Sage.

Hofstede, G. (1980). *Culture's Consequences: International Differences in Work-related Values*. Beverly Hills, CA: Sage.

Holloway, S.D. (1988). Concepts of Ability and Effort in Japan and the US. *Review of Educational Research*, 58, 327-345.

Jin, L. & Cortazzi, M. (1998). Dimensions of Dialogue, Large Classes in China. *International Journal of Educational Research*, 29, 739-761.

Kember, D. (1996). The Intention to Both Memorise and Understand: Another Approach to Learning? *Higher Education*, 31, 341-354.

Kember, D. (1997). A Reconceptualisation of the Research into University Academics' Conceptions of Teaching. *Learning and Instruction*, 7(3), 255-275.

Kember, D. & Gow, L. (1994). Orientations to Teaching and their Effect on the Quality of Student Learning. *Journal of Higher Education*, 65, 58-74.

Kember, D. & Kwan, K.P. (1999). Lecturers' Approaches to Teaching and their Relationship to Conceptions of Good Teaching. In Hativa, N. & Goodyear, P. (Eds.). *Teacher Thinking, Beliefs and Knowledge in Higher Education*. Dordrecht, the Netherlands: Kluwer Academic Publishers.

Kim, U., Triandis, H., Kagitcibasi, C., Choi, S.C. & Yoon, G. (Eds.) (1994). *Individualism and Collectivism*. Newbury Park, CA: Sage.

Larsson, S. (1983). Describing Teachers' Conceptions of their Professional

World. In Halkes, R. & Olson, J.K., *Teacher Thinking: A New Perspective on Persisting Problems in Education.* Proceedings of the first symposium of the International Study Association on Teacher Thinking, Tilburg, 1983, 123-133.

Lee, W.O. (1996). The Cultural Context of Chinese Learners: Conceptions of Learning in the Confucian Tradition. In D.A. Watkins & J.B. Biggs (Eds.), *The Chinese Learner: Cultural, Psychological, and Contextual Influences.* Hong Kong / Melbourne: Comparative Education Research Centre, The University of Hong Kong / Australian Council for Educational Research, 25-41.

Martin, E. & Balla, M. (1990). Conceptions of Teaching and Implications for Learning. *Research and Development in Higher Education,* 13, 298-304.

Marton, F. (1981). Phenomenography – Describing Conceptions of the World Around Us. *Instructional Science,* 10, 177-200.

Marton, F. & Booth, S. (1997). *Learning and Awareness.* New Jersey: Lawrence Erlbaum and Associates.

Marton, F., Dall'Alba, G. & Tse, L.K. (1996). Memorizing and Understanding: The Keys to the Paradox? In D.A. Watkins & J.B. Biggs (Eds.), *The Chinese Learner: Cultural, Psychological, and Contextual Influences.* Hong Kong / Melbourne: Comparative Education Research Centre, The University of Hong Kong / Australian Council for Educational Research, 69-83.

Marton, F., Dall'Alba, G. & Beaty, E. (1993). Conceptions of Learning. *International Journal of Educational Research,* 19, 277-300.

Marton, F. & Säljö, R. (1976). On Qualitative Differences in Learning – I: Outcome and Process. *British Journal of Educational Psychology,* 46, 4-11.

Marton, F. & Säljö, R. (1984). Approaches to Learning. In F. Marton, D. Hounsell & N. Entwistle (Eds.), *The Experience of Learning.* Edinburgh: Scottish Academic Press, 36-55.

Marton, F., Watkins, D.A. & Tang, C. (1997). Discontinuities and Continuities in the Experience of Learning: An Interview Study of High School Student in Hong Kong. *Learning and Instruction,* 7, 21-48.

Morris, P., Chan, K.K. & Lo, M.L. (1998). Changing Primary Schools in Hong Kong: Perspectives on Policy and its Impact. In P. Stimpson & P. Morris (Eds.), *Curriculum and Assessment in Hong Kong: Two Components, One System.* Hong Kong: The Open University of Hong Kong Press, 201-222.

Neill, A.S. (1960). *Summerhill.* New York: Hart.

Pratt, D.D. (1992). Conceptions of Teaching. *Adult Education Quarterly,* 42, 203-220.

Prosser, M. & Trigwell, K. (1998). *Understanding Learning and Teaching: The Experience in Higher Education.* Milton Keynes: Open University Press.

Salili, F. (1996). Accepting Personal Responsibility for Learning. In D.A. Watkins & J.B. Biggs (Eds.), *The Chinese Learner: Cultural, Psychological, and Contextual Influences.* Hong Kong / Melbourne: Comparative Education Research Centre, The University of Hong Kong / Australian Council for Educational Research, 85-106.

Salili, F., Chiu, C.Y. & Lai, S. (2001). The Influence of Culture and Context on Students' Motivational Orientation and Performance. In F. Salili, C. Y. Chiu & Y.Y. Hong (Eds.), *Student Motivation: The Culture and Context of Learning*. New York: Plenum.

Säljö, R. (1979). Learning in the Learner's Perspective: Some Common-sense Conceptions. Report from the Department of Education, University of Gothenburg, No.76.

Samuelowicz, K. & Bain, J.D. (1992). Conceptions of Teaching held by Academic Teachers. *Higher Education*, 24, 93-111.

Stevenson, H.W. & Lee, S. (1996). The Academic Achievement of Chinese Students. In M.H. Bond (Ed.), *The Handbook of Chinese Psychology*. Hong Kong: Oxford University Press, 124-142.

Stevenson, H.W. & Stigler, J. (1992). *The Learning Gap: Why our Schools are Failing and What We Can Learn from Japanese and Chinese Education*. New York: Summit Books.

Stigler, J. & Stevenson, H.W. (1991). How Asian Teachers Polish Each Other to Perfection. *American Educator*, 15(1), 12-21 & 43-47.

Tang, K.C.C. (1996). Collaborative Learning: The Latent Dimension in Chinese Students' Learning. In D.A. Watkins & J.B. Biggs (Eds.), *The Chinese Learner: Cultural, Psychological, and Contextual Influences*. Hong Kong / Melbourne: Comparative Education Research Centre, The University of Hong Kong / Australian Council for Educational Research, 183-204.

Trigwell, K., Prosser, M. & Waterhouse, F. (1999). Relations between Teachers' Approaches to Teaching and Students' Approaches to Learning. *Higher Education*, 37, 57-70.

Watkins, D.A. (1996a). Hong Kong Secondary School Learners: A Developmental Perspective. In D.A. Watkins & J.B. Biggs (Eds.), *The Chinese Learner: Cultural, Psychological, and Contextual Influences*. Hong Kong / Melbourne: Comparative Education Research Centre, The University of Hong Kong / Australian Council for Educational Research, 107-119.

Watkins, D.A. (1996b). Learning Theories and Approaches to Research: A Cross-cultural Perspective. In D.A. Watkins & J.B. Biggs (Eds.), *The Chinese Learner: Cultural, Psychological, and Contextual Influences*. Hong Kong / Melbourne: Comparative Education Research Centre, The University of Hong Kong / Australian Council for Educational Research, 3-24.

Watkins, D.A. (2001). Correlates of Approaches to Learning: A Cross-cultural Meta-analysis. In R.J. Sternberg & L.F. Zhang (Eds.). *Perspectives on Thinking, Learning, and Cognitive Styles*. Mahwah: Lawrence Erlbaum.

Watkins, D.A. & Biggs, J.B. (Eds.) (1996). *The Chinese Learner: Cultural, Psychological, and Contextual Influences*. Hong Kong / Melbourne: Comparative Education Research Centre, The University of Hong Kong / Australian Council for Educational Research.

Winter, S. (1995). Student Interaction and Relationships. In J.B. Biggs & D.A. Watkins (Eds.), *Classroom Learning: Educational Psychology for the Asian Teacher*. Singapore: Prentice Hall, 34-50.

Witham, S. (1999). Letter to the Editor. *South China Morning Post*, 19 November.
Yang, C.F. (2000). In the Wrong Places? Or with the Wrong People? *Journal of Psychology in Chinese Societies*, 1(1), 153-158.

TEACHER THINKING

2

Towards a Model of Teaching Conceptions of Chinese Secondary School Teachers of Physics

Gao Lingbiao and David A. Watkins

Both educational theorists and applied researchers have strongly advocated that learning is best viewed as a process of active construction and change within the learner, and that teaching should be oriented towards facilitating student learning (Greeno, Collins & Resnick, 1996). Experience has also shown that a change in teachers' conceptions of teaching is likely to be necessary before a real change in their teaching could occur (Calderhead, 1981). This led to increasing interest in studying teachers' conceptions of teaching in the past two decades (see also Chapters 1, 11 and 12). This chapter reports research exploring the teaching conceptions of Chinese secondary school teachers of physics and the interrelationships between different categories of teaching conceptions.

Developing a Conceptual Model

The first stage of the study reported in this chapter used an emic research approach which involved constructing a conceptual model of teaching conceptions held by Chinese school teachers of physics through in-depth interviews.

Semi-structured interviews were first conducted with 18 volunteers who taught senior secondary grade 1 physics in Guangzhou (to students about 16-17 years old). They represented a range of characteristics such as gender, qualifications, teaching experience, and school band. Episodes of the classroom teaching processes of all interviewees were videotaped before the interviews. These videotapes were used as an aid for promoting and 'warming up' the teachers, identifying the precise meaning of some ideas that were not clearly expressed during the interviews, and as an aid while re-coding the teachers' conceptual orientations to teaching.

The five commonly recognised dimensions proposed by Kember (1997) (see also Chapter 1) were used in this research for constructing the interview questions. Thirty-eight open-ended questions were constructed. Both 'key questions', eliciting teachers' responses about their opinions and values relating to teaching, and 'practical questions', eliciting teachers' responses about their teaching experiences and behaviours were asked.

The interviews lasted on average 50 minutes and were audio-recorded. Transcriptions of the interview records and two accuracy checks were done soon after the interviews. Two experienced researchers in the Division of Teaching and Learning in the Education Department of Guangzhou were invited to act as consultants for the data analysis and later construction of the questionnaire.

Analysis of the qualitative data involved three stages. Firstly the first author and the two consultants read the interview transcripts and identified key words and phrases independently. Those noted by all three persons were retained for further analysis. The next stage focused on coding the teachers' ideas to identify possible regularities. The final stage focused on identifying teachers' conceptions of teaching. Potential dimensions were sought according to whether the data relating to each dimension showed qualitative variations. Six dimensions were identified for delimiting and defining their conceptions: (1) the nature of learning and the roles of students, (2) the nature of teaching, (3) the roles of teachers, (4) the aims and expected outcomes of teaching, (5) the content of teaching, and (6) methods of teaching. Since most researchers accepted the 'bipolar' nature of the dimensions (Kember, 1997), teachers' ideas were coded to each of the dimensions and arranged in order from the most teacher-centred to the most student-centred. A mapping-plane was then designed (Figure 2.1). Comparisons of the key words and phrases were made to locate them in the 'mapping-plane'. Those identified as of the same dimension were arrayed in the same row from the most teacher-centred extreme to the most student-centred extreme. Thus, words and phrases implying the most teacher-centred views were located in the column at the far-left side of the 'mapping-plane' and the most student-centred at the far-right side. Each column implied one category of teachers' ideas or, say, a conception of teaching. From this analysis, five columns emerged in the 'mapping-plane', taken to represent five teaching conceptions were identified. Finally, the researcher and the consultants met with all interviewees to report the process and the analysis findings. All agreed with the coding and classification.

Figure 2.1
'Mapping-plane' for identifying teachers' ideas

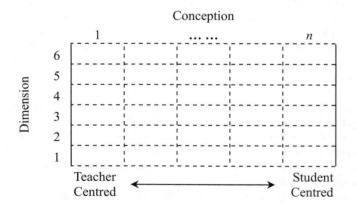

Conceptions identified

Five teaching conceptions were identified from the above analysis: Knowledge Delivery (KD), Exam Preparation (EP), Ability[1] Development (AD), Attitude Promotion (AP) and Conduct Guidance (CG). Table 2.1 lists the key words and phrases of these conceptions.

Table 2.1
An overview of conceptions of teaching

	Learning & Learner	Nature of Teaching	Role of Teacher	Expect Outcomes	Teaching Content	Method of Teaching
KD	Acquiring knowledge and skills; Passive receivers	Delivering knowledge and skills	Deliverer and resource	Accumulation of knowledge and skills	Follows the textbook closely	One-way lecturing plus demonstration
EP	Achieving exam requirements, Achievers, Competitive	Preparing for examinations; Drilling students	Trainer and director	High exam achievement	Conducted by the 'baton of exams'	Classroom drilling, Effective for preparing exams
AD	Internal construction; Explorers, Capable, flexible and creative	Facilitating learning	Guide, leader, and facilitator	Developing understanding and ability, knowing how to learn	Meets the needs of students and matches students' level	A variety of methods, emphasises activities & interactions
AP	Establishing good attitudes	Promoting and fostering good attitude	Model of good learner with good attitudes	Active and independent in learning	Contained implicitly in teachers' performance	Interactive and interesting; indirect manner
CG	Self-improvement	Facilitating and guiding good conduct	Role model of good conduct, friend of students	Qualified persons with good conduct	Related materials, contained implicitly in teachers' behaviours	Friendly and interactive indirect manner

Knowledge Delivery

The Knowledge Delivery conception is based on the view that learning is a process of acquiring or accumulating knowledge and skills. A teacher is both a deliverer and a bank of knowledge and skills. As teacher J said:

> "The nature of teaching, or say, the role of a teacher, is to deliver knowledge as well as methods and skills. No matter how many things are involved in the teaching process, it is still a delivery process." (Teacher J, SIR, 4-1)[2]

The teacher is at the centre of the classroom teaching-learning process. Learning is related to the quantitative accumulation of knowledge. A learner is no more than a passive receptor. The content of teaching is pre-determined by the course sylla-

---

[1] According to Chinese beliefs, ability is malleable so teachable.
[2] Here and later in this chapter SIR refers to the Selections of Interview Records. The number 4-1 is the serial number of that quotation.

bus and textbooks. Neither teachers nor students engage in making decisions about the teaching-learning content. Knowledge is something external to the students and transferred to them by teachers. Teaching proceeds in the direction from content (determined by course syllabus and the textbooks) to teachers, then to students, and finally to expected outcomes. Figure 2.2 shows a model of teaching based on the Knowledge Delivery conception. In this model, the teaching process starts from the syllabus and textbooks, and proceeds in a direct line to the expected outcome: the accumulation of knowledge.

Figure 2.2
A model of the knowledge delivery conception of teaching

Exam Preparation

The most important element of the Exam Preparation conception of teaching is students' achievement, especially in public examinations. As Teacher L said:

> "As a teacher, my main task in the classroom is to ensure that my students can get good marks in the matriculation examination. Because this is the most important, or in some cases, the only aspect by which the school authority assesses my teaching. As a result, the matriculation examination becomes the main focus of my teaching." (Teacher L, SIR, 4-5)

Teachers with this conception view learning and teaching from an exterior perspective in relation to students and teachers. Learning is a means to pass examinations and to attain required qualifications. Students are figures to be shaped according to the target of examinations. Teachers are trainers and directors to ensure that students can achieve the examination requirements. What is taught and the method of teaching are based on the content of and methods used in examinations. As in the case of the Knowledge Delivery conception, the content of teaching is pre-determined. Examinations act as a conductor's 'baton' conducting teachers, students and the teaching-learning process. This 'baton' determines the teaching content, pushing teachers and students to focus on solving a 'sea of items' in order to achieve better in examinations. Teaching is mainly a one-way procedure though there may be interactions between the teacher and students limited to solving exam-type items. Figure 2.3 provides a model of teaching based on the Exam Preparation conception of teaching. In this model, the teaching process starts from examinations and proceeds almost directly down to the expected outcomes. The dotted line between teachers and students indicates that there are limited teacher-student interactions as does that between student achievement and examinations.

Figure 2.3
A model of the exam preparation conception of teaching

Ability Development

The Ability Development conception is based on the view that learning is a process of internal construction. Students are not passive receptors but active builders who construct their own knowledge and understanding of the world. Students are at the centre of the teaching-learning process. Teaching is for facilitating student learning. A teacher is a guide to students, the teaching content must meet the needs of students and match the capacities of students. A variety of teaching strategies are encouraged. The development of student ability is the expected teaching outcome. As Teacher A said:

> "To develop students' abilities must be the most important aim of the school physics teaching. The ability to explore physics knowledge by experiment and to apply the physics knowledge in daily life, ... and the ability of analysing, thinking, ... and experimenting." (Teacher A, SIR, 4-7)

Although the course syllabus and textbooks still play important roles in determining the teaching content, both teachers and students contribute to the teaching content to some extent. Teaching and learning are not confined to the syllabus and textbooks but relate to the real world and match the students' ability levels. Teachers and students are involved in active interactions. The relationships among the content, teachers and students cannot be expressed as one-way but rather as two-way interactions. The model based on the Ability Development conception is shown in Figure 2.4. Here classroom teaching and learning form a complex system including multiple interactions among teachers, students and the course content. The dotted line implies that due to the school environment, the influence of teachers and students on the teaching content is rather weak.

Figure 2.4
A model of the ability development conception of teaching

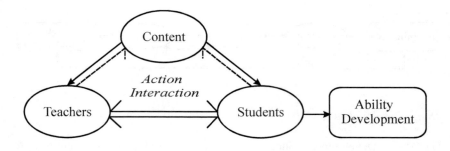

The Attitude Promotion conception is based on the view that learning skills and outcomes relate closely to learning attitudes. The products of learning are not only the accumulation of knowledge or development of academic abilities but also changes in students' attitudes to learning. For example, teacher I said:

> "I think if teachers can motivate their students and arouse their interests in the subject they teach, helping students to set up good habits and attitudes to learning, that's the most wonderful outcome you can expect." (Teacher I, SIR, 6-18)

This conception views teaching from an affective perspective. It emphasises the interactions between learning performance and attitude and focuses on motivating students and establishing good and 'correct' attitudes to learning. A good teacher is a model learner who model good attitudes to students. Teaching 'content' is not explicit as knowledge in the discipline, but a kind of implicit 'message' contained in the teacher's performance and in the teacher-student interactions. Teaching proceeds through the interactions between the teacher and students. Figure 2.5 shows a model of teaching based on the Attitude Promotion conception of teaching. In this model, students are at the centre of the teaching-learning process. Teachers influence students' attitudes in an implicit way. By actively interacting with students and providing exemplary roles, they help students to establish good learning attitudes.

Towards a Model of Teaching Conceptions

Figure 2.5
A model of the attitude promotion conception of teaching

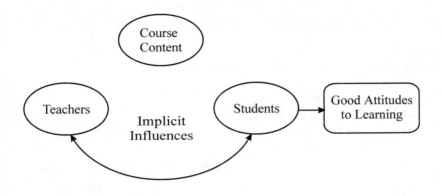

Conduct Guidance

The Conduct Guidance conception emphasises the implicit influences of classroom processes on student behaviour. Learning is now a process of conduct cultivation, a way to arrive at self-perfection. As teacher H explained:

> "By attending school and classes, students learn not only subject matter and skills, but also how to interact and communicate with their peers, teachers, school authorities and parents. Learn how to be a person and how to behave well." (Teacher H, SIR, 1-10)

Teaching aims at facilitating changes in students' conduct. A good teacher must be a good friend of students, and their conduct model. Teacher I claimed:

> "However, teaching should involve far more than knowledge delivery. It should include educating and cultivating students. Help them to learn how to be a person. That's what we call 'Jiao Shu Yu Ren'.[3] This should be much more important than the other things. ..." (Teacher I, SIR, 4-13)

The teaching content extends to novelistic, historical and all kinds of materials implying good conduct and values. However, as in the Attitude Promotion conception, the most important teaching 'content' is the implicit messages contained in the teachers' performance and teacher-student interaction. Teaching proceeds in an indirect manner. Figure 2.6, shows a model of the Conduct Guidance conception of teaching. In this model, teachers, students, teaching content and the im-

---

[3] "Jiao Shu Yu Ren": A set phrase means teaching as well as cultivating good persons.

plicit influence of teachers form a complex system. These elements interact with each other resulting in moving student behaviour towards a higher conduct level. Students are active in and at the centre of this system. The curves between teachers and students, and between the related materials and teachers and students, imply that influences on students' conduct occur in an implicit or indirect way.

Figure 2.6
A model of the conduct guidance conception of teaching

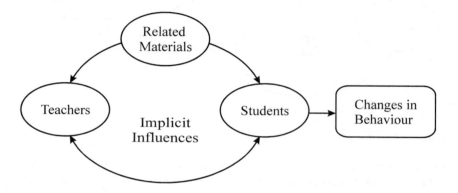

Relationships between categories of teaching conceptions

Comparing the meaning of the above conceptions, we can see that students are in a passive position in both the Knowledge Delivery and Exam Preparation conceptions. There teaching and learning are dominated by external factors: the course syllabus and textbooks or examinations. Classroom teaching and learning proceed in one direction from the content to teachers, then students, and finally the outcomes. What differentiates these two conceptions are, (a) who determines the content of teaching, the course syllabus and textbooks, or examinations; and (b) what are the expected outcomes: knowledge acquisition or high achievement in examinations.

We propose that it is reasonable to combine these two conceptions into a higher-order Moulding orientation (as described below both the first- and the higher-order models were later supported by confirmatory factor analysis). The common core is to mould students quantitatively and according to external demands. Students passively accept knowledge and are trained to meet external demands. The teaching-learning process is mostly one-way. Figure 2.7 shows a model of the Moulding orientation. The dotted line from students to teachers indicates that there are weak interactions between students and teachers and that from academic achievement examinations represents the feedback of examination results, which in turn would influence the examinations and the teaching-learning process.

Figure 2.7
A model of the moulding orientation of teaching

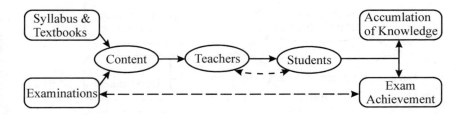

A comparison of the Ability Development, Attitude Promotion and Conduct Guidance conceptions shows that in each students are in an active position. Teachers act as guides or role models of student learning and behaviour. Active interactions and activities are encouraged in a variety of ways. The content of teaching is not confined to the course syllabus, textbooks and examinations. It includes daily life issues and methods of learning beyond acquiring knowledge and skills, as well as attitudes and conduct reflected in teachers' performance and behaviours. All these three conceptions expect qualitative changes in students as the outcomes of teaching and learning. Examination of the relationships among the major teaching elements under these three conceptions shows that they share similar elements. Teaching content, teachers and students interact in multiple ways and form a complex system. These three conceptions differ as while in the Ability Development conception the teaching content relates to students' cognitive abilities in the other two conceptions teaching 'content' appears in an implicit form and is related to non-cognitive aspects and the expected outcomes are different accordingly.

We propose a higher-order Cultivating orientation to underlie these three conceptions. The core of this orientation is the cultivation of students. Students are at the centre of the teaching-learning process. They learn by active interaction with teachers, peer students and the real world. The content of teaching not only includes academic knowledge, skills and underlying methods of learning and studying, but also the implicit influence on students' attitudes and conduct. External factors are not the only force in determining the teaching content. It includes the active involvement of both teachers and students. The expected outcome includes qualitative changes in academic quality, learning attitude and personal behaviour. Figure 2.8 shows the model of the Cultivating orientation of teaching.

Figure 2.8
A model of the cultivating orientation of teaching

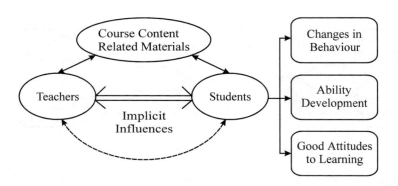

A general framework is then proposed for describing the categories of teaching conceptions held by school physics teachers in Guangdong China, and the relationship among these teaching conceptions (see Figure 2.9). At the lower level of this framework are the five first-order conceptions identified from the interview descriptions describing teachers' ideas about their teaching experience. The two higher-order orientations stand at the upper level of the framework. The Knowledge Delivery and Exam Preparation conceptions are covered by the Moulding orientation. Another higher-order orientation, the Cultivating orientation, covers three first order conceptions: Ability Development, Attitude Promotion and Conduct Guidance. The overlap between conceptions under the same higher-order orientation implies a strong relationship. The dotted line between the two higher-order orientations suggests a weak relationship.

Figure 2.9
A general framework of the conceptions of teaching

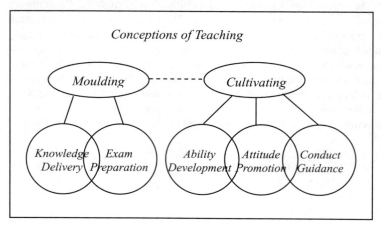

Further Research

Questionnaire development

Based on the above qualitative findings, a questionnaire titled School Physics Teachers' Conceptions of Teaching (SPTCT) was developed in Chinese. All items were constructed from the key ideas expressed by the teachers in the interviews. After four cycles of refinements and a pilot test, the final version of the SPTCT consisted of 37 items in five ordinary scales and two higher-order scales.

Scale KD related to the Knowledge Delivery conception (8 items), Scale EP related to the Exam Preparation conception (10 items), Scale AD related to the Ability Development conception (7 items), Scale AP related to the Attitude Promotion conception (7 items), and Scale CG related to the Conduct Guidance conception (5 items). Higher-order scale MO was the combination of scale KD and EP and tapped the Moulding orientation to teaching. Higher-order scale CU was the combination of scale AD, AP and CG, and tapped the Cultivating orientation to teaching.

The SPTCT was then distributed to 718 physics teachers in Guangdong with the help of the School Physics Teachers Association of Guangdong Province and 450 responses were returned. The internal-consistency coefficients were calculated as indicators of the reliability of responses to the SPTCT scales. The alpha coefficients for responses to the five first-order scales of the SPTCT ranged from .64 to .74 (median .73), and for the higher-order scales of the SPTCT were both .83. According to Nunnally (1978), values of alpha coefficients above .70 are considered as adequate for research purposes. Confirmatory factor analysis was applied to test the within-construct validity of the SPTCT at both item and scale level based on the conceptual model shown in Figure 2.9. All fit indices showed that the models were a good fit to the data (see Gao & Watkins, 1999 for details).

The above results indicate that responses to the SPTCT were reliable for assessing Chinese physics teachers' conceptions of teaching and also provided factor analytic support to the five teaching conceptions and two higher-level orientations identified qualitatively and the relationship among the teaching conceptions and orientations suggested by the qualitative analysis.

Multiple conceptions

Data from the SPTCT showed that about 66% of the respondents declared that they agreed with both Moulding and Cultivating orientations. This is in line with the interview data. A number of interviewees were found to base their responses to different interview questions on different or even conflicting beliefs and conceptions of teaching. For example, when responding to the question "what is your personal belief about the nature of teaching", teacher J emphasised that teaching is a process "to deliver knowledge as well as methods and skills (SIR, 4-1)". Then, to the question "what is the role of a school physics teacher", he replied that "teachers play an organising and leading/catalytic role" in helping student learning (SIR, 8-5). The former reflected clearly a Moulding orientation while the later implied a Cultivating orientation.

As Bowden (1988) also found, most of the teachers involved in this research did not realise that they had shifted their stance when they responded to different interview questions or the SPTCT items. However, they expressed no surprise when this was pointed out. Their explanations for these conflicts fell into two groups.

Firstly, several teachers explained that this was due to the big gap between the theoretical and the real world: the "ideal conceptions about what teaching should be" reflected the theoretical world and the "practical conceptions about what teaching really is" reflected the real school environment. This supported the view of Argyris & Schon (1978) that teachers might have two sets of personal theories: an "espoused theory" and a "theory-in-use". As a teacher said:

> "I find it impossible to try (the action learning approach in my class). How can I teach so little? How can I complete the school syllabus if I introduce only six new concepts in two weeks? How can I help students to prepare for the examinations if I don't drill them in solving exam-type items? I know that the action learning approach is good for student development. If I don't need to care about the performance of my students in public examinations, if I don't need to follow exactly the course syllabus and the textbooks, I think I will make a change." (SIR, 16-2)

Another group of teachers argued that teaching is a complex system processing in multiple ways and directions, "there are several parallel streams going down along the same slope, each stream defines one conception of teaching". For example, some teachers viewed the development of students' ability and the cultivation of good attitudes and good conduct as only one side of the picture. On the other side they felt that "as a good teacher you need to be responsible to your students. You need to help your students to perform well in the examinations so they can have a bright future" (SIR 1-4). Therefore, preparing students for examinations was also emphasised by the same teachers.

This research did not focus on examining why teachers have more than one conception of teaching. However, from the above descriptions, it was clear that teachers do have different models to support their conceptual framework about teaching. This might be an interesting issue for further study.

Discussion

Five conceptions and two broader area orientations were identified by interviewing school physics teachers in Guangdong, China. Parallels of these teaching conceptions and orientations could be found in previous studies, mainly of Western university lecturers.

Delivering knowledge is the most widely identified conception of teaching in the literature (Christensen, et al., 1995; Dall'Alba, 1990; Fox, 1983; Gow & Kember; 1993; Larsson, 1983; Martin & Balla, 1990; Pratt, 1992; Prosser, Trigwell & Taylor, 1994; Samuelowicz & Bain, 1992). Central to this concept is that teaching is a process of transmission, and that knowledge is something external to students that can be transmitted by teachers. Knowledge is determined by the course syllabus, stored in textbooks or teachers' brains, and is expected to accumulate in students through the delivery of teachers.

The Exam Preparation conception is similar to the 'organisational' conception proposed by Biggs (1990) which focused on institutional responsibility for knowledge and standards. While Biggs' suggestion was based on theoretical study, Fox (1983) identified a comparable 'shaping theory' from responses of polytechnic teachers to his question "what do you mean by teaching". This 'theory' focuses on shaping students according to the institutional standard, such as producing a competent engineer or developing a capacity to handle equipment, and views students "as raw material to be shaped, or moulded, or turned to a predetermined and often detailed specification" (p.153). The idea that students are something to be shaped by teachers is similar in both 'shaping theory' and the Exam Preparation conception, although the former focuses on general institutional standards and the latter focuses primarily on the demands of examinations.

The sharp focus on examinations among Guangdong school physics teachers must be given special attention since it may well be not only widely accepted by Guangdong school physics teachers, but also by teachers of other subjects throughout China. This emphasis has been identified as a weakness of the basic education system in China (Liu, 1995) and may be due to the effect of the educational evaluation system (Liu, 1996), the salience of examination in Chinese traditions (Gao, 1998), and the environment of Chinese society. Nowadays in China, schooling is still seen as an important and effective way of raising one's social and economic status. Success in public examinations, particularly the national university entrance examination, means that one can expect a secure, well paid career after graduation. To many students from poor rural areas, tertiary education represents "a distinctive line which decides whether they wear straw sandals or leather shoes later in their lives ". Most parents will reward their children if they get higher marks in examinations or punish their children for poor school records (Zhao, 1996). Student records in public examinations are treated as the most important indicator of the quality of schools by the community (Fu, 1996). There is thus great social pressure to push the teachers in this exam preparation direction.

Teaching conceptions identified by many previous researchers can be seen to parallel the 'Ability Development' conception identified in this research (Christensen, et al., 1995; Dall'Alba, 1990; Dunkin, 1990; Fox, 1983; Gow & Kember, 1993; Larsson, 1983; Martin & Balla, 1990; Pratt, 1992; Samuelowicz & Bain, 1992). When the term 'ability' was used by teachers in this research, it was repeatedly accompanied by other terms such as 'ability to explore', 'ability to learn', 'ability to understand', 'ability to think', 'problem solving ability', etc.. Ability was viewed as something underlying knowledge and skills that relate closely to human intellect. Ability could not simply be picked up from teachers through delivery, rather, it had to be developed by students themselves in the process of learning or practising.

Some conceptions identified by other researchers in the literature share ideas with the Attitude Promotion conception identified in this research. For example, Dunkin (1990) identified a conception viewing 'teaching as motivating learning', and Martin & Balla (1990) identified a category of conception viewing 'teaching as encouraging active learning'. These conceptions focus on motivating student learning by, for example, "providing enough interesting material to maintain stimulation (Dunkin, 1990, p.58)". However, the Attitude Promotion conception does not limit itself to involving merely 'facilitation' of cognitive progressing, but views the establishment of good learning attitudes as one of the aims of teaching and learning. This is an important point which differentiates the present conception from Pratt's (1992) 'apprenticeship conception' which encourages teachers' to demonstrate "modelling ways of being" to their students. The dominant elements of Pratt's apprenticeship conception are "teacher and content" (p.211) and it is based upon a belief that "a body of established wisdom and knowledge exists, in the form of expert practitioners, and is to be handed down from those who know, to those who don't know" (p.212). The Attitude Promotion conception does not mean that teachers 'hand down' good attitudes to students, rather, it emphasises an implicit manner of helping students to set up good learning attitudes through active interaction and by creating a proper learning environment. The teachers' modelling effect is only one of many environmental factors which foster good learning attitudes.

There is little in the literature to parallel the Conduct Guidance conception identified in this research. Pratt's (1992) 'nurturing' conception may be the closest. Pratt defined nurturing as "descriptive of a way of relating where genuine regard for the other person and a concern for the relationship bound the two together" (p.214). He argued that nurturing was not "reference to moral duty or obligation", instead, it 'has reference to relationship, caring, emotional support, and personal relationship" (p.214). He sub-labelled this conception as 'facilitating personal agency'. The Conduct Guidance conception also shares some ideas with Fox's (1983) 'growing theory' in that they both "place more emphasis on what is happening to the student as a person (p.158)". However, whereas Fox's 'growing theory' refers to intellectual factors the Chinese based conception refers to students' personal conduct.

Relating students' intellectual development to their moral and personal development, attending to the development of students' learning attitudes and personal conduct as an important aim of teaching, and expecting teachers to act as role models seem to be another aspect which differentiates the teaching conceptions of Chinese teachers from those of Western teachers (or at least those at university level). This may reflect another powerful tradition of Chinese educators, which emphasises that a good teacher should not only perform well in teaching and learning but also in other areas of life: the so called "Wei Ren Shi Biao (為人師表)". Given this tradition, it is not surprising that no participants rejected the Attitude Promotion conception in the quantitative part of this research.

The Moulding and Cultivating orientations are higher-order conceptions, each covering two or three of the ordinary conceptions of teaching listed above. These two orientations are similar to the 'knowledge transmission' and the 'learning facilitation' orientation identified by Gow & Kember (1993). While the 'learning facilitation' conception relates mainly to intellectual development, the Cultivating orientation identified in this research extends its domain from intellectual aspects to include the development of students' learning attitudes and their personal conduct.

From the above comparisons, it can be seen that in general, all teaching conceptions and orientations identified in this research reflect those identified in previous studies. However, the sharp focus on examinations, and the emphasis on relating teaching to developing good learning attitudes and good conduct, seem to characterise the teaching conceptions held by Guangdong school physics teachers. It is possible that parallel studies with Western secondary school teachers may provide similar findings.

Multiple conceptions of teaching

A number of researchers (Argyris & Schon, 1978; Bowden, 1988; Larsson, 1983; Marton & Säljö, 1984; Pratt, 1992) argued that an individual might have multiple or even conflicting conceptions and use them selectively, depending upon circumstances. In a survey assessing the teaching conceptions of 170 university lecturers, Kember and Gow (1994) reported that the departmental average for the 'learning facilitation' and the 'knowledge transmission' scale ranged from 4.2 to 4.7 and 3.4 to 4.0 respectively. According to the five-point Likert-type scale used in their study, this implied that on average, the lecturers' strongly agreed to the 'learning facilitation' orientation, and agreed to the 'knowledge transmission' orientation. This provided support for the above contention.

Conclusions

This is the first investigation of school physics teachers' conceptions of teaching from both qualitative and quantitative aspects in China. It is also one of the first in a non-Western context and amongst the first at secondary school level anywhere. Five conceptions of teaching and two higher-level orientations to teaching were found to be held by school physics teachers. A multiple-level model was constructed to describe the relationship among these five conceptions and two orientations. Based on the above findings, a questionnaire was developed to assess school physics teachers' conceptions of teaching in Guangdong China.

Qualitative findings of this research have provided insights which improve our understanding of teachers' conceptions of teaching:

(1) One teaching conception held by Guangdong school physics teachers seems to view students' examination performance, especially public examinations, as the most important indicator of good teaching and successful schooling. This seemed to be one of the major distinctions between the teaching conceptions held by Chinese school physics teachers and those held by Western tertiary lecturers. Western studies at school level may well find a similar conception (see also Chapter 4).

(2) Two other teaching conceptions held by Guangdong school physics teachers seem to combine classroom teaching with the cultivation of good learning attitudes and good conduct. These seemed to encompass both the Western 'facilitating learning' conception with the Chinese cultural focus on affective and moral development.
(3) Given the above differences, however, parallels of the five teaching conceptions and two higher-level orientations identified in this research could all be found in previous studies, though most of these studies were conducted at the tertiary level within a Western context. This supports the argument that most teaching conceptions found in the Western culture are likely to occur in other cultures, though some might emerge in one culture and not another (Prosser, et al., 1994; Watkins, 1997).
(4) A number of previous studies have suggested that an individual teacher might hold multiple or even conflicting conceptions of teaching. This research provided both qualitative and quantitative evidence to support this idea. Furthermore, it described two different pictures of these teachers. In one picture, a teacher might strongly support two conflicting conceptions because he/she took both "ideal" and "practical" considerations into account. In another picture, teachers saw teaching as a complex system, which could not be described simply by only one conception of teaching and so held multiple conceptions of teaching.
(5) This research also provides quantitative evidence to support a multiple-level model for describing the relationship among the teaching conceptions and orientations. This relationship is important for distinguishing between conceptions and for the clarification of the meaning of each conception.

Another contribution of this research was the questionnaire developed in this research, the SPTCT, for assessing school physics teachers' conceptions of teaching. Only two such questionnaires have been developed in the previous studies. Gow & Kember's (1993) questionnaire focused on university lecturers' conceptions of teaching in Hong Kong while Trigwell and his colleagues (1994) focused on university lecturers' approaches to teaching in Australia. The SPTCT is the first questionnaire in the field that focuses on secondary school teachers within the Chinese context that relates to a particular secondary school subject.

The SPTCT was carefully developed from the qualitative data collected in and the findings of the in-depth interviews and all items originate from the interview statements. Each scale relates to one teaching conception identified. Several scales combine into a higher-order scale related to a higher-level orientation. The structure of the SPTCT, and the relationships among the SPTCT items and scales were supported by a series of scale and item level confirmatory factor analyses. Therefore, the SPTCT questionnaire may not only be suitable for quantitative assessment, but also may be an instrument for linking qualitative and quantitative approaches.

Data collected by the SPTCT suggested a satisfactory reliability and validity for investigating school physics teachers' conceptions of teaching in Guangdong. With the SPTCT, it is possible to build the norms of teaching conceptions for all school physics teachers in Guangdong and probably in the most part of China. The SPTCT may be used for the development of questionnaires for assessing school teachers' conceptions of teaching in other subjects areas, too. The SPTCT may also act as a starting point for developing similar instruments to be used in other places within the regions that have a strong Chinese cultural context, for example, Hong Kong, Taiwan and Singapore and may also be useful in future cross-cultural investigations of teaching conceptions.

REFERENCES

Argyris, C. & Schon, D. (1978). *Organisational Learning: A Theory-of-action Perspective*. Reading, Massachusetts: Addison-Wesley.

Biggs, J.B. (1987). *Student Approaches to Learning and Studying*. Melbourne: Australian Council for Educational Research.

Biggs, J.B. (1989). Approaches to the Enhancement of Tertiary Teaching. *Higher Education Research and Development*, 8, 7-26.

Biggs, J.B. (1990). Teaching Design for Learning – A Keynote Discussion. Paper presented at the Annual Conference of the Higher Education Research and Development Society of Australia. Brisbane: Griffith University.

Biggs, J.B. (1992). *Why and How do Hong Kong Students Learn? Using the Learning and Study Process Questionnaires*. Education Paper 14. Hong Kong: Faculty of Education, The University of Hong Kong.

Biggs, J.B. (1998). Teaching across Cultures. A Keynote Speech on the International Conference on the Application of Psychology to the Quality of Teacher and Learning. Hong Kong: The University of Hong Kong, June.

Bowden, J. (1988). Achieving Change in Teaching Practices. In P. Ramsden, (Ed.), *Improving Learning: New Perspectives*. Great Britain: Kogan Page, 255-167.

Calderhead, J. (1981). Stimulated Recall: A Method for Research on Teaching. *British Journal of Educational Psychology*, 51, 211-217.

Christensen, C.A., Massey, D.R., Isaacs, P.J. & Synott, J. (1995). Beginning Teacher Education Students' Conceptions of Teaching and Approaches to Learning. *Australian Journal of Teacher Education*, 20(1), 19-29.

Dall'Alba, G. (1990). Foreshadowing Conceptions of Teaching. *Research and Development in Higher Education*, 13, 291-297.

Dunkin, M.J. (1990). The Induction of Academic Stuff to a University: Processes and Products. *Higher Education*, 20, 47-66.

Fox, D. (1983). Personal Theories of Teaching. *Studies in Higher Education*, 8(2), 151-163.

Fu, G. (1996). The Educational Environment should be Optimised by Doing away with the Practice of Emphasising Examinations but Neglecting Management (in Chinese). *Journal of the Chinese Society of Education*, 5, 22-23.

Gao, L. (1998). Cultural Context of School Science Teaching and Learning in P. R. China. *Science Education*, 82(1), 1-13.

Gow, L. & Kember, D. (1993). Conceptions of Teaching and their Relationship to Student Learning. *British Journal of Educational Psychology*, 63, 20-33.

Greeno, J.G., Collins, A.M. & Resnick L.B. (1996). Cognition and Learning. In D.C. Berliner & R.C. Calfee (Eds.), *Handbook of Educational Psychology*. New York: Simon & Schuster Macmillan, 15-46.

Kember, D. (1997). A Reconceptualisation of the Research into University Academics' Conceptions of Teaching. *Learning and Instruction*, 7(3), 255-275.

Kember, D. & Gow, L. (1994). Orientations to Teaching and their Effect on the Quality of Student Learning. *Journal of Higher Education*, 65(1), 58-74.

Larsson, S. (1983). Describing Teachers' Conceptions of their Professional World. In R. Halkes & J.K. Olson, *Teacher Thinking: A New Perspective on Persisting Problems in Education*. Proceedings of the first symposium of the international study association on teacher thinking. Tilburg, 123-133.

Liu, B. (1995). Some Ideas about Quality Education (in Chinese). *People's Education*, 7-8, 8-12.

Liu, W. (1996). Exploring into the Contradictions between Examination-oriented Education and Quality-orientated Education (in Chinese). *Journal of the Chinese Society of Education*, 5, 13-15.

Martin, E. & Balla, M. (1990). Conceptions of Teaching and Implications for Learning. *Research and Development in Higher Education*, 13, 298-304.

Marton, F. (1981). Phenomenography – Describing Conceptions of the World Around Us. *Instructional Science*, 10, 177-200.

Marton, F. & Säljö, R. (1984). Approaches to Learning. In F. Marton, D. Hounsell & N. Entwistle, *The Experience of Learning*. Edinburgh: Scottish Academic Press, 36-55.

Nunnally, J.O. (1978). *Psychometric Theory*. New York: McGraw-Hill.

Pratt, D.D. (1992). Conceptions of Teaching. *Adult Education Quarterly*, 42, 203-220.

Prosser, M., Trigwell, K. & Taylor, P. (1994). A Phenomenographic Study of Academics' Conceptions of Science Learning and Teaching. *Learning and Instruction*, 4, 217-231.

Prosser, M. & Trigwell, K. (1997). Relations between Perceptions of the Teaching Environment and Approaches to Teaching. *British Journal of Educational Psychology*, 67, 25-35.

Samuelowicz, K. & Bain, J.D. (1992). Conceptions of Teaching held by Academic Teachers. *Higher Education*, 24, 93-111.

Trigwell, K., Prosser, M. & Taylor, P. (1994). Qualitative Difference in Approaches to Teaching First Year University Science. *Higher Education*, 27, 75-84.

Trigwell, K. & Prosser, M. (1996). Congruence between Intention and Strategy in University Science Teachers' Approaches to Teaching. *Higher Education*, 32, 77-87.

Trigwell, K., Prosser, M. & Waterhouse, F. (1999). Relations between Teachers' Approaches to Teaching and Students' Approaches to Learning. *Higher Education*, 37, 57-70.

Watkins, D.A. (1998). A Cross-cultural Look at Perceptions of Good Teaching. In J. Forest (Ed.), *University Teaching: International Perspectives*. New York: Garland, 19-34.

Zhao, Z. (1996). *Current Educational Reform in China's Transitional Economy*. Seminar at the University of Hong Kong, December 6.

3

The Role of Assessment in Student Learning: The Views of Hong Kong and Swedish Lecturers

Bo Dahlin, David A. Watkins and Mats Ekholm

Twenty years ago, Elton and Laurillard stated that "the quickest way to change student learning is to change the assessment system" (1979, p.100). Since then, awareness of the significance of forms of assessment for students' learning processes has grown within the educational research community, and among practising teachers as well (cf. Knight, 1995; Brown & Glasner, 1999). Crooks (1988) in a comprehensive review of the area concluded that many assessment practices have detrimental effects on the quality of student learning, since they allowed and often even encouraged students to adopt surface learning strategies. The term "backwash effect" has been used for the phenomenon of the influence of assessment forms on learning strategies (see, for instance, Biggs, 1995). The backwash effect is generated by "the *student's* perception of the test, and the demands that it is seen to make" (Biggs, 1996, p.8). Awareness of this effect has led to an interest in exploring assessment methods which encourage students to develop study approaches which encompass more than the mere memorisation and reproduction of information (Biggs, 1995; Cheng, 1998; Hargreaves, 1997).

Another trend within research in higher education is the study of conceptions, based upon the phenomenographic approach (Marton, 1981). Starting with conceptions of learning (Säljö, 1982; Marton, Dall'Alba, & Beaty, 1993), it moved on to other basic educational concepts such as understanding (Entwistle & Entwistle, 1992; Dahlin, 1999), and teaching (Samuelowicz & Bain, 1992; Pratt, 1992). The basic rationale motivating these studies is that students' and teachers' conceptions of what they are doing and trying to achieve contribute strongly to how they act and behave in their learning and teaching practices, as shown by Van Rossum and Schenk (1984). Furthermore, there seem to be predictable correlations between teachers' conceptions of teaching and the learning strategies used by their students (Gow & Kember, 1993; Prosser & Trigwell, 1999; see also Chapters 2, 11 and 12).

The studies showing the backwash effect taken together with the phenomenographic studies indicate that there are systemic relations between teachers' and students' conceptions of the fundamental elements constituting academic studies. These elements include learning, teaching, subject matter, and assessment methods. In this chapter we take up the question of what variation of conceptions of the role of assessment in students' learning may exist among academic teachers. It seems plausible to assume, that the conceptions teachers have in this area constitute an important part of the systemic relations between conceptions and approaches described above. However, no phenomenographic study of such conceptions has yet been made to our knowledge.

The participants in our study come from two very different cultures, in very different parts of the world, viz. Hong Kong and Sweden. We took advantage of the opportunity to interview academic teachers in our respective working locations, because we thought this would increase the probability of finding a distinctive variation of conceptions.

Assessment practices in context

Hong Kong. Higher education in Hong Kong has expanded rapidly. While ten years ago there were two universities there are now nine and the percentage of the age cohort studying degree courses has over that period expanded from 5% to 18% (not including another 5% who study overseas). Today at universities in Hong Kong undergraduate courses are mainly taught in one semester modules with course grades awarded at the end of the module on the basis of a formal examination or more usually a combination of exam, assignment(s) and tutorial/practical performance (see Watkins, 1998). Hong Kong universities typically report assessment of undergraduate students on a five point letter-grade scale and guidelines of the percentage of students expected in each category are often provided (Watkins, 1998). On graduation students are awarded degrees of honours based on the British system. The assessment system at each university is monitored by external examiners many of whom come from outside Hong Kong.

Sweden. In Sweden also higher education has expanded during the last decade. As a reflection of this, in 1999 three polytechnical high schools were reformed into universities, making altogether 9 state run universities in the country (three are now private universities). During the 1990s the number of students in higher education increased, one of the reasons being increased unemployment and government policies to make access to higher education easier. Undergraduate modules are usually divided into smaller course units, which are assessed separately, at the end of 2, 5 or 10 weeks (in principle, any number of weeks between 1 to 20 is possible). The teacher(s) responsible for the course are generally free to decide which forms of assessment to use, even though there may be informal pressure from the institutional practice that has developed over the years. Grading is comparatively simple. In most fields there are three grades: Fail, Pass, and Pass with Honours. In Technical and Engineering subjects, a 1 to 5 scale is used, in order to be compatible with international grading systems. External examiners are called in only at the post-graduate level, that is for Masters and Ph.D. exams. They do not consider the assessment system as such, but the quality of the thesis produced. Graduation students are not awarded degrees and theses are not graded, but either pass or fail.

Method

The two samples

The Hong Kong sample consisted of 26 participants who volunteered to be interviewed after having answered a survey questionnaire sent out to 200 randomly chosen academic teachers in Hong Kong (Watkins, 1998). The Swedish sample consisted of 20 academics from a middle-sized Swedish university who volunteered to be interviewed. Both sets of interviewees held the position of Assistant Lecturer or higher, and represented a variety of disciplines from the Human, Social and Natural Sciences. Their teaching experience also ranged from 1 to 28 years in both samples.

Naturally, neither sample can be considered representative of the general population of academic teachers in Hong Kong or Sweden. Choosing to volunteer for an interview about the significance of forms of assessment presumably means that one has given the subject some thought, and finds it interesting to talk about. Since the two samples were not representative, any conclusions about the similarities and differences between academic teachers in Hong Kong and Sweden can only be tentative.

The interviews

The interviews were conducted by two Research Assistants (RAs), one in Hong Kong and one in Sweden. They were well informed about the style and purpose of phenomenographic interviewing, especially about the necessity of probing, asking for clarifications etc. As Prosser (1994) remarks, this is the most important aspect of using RAs in phenomenographic studies.

The interviews were semi-structured. The pre-established questions dealt with various aspects of assessment and student learning. The participants were asked to choose and reflect on one particular course, which they considered typical for their teaching work. Apart from the *direct* question of whether and how forms of assessment influenced students' learning, other, indirect questions were also put. These questions included the objectives of the chosen course; the forms of instruction and assessment used; and how examinations were graded. A question about whether "alternative" forms of assessment had been tried was also put.

The interviews were audio-taped and transcribed verbatim by the respective RA. The Hong Kong interviews were conducted in English, the Swedish ones in Swedish. The totality of the transcribed interviews consisted of approx. 600 pages. In the results section, quotes from the Swedish interviews are indexed with an "S," the Hong Kong interviews with "HK".

Analysis

The aim of phenomenographic interview analysis is to construct a range of categories of conceptions held by the group of participants at the time of the interviews. It is not assumed that the interviewees espouse the same conceptions, at different times or in different contexts. Nevertheless, *the variation* of conceptions obtained from the analysis is seen as generalisable across contexts.

Naturally, the answer to the *direct* question of whether and how forms of assessment influenced students' way of learning, was of central importance for the analysis. However, the whole interview was, in principle, taken as the unit of analysis. The answer to the direct question on the one hand, and answers to other questions on the other, were seen in relation to each other and as mutually illuminating.

The analysis was carried out in collaboration between the first author and each of the second and third authors. Many phenomenographic studies are the result of such team work, enhancing their validity. The person primarily responsible for the analysis proposes a system of categories, which is tested and probed by the other members of the group. As Bowden (1994) explains, this procedure "provides the discipline that ensures the full evidence of the transcripts is extracted and used to determine the final categories of description" (p.51).

In our case, the process of analysis had two major phases. In the first phase, the first and second authors worked closely together on analysing the Hong Kong interviews. The process followed the constant comparative method of Glaser and Strauss (1967) (a standard procedure in phenomenographic studies; see also Marton, 1986). The interviews were read and re-read and possible dimensions and categories of conceptions were suggested and discussed. When a particular category was provisionally established, another emerging category was compared to it and, if found to be critically different, was provisionally taken as yet another category.

The interviews were complex and many faceted. In the Hong Kong material in particular, some participants were very talkative. It was often hard to find unambiguous expressions of one single conception throughout such interviews. The phenomenographic analysis was confined to the *actual* role of assessment in student learning. Statements about ideal forms, and factors preventing them, were subjected to a thematic content analysis.

Two dimensions of the conceptions expressed emerged as clearly present in the interview data as a whole. These were the focus of the awareness of the backwash effect on the one hand, and the relation between curriculum and assessment on the other (see below). It also became clear that the interviews could be placed at definite "steps" along these dimensions. In this way, a two-dimensional outcome space was established, which constituted a structure in which the Hong Kong interviews were roughly positioned.

The second major phase of the analysis dealt with the Swedish interviews. This was primarily carried out by the first author. The preliminary outcome space, which was based on the Hong Kong interviews, was taken as a starting point for this analysis. However, from the Swedish interviews it seemed necessary to somewhat modify the steps along the two dimensions of the outcome space. (The major change was the adding of a middle position along the dimension "curriculum/assessment relation"). The third author then acted as a co-judge in trying to apply this modified structure to the Swedish interviews. The third author agreed that the structure as a whole was an adequate reflection of the Swedish interview material.

The Role of Assessment in Student Learning

However, it was sometimes difficult to agree on *one definite* position of a particular interview in the outcome structure. There were two reasons behind this difficulty: 1) the participants often expressed more than one conception; and 2) there was sometimes a lack of relevant and decisive interview statements.

Finally the Hong Kong analysis was reconsidered in light of the changes made on the basis of the Swedish material. In spite of the difficulties described, we feel that the outcome space as a whole is a reasonable and reliable description of both the inter- and intra-individual variation of conceptions that exists in this field.

Results

Conceptions of the actual role of assessment

The categories of conceptions of the actual role of assessment are described within the framework of a two-dimensional outcome space. The first dimension is called "curriculum/assessment relation" and concerns the relation between the assessment practice and the course curriculum, including forms of teaching and instruction. The second dimension is called "backwash effect" and is defined by which areas of student behaviour were seen as affected by assessment. This way of presenting the categories is in accord with what Marton and Booth (1997) has stated about the variations of experience studied in phenomenography:

> The variation in how a certain phenomenon is experienced, *between or within individuals*, can thus be understood in terms of the different ways of experiencing it *being different complexes of dimensions of variation*. (p.209; our italics)

The "curriculum/assessment relation" ranges from a completely external, over a partly external/partly internal, to a completely internal relation. By an external relation we mean that assessment is not viewed as part of the curriculum, but as something added on top of it, so to speak. Assessment then becomes an external device to measure the effects of the curriculum. Thus, the only relation between assessment and curriculum is that of measuring, checking and controlling the students' learning. When the relation is seen as internal, on the other hand, assessment is considered an essential part of the curriculum itself. Assessment is viewed as a learning experience in its own right, and it is intentionally used as such. This polarity of external versus internal curriculum/assessment-relation is (we believe) clear-cut and obvious in theory. In reality, however, what participants said in the interviews was not always easily categorised. For instance, one part of the assessment was seen as directed towards controlling the acquisition of so called basic knowledge, whereas the purpose of another part was to induce a reflective learning experience. The latter often took the form of more or less extensive project work, and was more common at higher course levels. Therefore, a middle position was constructed, in which the relation was seen as partly external, partly internal. The reason behind this may have to do with the notion of "basic knowledge," and the role that "memorising and reproducing" is perceived to play in the acquisition of such knowledge. We return to this issue in the discussion.

The dimension of backwash effect ranges over four positions. Its starting point is the view, that assessment affects students' motivation and effort. Knowing that one will be tested on one's knowledge, and possibly rewarded by a high grade, presumably stimulates students to work hard(er). Next, assessment can be seen as pointing out important knowledge areas. Students are very interested in getting to know what earlier assessments have looked like, in order to get an idea of what curriculum contents are important to focus on. Assessment make students read and study selectively: what is not likely to come up on exams is skipped over. Third, assessment can be seen as affecting the quality of students' understanding as a learning outcome (not as a learning strategy). Fourth, assessment can be seen as affecting the learning strategies and processes students use and go through during course work (naturally, this also affects the learning outcomes). We do not include "motivation and effort" in these processes and strategies. As used here, these are common sense notions, whereas "learning processes and strategies" signify more professional educational concepts.

The backwash effect dimension can also be seen in terms of the three phases of learning, as described by Marton, Watkins, and Tang (1997): acquiring, knowing and applying. The phase of acquisition is strongly related to learning strategies, that is, to actions used in order to "take in" new information. The second phase is more like a passive state of "knowing" something. It seems more connected with the result or outcome of the learning process. The third phase of application is both a process and an outcome. "Applying" can be part of the learning process, but it can also refer to the *ability* to apply, which is an outcome of learning. In these terms, the participants in our study were more eloquent about the backwash effect that assessment has on knowing and applying, than on the processes and strategies of acquiring. This is perhaps not surprising, since learning strategies is a field of inquiry within Educational Science, but seldom explored in detail by non-professional educationalists.

Figure 3.1 depicts graphically the two dimensional outcome space for conceptions of the actual role of assessment in learning, as well as where in this space the different categories are located, derived from analysis of our data. We have not been able to find a suitable name or label for each category. Instead, the characteristics of the conceptions in each category are summarily expressed by that category's position in the outcome space, and described in more detail below.

Figure 3.1
The two dimensional outcome space for conceptions of the actual role of assessment in student learning. The arrows indicate progressions towards more inclusive conceptions

The back-wash effect focus on	**Curriculum / assessment relation**		
	External	Partly external/ Partly internal	Internal
Motivation and effort	Category 1		
Curriculum content – facts – skills	Category 2	Category 4	
Learned Abilities	Category 3	Category 5	Category 7
Learning Strategies		Category 6	Category 8

Category 1. In this category, curriculum and assessment were seen as externally related. Awareness of the backwash effect was focused on students' motivation and effort, and assessments were often regarded as technical devices for measureing academic achievement. A lecturer in Organic Chemistry recounted how the introduction of brief but more frequent quizzes increased student performance:

> One point is that if we have more quizzes, I can see that the students spend more time during the semester year to do the revisions. [...] At the very last, the final exam, we found the absolute score is higher. (Organic Chemistry, 4HK)

This teacher also regarded it as "the spirit of examination to try to distinguish students according to their ability." The procedure of discriminating between high and low achievers sometimes seemed to be a very technical one, particularly among lecturers in Hong Kong, where the infamous "Bell curve" was often used more or less rigidly (see Watkins, 1998, for details). Assessment, from this perspective, becomes a technique for the presumably fair and objective measurement of student achievement, rather than an intrinsic part of the course curriculum.

Category 2. Here also the curriculum/assessment relation was seen as external, but awareness of backwash effect was focused on course content. By "course content" we refer to both theoretical knowledge as well as cognitive or practical skills. In subjects like Mathematics or Computer Programming, problem solving and the corresponding skills are essential parts of the curriculum and the course objectives. Such skills have mainly a technical, algorithmic nature, at least at the basic course levels. They can be acquired without any deeper cognitive changes, affecting personal thinking and attitudes. We therefore make a distinction between such skills and the "abilities" which are focused on in the next category.

As an illustration of this category, we quote a HK lecturer who talked about the backwash effect in terms of cue-conscious students:

> The questions that we give them in examination are limited to certain areas in the lectures and in some cases the topics that we choose for exam. When we give a lecture we know that certain parts are very easy to set questions on, others difficult to set questions. So if the students are careful enough they understand that, so that part is more popular. (Computer Studies, 17HK)

For this lecturer, class attendance was not obligatory. This in itself indicated that the relation between teaching and assessment was seen as external. About examinations he further said:

> (From) the responses on the examination's questions, I understand which part of the subject will be understood more easily, and which is more difficult for the students. So I can make a judgement on the lecture next year. But that would be two different sets of students, not the same. (Computer Studies, 17HK)

The only relation between assessment and curriculum seemed to be that examination results of one year influenced the teaching of next year's students. Altogether, these quotes imply that the curriculum/assessment relation was seen as external.

Examples of this category could also be found in the Swedish interviews. One lecturer in Mechanical Engineering (7S) talked about how assessment was used to check that students had acquired certain knowledge and skills, and his awareness of the backwash effect was primarily focused on students asking for previous assessment forms in order to familiarise themselves with the kind of questions that would come up in the exam.

Category 3. In this category the awareness of backwash effects was focused on the abilities that the students have developed during the course(s). Abilities in this context are not purely technical skills (as in category 2), but are based on a more internalised, personal understanding of a particular phenomenon. However, assessment was still seen mainly as a measuring device applied after the course.

One HK lecturer in English Literature was concerned that students learned to see the literature of a particular language group "as the culture and the thinking of that group of people in the world, incumbent in words." About assessment this teacher said:

> I am never content simply to set a discursive essay type question. I want that

kind of discussion but I also want close reading and specify text and want to know if a student can handle that, handle the vocabulary, handle what it actually means. Because it is quite easy for students to read books of criticism, get general notions about literature from them and spout these in essay without actually knowing much literature, without knowing really how to read literary texts very closely.... And of course I'm interested in also finding out who are the "A" students and who are the "B" students, who can do better and who are the "C's" and who are so poor at English that they have to, they really should have remedial English. (English Literature, 6HK)

In this quote, assessment seems to be mainly a means for the teacher to check whether the students have developed a certain ability to handle literary texts, and to diagnose which students need extra help.

A Swedish assistant lecturer in Nursing Science said there were never any disagreements among her colleagues about the form the assessments should take, because:

... often one has some thought about what it is that one conceives that the student should reach during this course, so to speak, in skills and in understanding... and as a rule we always agree [...] (Nursing Science, 14S)

Here also, assessment seems to be reduced to testing that the objectives of the course, in terms of acquired abilities, have been achieved.

Category 4. Here backwash effects were again seen as directed towards course content (concepts, facts or skills). However, the relation between curriculum and assessment appeared to be conceived simultaneously as external and internal. The internal view was expressed as an awareness of the possibility of using assessment as a learning experience in its own right. As an illustration, the HK lecturer quoted in the previous category at one (and only one) point in the interview said:

From my experience I can remember some of the questions I actually had on exams, certain exams when I was an undergraduate. That means that you are concentrating so fiercely in the exam that you tend to remember things about an exam, where you might forget other things from more casual attention in classes. So, I try to make the exam part of the learning experience. (English Literature, 6HK)

This lecturer is trying to make the exam a learning experience, but "learning" in this case seems to equal "remembering" some particular content or aspect of the course. It is not about developing an ability in the sense described in category 3.

A Swedish assistant lecturer in Chemistry expressed a similar view:

A: It's probably a lot of memorised knowledge [that is assessed] since it's on a basic level there is a lot of memorised knowledge, especially in Chemistry 1. But understanding is there too.

Q: In what way?
A: That they should put it into context, ... one can for instance ask them to solve something ... now that is a very open question, where they themselves have to account for what kind of material is needed, how you do the calculations, that you must do calculations... and here you can... also include for instance how accurately they can or want to work... (Chemistry, 11S)

Even though this teacher talked about "understanding," the focus seemed primarily to be on the *content* of this understanding. That is, assessment was used to check students' understanding of the course content in terms of Chemistry knowledge and laboratory skills. Still, in the area of skills, the described assessment form seems to have the potential for becoming also a learning experience.

Category 5. This is the major category in terms of the number of interviews that contained expressions of it. As in category 4, the relation between curriculum and assessment was seen as partly external, partly internal. However, awareness of the backwash effect included the abilities that students were expected to develop.

As an illustration we take some quotes from an HK lecturer in Mechanical Engineering:

The questions are primarily essay-based questions. ...., the intention is to make sure that the student understands the technology of the systems, in terms of how they are applied in industrial applications.... I do give students an indication of how I am going to structure the examination, because the examination is not just a case of regurgitating whatever notes I give them.... It is a matter of applying them in maybe some new scenario or recombining them in some alternative way to prove that they can apply that knowledge from different directions. [...] And I have told all the students that examination is a means of testing their understanding of the subject rather than testing their ability to reproduce notes. (Mechanical Engineering, HK)

Here, assessment seems intentionally designed to contribute to students' development of the capacity to understand and apply their knowledge in "new scenarios." In other words, assessment's backwash effect was used to influence the abilities that students were expected to develop. The form of assessment also had the potential of being a learning experience in itself. On the other hand, this lecturer also emphasised that an examination is "a means of testing", and in the interview he repeatedly said that he "told" the students that mere "regurgitating of notes" was not sufficient. This merely *telling* the students what is needed seems to implicate that there is still a lack in the integration between teaching and forms of instruction on the one hand, and assessment forms on the other. This, together with the emphasis on "testing," is our basis for saying that in this interview, the curriculum/ assessment relation was still seen as partly external in character.

A further example of this category are the following quotes from a Swedish lecturer who said the most important thing for an art historian "is precisely to learn to see and also to describe pictures and to be able to interpret them" (13S). Therefore, at higher course levels, assessment consisted in writing essays with such descriptions and interpretations. However, at the basic course level, examinations had a different purpose:

> ... in order for them to get any base at all to stand on I think it is necessary to memorise lots of factual knowledge because you have to test that in some way. (Art History, 13S)

Category 6. The difference between this and the previous category is that students' learning strategies were included in the backwash effect. Also the grounds of the "partly external/partly internal" categorisation were of different kinds. One was the view that higher scores were reserved for those students who showed understanding and abilities to apply. This was made explicit to the students, in order to stimulate deep strategies:

> My point to them [the students] was if you simply have a good memory, if you seem to reproduce the course notes, things that are taken strictly from books – that is not your own original thinking. You haven't got any value added to what is already there. Then you can't expect the top grades. (Public & Social Administration, 20HK)

The second basis for the "partly external/partly internal" categorisation was that there were cases where some forms of assessment, for instance short answer factual questions, were seen as devices for merely measuring reproduction of the discipline's "basic knowledge." Naturally, such examinations could not be regarded as particularly meaningful learning experiences. However, other assessment forms were seen as designed for stimulating students' development of deeper learning strategies, and as having the potential of being learning experiences. One HK lecturer in Business illustrates this view when he talks about memorising as the basis for more creative applications:

> I don't want the students to memorise everything, then it will affect their creativity. So that is why I am talking about I want a mix. But I think maybe, you know, in the primary, secondary education the students should memorise more. [...] So when they come into this college they already have a very solid foundation of basic knowledge. Then they can be exposed to creativity. And they can sort of forget about all the memorising things and try to talk about application, trying to relate it to real life. So I think I try somehow to make sure that the students memorise some things. But in terms of assessment I must confess that I don't encourage that sort of thing, because, take for example the case study, it is an open book. The student can prepare everything and bring it into the examination hall because we try to imitate real life. [...] But of course in the objective test [this was a MCQ test], ... the student should remember something. (Business, 1HK)

It seems clear from these quotes that this teacher envisages two kinds of assessment: one which simply measures already memorised "basic knowledge," and another which is designed as real life application in order to stimulate creative thinking. This interview subject was also very keen on trying to change the students learning strategies. He said he saw assessment as "a way of helping the student to learn," but that HK students most often "assume they come here to be taught." In response to the question how he tries to change the students' approach, he said:

> I try to make use of this sort of project [as a form of assessment]. I try to confront and I try to provoke. ... with a hundred students it is difficult to get students to respond. So we try to develop this sort of small class seminar project, what so ever. Try to confront the student, try to challenge. But most of the time you know you would be very lucky if you got 0.5% of the students to challenge you or come up. (Business, 1HK)

Even though he did not seem to be very successful, this teacher seems to do much more than merely *telling* the students what is expected of them: he is trying to make them *do* it in the very process of instruction, not only at the moment of examination.

A similar case was found among the Swedish interviews. This was a lecturer in Political Science. At the basic level courses he gave an examination with what he called "regurgitate-questions," because "if you are dealing with politics and administration you have to have the structure, you have to know about that [...] and then we have done that [examination] with a lot of a-b-c-questions so that it is easy to correct." However, he also used a kind of real life application task, which was discussed in groups:

> ... they get a material that shows the economy of a commune... They get a task that they shall on the basis of this commune's economy [...] they shall deliver a suggestion about how to increase the resources for child-care in this commune. (Political Science, 12S)

This teacher was clear about the backwash effect on learning strategies. The "regurgitate-questions" were intentionally designed to get the students to cram a lot of factual knowledge, whereas the group assignments were used in order to stimulate understanding, reflection and application both during course work and in the examination.

Yet another basis for the "partly internal/partly external" categorisation consists of interview cases where part of the assessment was designed to get away from mere "memorising and reproducing," but where the more important function of assessment still seemed to be the "fair and objective testing" of students performance. These interviews were characterised by much talk about the grading procedures, and a lot of effort seemed to go into them.

Finally, one HK lecturer (12HK) talked about having a final examination as being "like saying to the students that what is most important we keep secret to the very end." This teacher thought too much weight was given to final exams, but was not sure whether they could be abolished altogether. In his teaching he tried to change students' learning strategies by "asking questions and posing problems," and he used essays and group case studies as forms of continuous assessment. This issue is discussed in more detail below.

Category 7. This is the first category of conceptions in which the curriculum/assessment relation was seen as completely internal. In this view, the purely technical measurement of acquired knowledge, skill or ability was seen as irrelevant for genuine learning. Teaching and assessment were both geared towards developing understanding, even at the basic course levels. In the present category, "understanding" refers to the ability to relate and apply knowledge as an *outcome* of the learning process (not as a learning strategy). There is virtually no talk about the strategies students develop or use during course work.

This category is illustrated by some quotes from a Swedish lecturer in Literature. Similarly to the lecturer in Art History quoted in category 5, she emphasised the importance of being able to reflect and interpret works of Literature, but this was the objective already of the basic course level. In course work as well as in examinations, students were engaged in such activity. Reproducing basic factual knowledge played a very subordinate and insignificant role in her assessments:

> When it comes to Literature there is never a final answer but there are as I said different persons' suggestions for interpretation that you can put up against each other and that is why it is so important that they discuss these texts… and not just memorise from some handbook in Literature. (Literature, 4S)

The following quote was taken as an indication of her view of the relation between curriculum and assessment as internal:

> Well, I don't see… an examination as… a goal in itself, but every lesson is really a discussion, since we build instruction very much on group discussions and then make summaries of them. (Literature, 4S)

About the backwash effect she said:

> Q: Do you think the form of assessment influences the students' way of learning?
> [5-6 seconds silence]
> A: Well, of course, I suppose it does, … I mean they usually get hold of old examinations, we know that. And then at least they get an idea about the type of question we give and this thing that we say that it must be written in the form of an essay. That is, that they must follow up their thoughts, that there should be no mere listing of points but there must be a continuous discourse… and I think that makes them put an effort into thinking, even when they read an ordinary book. (Literature, 4S)

Admittedly, this teacher said the assessment form had an influence on students' thinking efforts, but this seems too vague and common-sensical to be taken as an expression of a clear awareness of the backwash effect on learning strategies (cf. also the long pause before answering).

Category 8. As in the previous category, here also the relation between curriculum and assessment was seen as completely internal. However, awareness of backwash effect included specific references to students' learning strategies, not only to the results of learning.

One HK lecturer in Computer Sciences said he let the students bring their textbooks, lecture notes and calculators into the examinations, because

> ... it forces me to set proper questions. I can't set questions like "give me the definition of..." because they can look it up in the book. (Computer Science, 8HK)

He also said that memorising had no important role in his courses "because of the way in which I do the assessment." In his teaching he used a lot of continuous assessment in order to influence students learning processes. At one point he had tried problem-based learning, but found that this approach was too "overwhelming" for the students. Still, he tried to use some of the ideas of problem-based learning in a more "structured and teacher directed" way.

Another HK lecturer spoke very frankly about the "children" who wanted answers to memorise and who "would never believe me when I told them what the exam was going to be."

> This is a third year final elective International Business, there are no answers! There's judgement, there's perspective, there's risk. It's a question oriented experience, not answers. [...] I am consistent that my assessment method is similar to my style and to the material that I teach. I teach what is my style. I could not teach factual answer oriented material. [...] I don't look for their answers [in assessment]. I look for how they develop whatever they are saying. Because there is no answer. (Business & Management, 2HK)

It seems clear from these quotes that this teacher used both teaching and assessment in order to influence students learning strategies. Merely measuring acquired knowledge was not really important to him.

The view that "there are no right answers" recurred in other interviews. In one, which was also placed in this category, the subject noted that the absence of right answers made students very anxious and uncertain. But he reassured them that this approach was "the way to learn. The alternative is rote learning." (Economics, 24HK) In order to change students' ideas about Economics he made them apply economic theories and concepts to all kinds of social phenomena, such as religion or the institution of marriage. These tasks were part of continuous assessment.

Finally, let us quote a Swedish lecturer in Sociology, who was acutely aware of the backwash effect on student learning strategies:

A: But I believe that this form of home assignment [writing a paper] quickens this learning. They notice that it doesn't work to just go home and copy the book, ... The teacher does not accept that you merely recount what is in the book, you have to take your position, you yourself have to say what you think is important and why and...

Q: So your view is that the way you assess can influence how the students, what study strategy they will...?

A: Yes, sure, oh yes, absolutely. ... it is a very important determining factor. ... I don't think there is anything wrong with the students. They adapt rationally to the system they have... that is why it is our task to design the examination so that they get the learning style that we want them to have. (Sociology, 15S)

This teacher said he always tried to arrange his teaching from his awareness of "what goes on in the students' heads." From the quote above it seems evident that the mere measuring of already acquired knowledge had no real significance for him, and that he saw an examination in itself as a learning experience for the students. He also questioned the significance of reproducing definitions of "basic concepts":

Traditionally, Sociology has basic concepts like "social norms," "social roles," "institutions," of course you can memorise those definitions verbatim but by doing that you will never understand what.... If you take a basic concept like "social role," you need an understanding of what question has been put so that one has arrived at this concept. [...] Basic concepts are in some way the results of human knowledge seeking activity. (Sociology, 15S)

The questioning of the notion of "basic concepts" which have to be acquired before one can move on to understanding and deeper learning strategies seems to be an essential characteristic of this category, as compared to category 6. There, the notion of basic knowledge seemed to justify an "after the fact" measuring of how much of this knowledge the students had acquired, even though one was aware that such tests encouraged surface strategies of memorisation and reproduction.

Ambiguities

As noted above, there were cases of vague or ambiguous interview statements which made categorisation difficult. For instance, some HK teachers recounted how a certain percentage of the grading points were reserved for "course work," such as tutorials or laboratory work (in Science). It could be argued that this illustrates an internal relation between curriculum and assessment, since assessment then in a sense becomes part of the course curriculum. On the other hand, this is not necessarily so, because it seemed in some cases to be based upon a fairly "technical" and quantitative point of view, as if merely saying that "course work must surely also be worth something." In such cases, there were no expressions of a more reflective educational rationale behind this procedure.

Another ambiguity is illustrated by the following statement:

> Then going into the final year of that degree student, we expect the student can learn or create it, the topic area, by themselves. So we have a dissertation or we call it a research project. It is also an important element. (Building & Real Estate, 21HK)

Is this lecturer saying that a dissertation or "research project" is used intentionally as a form of assessment in order to develop students' creative thinking? Or is she saying that since students at this level have to be in possession of this ability, we use this form of assessment? We opted for the latter interpretation. The reason for this choice was that the subject could not really answer the direct question on whether assessment forms had any influence on the way students learn.

Finally, the following quote raises the question of the contextual character of the conceptions described:

> We explain very clearly the structure of the course, what will happen and that first you will go into this and so on…and they become very conscious about their learning process, whereas in other courses I have which are not so well structured they are perhaps not as much aware about this […] it isn't self-evident that it always happens. (Assistant Lecturer, Art & Media, 8S)

This participant talked almost exclusively in terms of category 8. However, the quote above indicates that had she chosen to talk about another course, the conception expressed could have been different.

The disciplinary context

Conceptions are often contextual in character. Previous studies have indicated that faculty members from different disciplines often differ in their views of for instance course objectives and standards for grading student progress (Eljamal, Stark, Arnold, & Sharp, 1999). A dependence of assessment forms on disciplinary context has also been noted (Glasner, 1999). A plausible assumption would be, that this context also influences what functions assessment is seen to have in student learning. In some disciplines, for instance those belonging to Medicine or Engineering, serious consequences would arise if students did not acquire the knowledge and skills necessary for the work they are expected to do. In such cases, teachers may feel obliged to test, check and control that students have achieved the course objectives. This may influence the curriculum/ assessment relation (at least partly), making it more external, and students' learning strategies may fall out of focus. In one interview, placed in category 5, a HK Engineering lecturer said about the final examination:

> The questions are primarily essay-based … the intention is *to make sure that the student understands the technology in the systems*, in terms of how they

are applied industrially. (Mechanical Engineering, 16HK; our italics)

In contrast, in the Human and Social Sciences teachers often seem to be aware of the importance not only of the application of general theories to concrete cases, but also of theoretical and conceptual analysis, self-reflection and interpretation. In such a context it is presumably easier to realise the connection between the development of these abilities on the one hand, and course work and assessment forms on the other. Thereby, students' learning strategies also tend to come more into focus.

These two assumptions about the significance of the disciplinary area for the views expressed were partly confirmed by the interviews. There were more examples of categories 7 and 8 among teachers in Human or Social Science, whereas categories 1-3 appeared more frequently among teachers in "hard core" scientific or technological subjects.

On the other hand, cases pointing in the opposite directions were not completely absent. One HK lecturer in History (5HK) said he used to "mark off heavily" any mistakes in bibliographic entries, or even spelling, indicating that such basic skills were not to be compromised with, because according to his view History is a "public thing," and as an historian one is "working publicly." Another case was the HK lecturer in Computer Science quoted in category 8 above. Although Computer Science is a hard core subject with many algorithmic skills which simply must be tested, this teacher had developed a complex conception of the role of assessment in student learning.

Ideals and constraints

The results described so far have dealt with notions of the *actual* role of assessment in learning. However, the interviewed teachers frequently expressed views of the *ideal* role of assessment in student learning processes. Such ideals always showed themselves when talking about alternative forms of assessment which one had thought about but not tried; or had tried but given up. The ideal forms were often seen as more appropriate reflections of what students really had to work with in their future professional life. The reasons given for not having tried, or for going back to previous forms, had to do with perceived constraints of various aspects of the educational system. In this section, we will look closer at what these constraints were, and what ideal forms of assessment they were seen as preventing.

Physical space and resources

In one case, the lack of appropriate physical space was seen as preventing more authentic forms of assessment. A Swedish assistant lecturer in Electronic Engineering said:

> I believe very much in working with definite tasks that are relatively concrete, real problems or something like that and have that as... as some thread run-

ning through the whole course. But the problem is that then we would need rooms that are not booked by other... things, but where there were office landscapes or something... (16S)

Naturally, this type of constraint would be more commonly perceived in technological subjects, needing special instruments to test acquired knowledge and skills.

Class size

One ideal form of assessment sometimes mentioned was that of oral examinations. One Swedish lecturer was rather eloquent about this:

> Ideally I would bring in each student where you are sitting now, and talk to each student, that is more reliable than writing. [...] I get a much deeper understanding for when the student hesitates, reflects, answers directly, takes a chance, I can hear if he or she can follow an argument or construct an argument with knowledge, that is apply it linguistically... (Working Life Science, 9S)

The obvious constraint for this kind of assessment is the sheer number of students in classes. This prevented assessment forms where students could elaborate answers or produce long discourses – either in text or in speech – simply because of the time needed to read or listen and give feedback:

> We could be more group-based, more problem-focused [in assessments]. We could be more, a little bit more adventurous in some regard, but with the number of students we put in those big classes it is extremely difficult. (Health Science, 22HK)

Therefore, short answer questions or multiple-choice tests often have to be used instead, although it is recognised that these forms of assessment do not encourage deep learning.

The larger the number of students to assess, the more time is needed. Time equals money. In Sweden, no fees are paid by the students to the university. Resources for higher education are allocated by the state. Some Swedish lecturers perceived the state policy and budget for higher education to have serious effects on teaching and assessment:

> A: We looked at our economy the last four years and noted that we have increased our productivity with 33%... as it is called... and that, that... so now we are down at 5.8 hours per point [i.e., the students get 5.8 teaching hours per course week]. And that leads to some form of stress, chasing for effectiveness, which makes it very easy to cut...
> Q: What do you call effectiveness in this context?
> A: Well, yes... because it's so easy to take up the myth that as long as I stand

here and run through my part of the course it is effective, but that is, what worries me is that we loose so easily... our interest in designing education and teaching when we feel that we only get less and less teaching hours and larger and larger classes and more and more [students] who are not motivated...(Political Science, 12S)

Student characteristics

The perceived traits, characteristics, and abilities of students naturally influence what forms of assessment teachers consider possible to use. For instance, the fact that Hong Kong Chinese students study in a second language could be taken as a constraining factor:

> There are a lot of things that I would use more if their English ability was better. When I first came I used a lot of real world examples. They objected to that because it wasn't in the textbook. (Accountancy, 19HK)

Sometimes the knowledge students bring to basic courses is very limited and so teachers may feel forced to introduce a lot of "basic knowledge" material in their introductory courses. The assessment of such courses may tend to be external and quantitative in nature. As one Swedish lecturer said:

> Those who begin their studies here have not read very much, unfortunately, so then... it is always broadness against depth that we have to choose between. But there is something we call our literary canon and we think that if you are going to do Literature you ought to have read certain authors, it's like a must in some way, but that is at the cost of depth of course, but hopefully you get more depth [in advanced courses]. (Literature, 4S)

First-year students, in particular, were often seen as very dependent on their teachers. This it was argued prevented forms of assessment which presupposed independence, self-confidence, and initiative, for instance project work (but see Chapters 9 and 10):

> As we have run the project courses, those that I know of, they put *much* heavier demands on the students to run things themselves. And I think that one could perhaps change the teaching in other courses too a little in this direction but I don't know if that works with the beginning courses. There they are very... they are so dependent upon the teacher showing them what to do in some way... (Assistant Lecturer, Electronic Engineering, 16S)

Students were often seen as having acquired this dependency and lack of initiative in Primary and Secondary School. Both Hong Kong and Swedish lecturers complained that upper secondary schools did not encourage students to develop independence and initiative, and that their forms of assessment stimulated surface strategies of "memorising and reproducing." One Hong Kong lecturer was particularly explicit on this point:

> I'm not sure that the way we assess affects the way students learn. I think the way the students learn has been almost brain-washed by the time they get here, because no matter what we try to do to change it they seem to go back, they seem to want to go back into that same groove. (Accountancy, 19HK)

This teacher was very pessimistic about the possibilities to change her students' surface study approach:

> I know that what really works elsewhere doesn't seem to work here because it immediately gets put into this memorise and regurgitate routine. (Accountancy, 19HK)

Thus, the view that students would never change their learning strategies whatever was done, could perhaps dissuade teachers from attempting to change assessment.

Culture

Among the Hong Kong lecturers the cause of the habit of memorising and reproducing was not only taken to be previous school experience. It was also seen as a characteristic of Chinese culture (cf. Dahlin & Watkins, 2000). One Hong Kong lecturer compared Chinese and North American students thus:

> I think Hong Kong students think memorisation is very important; that is their whole... That's what they seem to have been taught. [...] I think the best North American students' concept of memorisation is, well, we want to memorise where you go to look stuff up, essentially. [...whereas] here [in Hong Kong] you find that people are more focused on *what* you look up rather than *how* to look it up, if you know what I mean. They would try and cram everything in and as a result not be very successful at it. (Business Management, 12 HK)

Another Hong Kong teacher saw the teacher-dependency of Chinese students as a further consequence of Chinese culture. From a North American/Western perspective, Hong Kong students could be seen as "immature," but from a Chinese point of view "they are disciplined, obedient children who do what they are told" (Business & Management, 2HK). This attitude made the students "just wait for the answers and give back the exact answers."

As already noted, some of the Hong Kong participants felt that they could not change these attitudes and habits of their students, no matter how hard they tried. Others, however, seemed to manage without difficulties:

> Q: How do you see the role of memorisation in your Hong Kong students?
> A: From my subject I don't think it is very important, because of the way in which I do the assessment. (Computer Sciences, 8HK)

The Role of Assessment in Student Learning

The grading system and institutional policy

Sometimes the grading system and institutional policy were perceived as limiting the possibilities to develop more suitable forms of assessment. One HK lecturer was very clear about this:

> We try to make examinations challenging but you are all the time constrained as well by the [Bell] curve and so in the end you wonder what you have achieved? [...] We have a very standard system for setting up the grades so that your assessment is pretty much set from the time the course is designed. So you are... it's not so easy to change, for example from 70% [final] exam and 30% [continuous] assessment to 50-50 or even 100%. There are [cases of] 100% or 50-50, but they had to be argued for very strongly in the beginning. Now that has become a little easier. I think there will be more flexibility, but still there is the sense of things needing to be the same. (Accounting, 19HK)

Thus, the necessity to pass a certain percentage of the students seems to have made "challenging examinations," where more students presumably could fail, impossible. This particular constraint was not found among the Swedish teachers, partly due to their much simpler grading system (see above). Forms of assessment were always up to the teacher to decide, even though there could sometimes be an informal pressure to conform and adapt to colleagues, particularly for more in-experienced assistant lecturers:

> Q: What freedom do you have in deciding forms of assessment?
> A: One could say we do as we please. There are some gruffs but I use "open book" and they may think what they like. (Ass. Lect., Electronic Engineering, 16S)

However, Swedish lecturers saw another constraint, which had much the same effect of making severe examinations impossible (see below).

Political and macrosocial factors

It is fairly obvious that the national educational politics as well as the structure and dynamics of society constitute the ultimate framework for what can and does take place within educational institutions. Aspects of this framework were also perceived as constraints on possible forms of assessment. In both Sweden and Hong Kong, the government's financial policy for higher education changed radically about ten years ago. In Sweden, pressure for fiscal efficiency was created by allocating resources to higher educational institutions according to the proportion of graduating students. Naturally, this made it economically impossible to fail more than a very limited number of students. One lecturer in Mathematics spoke very clearly about this:

> There are those who think that we should place the level so that most students pass. I think that, at least before we got the new funding system, there were

those who said that "we accept 100 students on a first-year course in Maths and only 15 will pass, but then I can't lower the level and lower the quality and pass a lot of extra students... if there are so many bad students that apply who should not study Maths, then I can't help that" [...] but that is completely meaningless, to spend one whole semester of both mine and the students' time, when only 15% have understood what it is all about [...] and now we do not get money for such things, that type of course, so there is no economy for that type of course... (2S)

Another type of external, macrosocial constraint was raised by a Hong Kong lecturer comparing the old British "final exam" system with the American practice of putting more emphasis on continuous assessment:

It seems to me that the final exam system applies to sort of an elitist band of traditional students or fraction of those. But I think it applies to a smaller and smaller fraction of, if you like, the new wave of students. Within the last 2-3 decades students have increasingly come to university, where the tendency in society is to say – well, you go to university in order to get this diploma in order to get this job. Industry and companies and government and the like in Hong Kong say you need a degree. [...] Well, America has for much much longer than the rest of the world faced up to the issue [...] that as education drifted away from being available solely to an elite, motivated, rich... that... that to guarantee that you grab the minds of the young people of the other kind you had to test them a lot in order that they at least for a few hours know this much in the expectation that then tomorrow and then the next day they know something relative to what you are saying to them. (Science & Technology, 25HK)

This lecturer seems to be saying that as higher education becomes mass education, the old British system with a final examination after several terms of study is no longer feasible. The "new wave" of students, lacking in motivation (and perhaps in ability), need to be kept on their toes with continual assessments. "There is no learning or scholarship tradition in our first generation working class students," as another Hong Kong lecturer said. (Such blunt "elitist" views were not expressed in the Swedish interviews, perhaps for ideological reasons.) He also pointed out that behind the increase in the number of students (with surface motivation) was society's need "to create lower level professionals, some of whom will be promotable over time" (Business & Management, 2HK).

Discussion

Three basic types of conceptions

From a global point of view, the two-dimensional outcome space could be summarised into three general types of conceptions. The first type would consist of categories 1-3. The common features of these conceptions is that there is virtually no talk about students' approaches to learning, or learning strategies. The focus is on course content, or the abilities students are expected to develop as a *result* of the course. Furthermore, assessment is viewed as something "very separate from the teaching and learning process, something to think about once the curriculum has been devised and plans for delivery finalised," as Brown (1999, p.3) describes what we have called the external relation between curriculum and assessment.

The second type of conception consists of categories 4-6. Here, teachers seem to have become aware of the teaching and learning *process* of the course, and sometimes even the strategies students use in order to learn. However, they also believe that there is a sort of "basic knowledge" which students simply have to acquire or internalise, *before* more sophisticated learning strategies can be usefully applied.

The third type of conceptions are the remaining categories 7 and 8. Here, the notion of basic knowledge to be accumulated has no, or a very subordinate role, to play. On the contrary, understanding, reflecting, interpreting, analysing, and relating – all such deeper strategies have an overriding importance from the start of the basic course.

This general characterisation of the conceptions described in this study suggests that there are two elements, the awareness of which would be critical for a *development* of teachers' conceptions of assessment: students' learning strategies and the notion of "basic knowledge." As long as teachers have the view that there is some basic knowledge to be acquired *before* understanding, relating and applying can take place, they will hardly come to the conception of a completely internal relation between curriculum and assessment. Similarly, teachers must become aware of the kind of learning strategies that various forms of instruction and assessment tend to evoke in their students.

The critical distinction: basic knowledge versus reflective understanding

Eljamal et al. (1999), in a study of US higher education teachers' goal statements, found that "intellectual development may be a low priority for instructors teaching introductory classes" and that "in introductory classes faculty focus on knowledge acquisition rather than on the relationships and connections with other fields" (p.21). They considered seeing "relationships and connections" as the core of intellectual development. The results of their study indicated that many US teachers in higher education do not see this kind of deeper learning as part of basic courses in their disciplines. It is saved for more advanced classes. The same point of view seems to be expressed by many of our interview subjects (see categories 4, 5 and 6).

The distinction between basic knowledge and higher order understanding is related to what Cole (1990) called two conceptions of educational achievement: "basic skills and facts" versus "higher order skills and advanced knowledge." The former goes together with a focus on the outcomes of learning, and the technical procedures for measuring these. The latter is relatively more focused on the processes of teaching and learning. Cole argued that these two conceptions are not sufficiently integrated, neither in educational research nor in teaching practice. In her own words, "the fact that we have two such different conceptions playing dominant and conflicting roles illustrates a major limitation that our field must overcome" (p.5). Overcoming this limitation may also play a significant role in overcoming the "double-tongued" views of categories 4 to 6.

Another parallel between conceptions uncovered in other studies, and the ones described here, concerns teachers' conceptions of teaching. A number of studies have found that teaching conceptions ranged from those which strongly advocated transmission of information from the teacher to the students to those which emphasised facilitation of understanding in students (see also Chapters 2, 11, and 12).

This basic polarity seems to reflect the polarity between external and internal views of the curriculum/assessment relation. That is, the notion of teaching as "transmission of information" is logically compatible with an external view of this relation; whereas the view of teaching as "facilitating understanding" seems more compatible with seeing assessment as an integral part of teaching and learning. It is also possible, even probable, that teachers adopt one conception or the other, depending on circumstances. The constraints of large classes may for instance "force" the teacher to act according to the information-transmission model, and apply an "after the fact", purely measuring form of assessment. This leads to the next theme of our discussion.

Ideal and working conceptions

Samuelowicz & Bain (1992) note that academic teachers might have both "ideal" and "working" conceptions of teaching:

> It seems [...] that the aims of teaching expressed by academic teachers coincide with the "ideal" conception of teaching whereas their teaching practices, *including assessment*, reflect their working conception of teaching. (ibid, p.110; our italics)

Our interview data suggest the same for conceptions of the role of assessment. In an interview situation, many participants would probably – for various reasons – rather talk about their "ideal" conception than their "working" one. Furthermore, Samuelowicz and Bain suggest that research may focus more on the factors that prevent teachers from acting according to their ideal conceptions. In this study, we have noted a number of constraints mentioned by the participant teachers, which were perceived as preventing them from realising their ideal forms of assessment. Most of these constraints were also related to forms of teaching and instruction.

As noted in the results, some participants expressed a wish for more authentic forms of assessment, where students would work with "real life" problems. As Biggs (1996) notes, this "ecological approach" to assessment has become a recent catch-cry, reflecting the fact that in general assessments are "detached and quantitative" in nature, and focused on "the declarative knowledge prerequisite to problem solving" (p.8). However, to implement more authentic assessment

The Role of Assessment in Student Learning

methods is not always easy, considering all the constraining factors that the participants in our study experienced. If, for instance, there is a perceived need for continuous assessment, this need may come into conflict with the large number of students, since continuous assessment is more time consuming. On the other hand, using self- and peer assessment methods could be a good way out of this predicament (Choy, 1997).

Towards a systems perspective on constraints

A moment's thought reveals that many of the forms of constraint perceived by the participants in this study are connected. For instance, the large number of students in each course, which prevents time consuming individual oral examinations, is connected with the economic rationalism (Biggs, 1996) of state educational politics. Another example is how macrosocial changes (e.g. increasing rates of unemployment among young people) contribute to larger groups of "unmotivated" students. "There is no learning tradition among first generation working class students," as one Hong Kong lecturer said. That is, "macrosocial factors", "student number" and "student characteristics" are linked. In engineering disciplines in particular the availability of physical localities with technical equipment sets limits for what forms of assessment are possible. Dominant political ideologies and judicial regulations also influence institutional policies. Within the degrees of freedom created by such regulations the perceived student characteristics may further contribute to which methods of assessment are chosen. Taking a systems perspective on educational practice (cf. ibid.), it seems clear that academic teachers are facing a system of interacting and constraining factors. Figure 3.2 intends to illustrate the interacting relations between the constraining factors presented in our results. The figure should be taken as tentative and intuitive only, we cannot develop it further here.

As a final remark, let us compare tertiary education with the primary and secondary levels, from a systems point of view. It may be argued that there are three systemic factors which continually warp all attempts to reform the lower level school system, viz. that it is a *mass education*; that it is *obligatory*; and that students are *graded*. Seldom if ever are these factors seriously considered when school or curriculum reforms are planned. Yet they are the basic conditions under which most lower level schooling takes place. In our time, higher education is slowly coming to work under virtually the same conditions. The growing number of students is turning it into a mass education of sorts. It is not obligatory in the judicial sense, but it is becoming a must from a practical, realistic point of view, particularly in countries with high youth unemployment. The competition for high grades is obvious in a place like Hong Kong, and is becoming more significant in Sweden too.

Figure 3.2
Some systemic interactions affecting forms of assessment in higher education. Arrows represent possible influences and constraints, not causal relations

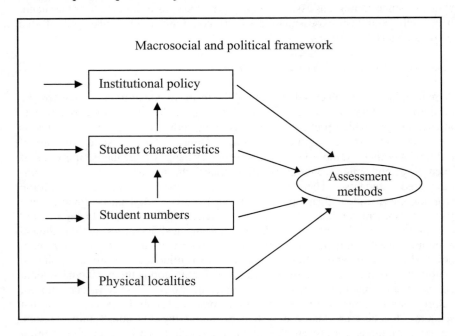

In trying to implement authentic forms of assessment one must also keep an eye on these systemic constraints. On the other hand, assessment forms *are* changing. As Glasner (1999, p.22) notes, the pattern of assessment experienced by today's students in higher education are more likely "to involve a variety of course work components as well as examinations than that of students' of even a decade ago." She even suggests that internal and external factors at work in higher education today "will combine to provide the revolutionary context in which assessment will be viewed as inextricably linked to learning" (p.27).

NOTE

The Hong Kong and Swedish sections of this research were supported by grants from the Hong Kong Research Grants Council and the Committee for Research and Conference Grants at the University of Hong Kong. The authors would like to thank Elizabeth Chan and Bjorn Eliasson for research assistance.

REFERENCES

Biggs, J.B. (1995). Assessing for Learning: Some Dimensions Underlying New

Approaches to Educational Assessment. *The Alberta Journal of Educational Research*, 41(1), 1-17.
Biggs, J.B. (1996). Assessing Learning Quality: Reconciling Institutional, Staff and Education Demands. *Assessment & Evaluation in Higher Education*, 21(1), 5-15.
Bowden, J.A. (1994). Experience of Phenomenographic Research: A Personal Account. In J.A. Bowden & E. Walsh (Eds.), *Phenomenographic Research: Variations in Method*. Melbourne: Royal Melbourne Institute of Technology, 44-55.
Brown, S. (1999). Institutional Strategies for Assessment. In S. Brown & A. Glasner (Eds.), *Assessment Matters in Higher Education*. Buckingham: Open University Press, 3-13.
Brown, S. & Glasner, A. (Eds.) (1999). *Assessment Matters in Higher Education*. Buckingham: Open University Press.
Cheng, L. (1998). Impact of a Public English Examination Change on Students' Perceptions and Attitudes toward their English Learning. *Studies in Educational Evaluation*, 24, 279-301.
Choy, S. (1997). Collaborative Assessment. In M. Hargreaves (Ed.), The Role of Assessment in Learning. *ASDU Issues*. Brisbane: Queensland University of Technology, 14-16.
Cole, N.S. (1990). Conceptions of Educational Achievement. *Educational Researcher*, 19(3), 2-7.
Crooks, T.J. (1988). The Impact of Classroom Evaluation Practices on Students. *Review of Educational Research*, 58, 438-481.
Dahlin, B. (1999). Ways of Coming to Understand: Metacognitive Awareness among First-year University Students. *Scandinavian Journal of Educational Research*, 43(2), 191-208.
Dahlin, B. & Watkins, D.A. (2000). The Role of Repetition in the Processes of Memorising and Understanding: A Comparison of the Views of German and Chinese Secondary School Students in Hong Kong. *British Journal of Educational Psychology*, 70, 65-84.
Eljamal, M.B., Stark, J., Arnold, G.L. & Sharp, S. (1999). Intellectual Development: A Complex Teaching Goal. *Studies in Higher Education*, 24(1), 7-26.
Elton, L.R.B. & Laurillard, D.M. (1979). Trends in Research on Student Learning. *Studies in Higher Education*, 4, 87-102.
Entwistle, A. & Entwistle, N. (1992). Experiences of Understanding in Revising for Degree Examinations. *Learning and Instruction*, 2(1), 1-22.
Glaser, B.G. & Strauss, A.L. (1967). *The Discovery of Grounded Theory: Strategies for Qualitative Research.* Chicago: Aldine Publishing Company.
Glasner, A. (1999). Innovations in Student Assessment: A System-wide Perspective. In S. Brown & A. Glasner (Eds.), *Assessment Matters in Higher Education*. Buckingham: Open University Press, 14-27.
Gow, L. & Kember, D. (1993). Conceptions of Teaching and their Relationship to Student Learning. *British Journal of Educational Psychology*, 63(1), 20-33.
Hargreaves, M. (Ed.) (1997). The Role of Assessment in Learning. *ASDU Issues*. Brisbane: Queensland University of Technology.

Knight, P. (Ed.) (1995). *Assessment for learning in Higher Education*. London: Kogan Page.

Marton, F. (1981). Phenomenography – Describing Conceptions of the World Around Us. *Instructional Science*, 10, 177-200.

Marton, F. (1986). Phenomenography – A Research Approach to Investigating Different Understandings of Reality. *Journal of Thought*, 21(3), 28-49.

Marton, F. & Booth, S. (1997). *Learning and Awareness*. Mahwah, N.J.: Lawrence Erlbaum.

Marton, F., Dall'Alba, G. & Beaty, E. (1993). Conceptions of Learning. *International Journal of Educational Research*, 19, 277-300.

Marton, F., Watkins, D.A. & Tang, C. (1997). Discontinuities and Continuities in the Experience of Learning: An Interview Study of High-school Students in Hong Kong. *Learning and Instruction*, 7, 21-48.

Pratt, D. (1992). Conceptions of Teaching. *Adult Education Quarterly*, 42(4), 203-220.

Prosser, M. (1994). Some Experiences when using Phenomenographic Research Methodology in the Context of Research in Teaching and Learning. In J.A. Bowden & E. Walsh (Eds.), *Phenomenographic Research: Variations in Method*. Melbourne: Royal Melbourne Institute of Technology, 31-43.

Prosser, M. & Trigwell, K. (1999). *Understanding Learning and Teaching: The Experience in Higher Education*. Buckingham, UK: Society for Research into Higher Education.

Samuelowicz, K. & Bain, J.D. (1992). Conceptions of Teaching held by Academic Teachers. *Higher Education*, 24, 93-111.

Säljö, R. (1982). *Learning and Understanding. A Study of Differences in Constructing Meaning from a Text*. Gothenburg: Acta Universitatis Gothoburgensis.

Van Rossum, E.J. & Schenk, S.M. (1984). The Relationship between Learning Conception, Study Strategy, and Learning Outcome. *British Journal of Educational Psychology*, 54, 73-83.

Watkins, D.A. (1998). Assessing University Students in Hong Kong: How and Why? In D.A. Watkins, C. Tang, J.B. Biggs & R. Kuisma (Eds.), *Assessment of University Students in Hong Kong: How and Why, Assessment Portfolio, Students' Grading*. Project Series, Volume 2. Hong Kong: City University of Hong Kong, 5-28.

TEACHER PRACTICE

4

Teacher-Student Interaction: Attributional Implications and Effectiveness of Teachers' Evaluative Feedback

Farideh Salili

The influence of teachers' classroom behavior on student motivation has long been documented. Until recently, however, the role of the teacher as a motivator was viewed in a narrow sense – a person who would dispense reinforcement for good behavior or successful academic work (Pintrich & Schunk, 1996). Recent research evidence in the West provided a wealth of evidence showing that the influence of teachers' classroom behavior on students is far more complex than was once believed. Teachers influence their students not only through reward and punishment, but also by the way they structure their classroom goals (Ames & Archer, 1988), communicate their expectations (Stipek, 1993), and other activities associated with instruction such as grouping practices, teaching, assessment, and feedback methods, and generally, the quality of their interactions with students (Brophy, 1981; Marshall & Weinstein, 1984; Pintrich & Schunk, 1996).

Studies also show that teachers and students have reciprocal effects on each other (see Pintrich & Schunk, 1996). Teachers' activities related to instruction affect students' learning and motivation, and in turn teachers' behaviors are affected by the way students respond to classroom activities.

While we now know a lot about teacher-student interactions in Western schools, relatively little research has been conducted in Chinese schools. Asians differ from their Western counterparts in their cultural values, beliefs and norms of behavior (Salili, 1994), so it is quite possible that the pattern of teacher-student interactions may be different in Asian cultures. This chapter is based on such an assumption. I will explore teacher-student interactions in Hong Kong schools and argue that culture and context of learning has a profound impact on the way teachers interact with their students and in turn on their motivation to learn.

The first part of the Chapter will present a review of the existing literature and research on the influence of Chinese culture on the nature of teacher-student interaction. The second part will report major findings of a research program in Hong Kong focusing on teachers' performance feedback, reward and punishment, and their effectiveness and influence on students' motivation and behavior.

The Culture and Context of Teaching and Learning in Hong Kong Schools

In any culture, teacher-student interaction is influenced by norms of behavior, values, and beliefs that exist in that culture. These cultural characteristics are not stable over time and will change as people are exposed to other cultures through geographic mobility, media and information technology. The exposure to Western cultures and increased affluence are bringing about some changes in the style of parenting and educational practices in Asian countries. Child-rearing and education is becoming more democratic, creating a challenge to the absolute power of parents and teachers. However, while new ideas and practices are introduced, the old cultural values and practices still exist side by side at the same time, causing conflicts between generations and within the individuals.

Teacher-student interaction in Hong Kong is influenced by the same forces. The author, in the course of her 23 years of teaching and research in Hong Kong, has observed dramatic changes in the way teachers and students interact with each other. Many of these changes are brought about by Western educated teachers and educators who are active in trying to change the education system of Hong Kong from teacher-centered, examination and textbook driven to a more student-centered, broader-based and analytical system. The introduction in 1995 of the Target Oriented Curriculum (TOC) in elementary schools is an example of such a change.

In spite of new innovations, however, the influences of the traditional cultural values still exist and can be observed in Chinese classrooms. Hence, it is important to understand cultural values that shape teacher-student interactions.

Influence of traditional child rearing practices

Child rearing and education in the Chinese culture is characterised as being generally harsher and more authoritarian than that in North America and Western Europe (Salili, 1995; Wong, 1992). As an example, it is a tradition that parents do not praise their children within their earshot so that they are not spoiled. It is believed that praise undermines character. According to Wong (1992), "When an outsider praises the child, it is considered modesty to speak ill of the child by pointing out his faults and shortcomings" (p.36). Teachers affected by this philosophy seldom praise children in their classroom.

Punishment on the other hand is considered beneficial to children and administered frequently (Ho, 1986). Corporal punishment in particular has a long history as "the best way to educate a son" (Wong, 1992, p.37). Chinese believe that the cane breeds filiality and it is not uncommon even today for parents to corporally punish their children. Chen, Lu, Hung, & Chen, (1980) in a Taiwan study found that a great majority of teachers, parents and students thought that corporal punishment should be allowed as long as no injury was inflicted on children. The most popular form of punishment used by the teachers included standing in a corner, hitting on the palm and extra school work. Teachers in Hong Kong may also be influenced by the mentality that pain on the body is good for the child and punishment strategies that inflict exhaustion is common although the cane is not used (Wong, 1992). However, more recently, at least officially, corporal punishment is not allowed in good schools.

The school context

Although teachers in Hong Kong are still among the lower paid professionals compared with lawyers and medical doctors, they enjoy a high degree of respect from the students and their parents. This is because Chinese attach great importance to education and teachers are at the heart of educational establishments.

The value that a society places on education reflects both historical tradition and the current social structure of that society. These forces influence the structure of the education system as well as teaching and learning processes. The competitive examination system that exists in most Asian countries, for example, is rooted in the ancient practices used by governments to select civil officials (Chen & Stevenson, 1995). Cultural values are also reflected in educational policies such as the length of the schooling, the type of role models the textbooks promote, as well as the manner in which students and teachers interact.

In Chinese societies there is a set of rules of behavior which people learn early in life, which influence their behavior. One such rule, according to Liu (1986), is to respect and obey one's superiors under all circumstances. "If your superiors are present, or indirectly involved, in any situation, then you are to respect and obey them" (p.78). Teachers in typical Chinese schools are considered authorities and superior. Students are taught to respect, obey, listen, and follow their instruction, and not to challenge them. Any deviations from these rules are met with punishment. One of the roles of a teacher is to enforce strict discipline in students. Speaking loudly or talking to each other are forbidden. Students are only allowed to talk when they are asked questions by the teacher. Questioning the teacher could be perceived as a sign of disrespect.

Lam (1996), in an interesting study of 690 teachers in 93 primary schools in Hong Kong, asked teachers to indicate their conception of ideal pupils compared with their conception of creative pupils. Regardless of their method of teaching, "Teachers' conception of an ideal pupil fit the typical Chinese good child model" (p.39) and in line with Confucian values. The top-ranking characteristics of ideal pupils for all the teachers were: being honest, self-disciplined, respecting parents, being responsible, and healthy. Other traits teachers wanted their students to have were: being diligent, not-selfish, humble and obedient. This study clearly shows that the influence of the traditional values are still quite strong in present day Hong Kong despite Western influences.

Similarly, teachers' interaction with their students follows cultural norms of behavior in Chinese culture. A common belief among school teachers is that, until they are in full control, they should keep a straight face, avoid talking to or smiling unnecessarily at the students when they start a new class. Smiling and talking to the students could encourage discipline problems (reported by a group of teachers in an informal focused interview in 1998). Hence, teachers should keep their distance with students so that they could control and manage the class more effectively.

Chinese also believe that the best way of learning is through memorisation and repeated practice (Biggs, 1992; Liu, 1984, cited in Liu 1986). The effect of this widespread belief is the extraordinary amount of homework and assignments, and the frequent tests and examinations that teachers give students to ensure adequate practice and learning. A survey by Liu (1984) in Taiwan revealed that teachers in most public schools (grades 1 to 6) required students to memorise every lesson in the Chinese language textbook. A similar trend was also observed in junior high schools. Stevenson and his colleagues (cited in Liu, 1986) reported that Taiwanese grade 1 pupils spent 77 minutes each week doing homework, more than five times longer than their American counterparts. In our recent study (not yet reported) we also found that memorisation was prominent among ways thought to ensure learning and often synonymous to learning.

Teacher's feedback

One of the major functions of a teacher is to give feedback to students on their performance. According to Pintrich & Schunk (1996), feedback can provide important information to students and motivate them to work harder, use more appropriate strategies, improve their work, as well as give them a sense of competence and self-efficacy. Feedback provides information about accuracy of students' work and ways of correcting mistakes. Constructive information concerning errors can increase self-efficacy and enhance motivation. Feedback indicating that answers are correct may motivate students by showing them that they are becoming more competent.

Feedback can also provide motivational information such as comments on the progress made and the level of competence. This may include comparisons with or observation of peers (e.g., "see how John is doing"), and persuasive feedback such as, "I am sure you can do better than this" or "keep up the good work". According to Bandura (1986) such feedback increases students' sense of self-efficacy.

Information, linking students' performance with attributions such as effort is likely to increase students' motivation (e.g., "you need to put more effort and change your strategies"). Furthermore, giving information as to how appropriate their strategies are, and how they could improve them, helps students to focus on important aspects of the task, organise the learning material, and use appropriate learning strategies. Learning an appropriate strategy enhances the chances of success and in turn increases self-efficacy and motivation (Pintrich & Schunk, 1996).

The type of feedback and their consequences outlined above is normally based on formative evaluation of students' work which is more common in Western schools. The type of feedback that students receive in Hong Kong is mainly in the form of marks and grades which are based on competitive examinations. Hence the amount and type of information provided by the teacher is at best limited.

In 1995 the Education Department of the Hong Kong Government introduced Target Oriented Curriculum (TOC) with the goal of reforming and changing the orientation of the school curriculum, pedagogy and assessment. TOC was designed to promote individualism, all-rounded development of the students, child-centered, task-oriented learning and criterion-referenced assessment (Morris, 1999).

A key component of TOC is that target oriented assessment is supposed to replace frequent competitive examinations with formative evaluation. It was hoped that such an assessment would identify areas of strength and weakness and provide constructive feedback for students, teachers and parents. However, other structural aspects of the education system, such as aptitude testing, allocating students at the end of grade 6 to different secondary schools according to their academic performance, and classifying schools according to their academic standards, continued to co-exist parallel to TOC.

Morris (1999) reported that the primary form of feedback to students before the introduction of TOC was in the form of reporting examination results with percentage marks and ranking the pupils within the class. With the introduction of TOC in primary schools, a combination of marks/grades and checklists which show pupil's performance on assessment targets is used, with less use of comparisons between the pupils. "Ticks and crosses were used to indicate pupils' ability to perform a specific skill or their level of performance was differentiated on a quantitative scale (e.g., outstanding–poor). There was little evidence of feedback designed to identify what the pupils' needed to do to improve their learning (p.17)". Morris reported instances where teachers provided extensive (verbal) comments and feedback on pupils' progress. However, these forms of assessment were not seen as legitimate as it was not considered objective evidence of students' performance. Teachers still continued to rely on tests and exams in giving feedback and reporting the students' progress, and considered examination results as the most reliable and objective feedback.

Morris interviewed 34 students in five primary schools to explore students' views on the type of feedback they received. The majority of students claimed that they did not receive any feedback other than grades/ marks, and ranking within the class. Some students in each school, however, reported that they had received feedback in varying forms including praise and stickers when they performed well (e.g., "good boys/girls") and punishment when they behaved badly.

Hence, new innovations from the West may be accepted, but only to be incorporated into the old and traditional structure. The feedback to the students most of the time provides information as to how they performed compared to their peers.

Teacher Praise and Criticisms

According to Brophy (1981), praise is a positive feedback expressing teacher's approval of students' behavior or academic work. It is an indication that "the behavior is appropriate and that answers are correct" (cited in Pintrich & Schunk, 1996, p.343). Praise goes beyond a simple feedback on performance as it conveys teacher's positive affect as well as providing information about the value of the student's behavior.

From a behaviorist perspective praise can be an effective reinforcer if given immediately for a specific behavior or performance and if it is perceived as credible and sincere. Brophy (1981), in a review of research literature on praise, reported that praise does not always act as a reinforcer because it is often administered inconsistently, non-contingently, and not for a specific behavior. Teachers often praise students because they perceive that students need to be praised, not necessarily for good behavior or performance. Brophy's (1981) review of research also showed that praise was more effective in young children because they liked to please adults, but it was not as powerful with older children.

Criticism is defined as expression of disapproval of students' academic work or behavior (Pintrich & Schunk, 1996). It indicates that the behavior is inappropriate or the performance is poor. Research shows that criticism in moderation can be motivating but its effectiveness diminishes when it is given frequently. Criticism is given more frequently to boys than to girls, and more to lower socio-economic class students and blacks. Teachers also criticise students for whom they hold low expectations (Brophy & Good, 1974). The effectiveness of criticism for motivating students depends on whether it involves motivational processes. It is effective when it indicates to the students that they are competent and they could do better if they expend more effort and use better strategies (Pintrich & Schunk, 1996).

Both praise and criticism may convey attributional information to the students about what the teacher thinks of their ability and effort (Pintrich & Blumenfeld, 1985). Since praise and criticism convey teachers' belief about ability they could be detrimental to students' motivation if given indiscriminately. Praise for success at an easy task, for example, will convey the message that the teacher thought the student has low ability and that he or she is not expected to learn much. Criticism conveying the message of low ability (e.g., "you will never be able to figure this out") could have a similar effect and lower the students' self-efficacy.

The attributional implication of praise and criticism on student learning and self-evaluation has been the focus of much research in the past two decades (see Brophy, 1981; Marshall & Weinstein, 1984; Meyer et al., 1979; Meyer, 1982; Barker & Graham, 1987; Schunk, 1989). Several studies have examined how individuals combine information from various sources to make judgements about the consequences of success and failure. The results of these studies indicate that, generally, a successful outcome is rewarded more when the student's ability is low than when it is high, and failure is punished more when the ability is high than when it is low. Since ability and effort are perceived to have a compensatory relationship, this indicates that effort may be the primary determinant of reward and punishment (Weiner, 1986).

Based on these findings Meyer et al. (1979, 1982) conducted a series of studies to examine the effect of teacher's praise and blame on students' self-evaluation of ability. They hypothesised that since teacher's praise and criticism reflect the amount of effort students spend on the task, if the difficulty level of the task is known, then students should be able to draw conclusions as to how their abilities are estimated. These hypotheses were tested among German students of different ages. The results showed that older students perceived praise after success, or neutral feedback after failure, as an indication that the teacher perceived their ability to be low. On the other hand, when they were given criticism after failure and neutral feedback after success, they perceived that the teacher had estimated their ability to be high and their effort low. However, younger students who were given similar scenarios perceived praise after success as an indication of high ability and criticism after failure as a sign of low ability.

These findings suggest that praise, often given for reinforcement, may have negative consequences on students' perception of ability. Research findings, however, suggest that ability is a much more important factor to students (Covington & Omelich, 1979; Nicholls, 1978). Furthermore, reaction to evaluation may be determined by many personal as well as situational and contextual factors, such as the individual's achievement goal (Jagacinski, Nocholls, & Burton, 1983), classroom task structure, grouping practices, feedback and evaluation procedures, information about ability, and quality of interactions (Marshal & Weinstein, 1984). Teacher and student personality characteristics, perceived merits of one's actions, cognitive maturity and a host of other factors have all been found to influence self-evaluation (see, for example, Brophy, 1981; Schunk, 1989).

Hong Kong studies

The above studies were all conducted in Western countries and their applicability to the Chinese culture is doubtful. There is now a wealth of evidence showing that sociocultural, situational and contextual factors mediate achievement attributions (see Salili, 1995). As noted above, the education context in Hong Kong is very authoritarian and more teacher-centered than in the West. Believing that praise would spoil children, Hong Kong teachers seldom praise students, while criticism and other forms of punishment are administered quite frequently. Classroom observations in Hong Kong shows that secondary school teachers used more disapproval than approval as control technique (Winter, 1988). Hence, it is possible that praise and criticisms have different meanings and effect differently on students' perception of ability, compared to that in the West.

In order to test these hypotheses several experiments were conducted (see Salili, Hwang & Choi, 1989; Salili & Hau, 1994). The findings of some of these studies are presented in the following sections.

Study 1: Experiment 1

The aim of this study was to see if the results of Meyer et al. (1979) could be replicated among Chinese students in Hong Kong (Salili, Hwang & Choi, 1989). Participants were 240 undergraduate students, aged 18-25 studying in the University of Hong Kong. The background of these students was similar to University students in Meyer et al.'s (1979) study.

There were a total of eight hypothetical situations. Each group of 30 students was randomly assigned one of these situations. Participants were told to "imagine themselves in a math class solving a math problem. The problem is so easy that everyone can solve it (so difficult that very few can solve it). The teacher will allow enough time to think it over. The solution must be written down. After all the students are finished. The teacher looks at your notebook and that of your fellow student. Both of you have given the correct (incorrect) solution to this very easy (very difficult) problem" (Meyer et al., 1979, p.266).

In the neutral condition the teacher's comments were: "The teacher says to you (to your fellow student) the answer is correct (or, no the answer is not correct)".

In the praise or criticism conditions teacher's comments were: "The teacher says to you (to your fellow students), you have done very fine; I'm very impressed", or "What have you done there! The answer is not correct". Participants were then asked to rate how they thought the teacher was evaluating their own and their friends' ability and effort using 9-point scales.

As can be seen from Table 4.1, the results of this study showed that teachers' ability's estimates were perceived to be significantly higher when the task was difficult than when it was easy. Table 4.1 also shows that the successful student (both oneself and fellow student) was rated significantly higher on ability than the unsuccessful one. A student who was blamed was perceived to be significantly higher in ability than a student who received neutral feedback after failure. No such difference was found in the case of the fellow student. The results also showed no significant difference between student's ability estimate in praise vs. neutral condition. Thus, Meyer et al.'s findings were replicated only in the case of failure and only for oneself.

Similar results as in Meyer et al.'s (1979) study were found for effort ratings. Teacher's effort estimate was perceived to be higher in the success condition than in the failure condition. Perceived estimate of effort was higher for the difficult than for the easy task. The results also showed that the student who was praised by the teacher was perceived to have expended significantly more effort than the student who received neutral feedback. In addition, the student who received criticism after failure was perceived to have expanded less effort on the task than the one receiving neutral feedback.

Study 1: Experiment 2

One problem with the above experiment is the methodology employed. The experiment used the exact procedure employed by Meyer et al. (1979). Participants in these studies were given feedback on the performance of themselves as well as their fellow students and had to rate the ability and effort for both. Such an evaluation and feedback procedure is rarely used in the Hong Kong classroom context. Hence, students' response may be different in the real situation (see Fontain, 1975). In Experiment 2, a slightly different methodology was used in order to make it more realistic in the local educational settings.

Participants were 151 male and female students aged 18-25, studying in two post-secondary colleges in Hong Kong. The backgrounds of these students were very similar to those in the first experiment.

Table 4.1
Mean ratings of effort and ability in various situations

		Experiment 1 Post-secondary students				Experiment 2 Undergraduates			
		Success		Failure		Success		Failure	
	Task	N	P	N	B	N	P	N	B
Own ability	Easy	6.2	6.9	4.6	4.6	2.7	2.8	2.6	2.3
	Difficult	6.3	7.1	5.6	6.2	3.5	3.8	3.0	3.0
Own effort	Easy	5.7	7.3	4.7	3.6	2.4	4.2	2.9	2.0
	Difficult	6.1	7.5	5.7	4.0	2.3	4.2	2.7	1.6
Partner's ability	Easy	6.7	6.0	4.7	5.9				
	Difficult	6.9	6.3	4.8	6.3				
Partner's effort	Easy	6.0	6.9	5.4	3.6				
	Difficult	6.2	7.7	6.1	3.1				

Note. N = neutral feedback, P = praise, B = blame
Adapted from Salili & Hau (1999).

Two changes were made to the procedure used in the first experiment. The first change was in the actual scenarios used. In this experiment we omitted the fellow student but no other changes were made. Hence, participants estimated the teacher's perception of their own ability and effort only. The second was the comments made by the teacher to represent praise and blame. In this study comments frequently used by the teachers in Hong Kong to represent praise, criticism and neutral feedback, identified in a survey by Mak (1982), were used. Teacher's comments in praise for success and blame for failure were as follows:

> "The teacher says to you, "You have done well" (praise), or "What have you done! How could you have got it incorrect!" (criticism) (Salili, Hwang & Choi, 1989, p.120).

The results of this experiment showed that ability was perceived to be higher in the difficult task than in the easy task and successful students were perceived to have higher ability than the unsuccessful ones (see Table 4.1). No significant difference was, however, found between ability ratings in praise and neutral feedback after success, and between ability ratings in criticism and neutral feedback after failure.

Similar results as in Experiment 1 were found with regards to perceived effort.

Our findings above showed that when we used a different procedure to that of Meyer et al.'s (1979) (in Experiment 2) so as to reflect the local classroom context more realistically, the results of ability perception also changed. Our adult participants in Experiment 2, responded similarly to Meyer's (1982) study with young children, suggesting that ability perception may be sensitive to the changes in the learning context. Both experiments used scenarios which explores University students' perception in an imaginary situation. Studies have shown that scenarios usually encourage logical responses from the participants, whereas, reactions to a real situation are also affected by the participants' emotions (see Hau & Salili, 1993 for a review of measurement issues). Hence, it was not clear whether the findings of these experiments would apply to the real classroom situation and to the younger students.

In order to explore these issues, we conducted two further experiments (See Salili & Hau, 1994 for details of these studies). In brief, participants in both experiments were Grades 2-10 Chinese students, In the first experiment we replicated Meyer's (1982) study using the same scenarios, and in the second experiment we used the actual classroom situation. In the latter experiment, students were given a mathematics' test and after they received teacher's feedback about their performance, they were asked by the experimenter

> "From the comments you just received, how do you think your teacher would rate your (your friends') ability and effort".

The results of the replication study showed younger children perceived that students receiving praise (cf. neutral feedback) for success, or neutral comments (cf. criticism) after failure had higher ability estimates, thus confirming Meyer's (1982) findings with younger children (see Table 4.2).

As can be seen from Table 4.2, the results for older students in the praise condition tended to be reversed. Older students perceived that praise for success indicated lower ability. However, contrary to Meyer et al's (1979) findings, those who were blamed after failure were perceived to have similar ability to students given neutral feedback. The findings with regards to effort and task difficulty confirmed our previous findings.

The results of the second experiment in real classroom situation confirmed our previous findings with younger children. However, no differences were found between ability of praised (or blamed) students and those receiving neutral feedback in the case of older students. Those who were praised following success or who were blamed for failure were perceived to be higher in immediate effort than those who received neutral feedback.

In both success and failure situations there was a tendency for participants to give higher ratings for ability and effort of their partner than themselves regardless of the type of feedback received.

The results also showed that high achievers perceived their own and their partners' (who were high achievers) immediate effort, usual effort and ability higher than the low achievers.

Table 4.2
Means of students' perception of ability and effort

Scale/Treatment	G. 2	G. 4	G. 6	G. 8	G. 10
			Educational Level		
		Praise/Neutral Feedback Experiment			
Own Immediate Effort					
Neutral	5.27	6.14	5.96	5.18	5.76
Praise	6.25	7.21	6.83	6.71	6.67
Own Ability					
Neutral	5.13	5.79	6.13	5.71	6.24
Praise	6.56	7.07	6.57	6.35	6.05
Own Usual Effort					
Neutral	5.40	5.79	5.87	5.18	5.14
Praise	5.88	6.64	6.17	5.88	5.71
Partners' Immediate Effort					
Neutral	6.40	6.57	7.09	7.18	7.05
Praise	6.44	7.14	7.39	6.88	6.81
Partners' Ability					
Neutral	5.80	6.71	7.13	7.06	7.10
Praise	6.25	7.14	7.17	6.82	6.57
Partners' Usual Effort					
Neutral	5.87	5.93	6.83	6.59	6.86
Praise	6.06	6.93	6.96	6.35	6.71
		Blame/Neutral Feedback Experiment			
Own Immediate Effort					
Neutral	5.56	5.27	5.65	4.65	4.26
Blame	4.63	4.33	3.80	2.95	2.74
Own Ability					
Neutral	4.81	4.47	4.40	4.40	4.32
Blame	4.06	5.33	4.85	4.20	4.16
Own Usual Effort					
Neutral	5.50	5.07	5.10	4.60	4.11
Blame	5.13	5.47	5.60	3.95	3.79
Partners' Immediate Effort					
Neutral	4.88	5.07	5.05	4.65	4.53
Blame	5.25	5.40	4.90	4.05	4.32
Partners' Ability					
Neutral	5.31	4.73	5.05	4.65	4.84
Blame	4.94	6.07	5.25	5.00	4.84
Partners' Usual Effort					
Neutral	4.88	4.93	5.15	5.05	5.11
Blame	6.00	6.07	5.40	4.80	4.89

Adapted from Salili & Hau (1994)

General discussion

The results of all these experiments were similar to the findings of studies conducted in the West by Meyer et al. (1979) and Barker & Graham (1987) with regards to effort and for younger children. Regardless of educational level, students who were praised for success were perceived to have expended greater effort. Similar to their Western counterparts, younger Chinese students also thought that students praised for success had higher ability and those who received criticism were lower in ability. Apparently younger children had difficulty distinguishing between effort and ability (Nicholls, 1989). Younger students also based their judgments more on the performance outcome in both success and failure situations, while in the case of older students, task difficulty was also used as an important cue for ability and effort. This reflected differences in the level of cognitive maturity between younger and older students.

There were differences with regard to ability perception in older students. In contrast to their Western counterparts, older Chinese students did not perceive blame as an indication of higher ability. This suggests that ability perception is more influenced by contextual and cultural variables than effort. Barker & Graham (1987) hypothesised that older children can perceive a compensatory relationship between effort and ability, whereas younger children cannot perceive such a relationship. This suggests that the correlation between effort and ability would be negative for older students and positive for younger children, as they found. In our study among the Chinese students, however, perception of ability was always positively correlated with perception of effort, although this relationship was weaker for older students, suggesting a strong cultural influence.

Chinese people believe that working hard and expending effort increases one's ability. That is, ability can be controlled by effort. This is different from the Western belief that ability is a stable characteristic which is given rather than achieved (Salili & Hau, 1994). Thus, in the mind of Chinese those who have worked hard have higher ability and those who have the ability must have worked hard. This also confirms our hypothesis that the meaning of ability for the Chinese may be different to that for the westerners.

The results also showed that ability may be perceived as a less important determinant of praise or blame than effort. This may be related to the fact that praise is seldom used as a feedback in Chinese schools and is usually given for outstanding achievement and other good qualities. Criticism, on the other hand, is used frequently and is believed to be good for the students.

Hence, in such a learning context negative feedback, if not excessive and if it is followed by appropriate explanations and guidance, may have a positive effect of motivating students to work harder (Salili & Hau, 1994). On the other hand, praise that is given for trivial reasons or for success in easy tasks may not be beneficial and in the long-term interest of students.

Effectiveness of Reward and Punishment

Reinforcement strategies in schools are often not used according to what the behaviorist model prescribes (McNamara, 1986). Shaping, for example, which is an effective strategy for helping students acquire a desirable behavior, is not adopted in schools. The schools usually reward only students who perform well over the school year. Low achievers are deprived of institutionalised rewards, such as certificates of merit and everyday teacher-related reinforcement (Good & Brophy, 1987).

Wong (1992) observed that teachers in Hong Kong schools did not seem to be very efficient in their incentive (reward) and sanction (punishment) strategies. To control the class, secondary school teachers often made public disapproval comments. There were also heavy reliance on institutional procedures outside the classroom to punish and reward (rarely) students. Research in the West has shown that both methods are ineffective in controlling students' behavior (McNamara, 1986). High prevalence of unruly and inappropriate classroom behavior have been reported both in Hong Kong and in the West (van Houten et al., 1982; Education Commission Report No 4, Hong Kong, 1990). Thus the reward and punishment strategies being used in schools do not seem to work.

Western research shows that students and teachers may have different perceptions of the severity and effectiveness of incentive and sanction strategies (see Merrett, Wilkins, Houghton and Wheldall, 1988 for a review). Thus, teachers' attempts to change the behavior of misbehaving or underachieving students may miss the mark.

The earliest research on the effectiveness of reward and punishment in secondary schools was conducted by Highfield & Pinset (1952). The researchers asked 94 secondary school students about their opinion of 15 deterrents and 12 rewards commonly used in their school. They reported that the most disliked deterrents were sending an unfavourable report home, being closely watched by the teacher, and deprivation of games and favourite lessons. The rewards that students liked best were marks and sending a favourable report home. Teachers, however, considered a good telling off, extra work, sending the student to the principal's office, and urging the student to make more effort as the most important deterrents, while the most effective reward was posts of responsibility and quiet appreciation.

More recent studies have also reported similar findings (see for example, Branwhite, 1988; Caffyn, 1987; Sharp, 1985). Despite methodological differences the results of these studies were consistent with regards to students' perception of effective reward and punishment strategies. Incentives that were considered effective included personal success (e.g., doing well on a test, good term report) and those that involved parents (e.g., sending letter home). Effective sanction strategies were those that helped bring about alternative behavior and parental involvement. Ineffective reward strategies included praise, especially public praise and posts of responsibility. Ineffective punishment strategies were reprimands, especially loud reprimands and other traditional strategies (e.g., writing lines, extra work, detention, debits, and being sent out of class). However, students did not seem to appreciate teacher's praise, but seemed to place high value on the teacher's opinion of them (Sharp, 1985). Knowing that the teacher is pleased with students' work was considered an effective motivator for good work and good behaviour (Caffyn, 1987).

The effectiveness of incentive and sanction strategies may also depend on individual characteristics such as gender (Adler, 1988, cited in Wong, 1992) and achievement level (Brophy & Good, 1974) as well as the relationship between the student and the administrator of reward and punishment. Patterns of teacher interaction with students, their expectations and standards differ according to students' characteristics. It is commonly believed that boys engage in more aggressive and problem behaviors than girls. In a study Hartle (1979, cited in Wong, 1992) reported that teachers and students rated the behavior of boys less appropriate than that of girls. However, Slee (1988, cited in Wong, 1992) found that boys and girls had similar quantities of deviant behavior, but girls were more inclined to tell the teacher what they think of them, whereas boys were more likely to show aggressive behavior such as fighting and damaging things.

Boys and girls are also subjected to different discipline practices and standards of tolerance for misbehavior (Slee, 1988). Teachers, for example, are found to use femininity to form standard of behavior for girls (Adler, 1988). Dweck et al. (1978) reported that when teachers criticise girls' work, it is more frequently about the content, whereas criticisms for the boys was more directed at both form and content.

The Hong Kong context

In Hong Kong misbehaving students are not dealt with by the teachers directly, but rather they are usually referred to discipline teachers or the head master for intervention (Wan & Salili, 1996). The behavior code for students is a list of "thou shall not" and the consequences of misbehavior or disobedience is in the form of black marks, demerits and punishment that inflict exhaustion (e.g., writing lines, standing in class and extra work) (Wong, 1992). The rewards can be in the form of service to the school (e.g., becoming monitors, and prefects) and only outstanding achievement such as being first in the grade, or champion in a competition can qualify for such rewards. They can also be in the form of merits, certificates and book coupons. No empirical research, however, existed on the effectiveness of these strategies.

Wan & Salili (1996) investigated students' perception of the effectiveness of common reward and punishment strategies used in Hong Kong and the effect of gender and achievement level on these perceptions. Participants were a total of 372 (167 male and 205 female) students aged 13-18. They were randomly selected from 11 classes in four co-educational Anglo-Chinese schools in Hong Kong. The schools were similar in curriculum and standards. Within each class, participants were divided into three groups of high, medium and low achievers.

A questionnaire based on an instrument used by Caffyn (1987) was adapted for use in Hong Kong. This included 50 scenarios in two different contexts: work-related and behaviour-related (reward and punishment situations). The following is an example:

> "Imagine someone in your class has been trying very hard for sometime and has been doing much better work. How successful would the strategies listed

bellow be encouraging that person to keep working hard? Please read each statement carefully and circle the box for each to show the degree of effectiveness. One indicates very effective and 4 not effective at all. A lower rating means greater effectiveness of the strategy" (Wan & Salili, 1996, p.264).

Students were provided with a list of reward and punishment strategies developed through interviews with a group of experienced secondary school teachers. They were asked to rate effectiveness of each reward and punishment situation on a 4-point scale.

Results and Discussions

T-test comparisons between strategies or group of strategies and separate ANOVAs exploring the effects of gender and level of achievement on effectiveness of strategies in different situations were conducted (details in Wan & Salili, 1996). The results showed that overall, reward is perceived to be more effective than punishment in bringing about both good behaviour and in improving performance. Some of the strategies that teachers use both in reward and punishment situations, such as feedback on school work, term report, communication with parents and merits or demerits were reported to work better in the reward situation than in the punishment situation. These findings are in line with findings in the West that confirm the theoretical position of behavior modification approach that positive reinforcement is more effective than punishment.

We also found that reward strategies that reflect performance (e.g., term reports, certificates) were the most effective strategies and more so in work-related than behavior-related situations. Similarly, punishment strategies that are aimed at changing conditions that cause poor performance (e.g., private discussions with teacher, teacher-parent talk, extra work) were perceived to be more effective as they helped students to understand the nature of the problem and led to remedial work. This reflects the importance of school success in Hong Kong. It is also in line with normal school practice where reward is usually given for good performance rather than good behavior. In order to receive reward for good behavior students must show leadership and contribute significantly to school life through performing various duties. Contrary to the findings in the West (see McNamara, 1986), Hong Kong students rated term reports and certificates as very effective reward strategies. The importance of these rewards may be related to formal recognition of performance to which parents have access. They may be valued because they are considered proofs of students' filial piety.

Despite the emphasis on academic success, only slightly more than half the students considered marks and good comments effective feedback, possibly because teachers seldom give good grades or good comments to the students. In addition, often due to teachers' heavy workload, grades are not given early enough to act as reinforcement. However, students rated comments as more effective than marks even though marks are indications of academic performance, possibly because comments are more personal and indicate teachers' attention to students' work.

Contrary to Western findings students in this study found public praise more effective than private praise. Again this could be due to the fact that verbal or public praise are seldom given. Hence, students may associate public praise with great honour, particularly in the presence of parents (Salili, Hwang & Choi, 1989).

Informing parents as a reward strategy was considered effective but not as much as the above strategies, possibly because in Hong Kong schools such communications are rare. Similar conclusion can be drawn about small gifts which is rarely given to students. High achievers considered the strategy of involving parents as a punishment more effective than low achievers, probably because low achievers are frequently punished by parents, making this strategy less effective for them.

As in Western studies, awarding posts of responsibility appeared to be more effective in behavior-related than in work-related situations. This may be due to the fact that posts of responsibility are often given to outstanding students and other students may find them unobtainable. High achievers who are usually given such posts did not find them more effective than low achievers, possibly because they find such responsibility a burden rather than an effective reward.

Referral of the student to a higher authority was perceived to be more effective for changing bad behavior than for poor academic work, but seating the misbehaving student near the teacher was considered more effective than referring the student to a higher authority, or isolating from other classmates.

Punishment related to poor performance (e.g., demerits) was perceived as ineffective, probably because teachers use these strategies too frequently while they rarely reward the students for good behavior or good performance.

In this study we also found a trend for the girls to perceive greater effectiveness for reward and punishment strategies. In line with female sex-role orientation, girls also found person-oriented strategies such as private praise and comments more effective than boys did. Low achieving females also found negative comments on their school work more effective than boys did.

Level of achievement seemed to have some influence on the perceived effectiveness of the strategies. High achievers reported greater effectiveness of reward strategies than low achievers. The strategies that were considered more effective by high achievers were private praise and teachers' expression of satisfaction with students' performance. This difference between high and low achievers could be attributed to their differential exposure to rewards, suggesting that one has to be rewarded to appreciate it.

Overall, behavior-related strategies were considered more effective than work-related strategies, suggesting that misbehavior may be more amenable to intervention than poor school work, possibly because poor performance may be perceived to be related to low ability which is relatively more stable.

The results of this study showed that teachers are considered the most effective agents in administering reward and punishment, hence they have greater responsibility in learning to administer them appropriately and for the benefit of their students.

Summary and Conclusions

Exposure to Western culture and affluence has introduced new ideas and brought changes to the lives of the Chinese people in Hong Kong. New changes in the school curriculum are accepted but the old system of assessment and feedback still continue to exist side by side. Teacher-student interaction still follows the traditional values and norms of behavior of the Chinese culture. This chapter examined teacher-student interaction by focussing on teachers' feedback, praise and criticism and the effectiveness of various methods of incentives and reprimands that Chinese teachers may use in their classrooms.

Studies in the West have reported that when teachers praise students after success or give neutral feedback after failure, students may perceive that their ability is estimated to be low by the teacher (Meyer et. al., 1979). Such comments may influence the students' conception of ability, and their beliefs about their own competence.

Based on the empirical evidence that causal attributions for achievement are influenced by situational and contextual factors (Salili, 1995), we hypothesised that Chinese teachers' evaluative feedback may have different meaning for Chinese students and may not have the same effect on their perception of ability as it does with their Western counterparts.

The results of our studies showed that, indeed, perception of ability is different among Hong Kong Chinese students. Younger primary school students behaved like their counterparts in the West. They based their judgements more on performance outcomes, believing that praise for success and neutral feedback for failure indicated high ability, and criticism for failure indicated low ability. Our findings with regards to effort perception were also similar to the findings in the West across all ages and situations.

As expected, we found that ability perception was more influenced by the context in which reward and criticism were administered. When we replicated the Meyer et al. (1979) study results were mixed. Although we found a tendency for older students to perceive a compensatory relationship between effort and ability in some situations, the correlation between effort and ability was always positive for the older Chinese students while it was negative for Western students.

When scenarios resembling the real situation and when actual classroom situations were used, older Chinese students perceived praise or neutral feedback for success as an indication of high ability. Otherwise, there were no differences between perception of ability after blame for failure, praise for success or neutral feedback. This suggests that the meaning of ability for Chinese students is different from that of the Western students. In the West, ability is considered a stable and uncontrollable disposition, but for the Chinese it is more malleable and under one's control. This is in line with Chinese cultural beliefs that with studying hard and gaining knowledge one's ability can be increased. Hence, for the West, teacher blame carries the message "You have not worked hard enough but your ability is high", whereas for the Chinese, blame carries the message "You have not worked hard enough, and your ability is not particularly high". However, since ability is controllable for the Chinese, teacher blame should be interpreted as "You have been lazy, and that is why your ability is not particularly high" (Salili & Hau, 1994, p.234).

Such a pattern of attribution, according to Western literature, is adaptive and minimises the chances of learned helplessness. However, the strong emphasis on academic excellence and pressure to succeed from parents and teachers together with such attributional disposition may cause great stress and anxiety, resulting in feelings of shame and despair in low ability as well as some average students. More research is however needed to explore the impact of teachers' praise and criticism among low ability students.

The findings of our studies also show that Chinese students depend less on praise or external reward than Western students, possibly because teachers seldom praise students. Praise, which is rarely given, is usually for outstanding achievement and a host of other virtues. Hence, the student who receives praise may consider it a high honour which is related to both ability and effort.

Our investigation of the effectiveness of incentives and rewards also showed the influence of culture and context of learning. While there were a lot of similarities between the results of our study and the Western findings, there were also interesting differences. Generally, students found reward as more effective than punishment. Referral to higher authorities was perceived more effective for behavior problem than for academic performance. Also, punishments such as demerits and sending notes to parents were considered ineffective, probably because teachers administer them very frequently. The strategies that informed students of their performance, and had problem solving value, were considered most effective.

Contrary to Western findings Chinese students considered public praise more effective than private praise, probably because students seldom receive it. Public praise is an indication of both high ability and effort and would make their parents proud. Similarly, term reports and certificates were also considered very effective, especially by high achievers, for the same reasons.

We also found some differences between high and low achievers with regards to what was perceived as effective reward or punishment. Posts of responsibility which are often given to high achievers were perceived to be more effective by low achievers than by high achievers. This may suggest that low achievers associated posts of responsibility with power and prestige, whereas high achievers considered them a burden. Reward was considered more effective by high achievers than by low achievers, especially private praise and expression of satisfaction from teachers. As noted above, this may be due to the fact that low achievers had never experienced praise and hence did not appreciate it.

Overall, girls perceived both reward and punishment more effective than boys, particularly person-oriented strategies such as private praise or comments from their teachers. This finding is in line with conventional views of feminine characteristics.

The results of our studies above showed that teachers have great influence on students' behavior. Performance feedback given by the teacher has an important implication for students' ability perception. Particularly, praise or reward for good performance, if it is not given for trivial reasons, can enhance students' perception of ability and self-competence. Teachers are also perceived as the most effective administrators of reward and punishment. Hence, it is important that they should use them effectively.

Our study also showed that teachers should use strategies that have problem solving values and refrain from frequent punishments. The practice of sending student to head master was considered particularly ineffective. This means that the role of these experienced teachers need to be redefined. They could use their experience more effectively by teaching effective classroom management skills or devising school-wide policies for the use of effective incentive and sanction strategies.

Finally, we found a great cultural difference in the way Chinese students perceive teachers' comments compared to their Western counterparts. These differences can be attributed to their differences in cultural values as well as the context of learning. According to the Western literature, attribution of failure to effort is adaptive. However, in the context of Hong Kong Chinese culture, such an attribution pattern may not be so adaptive in the case of genuinely low ability students who repeatedly fail no matter how hard they work. Teachers' comments conveying the message that students' failure is due to laziness may cause them feelings of shame and guilt which may result in depression with dire consequences.

REFERENCES

Alder, C. (1988). Girls' Schooling and Troubles. In R. Slee (Ed.), *Discipline and Schools: A Curriculum Perspective*. Australia, Melbourne.

Ames, C. & Archer, J. (1988). Achievement Goals in the Classroom: Students' Learning Strategies and Motivation Processes. *Journal of Educational Psychology*, 80, 260-267.

Bandura, A. (1986). *Social Foundations of Thought and Action: A Social Cognitive Theory*. Englewood Cliffs. NJ: Prentice Hall.

Barker, G.P. & Graham, S. (1987). Developmental Study of Praises and Blame as Attributional Cues, *Journal of Educational Psychology*, 79, 62-66.

Biggs, J.B. (1992). *Why and How do Hong Kong Students Learn? Using the Learning Process Questionnaires*. Education Papers 14. Hong Kong: Faculty of Education, The University of Hong Kong.

Branwhite, T. (1988). The PASS Survey: School-based Preferences of 500+ Adolescent Consumers, *Educational Studies*, 14, 165-176.

Brophy, J. (1981). Teacher Praise: A Functional Analysis. *Review of Educational Research*, 51, 5-32.

Brophy, J. & Good, T.L. (1974). *Teacher-student Relationships: Causes and Consequences*. New York: Holt, Rinehart & Winston.

Caffyn, R. (1987). Rewards and Punishments in Schools: A Study of their Effectiveness as Perceived by Secondary School Students and their Teachers. *School Psychology International*, 8, 85-94.

Chen, C. & Stevenson, H.W. with Hayward., C. & Burgers S. (1995). Culture and

Academic Achievement: Ethic and Cross-national Differences. In M.L. Maehr & P. Pintrich (Eds), *Advances in Motivation and Achievement*. Greenwich CT: JAI Press. Vol. 119-152.

Chen, Y., Lu, C., Hung, Y. & Chen L. (1980). A Survey on the Opinions about Corporal Punishment by Teachers, Students and Parents. *Bulletin of Educational Psychology*, 13, 57-74.

Covington, M.V. & Omelich, C.L. (1979). Effort: The Double-edged Sword in School Achievement. *Journal of Educational Psychology*, 71, 169-182.

Dweck, C.S., Davidson, W., Nelson, S. & Enna, B. (1978). Sex Differences and Learned Helplessness: The Contingencies of Evaluative Feedback in the Classroom and III. An Experimental Analysis, *Developmental Psychology*, 14, 268-276.

Fontain, S. (1975). Causal Attribution in Simulated versus Real Situation: When People Are Logical, and When Are They Not? *Journal of Personality and Social Psychology*, 32, 1021-1029.

Good, T. & Brophy, J. (1987). *Looking in Classroom Relationship: Causes & Consequences*. New York: Holt Rinehart & Winston.

Hau, K.T. & Salili, F. (1993). Measurement of Achievement Attribution: A Review of Instigation Methods, Question Content, and Measurement Format. *Educational Psychology Review*, 5(4), 377-422.

Highfield, M. & Pinset, A. (1952). *A Survey of Rewards and Punishments in Schools*. London: Newnes.

Ho, D.Y.F. (1986). Chinese Patterns of Socialization: A Critical Review. In M.H. Bond (Ed.), *The Psychology of Chinese People*. Hong Kong: Oxford University Press, 1-35.

Jagacinski, C., Nicholls, J. & Burton (1983). Conceptions of Ability and Related Affects in Task Involvement and Ego Involvement. *Journal of Educational Psychology*, 76, 909-919.

Lam, M.O.L. (1996). *Conceptions of an Ideal and Creative Pupil Among Primary School Teachers, using Different Teaching Approaches*. Master of Social Science Thesis. Submitted to the Department of Psychology, The University of Hong Kong.

Liu, L.M. (1984). *A Survey of Memorization Requirement in Taipei Primary and Secondary Schools*. Unpublished manuscript.

Liu, L.M. (1986). Chinese Cognition. In M.H. Bond (Ed.), *The Psychology of Chinese People*. Hong Kong: Oxford University Press, 73-102.

Mak, S.M.I. (1982). *Teachers' Evaluative Comments: What Do They Tell Students about Teacher Perception of their Ability and Effort?* Unpublished Certificate of Psychology Thesis, The University of Hong Kong.

Marshall, H. & Weinstein, R.S. (1984). Classroom Factors Affecting Students' Self-evaluations: An Interactional Model. *Review of Educational Research*, 54, 301-325.

McNamara, E. (1986). The Effectiveness of Incentive and Sanction Systems Used in Secondary Schools: A Behavioral Analysis, *Durham and Newcastle Research Review*, 10.

Merrett, F., Wilkins, J. Houghton, S. & Wheldall, K. (1988). Rules, Sanctions and

Rewards in Secondary Schools. *Educational Studies*, 14(2), 145-157.

Meyer, W., Bachmann, M., Biermann, U., Hempelmann, M., Ploger, F. & Spiller, H. (1979). The Informational Value of Evaluative Behavior: Influences of Praise and Blame in Perceptions of Ability. *Journal of Educational Psychology*, 71, 259-268.

Meyer, W.U. (1982). Indirect Communication about Perceived Ability Estimates. *Journal of Educational Psychology*, 74, 888-897.

Morris, P. (1999). *Final Report: The Project on Feedback and Assessment*. Submitted to Curriculum Development Institute, Hong Kong Government.

Nicholls, J. (1978). The Development of the Concepts of Effort and Ability, Perception of Academic Attainment, and the Understanding that Difficult Tasks Require More Ability. *Child Development*, 49, 800-814.

Nicholls, J. (1989). *The Competitive Ethos and Democratic Education*. Cambridge, MA: Harvard University Press.

Pintrich, P.R. & Blumenfeld, P. (1985). Classroom Experience and Children's Self-perceptions of Ability, Effort and Conduct. *Journal of Educational Psychology*, 77, 646-657.

Pintrich, P.R. & Schunk, D.H. (1996). *Motivation in Education: Theory Research, and Applications*. Englewood Cliffs, N.J.: Printice Hall.

Salili, F. (1994). Age, Sex, and Cultural Differences in the Meaning and Dimensions of Achievement. *Personality and Social Psychology Bulletin*, 20(6), 635-648.

Salili F. (1995). Explaining Chinese Students' Motivation and Achievement: A Socio-cultural Analysis. In M.L. Machn & P. Pintrich (Eds.), *Advances in Motivation and Achievement*. Vol. 9. Greenwich, CT: JAI, 73-118.

Salili F. & Hau K.T. (1994). The Effect of Teachers' Evaluation Feedback on Chinese Students' Perception of Ability: A Cultural and Situational Analysis. *Educational Studies*, 20, 223-236.

Salili, F., Hwang C.E. & Choi N.F. (1989). Teachers' Evaluative Behavior: The Relationship between Teachers' Comments and Perceived Ability in Hong Kong. *Journal of Cross-Cultural Psychology*, 20, 115-132.

Schunk, D.H. (1989). Self-efficacy and Achievement Behaviors. *Educational Psychology Review*, 1, 173-208.

Sharp, P. (1985). Behavior Modification in the Secondary School: A Survey of Students' Attitudes to Rewards and Praise. *Behavioral Approaches with Children*, 9, 109-112.

Stipek, D.J. (1993). *Motivation to Learn: From Theory to Practice*. Boston: Allyn and Bacon.

van Houten, R., Nau, P.A., MacKenzie-Keating, S., Sameoto, D. & Colavecchia, B. (1982). An Analysis of Some Variables Influencing the Effectiveness of Reprimands. *Journal of Applied Behavioral Analysis*, 11, 91-94.

Wan, F. & Salili, F. (1996). Perceived Effectiveness of Reward & Punishment Strategies by Hong Kong Secondary School Students. *Psychologia*, 39, 256-275.

Weiner, B. (1986). *An Attributional Theory of Motivation and Emotions*. New York: Springler-Verlag.

Winter, S. (1988). Teacher Approval and Disapproval in Hong Kong Secondary School Classrooms. *British Journal of Educational Psychology*, 60, 88-92.

Wong, O.H.F. (1992). *Perceived Effectiveness of Reward and Punishment by Secondary School Students*. Master of Social Sciences Thesis, The University of Hong Kong.

5

Are Chinese Teachers Authoritarian?

Irene T. Ho

In Chinese societies under the influence of the Confucian culture, teacher authority and the suppression of individuality have deep-seated cultural roots. As a result, teacher-centred pedagogy and student compliance are still prevalent in many modern Chinese societies despite the fact that some of them have a long history of Western influence (Biggs, 1996a; Ho, 1993; Scollon & Wong-Scollon, 1994). Western research has shown that humanistic or student-centred orientations in student control are associated with higher intrinsic learning motivation in students and better classroom climate (Bean & Hoy, 1974; Deci, Schwartz, Sheinman & Ryan, 1981; Lunenberg, 1983). Nevertheless, it is a common perception that Chinese teachers are able to conduct their classes with less disruption than their Western counterparts, with students showing higher academic motivation (Salili, 1996). It appears that Chinese teachers are able to achieve good results in both student achievement and behaviour with their authoritarian approach, and this raises doubts about the universality of humanistic approaches to education as advocated in the West, at the same time making many Western theories appear irrelevant in the training of Asian teachers.

The extent to which teachers are authoritarian or student-centred in their approaches to students could perhaps be most clearly seen in how teachers manage everyday classroom situations and discipline their students. Despite the available evidence that disciplinary approaches in the Confucian tradition are mainly teacher-centred and punitive (Cheung & Lau, 1985; Ho, 1981, 1986; Leung, Salili & Baber, 1986; Salili, 1996), recent studies have shown that observations about Chinese teachers being authoritarian might have been over-generalised, with elements of student-centredness also seen in their management of student problems (O'Connor, 1991, Ho, 1999). In the following sections, research findings regarding the cultural characteristics and teachers' discipline approaches in the Chinese tradition are discussed for a better understanding of the nature of alleged authoritarian practices in Chinese schools.

Authoritarian Practices in Chinese Education

In contrast to the elaborate and varied theories and models of classroom management and discipline in the West (Jones & Jones, 1995; Lewis, 1997; Wolfgang & Glickman, 1995), student discipline in the Confucian tradition has been guided largely by a few general principles. These principles, detailed below, should be understood in the light of the Confucian collectivistic culture characterised by hierarchical social relationships with mutually obliging responsibilities as well as clearly stated norms for behaviour.

Expectations for conformity

In collectivistic societies there is usually greater expectation for members to conform to more uniform standards of behaviour. Ho (1996) argues that authoritarian moralism, with its two salient features of hierarchical ranking of authority and "a pervasive application of moral precepts as the primary standard against which people are judged" (p.161), is a central characteristic of Chinese patterns of socialisation guided by filial piety. As a result, the overriding emphasis is on the development of moral character through education, and it predisposes parents and teachers to be moralistic: to ensure that children's conduct meets external moral criteria, rather than be sensitive to their internal needs, feelings and aspirations. Unlike individualistic Western cultures, where harmonious social relations rest upon the balance between the satisfaction of individual goals or individual rights and a sense of fairness to all, proper behaviour in the Confucian collectivistic culture is defined by social roles, with mutual obligation among members of society and the fulfilment of their duties for each other being emphasised. Self-expression, independence, creativity and all-round personal development in the Western sense are often neglected if not inhibited by Chinese parents and teachers (Ho, 1994; Ho & Kang, 1984).

In a recent study comparing Hong Kong and Australian teachers' approaches to student discipline (Ho, 1999), twelve experienced secondary school teachers in each cultural setting (collectivistic and individualistic respectively) were asked to respond to a number of student problem behaviours. When judging whether a behaviour adversely affected other people, Australian teachers evaluated the behaviour more in the light of the balance between individual rights and a sense of fairness, while Hong Kong teachers considered it more in terms of the violation of group norms. Hong Kong teachers tended to resort more to moralisation (asserting what is right and what is wrong) and emphasised consequences for their actions when attempting to enhance students' awareness about the inappropriateness of certain behaviours, while Australian teachers often appealed to a sense of fairness in that inappropriate behaviours often represented violations of other people's rights. An example was seen in teachers' comments about the use of foul language.

Hong Kong Teacher C:

> "First it reveals poor self-cultivation, secondly he openly challenges school regulations, also challenging the teacher ….."

Hong Kong Teacher F:

> "Foul language is usually aggressive,….is not accepted by society generally …. Language is…not something personal…."

Australian Teacher A:

> "*If they are using it within their own small group and is acceptable to everyone else, then fine. But if it's not acceptable to everyone around you, you shouldn't use it. You should respect other people's rights.*"

Moreover, students' individual differences as well as their choices and rights were more respected in the Australian context, whereas requirements for students in the Hong Kong context were less flexible, as revealed in the management of homework problems. All Hong Kong teachers interviewed agreed that students should complete homework as expected, and detention was a common means to make students do uncompleted work, sometimes requiring them to do more than what was originally required.

Hong Kong Teacher L:

> "*If he comes to school not wanting to learn, it is very troublesome....you have to make him do what he has missed.*"

Australian Teacher D:

> "*A daydreaming child could often be quite bright or gifted; a student not doing homework could often turn out to be a responsible and worthwhile human being.....It's just one aspect of the person....No, I don't get terribly upset. (There are) people out there with remarkable achievement without getting homework done in the past....Society's going to have all types. So if they make a contribution later in life, it's fine.*"

While Australian teachers were more prepared to consider student background factors or differential expectations and adjust their requirements accordingly (Teacher E: "*Sometimes it's a good idea to try and change the goals 'cos not all students are going to achieve the same level in your class.*"), Hong Kong teachers emphasised close supervision with constant reminding and intensive help to ensure students meet the uniform requirements.

Teachers' moral responsibility in student guidance

One important tenet in Confucian schooling is that teachers, like parents, are very much responsible for good behaviour in students, as indicated in the Chinese aphorism "Rearing without education is the fault of the father, teaching without strictness is the negligence of the teacher." Teachers should conduct themselves with "exemplary virtue" (Yuan, 1984, p.57) and be responsible for guiding student behaviour (Ho, 1996; Meyer, 1988, in Wu, 1996). They should "set themselves as an example…; they must not only teach the students culture and science but also educate them morally" (Jiaoyu, 1981, cited in O'Connor, 1991). With such important duties come ascribed high status and authority as well as the requirement to be strongly committed to not just teaching but the overall development of the student (Lee, 1996). More precisely, the emphasis is on the cultivation of moral or proper behaviour rather than overall development in the Western sense, where emotional adjustment and positive self-perceptions play a more important part.

In Ho's (1999) interviews with teachers, when talking about how they would manage student problem behaviours, Australian teachers tended to view their involvement more within the framework of professional responsibilities, with more clearly defined roles and responsibilities. They set limits to the extent of their involvement and were more prepared to let students choose their own course of action or make referrals after teacher efforts had been made up to a certain point.

Australian Teacher I on homework problems:

> "Leave them to get a perfect zero....I have no problem at all in its management....The only responsibility I have (is to) notify the parents...If I consider that perhaps the school environment is not the place for the kid to be, why stress them out even more. Why perhaps make them suicidal or turn to drugs and alcohol....I'd probably speak to the careers advisor and try to create apprenticeship training for them....You may find...that there is some underlying family problem or cause to it but it's certainly not within my role to (deal with) it."

Another Australian teacher commented on the fact that some authoritarian teachers did spend more time going after students when they did not hand in homework: *"That just punishes yourself as well as the student."*

In contrast, Hong Kong teachers tended to regard themselves as having the moral responsibility to guide students on the right path and were more prepared to go all the way to rectify misbehaviour, spending as much time as they could and often getting personally involved.

Hong Kong Teacher C on student arriving late:

> *"Give him morning calls to make sure he comes to school on time."*

Hong Kong Teacher A on student's schoolwork problems:

> "...doing revision with him during recess, stay with him during lunch and after school while he does his homework, teach him how to study...."

While most Australian teachers interviewed did not show too much concern about students using bad language as long as it was not used on school grounds, a few Hong Kong teachers indicated that it was their responsibility to teach students not to use foul language even outside the school environment, if it became known to them.

Hong Kong Teacher K: "*Sometimes discipline teachers walk around nearby shopping malls after school to make sure that students do not gather there to get into bad company or behave inappropriately.*"

All these reflect the Chinese concept of teachers being like parents to students: "Teacher for a day, parent for life."

This cultural difference in perceptions of teachers' role was also reflected in investigations of teachers' causal attributions for various types of student problem behaviours (Ho, 1999). Interview results as well as questionnaire data showed that Australian teachers were more prepared to see teacher or teaching-related factors as causes for students' learning problems (daydreaming in class, not completing homework) or classroom discipline problems (talking in class, lesson disruption) but not so much for students displaying inappropriate social behaviours (being rude to teachers, bullying). On the contrary, Hong Kong teachers made higher self-attribution for students challenging teachers than failing to complete homework. In other words, Hong Kong teachers assumed more responsibility for bringing about a good teacher-student relationship than for students failing in schoolwork, whereas Australian teachers focused more on their professional responsibility to maintain classroom order and motivate students to learn.

Furthermore, in factor analytic studies of teacher efficacy in the two cultural contexts, Hong Kong teachers exhibited an integrated personal teaching efficacy pertaining to the areas of discipline, instruction and guidance; whereas for Australian teachers, guidance efficacy turned out to be separate from discipline and instruction efficacy (Table 5.1).

It appears that in the Chinese context, teachers have the moral responsibility to ensure good behaviour in students not only regarding discipline in the classroom but also guidance in daily life, with teachers being concerned about student behaviour both inside and outside the school environment. On the other hand, in the Western context, except for those with a personal commitment to student guidance, teachers' perception of their professional responsibility focuses more on instruction and classroom management, with student discipline being associated more with minimising disruptions to instructional and social processes in school. Western teachers generally do not pay attention to student behaviour and problems outside the school environment as much as Chinese teachers would, and student guidance is often more the responsibility of specialised personnel such as counsellors.

Harsh measures in discipline

An important consequence of the great concern about proper behaviour is the sanction it gives for the use of harsh methods, with impulse control and strict discipline being emphasised in the socialisation of Chinese children. Ho (1981) found that Chinese parents and teachers in Hong Kong tended to restrict and control their children's behaviour from a very young age, often employing harsh methods of discipline to ensure compliance, such as the use of ridicule and shaming in front of other students. Chinese schools are often characterised by a high

Table 5.1
Dimensions of teacher efficacy for Australian and Hong Kong teachers: standardised loadings for best-fit models in confirmatory factor analysis

Item	Australian sample			Hong Kong sample	
	Personal discipline/ instruction efficacy	Personal guidance efficacy	Beliefs about external influences	Personal teaching efficacy (discipline/ instruction/ guidance)	Beliefs about external influences
I have very effective classroom management skills.	0.74			0.77	
I can communicate to students that I am serious about getting appropriate behaviour.	0.74			0.68	
My teaching methods are very effective in helping students learn.	0.72			0.78	
I am effective in making students observe rules and regulations.	0.69			0.72	
I have a good grasp of teaching approaches that help to maintain students' learning motivation.	0.64			0.76	
I find it easy to make my expectations clear to students.	0.62			0.64	
If a student in my class becomes disruptive and noisy, I am usually able to redirect him/her quickly.	0.62			0.61	
When a student does better than usual, many times it is because I exerted a little extra effort.	--			0.45	
I know how to teach a new concept so that students will master it quickly.	0.60			0.68	
When the grades of my student improve, it is usually because I found more effective teaching approaches.	0.39			0.51	
I am usually able to help students with emotional problems to adjust better in life.		0.80		0.62	
Students would come to me when they have problems in their daily life because they know I can help.		0.73		0.42	
I am good at understanding students' psychological needs and how they cause problem behaviours.		0.71		0.70	
I am good at counselling students.		0.64		0.73	
I find some students to be impossible to discipline effectively.			0.80		0.75
There are some students who won't behave no matter what I do.			0.74		0.72
A teacher is limited in what he/she can achieve in student discipline because of the current values in society.			0.67		0.68
Student behaviour in classrooms is influenced more by peers than the teacher.			0.50		0.49
A teacher is very limited in what can be achieved because a student's home environment is a large influence on achievement.			0.47		0.59
If students aren't disciplined at home, then they aren't likely to accept it at school.			0.33		--

level of discipline and strict teachers (Cheung & Lau, 1985; Leung, Salili & Baber, 1986). In a survey by Wong (1992, in Salili, 1996) of Hong Kong secondary school teachers and students, it was found that "the banning of corporal punishment (since 1991) remained an isolated attempt to improve the pastoral system. Sanction strategies still operate at the level of 'what fits the crime'" (p.36). Wilson (1974, in Ho, 1986) suggested that the common use of shaming, ostracism and moral education in Chinese homes and schools led to the development of strong internalised control, conformity and reluctance to express hostility towards authority among Chinese students. This perhaps explains why Chinese students are often observed by Westerners to be passive learners who remain quiet in the classroom and seldom challenge their teachers (Biggs, 1996a; Ho, 1993; Scollon & Wong-Scollon, 1994).

Ho's (1999) study showed that especially when dealing with inappropriate interpersonal behaviour, some Hong Kong teachers would more readily use social pressure or group disapproval through discrediting the offender in front of the whole class, sometimes also by enforcing collective responsibility for individual students' faults. Australian teachers, on the other hand, would avoid shaming students in front of others out of consideration for their self-esteem, preferring to deal with problems on a more individual basis.

In face of a student challenging the teacher, most Hong Kong teachers interviewed in the study saw the need to deal with this in front of the whole class (e.g. by direct reprimand, asking the student to express his/her ideas politely once more, pointing out his faulty reasoning) so that he/she did not gain status through this behaviour or become an example to others. Some would deliberately use group pressure to achieve this by asking classmates to comment on his/her behaviour. Similarly, when dealing with bullying, Hong Kong teachers considered it important to discredit the bully in front of his/her classmates if the incident was known to other students. Actions to be taken could include an open discussion of the vice of such behaviours (to forestall similar behaviours by students and to "restore the victim's confidence"), demanding an open apology from the offender ("to restore the victim's 'face'"), or even teasing the offender about his/her own weaknesses to make him/her lose status (Teacher J: "*Using the person's own way to deal with the person*"). Only two Australian teachers indicated that they would deal with the matter in front of the whole class and most would remove or isolate the bully immediately, followed by talking to him/her to create awareness about the inappropriateness of the behaviour. Hong Kong Teacher J indicated that both the offender and the victim should face punishment, since both had contributed to the situation. According to her, an appropriate punishment for the victim would be to "*face the wall and reflect on own faults*".

Likewise, one Hong Kong teacher mentioned that when a student became talkative in class, she would use group pressure or isolation strategy to stop the problem by warning other students not to pay attention to the talkative one, or else they would be punished. If a student was repeatedly late to school, a few Hong Kong teachers said they would readily involve the family or other students to help him/her, such as having other students give him/her morning calls (Teacher H: "*...to help him/her have greater self-control arising from not wanting to bother* *classmates or family .... see if he/she has this conscience..."*). All these indicate a sense of collective responsibility for individual problems, which is not uncommon in collectivistic societies.

Closely associated with this strictness in discipline is the little use of praise and encouragement, which stands in sharp contrast to practices in Western schools. Despite their hard work, Chinese students are seldom praised for their effort and achievement, since the traditional view is that praise may be harmful to children by spoiling them (Salili, Hwang & Choi, 1989). Wong's study (1992, in Salili, 1996) showed that in Hong Kong schools, usually only very outstanding achievement or performance, such as coming first in class or service to the school, qualified for awards of recognition, and it was more common to reward students for making improvement in their schoolwork than for good behaviour. In fact, even if praise is given, it is often accompanied by caution to avoid complacency and to prevent them from getting "carried away" (Salili & Hau, 1994). On the other hand, criticism and punishment are widely used (Ho, 1981) and considered beneficial to children by making them aware of their shortcomings (Salili et al., 1989). This apparent preference for punitive measures rather than praise seems to be rooted in the notion of duty. Since doing well in school and behaving properly are just fulfilling duties intrinsic to one's role as a student, there is no need to praise one for displaying normative behaviour. On the other hand, misbehaving is deviant, disrupts the social order, and has to be dealt with harshly.

Alternative Views on Chinese Teachers' Approaches to Students

Despite all these indications of an authoritarian approach to discipline, some authors have recently suggested that such observations might not have reflected the full picture of teachers' approaches to students in the Confucian tradition. Discussions and findings that support this position focus mainly on the different meanings and functions of authority and punishment in Confucian versus Western cultural contexts (Ho, 1999; Scollon & Wong-Scollon, 1994) as well as the nature of teacher-student relationships in Confucian educational contexts (Biggs, 1996b; Ho, 1999). Evidence showing Chinese teachers to be student-centred in solving daily problems has also been provided (Ho, 1999; O'Connor, 1991).

Meaning of teacher authority and punishment in the Confucian context

In their discussion of misperceptions about authority relationships in the Confucian culture, Scollon and Wong-Scollon (1994) point out the importance of distinguishing Western and Confucian concepts of authority:

> "...western concepts of authority are set against the background of the western concept of the free, autonomous individual whereas Asian concepts of authority are set within a context of the part-whole relations of Confucian thought. When a westerner views Confucian or Post-Confucian authority structures, all that is seen is the restriction on the freedom of choice of the individual. An Asian looking at the same phenomenon is more apt to focus on

the responsibility of the person in the position of authority to look after the interests of the one or ones over which the person's authority applies. The Asian focuses on the care, nurture, and benevolence (or their absence) of the person in authority while the westerner tends to focus on the restriction, limitation, and dependence of the person over which the authority is exercised. An Asian tends to acknowledge the pervasive hierarchical relations in society...while the westerner tends to deny one's own authority over others at the same time as feeling the restrictions of authority over oneself." (p.21)

In the context of education, Chinese teachers exercising authority over students is seen as appropriate since this primarily reflects care for and nurture of the student. On the contrary, Western teachers may play down their authority over students for fear of stifling their freedom of expression and threatening a warm teacher-student relationship. In the same light, while Westerners would react to the ostracising and shaming of a misbehaving child by focusing on the damage done to his/her self-esteem, Chinese people would focus on its effects of making clear to the child how his/her behaviour violates the norms and moral requirements of the group. In other words, while it is legitimate to compare the relative occurrence of various phenomena in different cultural groups, care should be taken in the interpretation of the meaning they carry in the respective cultures.

The use of punishment for inappropriate behaviour is often a means to exert teacher authority in Chinese schools, as related in previous sections. However, in Ho's (1999) study, it was found that the use and meaning of various forms of punishment could be different between Hong Kong and Australian teachers. Punitive measures reported in the Australian context were mostly meant as deterrents to the re-occurrence of unacceptable behaviour and were largely in the form of detentions, time-out or isolation, community services (e.g. picking up papers), or suspension in more serious cases. In contrast, some Hong Kong teachers alleged that the meaning of punishment did not lie in its effectiveness in changing student behaviour, but rather in re-asserting norms for behaviour, or, as Teacher B (HK) put it, "*a declaration of the system*". They would employ a greater variety of punitive measures, sometimes quite innovative ones, such as having the student check out the meaning of foul language in the dictionary and then write an essay about it if he/she was caught using inappropriate language.

In other words, sometimes the widespread use of punishment in the Chinese context is not so much to bring about genuine change in behaviour but to show that someone has done something wrong. Thus misbehaviour is almost always followed by some form of punishment. Hong Kong Teachers D and I alleged that since detention often involved teachers spending out-of-class time with the student on a one-on-one basis, it provided good opportunities for establishing a more personal teacher-student relationship, which would foster greater self-control in student behaviour as a result of greater respect for the teacher arising from a better relationship. In this sense punitive measures in the Chinese context could have positive rather than negative effects on the teacher-student relationship, and some teachers stressed that punishment was always accompanied by some efforts at pacifying to ensure that the student fully understood and accepted the form and severity of the punishment.

Teacher-student relationships in Chinese schools

Observations by Chan (1993) and Biggs (1996b) in Chinese and Hong Kong universities revealed that despite the relatively little interaction and lack of response to the teacher in the classroom, there was much teacher-student interaction outside the classroom with a lot of informal discussions and collective activities, which were "typically marked if not by warmth then by a sense of responsibility and mutual respect" (Biggs, 1996b, p.274). Such contrasting relationships could be explained in terms of the complex nature of social roles and relationships in collectivistic cultures: in the formal class situation, the more formal and hierarchical relationship is in operation, which enables the teacher to be authoritarian and thus facilitates the teaching and learning process, whereas outside the classroom, relationships are informal and the social climate could be warm. Biggs (1996b), drawing on his experience in Hong Kong, asserted that as soon as class was over, the number of Chinese students seeking interaction with the teacher was much higher than was the case with Western students.

Therefore while authoritarian approaches in the West are always associated with a sense of oppression and the lack of warmth in the teacher-student relationship, which inevitably hinder the teacher and learning process, similar effects may not be seen in the Confucian culture context, where teacher authority is an ingrained feature in the formal classroom and is accepted by all parties concerned, with warm teacher-student interactions being encouraged in other settings.

Further insights regarding these two aspects of teacher-student relationships were provided in Ho's (1999) study. When commenting on what an ideal teacher-student relationship should be like, both Hong Kong and Australian teachers stated that teachers should maintain some authority over students and yet be approachable, emphasising the fact that they were more effective with students with whom they had a good relationship, characterised by mutual respect, understanding, and the student perceiving care and concern on the teacher's part. However, there appeared to be a difference between the two groups of teachers regarding the basis for such a relationship. Among Australian teachers, respect from students was allegedly earned through good teaching and demonstration of teacher competence, and this respect in turn enabled the teacher to exercise the necessary authority over students.

Australian Teacher E:

> "They see the teacher as someone who could help them in achieving what they're here to do and learn, so that would be the base behind the relationship."

Australian Teacher J:

> "(They respect you because you) work for them, you prepare these lessons,

you know your subject, and they know that you're going to help them as much as you can."

In the Hong Kong context, teachers were respected for being able to exercise authority in the classroom as well as having an affectionate relationship with students, and this respect from students enabled the teacher to teach without disruption.

Hong Kong Teacher E:

"Chinese people say, 'Discipline (control) first and then teach.' If you can't discipline then you can't teach."

Hong Kong Teacher K:

"We learn to respect each other. There must be some affection between teacher and student....for the teacher to be effective. At the same time some degree of authority has to be maintained."

This dual emphasis on the apparently contradictory elements of authority and affection in the teacher-student relationship was clearly indicated among Hong Kong teachers, who used phrases such as *"dual emphasis on mercy and authority"*, *"simultaneous use of hard and soft measures"* and *"being a teacher, at the same time being a friend"* to describe their approaches to students.

The way Chinese teachers reconcile these seemingly opposite approaches to students is to emphasise different roles in different situations. In the Chinese classroom teacher authority characterises the teacher-student relationship, but after class there are opportunities for establishing a warm and affectionate relationship through informal activities. During the interviews quite a few Hong Kong teachers remarked that those who were prepared to devote more time to establish rapport with students would be more effective in dealing with student problems.

Hong Kong Teacher J:

"Join them in their after-school activities, play basketball with them, visit the museum with them....These are ways to establish understanding and a good relationship."

Thus teacher-student relationships in the West are again more professional in nature, with respect for teachers and classroom order being closely associated with and often a result of good instructional and classroom organisation skills (Jones & Jones, 1995). In the Chinese context, teacher authority in the classroom is ascribed, and the ability to exercise this authority to keep the class under control is considered a prerequisite to effective teaching ("Discipline first, then teach."). On the other hand, it is common for Chinese teachers and students to establish personal and warm relationships outside the classroom learning context, which contributes to the affective quality of the teacher-student relationship.

Evidence for student-centredness in teacher thinking

In a study by O'Connor (1991), carried out in the People's Republic of China, ten veteran elementary school teachers were presented a number of vignettes depicting behaviour problems such as disruption in class, bullying, and daydreaming, and were asked to think aloud while they analysed the problem and decide on management strategy. It turned out that they were very humanistic and student-centred in their approach, using methods that focused on promoting student self-esteem and self-respect and taking care not to make students "lose face". They were even found to rely on reasoning and persuasion more than American teachers did in other similar studies by the same author. These results may seem to contradict those of many other studies conducted in various Chinese societies, as discussed earlier. This study analysed what the teachers thought about the problems rather than observing what they did in their daily practice, while most other studies examine teacher behaviour, but perhaps more importantly in the Chinese context authoritarian behaviour and student-centred thinking are not necessarily incompatible, as Western theorists would assume.

Further evidence of student-centred elements in Chinese teachers' approaches to students was provided in Ho's study (1999), where factor-analytic studies of teachers' management strategies for student problem behaviours revealed that just as in the case of their Australian counterparts, there was a student-centred dimension to Hong Kong teachers' disciplinary strategies (along with a rule-based dimension and a punitive dimension), characterised by respect for students' own aims and choices, listening to students' point of view, providing choices for students, showing empathy, and developing plans for change with students (Table 5.2).

Table 5.2
Discipline strategies for Australian (Aus) and Hong Kong (HK) teachers: standardised loadings for best-fit models in confirmatory factor analysis

Item	Student-centred approach		Rule-based approach		Punitive approach	
	Aus	HK	Aus	HK	Aus	HK
Provide choices for student	0.63	0.85				
Listen to student's point of view	0.84	0.59		0.36		
Respect student's own aims and choices	0.87	0.82				
Show empathy	0.81	0.74				
Develop plans for change with student	0.53	0.66	0.38	0.25		
Establish clear rules			0.92	0.93		
Clarify rules and consequences with student			0.90	0.85		
Consistent enforcement of rules			0.88	0.73		
Warn about disciplinary action			0.35		0.56	0.76
Reprimand					0.81	0.76
Punish					0.74	0.84

When teachers were asked to indicate the extent to which they were likely to use each of the approaches in response to a number of common student problem behaviours in the same study, Australian and Hong Kong teachers generally did not differ in their emphasis of the student-centred approach ($F(1,888)=1.19$, $p>0.017$). What appeared surprising was that Australian teachers actually displayed a greater tendency to use the rule-based and punitive approaches than their Hong Kong counterparts ($F(1,888)=71.63$ and 72.10 respectively, $p<0.017$, means given in Table 5.3).

Table 5.3
Adjusted composite likelihood ratings for management approaches

Management approach	Australia (N=195) Mean	(SD)	Hong Kong (N=255) Mean	(SD)
Rule-based	31.43	(3.38)	28.36	(4.07)
Punitive	27.36	(4.40)	24.37	(4.62)
Student-centred	23.87	(4.88)	23.40	(4.47)

Detailed analysis of variation in discipline approaches for different types of problem behaviours in the two cultural contexts threw light on how these results might be interpreted. Among Australian teachers, there was a distinct emphasis on the rule-based and punitive approaches for interpersonal problems (being rude to teacher, bullying) and lesson disruption (talkative, calling out in class), whereas Hong Kong teachers were more stable in their emphasis on these approaches across different types of problems. Probably in the Hong Kong collectivistic context, rules for behaviour and punitive consequences for the violation of such rules are similarly relevant across all situations. There is greater consensus about group norms concerning interpersonal and classroom behaviours, such as showing respect for all teachers, and these norms do not even have to be stated explicitly in order to be followed. On the contrary, in the Australian individualistic culture, what is acceptable individual behaviour is more subject to negotiation between the parties concerned. Teachers cannot rely on students automatically complying with norms for behaviour in school, yet they are given the responsibility to manage student behaviour so that teaching and learning could take place in school. As a result it might be necessary to have very clearly stated rules and punitive measures in order to keep students under control, especially for behaviours that significantly disrupt group processes, as in interpersonal conflicts and lesson disruption.

Conclusions

Judging from the evidence available so far, the answer to the question "Are Chinese teachers authoritarian?" should be "Yes and no." On the one hand, teacher authority remains an important basis for classroom discipline and control of student behaviour, characterised by strict codes of behaviour, use of punitive or other harsh measures, and teachers having a strong moral responsibility to guide students on the right path. Nevertheless, these apparently authoritarian practices might not generate the same negative effects as they would in Western contexts when evaluated in the light of the concept of authority and punishment in the Confucian context as well as the nature of teacher-student relationships in this tradition, where there is a strong emphasis on an affective and personal relationship established through informal interactions.

It is likely that most previous observations emphasising authoritarianism in Chinese teachers have not distinguished between formal and informal settings in the Confucian school context. While Western teachers display a more integrated approach to students in various situations, and lessons could be conducted in a regimented or informal manner according to the teacher's personal orientation, Confucian classes are mostly quite formal (a situation for students to receive knowledge from the teacher), where teachers could be highly authoritarian if necessary in order to keep absolute control over the situation. Personal needs are not addressed in the classroom and both teachers and students share these expectations. However, once out of the formal class situation, where the demand for orderliness is no longer relevant, teachers may interact with students on more friendly terms, attending to their personal needs on a more student-centred basis.

Thus Chinese teachers could appear very authoritarian or student-centred, depending on the context (formal or informal) in which they are observed or whether their thinking or behaviour is being assessed. Put in another way, while Western teachers are to a larger extent allowed to be themselves (expressing different personalities and values) in all situations, the concept of behaving differently according to different role requirements is more entrenched among Chinese teachers. One of the more striking examples of how Chinese teachers may reconcile authoritarian and student-centred approaches to students is seen in Hong Kong teachers' use of detention, as mentioned earlier. While detention is without doubt a punitive measure, some teachers actually make use of this after-class informal situation to establish better communication and relationship with students. In other words, student-centred methods as postulated in the West appear to be also relevant in the Chinese school context although they may be operationalised in different ways.

REFERENCES

Bean, J.S. & Hoy, W.K. (1974). Pupil Control Ideology of Teachers and Instructional Climate in the Classroom. *High School Journal*, 58, 61-69.

Biggs, J.B. (1996a). *Academic Development in Confucian Heritage Culture*. Paper presented at the International Symposium on Child Development, Hong Kong.

Biggs, J.B. (1996b). Western Misperceptions of the Confucian-Heritage Learning Culture. In D.A. Watkins & J.B. Biggs (Eds.), *The Chinese Learner: Cultural, Psychological and Contextual Influences*. Hong Kong/Melbourne: Comparative Education Research Centre, The University of Hong Kong/Australian Council for Educational Research, 45-67.

Chan, S.L. (1993). *Approaches to Learning of Medical and Economics-law Students in a Guangzhou University*. University of Hong Kong: M.Ed. Dissertation.

Cheung, P.C. & Lau, S. (1985). Self-esteem: Its Relationship to the Family and School Social Environments among Chinese Adolescents. *Youth and Society*, 16(4), 438-456.

Deci, E.L., Schwartz, A.J., Sheinman, L. & Ryan, R.M. (1981). An Instrument to Assess Adults' Orientations toward Control versus Autonomy with Children: Reflections on Intrinsic Motivation and Perceived Competence. *Journal of Educational Psychology*, 73(5), 642-650.

Ho, D.Y.F. (1981). Traditional Pattern of Socialization in Chinese Society. *Acta Psychologica Taiwanica*, 23(2), 81-95.

Ho, D.Y.F. (1986). Chinese Patterns of Socialization: A Critical Review. In M.H. Bond (Ed.), *The Psychology of the Chinese People*. Hong Kong: Oxford University Press, 1-37.

Ho, D.Y.F. (1993). Cognitive Socialization in Confucian Heritage Cultures. In P. Greenfield & J. Cocking (Eds.), *Cross-cultural Roots of Minority Children Development*. Hillsdale, NJ: Erlbaum, 285-313.

Ho, D.Y.F. (1994). Filial Piety, Authoritarian Moralism, and Cognitive Conservatism in Chinese Societies. *Genetic, Social and General Psychology Monographs*, 120, 347-365.

Ho, D.Y.F. (1996). Filial Piety and its Psychological Consequences. In M.H. Bond (Ed.), *The Handbook of Chinese Psychology*. Hong Kong: Oxford University Press, 155-165.

Ho, D.Y.F. & Kang, T.K. (1984). Intergenerational Comparisons of Child-rearing Attitudes and Practices in Hong Kong. *Developmental Psychology*, 20(6), 1004-1016.

Ho, I.T. (1999). *Teacher Thinking about Student Problem Behaviours and Management Strategies: A Comparative Study of Australian and Hong Kong Teachers*. Unpublished doctoral thesis, the University of Sydney.

Jones, V.F. & Jones, L.S. (1995). *Comprehensive Classroom Management*. Boston: Allyn and Bacon.

Lee, W.O. (1996). The Cultural Context for the Chinese Learner: Conceptions of Learning in the Confucian Tradition. In D.A. Watkins & J.B. Biggs (Eds.), *The Chinese Learner: Cultural, Psychological and Contextual Influences*. Hong Kong/Melbourne: Comparative Education Research Centre, The University of Hong Kong/Australian Council for Educational Research, 25-41.

Lewis, R. (1997). *The Discipline Dilemma*. Melbourne: The Australian Council for Educational Research Ltd.

Leung, P.W.H., Salili, F. & Baber, F.M. (1986). Common Adolescent Problems in Hong Kong: Their Relationship with Self-esteem, Locus of Control, Intelligence and Family Environment. *Psychologia*, 29, 91-101.

Lunenberg, F.C. (1983). Pupil Control Ideology and Self-concept as a Learner. *Educational Research Quarterly*, 8(3), 33-39.

O'Connor, J.E. (1991). *A Descriptive Analysis of Chinese Teachers' Thought Processes*. Paper presented at the Conference of Chinese Education for the

21st Century, Honolulu, Hawaii.
Salili, F. (1996). Accepting Personal Responsibility for Learning. In D.A. Watkins & J.B. Biggs (Eds.), *The Chinese Learner: Cultural, Psychological and Contextual Influences*. Hong Kong/Melbourne: Comparative Education Research Centre, The University of Hong Kong/Australian Council for Educational Research, 85-105.
Salili, F. & Hau K.T. (1994). The Effect of Teachers' Evaluative Feedback on Chinese Students' Perception of Ability: A Cultural and Situational Analysis. *Educational Studies*, 20(2), 223-236.
Salili, F., Hwang, C. & Choi, N.F. (1989). Teachers' Evaluative Behaviour: The Relationship between Teachers' Comments and Perceived Ability in Hong Kong. *Journal of Cross-Cultural Psychology*, 20(2), 115-132.
Scollon, R. & Wong-Scollon, S. (1994). *The Post-Confucian Confusion*. Hong Kong City Polytechnic University, Department of English Research Report No.37.
Wolfgang, C. & Glickman, C. (1995). *Solving Discipline Problems*. Boston: Allyn & Bacon.
Wu, D.Y.H. (1996). Chinese Childhood Socialization. In M.H. Bond (Ed.), *The Handbook of Chinese Psychology*. Hong Kong: Oxford University Press, 143-154.
Yuan, G. (1984). Six Measures to ensure the Success of Key Middle Schools. *Chinese Education*, 17(2), 57-60.

6

Large Classes in China: 'Good' Teachers and Interaction

Martin Cortazzi and Jin Lixian

Given the size of China and its population of over 1.2 billion, it is perhaps not surprising that class sizes are also large, certainly in comparison with Western countries. At primary (ages 7-11/12) and middle school (ages 12/13-18/19) levels, class sizes can range from fewer than 30 to 70 or more. Classes commonly have 50 or 60 students. University classes may have fewer than 20 students but often have 30-50 and can rise to over 100, even in such subjects as foreign languages. Schools can be large: there may be 1,000-3,000 students in a primary school, and 1,500 to well over 3,000 students in a middle school. Staffing levels are therefore 50-100 or more teachers in a primary school and 100-200 or more in a middle school. Western observers seem to quote quite different numbers in the class sizes they observe (Jin & Cortazzi, 1998a). This probably depends on when and where they visit schools, and the number and range of schools they look at: rural and urban schools may have quite different class sizes, the former may fluctuate at planting or harvest times, and there are some urban variations from school to school. As examples from our own visits in Tianjin and Wuhan in 1996, we saw: a class of 21 nursery children aged 1-2; classes of 27 three year olds and 44 five year olds in a kindergarten; primary classes of 64 seven year olds, 56 eight year olds and 72 eleven year olds; middle school classes of 58 twelve year olds and 57 fifteen year olds. These numbers are large enough to surprise many Western teachers.

What is certainly surprising is that when teacher-student ratios are examined it seems that many schools could in fact reduce their class sizes but choose not to do so. Chinese teachers in large schools give four reasons for this (Jin & Cortazzi, 1998a). First, physical conditions often do not permit the extra classrooms that would be necessary to reduce class sizes. Second, given the large numbers of teachers in most schools, teachers specialise and teach only one or sometimes two subjects even at primary level (except in smaller schools). Smaller classes would make it difficult to maintain this specialization without recruiting more teachers. Third, if classes are larger this allows each teacher to teach fewer lessons per week. Thus, primary teachers generally teach a maximum of eighteen 40 minute lessons per week, junior middle school teachers have between ten and twelve 45 minute class periods each week, and senior middle school teachers twelve such classes per week. This is important because it has an effect on the classroom interaction and on the quality of teaching. It means that more non-teaching time is available for lesson preparation. In large schools (i.e. with 2-

3,000 students), a teacher can teach the same lesson to several classes of the same age group in the same week. Time can also be given to supervise students' daily self-study sessions, to help individual students after class in breaks or lunch hours, to make home visits, or to observe colleagues teach. Finally, many Chinese teachers simply do not put such an emphasis on reducing class sizes as has become commonplace in the West. They would rather give attention to finding the best ways to present knowledge and concepts, illustrated with good examples and taught in a vivid manner to facilitate learning.

There are remarkably few published articles on the topic of large classes written by Chinese teachers or researchers; we found just one in a sample of 707 articles recently published in China and Taiwan (Jin & Cortazzi, 1998a). On the other hand, Chinese teachers (when they are asked in questionnaires) do place 'large classes' in a list of recognised constraints, ranked fourth after 'limited resources', 'exams' and 'textbooks' (Ward et al., 1995). However, for many who teach the large classes there is a quiet acceptance for what they personally cannot change. The 1999 discussion on promoting 'quality education' in China in schools and in the media (e.g. *China Daily*, May 31-June 4th, 1999) has not notably featured large classes, although universalising compulsory education, eliminating illiteracy, extending facilities and technical resources (especially at tertiary level), and raising teaching standards have been identified as key areas. To raise teaching standards in Hunan schools, for example, teachers were required to attend summer courses in 1999 focussing on professional skills and ethics. This suggests that teaching quality is seen as crucial to quality education.

Thus while many Western policy makers see large classes as essentially a barrier to quality learning, their Chinese counterparts probably see the quality of the teachers, teachers' preparation and their performance in classroom interaction as keys to the quality learning of students, even in classes where the normal size is considerably larger than the normal Western definition of 'large'.

And yet, despite teaching large classes, there is a general recognition that the academic achievement of Chinese students is high (Stevenson & Lee, 1996; Reynolds & Farrell, 1996), even by those who have doubts about the testing widely used to measure such achievement (Galton, 1998). While achievement motivation, hard work and effort are important factors in Chinese students' attainment, the learning environment is also important (Biggs, 1994, 1996). There are clearly cultural and contextual influences which make up what seems in many ways to be an effective learning environment (Watkins & Biggs, 1996) and a key figure in a Chinese culture of learning is the Chinese teacher (Cortazzi & Jin, 1996a).

This chapter focuses on interaction in large classes in China by looking at the role of the teacher and how the teacher organises learner participation. We draw on questionnaire and interview data obtained from Chinese students and teachers (all quotations are from our research interviews or classrooms) and on our observations and video-recordings of kindergartens, primary and middle schools made between 1992 and 1999. First, we explore Chinese concepts of a 'good teacher'; these are important because students' and teachers' expectations of classroom interaction will in part derive from such concepts. We draw attention to aspects of teacher preparation and teacher development which are rarely discussed outside China, yet these turn out to be key supportive elements for teaching large classes effectively. We draw on transcripts of classroom interaction to summarise the participation patterns and sequences of some Chinese language lessons at primary and kindergarten levels. In the analysis and discussion, we highlight the ways in which Chinese teachers seem to employ a number of key elements which we put into a framework of interactive activities.

A 'Good' Teacher in China

Classroom interaction essentially encompasses teacher-student talk and classroom activity and how they are organised. This is heavily influenced by concepts of expected characteristics of a 'good' teacher, whether such concepts are those of the teacher or the learners, because to a large extent this defines what teachers do and what learners expect them to do. To investigate Chinese students' perceptions of good teachers (Cortazzi & Jin, 1996a) we first asked 135 university students in Tianjin to write essays on this topic. In their open-ended responses, 67% of the writers mentioned that a good teacher *has deep knowledge* or a similar phrase, 25% included *is patient*, 23.7% *is humorous*, 21.5% *is a good moral example* and *shows friendliness*. Other qualities commonly mentioned were that a good teacher *teaches students about life* (17.5%), *arouses students' interest* (17%), *is warm-hearted and understanding* or *uses effective teaching methods* (16.2%), and *is caring and helpful* (14.8%) and *explains clearly* (6.7%). The frequent mention of teachers' knowledge supports a general recognition that a large part of the interaction in Chinese classes (with variations in different subjects and age ranges) is teacher-centred and text-based; both the teacher and the textbook are regarded as authoritative sources of knowledge. This is most evident in the teaching of reading, both for Chinese and English or other foreign languages (Cortazzi & Jin, 1996b).

To locate these ideas within a more international context we then developed a questionnaire based on the essay analysis. This was administered to a further 129 Chinese university students in Tianjin, Beijing and Wuhan and to groups of similar university students in other countries, allowing comparisons with Britain (Jin & Cortazzi, 1998a), Japan (Jin & Cortazzi, 1997-8), and Malaysia (Cortazzi & Jin in press) and Turkey. The data here are extensive but we have selected a few examples, shown in Figure 6.1

The figures in Figure 6.1 show mean scores derived from a 5 point scale which represents the extent of subjects' agreement with the statements about teachers (1 signifies strong disagreement, 5 indicates strong agreement). At first sight, the students in the five countries all seem to agree with the statements but the extent of this agreement can differ dramatically, as statistical tests of significant differences show. The results indicate that there are quite different emphases in students' expectations and perceptions of good teachers. Taking the Chinese concepts of the teacher as a baseline (since the original essays were written by Chinese), the Chinese students' expectation that a good teacher *has deep knowledge* is shared with students in Japan, Malaysia and Turkey but not with British students; the latter rate this aspect significantly lower (p<0.0000). The Chinese perception that a good teacher *is patient* is significantly lower than that of the British (p<0.0000) or Turkish (p<0.022), but significantly higher than that of the Japanese (p<0.0000) or Malaysians (p<0.017). The Chinese perception that a good teacher *is a good moral example* is significantly higher than that of the British (p<0.0001) and Japanese (p<0.0002), about the same as the Malaysians yet significantly lower than that of the Turkish students (p<0.0029). The Chinese belief that a good teacher *is friendly* is shared with the Japanese; it is significantly higher than that of the Malaysians (p<0.008) and British (p<0.010), but significantly lower than that of the Turkish students (p<0.016).

The Chinese emphasis on the teacher as a friend is consistent with other data from students obtained using a metaphor elicitation technique (Cortazzi & Jin, 1999), where Chinese students frequently say the teacher is a friend using such phrases as *'a respected friend,' 'a close friend,' 'a strict friend,'* or *'a kind friend.'* Less frequently, they mention a parent, *'a strict father and a patient mother'* or *'my mother'*. Some students apparently see the teacher as a combination of friend and parent: *'a father and a friend,' 'a strict mother and a good friend'*. Such epithets are shared with many Japanese respondents, but are rare in our data for British students; however, they are common among Turkish students and among Malaysians.

Figure 6.1
Selected items showing students' ratings of aspects of a 'good teacher'

A 'GOOD' TEACHER ...	Means CHINA (n=129)	Means BRITAIN (n=205)	Means JAPAN (n=93)	Means TURKEY (n=165)	Means MALAYSIA (n=101)
Has deep knowledge	4.535	3.548	4.484	4.494	4.337
Is patient	4.307	4.571	3.696	4.344	4.020
Is a good moral example	4.181	3.808	3.802	4.337	4.257
Is friendly	4.372	4.177	4.333	4.472	4.141
Explains clearly	4.271	4.730	4.516	4.475	4.564
Organises a variety of classroom activities	3.884	4.200	3.946	4.242	3.554
Has an answer to students' questions	3.884	4.200	3.946	4.242	3.554

We would argue that the differences in emphasis here affect classroom interaction so that, for example, the interaction typical of Chinese classrooms has some characteristic qualities which are different from those typically found elsewhere. This is implied in other examples of findings which are more clearly associated with classroom interaction. Chinese students hold that a good teacher *explains clearly* significantly less than the Japanese (p<0.0098), Malaysian (p<0.0006), Turkish

($p<0.0001$) or British ($p<0.0000$) students. Of course, this does not necessarily mean that respondents think Chinese teachers do not explain well when they teach; perhaps the Chinese students believe that a good student should listen carefully and make a strong effort to learn. Thus Chinese students have told us, *'Listen and remember, that is most Chinese students' conception of study.'* This is sometimes likened to stuffing a Peking duck, *'We Chinese get used to a pouring and filling way.'* In this picture, it is the teacher who is 'pouring and filling', explaining and giving knowledge in a transmission process.

The results for the characteristic that a good teacher *organises a variety of activities* (not featured in the essays but added to the questionnaire later) shows that the Chinese rating is about the same as that of the Japanese but significantly lower than that of the British ($p<0.001$) and Turkish ($p<0.0000$) groups but significantly higher than that of the Malaysians ($p<0.0044$). As another example, the Chinese belief that a good teacher *has an answer to students' questions* is significantly higher than that of the British ($p<0.0000$) but significantly lower than that of the Japanese ($p<0.001$), Turkish ($p<0.007$) and Malaysian ($p<0.0312$) students. A possible explanation of this may be that Chinese teachers are likely to be seen as sources of knowledge more than British teachers are (by their respective students). Perhaps British students think British teachers do not need to know answers, but they do need to be able to find out (Cortazzi & Jin, in press). However, this leaves the question of why the Chinese rating here is significantly lower than the Japanese, Turkish and Malaysian ones. Elsewhere in the data, the Chinese rating that good students study independently is significantly higher than all the other groups here, so perhaps if the teacher cannot answer a question the Chinese students believe they can study independently to find the answer themselves. Perhaps with this belief they ask few questions. The Chinese handling of student classroom questions is a complex matter. It involves the students' own sensitivity to lesson timing, pace and prediction of teacher talk, plus self-reflection and an element of regard for the 'face' of both student and teacher (Cortazzi & Jin, 1996a; Jin & Cortazzi, 1997-8).

Chinese teachers' own characterisations of 'good' teachers also tend to emphasise the extent of knowledge required, along with friendliness and professional morality. In interviews, teachers in responsible positions have no hesitation in characterising good teachers. Thus a senior teacher in a middle-school said:

A good teacher has professional responsibility, a good basis of knowledge, is able to interact with students, solve their problems, is able to explain difficult points to them. A good teacher will treat students as friends. Students will accept a good teacher because the teacher has the ability to help them.

The head teacher of another middle school said:

Good teachers are dedicated. They work hard, have a good spirit and love their profession. They have professional morality. They are responsible and self-sacrificing. A good teacher is like a burning candle; it gives light through self-sacrifice. They have professional knowledge and skills and are expert. They should also have good health.

The head of a large primary school said:

A good teacher has good knowledge of the subject, is polite and courteous, has a teaching ability in other teachers' opinion, is a good friend in students' opinion and talks to them after class, is interested in students, helps them to get knowledge easily with a good teaching manner.

The head of a large kindergarten readily listed the following:

A good teacher loves children and her career; she is clear about educational goals for children and what children should become; she has good qualities herself, has a professional morality, is a good example and a friend of the children; she is patient; she has profound knowledge, both general knowledge and professional knowledge, has a good educational background and good ways of perceiving children.

The head of a language department in a preschool normal school (which trains kindergarten teachers in a full time 3 year course) commented:

Our students need a special knowledge of child development and of methods of cultivating children's abilities. Good teachers must use the standard language (Putonghua) *and clear speech. They must be a good model of language not only for language development itself but also because language development is also social learning so being a model is important. This is input for children's learning. Good teachers need strong training in organisational skills so their training is very strict. The teacher as a model is important for everything. For instance, children must develop a sense of beauty and aesthetics so teachers must combine strictness with helping children to be individually creative. Teachers have to give models of this in their own example.*

A senior colleague in another department of the same institution added:

A good teacher must love children and have a professional conscience. She must use good educational methods. She must show respect for children and in part feel close to them. She needs skills, like dancing or musical ability, and a sense of humour and patience. It is very difficult for a teacher to be good at every aspect.

Such comments are readily forthcoming. They are representative of many others and, allowing for differences across phases, they seem quite consistent.

The human tone of many comments is striking: Chinese teachers aim to combine *jiao shu* (literally, 'teaching the book', or perhaps giving knowledge) with *yu ren* ('cultivating the person') and both these Chinese terms translate the English word 'education'. This combination is clear in one primary head-teacher's comment on a phrase which is currently emphasised, 'quality education': *'It means create students' ability or capacity. Students should not only learn from books but from society.'* He added that this includes enhanced education in music, arts, sports, and vocational fields and that crucially it depends on the quality of good teachers, who need to be *'well-rounded real people with professional ethics'* in order to develop students with similar qualities. A huge poster in a preschool normal school proclaims *'Education creates a real person. This is your profession'*.

Teacher Development and Preparation

Good teachers in China may be honoured with titles (and salary bonuses). Such titles are awarded after they have been observed and have given demonstration lessons in a competitive situation, at one to three days' notice, in front of tens or hundreds of their peers. The audience of teachers may come from other schools in the area or from the whole district. This system has an important modelling effect since many young teachers attend these public presentations of good lessons (attendance is required for promotion). The teachers who win such titles as 'advanced', 'senior', 'special' or 'model' teacher act as mentors to younger teachers and their mentoring role includes giving further demonstration lessons. Their performance therefore has a key role in the preparation of other teachers who observe it and to some extent seeing such acknowledged good examples models the later teaching performance of others.

In Wuhan, the recognised criteria for an able teacher include five abilities: to show effective preparation; to deliver an effective teaching performance; to express the rationale underlying their teaching; to observe other teachers; and to evaluate others' teaching. In this system it is not surprising that, in general, senior teachers can readily list characteristics of good teachers, nor is it surprising to observe considerable consistency of practice in the lessons in Chinese schools which other teachers also observe.

These same criteria can be used at school level too. Many Chinese schools have now instituted their own system of peer teacher observation. Each teacher observes six to ten classes taught by other teachers each term, mostly in their own school but sometimes in other schools in the district. Any teacher can therefore find that their class is observed on a regular basis by several colleagues and sometimes by ten or more (apart from classes specifically seen by their mentor if they are newer teachers). This has a major function of teacher development for two reasons: the observed lessons will tend to be the best that the performing teacher can arrange, and many teachers will feel encouraged to take up specific classroom practices which they see being managed effectively in their own context. Some teaching methods and approaches can spread rapidly in this way, in a kind of cultural epidemiology through observation (Sperber, 1996). This would mean that observations may change a teacher's mental representation of teaching, which affects their classroom behaviour; this is observed by others, and the chain continues, consciously or not, until at some stage certain aspects of teaching are held as mental representations or common values by large groups. Observers may choose which class to observe according to whether they themselves teach that class at other times, or whether the class will demonstrate a particular type of lesson (e.g. it may feature pair or groupwork). Sometimes teachers will observe the teaching of subjects other than their own. Observers take notes and often use a checklist or teaching evaluation form. Checklists may invite comments and grades on the use of teaching, teaching arrangements, teaching methods, teaching quality and effect on learning. Observers usually talk over the lesson later with the teacher of the lesson, who is encouraged to engage in self-reflection and evaluation. Post-lesson discussion and the checklists themselves tend to focus on the teacher, although comments on student participation are invited. There seem to be two reasons for this focus: many lessons are indeed teacher-led or teacher-centred (this is not surprising in large classes), and observers usually sit at the very back of the classroom (given crowded classrooms with little space for movement there is little choice about this) so their view is predominantly to see the teacher over a sea of students' heads.

The knowledge that lessons can be observed in this way underlines the writing of lesson plans. In many schools these must be made available to mentors or senior teachers. However, planning is made easier and more effective in group sessions. These sessions represent a collective approach to teacher planning: in subject groups, the teachers establish a weekly meeting in which by arrangement teachers take turns to discuss their preparation and present lesson plans to each other before they use them in class. They discuss the key points of a lesson, any interesting activities or background research, and different ways to make the best use of the class time available. Among other issues they may talk about ways to teach large classes and how to involve students in active participation. Group co-ordinators ensure that all teachers are involved and that the group supports new teachers. This process encourages consistent high quality teaching. The next section relates the 'good teacher' and preparation and planning to interactive activities in the classroom.

A Framework of Interactive Activities in Large Classes

Our observations of large classes in China and subsequent analysis of photographic and video evidence that we have gathered have so far led us to identify a number of features which together make up a tentative model of influential features in classroom interaction in many Chinese contexts (see Figure 6.2).

The model in Figure 6.2 makes reference to Chinese teachers' (or learners') ideological background and cultures of learning. These ideas are elaborated elsewhere (Cortazzi & Jin, 1996a; Jin & Cortazzi, 1998b) and relate to further models which attempt to analyse Confucian and Taoist influences and cultural expectations about what learning means. The basic premise is that much learning is fundamentally cultural and that therefore the ideas about expectations, values, beliefs and behaviour associated with learning may vary across cultural groups (as may be interpreted from the data about 'good' teachers presented earlier).

Figure 6.2
A tentative model of influential features in interaction in large classes in China

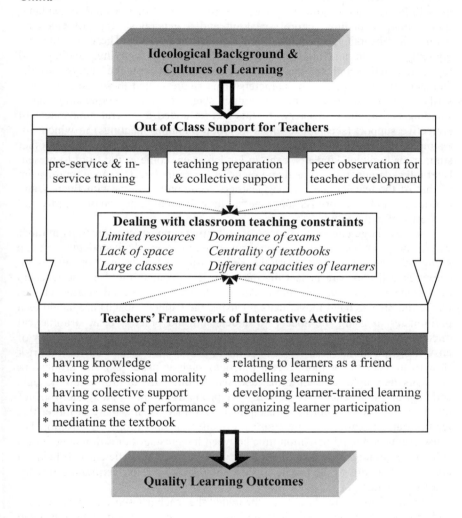

This model here includes a teacher's framework of interactive features, some of the elements of which appear in the questionnaire and interview data cited earlier.

The framework includes the knowledge and expertise of the teacher, and the relationships established with learners (in which the teacher is a friend, warm-hearted and understanding, showing a kind of parental care and concern). An out of class support element in the model includes the extensive preparation that teachers carry out in advance (in groups and individually through lesson plans and extensively teacher-annotated textbooks) and peer observation for teacher development. The framework also includes the professional morality expected of teachers, which encompasses the role of modelling learning to students. This modelling can lead to quite extensive classroom use of demonstration, explanation, imitation, drilling, choral speaking and a general strategy of engaging learners in rehearsing, repeating, practising, and memorising. These activities are typically seen in teaching children to write through copying, tracing, and repeated practice and yet this is often accompanied with the analysis of the elements of Chinese written characters. This suggests that these are not necessarily goals in themselves but are rather stages towards internalising understanding and attaining mastery. To this can be added a general atmosphere of collective support (seen for teachers in group planning meetings) in which, for example, teachers use a learner's errors to elicit the correction from another student, or in which students, even in kindergarten, come to the front to present brief talks, demonstrate or read and recite in a prepared performance reminiscent of that of the teacher. That young learners commonly do this with fluency and confidence and without fuss suggests that they feel a high degree of security and support within the group.

In these large classes this sense of collective support also functions in other ways. There is a measure of 'learner-trained learning' in which students are quite stringently taught certain learning skills, ways of working, or classroom activities. All these are in fact the means to learn something else (and teachers help students to understand this). This is clearly seen in kindergarten classes where the precise hand movements for using the Chinese abacus are taught as a preliminary to using the abacus to understand and practise basic arithmetical operations. This also seems to be the case with the traditional disciplined way of answering questions (students raise a hand, stand, answer, and sit in one brisk flow of movement) or more recent practices such as using pair and groupwork (students are taught to listen to instructions, get into pairs or groups, do the task, and stop on the teacher's signal – all very promptly). While to a Western visitor this may seem either dutifully disciplined or rather robotic there is more: this learner-trained learning is immensely effective in classroom organisation because it cuts down the transition time between lesson stages or different activities. It helps to get large numbers of students working together efficiently. It helps to ensure a basic aim of the teacher: to use the lesson time to maximum effect for quality learning.

To this framework should also be added the teacher's sense of performance and the use of the textbook. The performance element includes the rehearsed presentation of information, explanations, or demonstrations but also a kind of virtuoso conductor's sense that the lesson has clear stages, a variety of often brief student activities, and a sense of pace. The textbook embodies knowledge and that which is to be learned (sometimes quite literally in the memorising and reciting of texts). It can form the third part of the triangle between teacher-students-text where much of the teacher's effort is to mediate between students and text. This can be physically enacted when students read aloud collectively: the textbook is held up at chin or chest level by the teacher and class alike – they see each other past the book and see the book of the other. This sense of performance and text mediation is evident in this middle school teacher's comment made after a high quality Chinese language lesson with 53 students:

> *When I prepare I see the text in my imagination and I imagine myself performing the text. My teaching is like acting on stage with the text to bring it alive to students. I have this image of performing in my mind. Teaching is a kind of recreating of the text to bring the text alive through performance.*

The elements of this framework seem to form a system inasmuch as they interact with each other; each element is part of a system of cultural practices. A further element to be added is how teachers organise learner participation.

Organising Learner Participation in Primary Schools

A major challenge for the teacher of large classes is how to organise the participation of learners. This does not necessarily mean simply verbal activity for different kinds of verbal activity can have different interpretations, if common Chinese and Western classroom activities are compared (Cortazzi & Jin, 1996a). Some Chinese students consciously learn through concentration and listening. This point was emphasised by a Chinese student at a British university after someone had mentioned that Chinese students were 'passive':

> *We are active in our minds. We are thinking all the time. Our minds follow the lecturer with questions and challenges. We are just not used to speaking out. But all of us know very well what is going on and we know the answers to the questions those lecturers asked or other students raised.*

This listening-oriented learning can be quite conscious among young Chinese learners, too, as is shown in this explanation from an eight year old:

> *I may be listening but I am not passive. I am learning in my head. I learn from my teacher. I also learn from what my friends do. If they make a mistake, I learn from that too.*

For the Chinese teacher, then, the challenge is to arouse and maintain learners' attention, concentration, listening and interest (as mentioned previously in the essays) and also to enable as many individuals as possible to speak, even if this is brief.

In handling a text, for example, the range of commonly employed interaction patterns includes:

- the teacher reads or explains, students listen; one student reads or comments;
- several students read in a pre-set sequence (reading a paragraph or dialogue);
- the whole class reads in chorus;

- half the class reads in chorus (by seating rows or gender);
- the whole class reads aloud but each student reads at his or her own pace;
- students read silently (usually with a pre-set task).

Clearly there are many other ways of using texts in class (we have seen effective use made of drawings, photos, posters, flashcards, puppets and toys, or simple models in large classes), but these basic elements are often used briefly in rapid, prepared sequences, usually interspersed with focused question-answer exchanges or blackboard explanations and occasional explanations by students. More recent practices of using pair or group tasks and discussion can greatly extend the range, and even without technological aids this repertoire of organising strategies allows Chinese teachers to use texts in a mediated manner to get a surprisingly high participation rate.

This kind of participation must ultimately be measured by assessments of learning (perhaps through the heavy homework output or daily tests experienced by many middle school students), but the following summaries of the interaction from video recordings of Chinese language lessons give some idea of what the participation in these lessons is like.

A teacher working with a class of 49 primary children, aged 8-9, not only herself read, explained, and thoroughly illustrated the meaning of the target text in 30 minutes but in that time she also got 20 individual learners to speak to the whole class. Additionally, by the end of the half hour the whole class had spoken or read in chorus three times and had further discussed, read and retold the story three times in pairs.

In another primary class of 56 children, aged 8-9, a teacher working with a text had managed, within the first 25 minutes, to get 12 children to read and 3 to recite parts of the text, while a further 7 children answered questions and 21 explained the use of words and phrases. Additionally the whole class read 5 sections of the text in chorus and the teacher herself read the text twice, gave three explanations, and made four comments on children's explanations.

In a third primary class with 64 children, aged 6-7, the teacher working with a text involved 53 individual children in answering questions and giving explanations or examples and had 34 brief rounds of whole-class choral answers to confirm individual learner's answers, correct other's mistakes or give class answers to the teacher. In addition she read the whole text herself, re-read a paragraph and explained the structures of different words. All this took place in the first 21 minutes; the lesson continued at this intensive, involving, fast pace but with different activities for another 19 minutes but this included a one and a half minute break for an action song led by a child. Clearly such lessons are well-thought out, carefully timed, and broadly planned within the framework of interactive activities as we have analysed it.

The following lesson outline of the first 20 minutes of a fourth primary lesson with a class of 50 children, aged 9-10, gives a further idea of how tightly organised such lessons are in terms of having a carefully structured series of activities. These activities are packaged, as it were, by preparation, timing, pace, variety but often brevity of activity, and the efficient transitions between activities. These lessons are teacher-controlled but they involve learners quite heavily. They depend crucially on what we have called learner-trained learning:

- The teacher (T) introduces the topic of the lesson: to study the text 'There's only one earth'
- T nominates several students (Ss) to stand up and read a character or word aloud (2 mins)
- T asks questions: several Ss answer when nominated; T gives a follow-up explanation to two answers (1 min)
- A writing task: T gives some Ss an individual card on which to write answers, other Ss write in their books. T gives encouragement, 'You all write very well'. T collects some of the cards and sticks them on the board while the rest finish writing (3 mins)
- T tells Ss to stop writing and to read the examples on the board; T asks a question (1 min)
- T gets Ss to engage in peer discussion on a further question. T asks some who finish to write on the board one by one (1 min)
- T follows up with further questions; 'Any other answer? Why?' Ss stand to read their answers from their books. T elicits further confirmation from the class (1 min)
- Ss read a section from their books aloud, individually (1 min)
- T gets Ss to discuss in groups of four: the fixed seating arrangements will only allow this if pairs turn round in their seats to face the pairs behind them (2 mins)
- T asks group representatives to report back on their discussion to the class; T intersperses reports with praise and comment (2 mins)
- T again asks Ss to read a section aloud, individually (1 min)
- T asks Ss to read aloud to each other in pairs (1 min)
- T nominates one S to stand and read aloud to the class (1 min)
- T asks questions about the text; Ss stand and answer from the text (1 min)
- T plays recorded music and asks all Ss to read the whole text aloud in chorus to the rhythm of the music (2 mins)

This segment shows the brief use of pairs and groups as a particular way of organising learner participation. Using them co-operatively would fit into the collective support element of the framework of interactive activities.

Using co-operative pairs and groups

The classroom activity of using co-operative pairs and groups is a relatively recent practice which can now be seen in a range of curriculum subjects. A few years ago it was probably only used systematically in a few English classes as Chinese teachers attempted to apply Western communicative approaches to language teaching (Cortazzi & Jin, 1996b). This was initially held to be problematic because of large classes. Instead of splitting the entire class into pairs or groups to talk simultaneously, as in the example above, Chinese teachers often use pairs sequentially. Two students stand in different parts of the room and one asks the other a question or comments on or corrects the answer of the other. Then another pair similarly interacts while the rest of the class observe and listen, and the sequence continues. As shown earlier, transition times as pairs change over is minimal because of the learner-trained learning: students know the procedures and react promptly to teachers' cues. In this way, pairs or groups (whose members are usually well prepared individually in advance) may come to the front and perform to the teacher and class without raising anxieties about noise or wasting time or the inability to monitor student talk. This has the further advantage that feedback from the teacher is simultaneously to those who have spoken and to the rest of the class, who have also heard the original utterances. This provides a clear possibility for vicarious learning, providing students listen and concentrate. Since, as we have seen, such activities tend to be brisk and short, this is not much to ask. It fits the listening-oriented learning of many Chinese learners and, in fact, our photos of classrooms show that lack of such attention is extremely rare: direction of gaze, body stance, and subsequent activity all indicate very high levels of concentration at such times.

Increasingly, however, simultaneous pair and group organisation is used: the entire class divides into pairs or groups with the same (or less commonly a different) task and proceed to discuss it simultaneously, and often spontaneously. This is now fairly common as a paired reading task. A primary teacher commented:

Pairs seem to be very useful. The children always feel some distance when they interact with the teacher but this is much less so when they interact with each other. Weaker students get help from other students.

This use of pairs to support learners of a wide range of abilities is being seen as increasingly important because more and more Chinese teachers are conscious that catering for different learning capacities is a constraint on their interaction. How to plan for different levels of abilities is on the agenda for group planning meetings.

Fixed furniture and lack of space for movement makes groupwork less free than it might otherwise be but Chinese teachers get students to rotate in their chairs to make up a group with others behind them. We have seen primary teachers in Taiwan employ co-operative groupwork particularly effectively in such curriculum areas as maths, social studies and Chinese: the teacher sets the class a problem; the children split into groups and huddle together to discuss alternative solutions; after decisions are reached, the chairperson from each group in turn presents the main points to the whole class. Further, during each presentation the teacher temporarily abdicates turn-taking control so that children in other groups ask questions or give comments to the chairperson directly and sometimes extensively. The collective support from what we have called the framework of interactive activities is being used here to develop the learners' sense of group co-operation and organisation with a measure of autonomy. This includes evaluating the work of other groups without teacher mediation, which interestingly provides an opportunity for the children to construct or internalise criteria of assessment. Again, the effective use of this pattern depends on learner-trained learning. The teachers throughout one school had learned how to use this form of groupwork by observing their peers.

A kindergarten model

We now present a further example of a 'good' teacher interacting with a kindergarten class. This may seem like a counter-example compared to those previously discussed since the class is not actually large: it has 25 five year olds. This compares to other classes of 44 five year olds which we observed in the same year in the same area in north China. However, in some other ways the class can be taken as typical of those conducted by a teacher regarded as 'good' and not untypical of those which can be conducted with large classes. The main reason for this is that this lesson was also observed by a panel of ten senior teachers who were assessing a series of demonstration lessons in the area in order to select only a few teachers for the award of the special titles mentioned earlier. The panel members include assessors from a renowned kindergarten in Beijing, whose judgement will be highly respected. In this competitive context, therefore, the teacher cannot afford to use an approach or teaching strategies which the panel believe can only be used with such a small class. In this sense this lesson can be taken as representative of lessons which, in the view of the senior kindergarten teachers observing it, could be taught elsewhere, including in those common situations where the numbers are nearly double those actually seen here.

It is the spring of 1997. The class is small because the kindergarten is an experimental one situated in a village outside Tianjin. There are so far 5 classes and 150 children, yet 33 teachers. However, the kindergarten is rapidly expanding its intake because it has become very popular with parents in the two years since it was established, so the luxurious teacher-child ratio is unlikely to continue for long. One reason for needing this number of teachers is that the kindergarten offers extra classes in the evenings for the children. That these are also popular indicates patterns of long working hours among parents and the strong desire to give their children a sound early start in education (if they can afford it, but many villages in this area are prosperous). The buildings are new and the conditions are good (many Chinese kindergartens are located in older buildings where it is difficult to provide a bright and colourful environment).

The classroom is not particularly large and with the visitors present it is crowded. The children are seated in a V pattern with the teacher standing at the open end. There is an assistant teacher, as is normal in kindergartens, but she takes no part in this lesson. The walls are colourfully decorated with fabrics, flowers, wallcharts, and the flag of Hong Kong (to celebrate the 1997 return to China). This is a Chinese language lesson which lasts for 20 minutes. It is probably a revision lesson. This fits the cycle of three lessons which is common at primary and middle school levels: first, preparation and initiation; second, extension, expansion and involvement; third, application, revision and feedback through activity or testing.

There are 12 cards pinned to the board with large characters written on them. In stage one, the teacher gets children in turn to come to the front and choose the card which matches the word she says. Children turn to address the class to say something about their word. Some other children stand in their places to give help and support as needed, cued by the teacher.

In stage 2, children in turn come to the front and silently read a card which the teacher holds so that others cannot see it; each child has to mime the phrase written in Chinese, such as 'walk', 'wash face', 'kick ball'. The class have to guess the words, which are then revealed by the teacher. The children mime with clear confident gestures. The class responds with enthusiasm.

For stage 3, all children sit and the teacher passes series of cards with words along the rows to the rhythm of a tambourine; when the sound stops, the child holding the card has to make a sentence using the target word. One card has the character 'love'; a child says 'I love my teacher'. The pace is very fast; children stand straight and speak fluently. Every child is involved and the class clearly enjoy the activity.

Next, all children in the two large groups (on either arm of the V seating arrangement) are given individual cards. Each child reads his or her own card silently, shows it to others in the team in turn and calls out the words; the other team reveal their cards across the room so that the caller can find the matching card. Matching pairs are antonyms ('tall': 'short') and the child making the match then has to use the words in a sentence to get a team point. The children seem highly involved, a large measure of concentration and attention is evident in the way they sit, stand, rapidly switch gaze direction and read quickly as the game proceeds at a smart pace. Apparently all the children can read, understand, match, and use the set of words.

The final stage involves character analysis and problem solving – a challenging task for five year olds. On the board are displayed 32 large cards with two-character phrases (most Chinese characters are made up of two or more components, e.g. 'radicals' indicating general meaning, or 'phonetics' giving a clue to pronunciation; many characters are composed of several semantic elements). Here, each card has a character element, such as the radical, missing. The class have been given these missing elements on cards and the task is now to match these with the corresponding card from the array displayed, place the character component in a semantically correct position (according to both elements either side), turn to the class and read the whole phrase. The teacher explains the task very carefully and most cards are matched by children spontaneously working in pairs to help each other, aided by others calling out.

The element of preparation here is obvious; the teacher is well-prepared and so are the children. They have learned to read most of the words beforehand, but the fifth activity is not easy for any of them. The steps have been graded to lead to this clear challenge. There is a sense that the lesson is a performance but it is clearly not routine. The teacher's instructions are clear. She has a kind, friendly manner. The activities are brisk, promptly and almost seamlessly sequenced. This can only happen with children of this age because they have been trained in the relevant classroom routines (i.e. learner-trained learning) before these routines can be used in creative interaction. The 20 minutes are used very intensively and the learner participation is very high throughout. The collective support, initially elicited by the teacher but spontaneous later, is also evident.

After a short break at the end of the class, an evaluation meeting was called. The observers commented on this (and another lesson):

> *The teachers are smiling. The children are lively and active. Everyone participates in the class activities. The activities and formal learning are well-balanced. The teachers have professional ability and good feelings for the children. We can see that there are good relations between teachers and children. The conditions here are good. You have a new building, clean classrooms and nice facilities. You have made the classrooms very colourful. The conditions are good, but in the end we know it is the teaching quality that counts. Teachers need to be disciplined and children need to be taught before they can be creative. You also give them a lot of free play and free outside activities.*

There are resonances here with some of the comments on good teachers quoted earlier.

Apart from the dimensions of quality teaching, the general push for education has often been discussed in China in terms of increasing facilities, including the use of technology, as part of the drive towards modernisation.

Further support from technology

New technologies can clearly be of great assistance in teaching large classes, indeed, potentially they can make large classes unnecessary. Overhead projectors have come to be used in many schools in China; they seem to be especially used rather briefly to present single words or phrases, texts, or illustrations by using masking techniques, colour, and occasionally overlays. The use of tape recorders, television and video-recorders is well-established, though hardly found in every classroom. However, like the use of overhead projectors such facilities tend to be briefly used for illustration only. Reasons for this may be that in teachers' minds they cannot replace the book (certainly while the present system of tests and exams continues to dominate middle school activity), that they do not seem interactive, or simply that such resources are expensive or scarce and should be treated with caution. A few schools, experimentally, use close circuit TV but mostly to focus on the teacher for later peer observation and discussion of good practices for teacher development. Others have begun to use computers (usually one near to and controlled by the teacher) to present ideas and information, but so far the application to most subjects is limited to demonstration, apart from the predictably popular computer and information technology classes as such. A few schools are using multimedia systems, for example in maths and languages classes, where large screens, sound, text and images can be exciting and helpful for large classes. However, although many Chinese teachers are clearly on the threshold of change in this respect (4,000 schools were linked to the internet in

1998-9), lessons we saw in 1999 showed teachers using multimedia for traditional drills, matching, gap filling, and question and answer exercises which do little more than replicate what is in the textbook. Apparently, and unsurprisingly, cultural change among teachers is slower than technical change.

To some extent the multimedia replace the teacher's voice but this could carry the risk of losing the human dimension of much classroom interaction. This seems to be the very dimension which makes Chinese interaction effective. Perhaps technology should be seen as offering possibilities of alternative teaching and learning strategies which parallel but do not replace the best existing practices, some of which may stem from strong traditional values (like aspects of the 'good' teacher). The issue of technology is therefore not just a matter of cost, provision and training in use but a resurfacing of the nineteenth century *ti-yong* debate: whether and how far modern Chinese teachers and students should pursue the use of Western technology, and more generally Western pedagogies, for *yong* ('function', 'utility'); or whether and how far to keep Chinese learning for *ti* ('substance', 'essence') (Levenson, 1958, pp.59-78).

What others can learn from examining interaction in Chinese classes

Perhaps the outstanding implication arising from this kind of study is that it raises questions about the essential arguments that have been persistently made about the need to reduce class sizes in the West. Chinese classes are demonstrably large yet the teachers we have observed and interviewed are clearly successful in coping; more, their students are clearly successful and they participate actively. Yet care needs to be exercised if other countries are tempted to transfer some of the principles and practices which we have described and analysed in the framework of interactive activities. We have emphasized the cultural notions of 'good' Chinese teachers to underline the general proposition that it may not be easy to undertake a successful transfer of part of the system without considering how it fits into a whole network of social practices and expectations. Still, this study draws attention to the importance of:

- teacher preparation and group support;
- peer observation;
- aspects of structuring classroom presentation, practice, and participation;
- and learner-trained learning.

Evidently the lessons we have observed illustrate some general principles which any teacher could further reflect on, such as how to use short amounts of available time for intensive learning. Evidently in looking for general principles or common practices we need to be properly cautious about generalising to the huge number of schools in China on the basis of limited evidence (almost any study, of course, however large scale, will still have this limitation in China because of the size of her educational enterprise). While some aspects of interaction in large classes in China include rather traditional aspects of direct instruction, the teachers themselves (despite daunting, often difficult circumstances and meagre financial rewards) seem eager to develop their teaching. They are keen to learn of new ideas such as those of co-operative learning. They remain deeply concerned for all the learners they teach (even with very large numbers). And yet they have much to offer others who may teach in more fortunate circumstances.

Interaction in large Chinese classes can be seen as having several layers. The mediation and participation patterns between teacher and class, among learners, and between learners and texts are but one layer. This layer is supported by another layer of interaction between teachers across classrooms in planning and modelling performance. There is a third less visible layer which is influential: the interaction between the past in educational, philosophical and cultural traditions and the present in change, development and technological innovation. A fourth layer is the interaction across cultures, between Chinese practices and others from elsewhere. In the spirit of this intercultural dialogue, Chinese teachers strive to learn from others. Those from outside China may also have something to learn from Chinese interaction, whether this takes place in small or large classes.

REFERENCES

Biggs, J.B. (1994). What are Effective Schools? Lessons from East and West. *Australian Educational Researcher*, 21(1), 19-39.

Biggs, J.B. (1996). Learning, Schooling and Socialization: A Chinese Solution to a Western Problem. In S. Lau (Ed.), *Growing Up the Chinese Way*. Hong Kong: The Chinese University Press, 147-167.

Cortazzi, M. & Jin, L. (1996a). Cultures of Learning: Language Classrooms in China. In H. Coleman (Ed.), *Society and the Language Classroom*. Cambridge: Cambridge University Press, 169-206.

Cortazzi, M. & Jin, L. (1996b). English Teaching and Learning in China (State of the Art article). *Language Teaching*, 29(2), 61-80.

Cortazzi, M. & Jin, L. (1999). Bridges to Learning: Metaphors of Teaching, Learning and Language. In L. Cameron & G. Low (Eds.), *Researching and Applying Metaphor*. Cambridge: Cambridge University Press, 149-176.

Cortazzi, M. & Jin, L. (in press). Cultures of Learning: The Social Construction of Educational Identities. In D.C.S. Li (Ed.), *Discourses in Search of Members*. Norwood, N.J.: Ablex.

Galton, M. (1998). What do The Tests Measure? *Education 3-13*, 26(2), 50-59.

Jin, L. & Cortazzi, M. (1997-8). Expectations and Questions in Intercultural Classrooms. *Intercultural Communication Studies*, 7(2), 37-62.

Jin, L. & Cortazzi, M. (1998a). Dimensions of Dialogue: Large Classes in China. *International Journal of Educational Research*, 29, 739-761.

Jin, L. & Cortazzi, M. (1998b). The Culture the Learner Brings: A Bridge or A Barrier? In M. Byram & M. Fleming (Eds.), *Language Learning in Intercultural Perspective, Approaches through Drama and Ethnography*. Cam-

bridge: Cambridge University Press, 98-118.
Levenson, J.R. (1958). *Confucian China and its Modern Fate, The Problem of Intellectual Continuity*. London: Routledge and Kegan Paul.
Reynolds, D. & Farrell, S. (1996). *Worlds apart? A review of International Surveys of Educational Achievement Involving England*. London: Office for Standards in Education (OFSTED) Reviews of Research, HMSO.
Sperber, D. (1996). *Explaining Culture, A Naturalistic Approach*. Oxford: Blackwell.
Stevenson, H.W. & Lee, S-Y. (1996). The Academic Achievement of Chinese Students. In M.H. Bond (Ed.), *The Handbook of Chinese Psychology*. Hong Kong: Oxford University Press, 124-142.
Ward, T., Barr, B., Chai, M., Hua, D., Kong, X. & Lu, H. (1995). *A Crane among the Chickens? Evaluating a Training Programme for English Teachers in China*. Shanghai: Shanghai Foreign Language Education Press.
Watkins, D.A. & Biggs, J.B. (1996). *The Chinese Learner: Cultural, Psychological and Contextual Influences*. Hong Kong / Melbourne: Comparative Education Research Centre, The University of Hong Kong / Australian Council for Educational Research.

7

Two Faces of the Reed Relay: Exploring the Effects of the Medium of Instruction

Dorothy F.P. Ng, Amy B.M. Tsui and Ference Marton

In Hong Kong, the Chinese language (the spoken form of which is Cantonese) is the mother tongue of over 96% of the population and is the major inter-ethnic lingua franca in the daily lives of the people. However, because Hong Kong was a British colony, all official communications were in English despite the fact that both English and Chinese were the official languages. After the change of sovereignty in 1997, English was retained as one of the official languages in order to maintain the economic competitiveness of Hong Kong as an international city. The Hong Kong Special Administrative Region (HKSAR) government declared that one of the goals of education in Hong Kong is to produce graduates who are bi-literate (English and Chinese) and tri-lingual (Putonghua, English and Cantonese) (The Chief Executive's Policy Speech, 1997, para 84). There is a general agreement in the community that Hong Kong needs students who graduate with strong skills in both Chinese and English, particularly the latter. As the result of this bilingual nature of Hong Kong society, there has been considerable debate about which language should be the medium of instruction in schools.

Historically, there has been a common belief among parents, principals and teachers in Hong Kong that using English as the medium of instruction (EMI) can facilitate English language learning and lead to a higher standard of English. Overseas, similar beliefs have been reported about the use of the second language as the medium of instruction in bilingual societies. For example, the Canadian Immersion Programs have been quoted as a successful example of second language acquisition through using the second language as a medium of instruction (Cummins & Swain, 1986). Since English is considered the golden passport to success, English medium schools have always been the preferred model of schooling of parents rather than Chinese medium schools.

The effect of using a second language of which learners do not yet have a full command as a medium of learning has always been a cause for concern. As early as 1973, a group of academics expressed their concern about its detrimental effects on students' intellectual development in a booklet with the powerful title "At What Cost?" (Cheng et al. 1973). After the introduction of the nine year compulsory education in 1978 which changed the education system from elitist to universal, the continued use of English as a medium in the majority of schools exacerbated the problem. In order to help students learn, teachers had to resort to mixed code. In some cases, the teachers' own English was not proficient enough to conduct lessons entirely in English (Johnson 1994; Tung 1990). In the eighties, a number of studies were conducted on the effect of the medium of instruction on academic achievement and on classroom teaching. Brimer et al. (1985), one of the most widely cited studies, examined the academic achievement of students of different English proficiency levels in History and Integrated Science. The study showed that only those students who have attained a high level of English proficiency (estimated to be about 30% of the total student population) could benefit from English medium instruction. It also showed that students with low English proficiency would be seriously disadvantaged when they are required to display in English what they had learnt.

In the nineties, the debate on the medium of instruction policy was spearheaded by the fourth report of the Education Commission, an advisory body to the government on education policy, which recommended that mixed code be stamped out in classroom teaching and that by 1998 schools be "firmly guided" to use either Chinese or English as the medium of instruction. This recommendation culminated in only 114 schools out of 421 public sector schools being allowed to use English as a medium of instruction in 1998.

The negative effect of using a weaker language as a medium of learning on academic achievement is convincingly demonstrated by a recent longitudinal study reported by Marsh, Hau and Kong (in press) on the effect of the different media of instruction on students' achievement in Chinese, English, Geography, History, Mathematics and Science from secondary 1 to 3 (grades 7 to 9), involving 12,784 students. English as a medium of instruction had positive effects on students' English proficiency, mildly positive effects on their proficiency in Chinese, weakly negative effects on their achievements in Mathematics and – in the words of the authors – "incredibly" negative effects on achievement in Geography, History and Science. These negative effects persisted mainly throughout all three years and they hit basically students at all initial levels of ability. The size of the effect was "incredible", indeed. The medium of instruction made at least as much difference as the initial differences between the students (which were largely in favour of EMI students). It seems that Hong Kong students being taught the different subjects in English at high school level are seriously disadvantaged.

In a way this is hardly suprising. Being taught in a language which you do not know very well enough for handling complex concepts and being taught by teachers who mostly do not have a sufficient degree of mastery in this language either, can hardly be an advantage. (With the possible exception of learning that language itself). The studies cited above have shown this to be the case.

Previous studies on the effect of the medium of instruction in classroom teaching have focused on the interaction between students and the teacher. Little attention has been paid to the impact of such interactions on learning. The question which intrigued us is how this effect is mediated in the classroom.

Studying teaching

As our interest is how the medium of instruction effects student achievement in non-language subjects, we have to look at what is happening in the classroom from the point of view of what is possible to learn there. So how can this problem be addressed at all? Let us start with a minimal assumption: In order to learn the learner has to experience something – consciously or unconsciously. We can only experience that which we discern and discernment presupposes variation. If a child has a weak sight she will not become aware of her own way of seeing the world until she gets spectacles and discovers another way of seeing the world. The minimum variation is the appearance of something that was not present before or the disappearance of something that was present before. Through more extensive variation different aspects become visible, instances are linked to each other; through simultaneous variation simultaneous awareness is afforded, through the contrast of what is invariant and what varies various aspects can be separated. Marton & Booth (1997) and Bowden & Marton (1998) argued that in relation to every object of learning a necessary pattern of variation, inherent in the learning environment, can be identified. We have taken this line of reasoning as our assumption when observing classroom interactions and we set out to identify differences in the pattern of variation in learning environments differing with respect to the medium of instruction used.

The study

When you compare classrooms characterized by the medium of instruction they are likely to differ in other respects as well: different teachers are teaching different things to different students.

Now, the students can not be the same if you wish to compare the effects of Chinese versus English as the medium of instruction, of course, but as we are interested in how the object of learning is dealt with, this object should be identical across comparisons. And having the same teacher too would no doubt be a great advantage. So in this first study in which we try to illuminate how the object of learning is dealt with when the medium of instruction differs, we tried to find a teacher teaching virtually the same thing in Chinese as well as in English. And we found such a teacher in a school where Chinese and English were used in different classes in the same grade.

The School. The school is divided into Chinese and English sections. For each form, there are 4 English classes and 2 Chinese classes. Students in the English section are usually from Band 1 and Band 2 groups (that is of above average ability). For those students in the Chinese section, they are usually from Band 2 and Band 3 groups (that is of above to slightly below average ability). The curriculum in both sections is virtually the same.

The Teacher. This teacher, with six years of teaching experience, taught Physics in one class of Form Three using Chinese as a medium of instruction (hereafter CMI) and to another class using English as a medium of instruction (hereafter EMI). Two lessons were observed in which the lesson content (Reed relay switching), planning procedures, textbooks and worksheets used were the same for both classes.

One content two lessons

The lesson was about the Reed relay. This is a device which allows an electric circuit with weak current to control another electric circuit with strong current without the two being connected with each other. This means that if you touch the electric circuit with the weak current, you will not get a shock from the circuit with the strong current in spite of the fact that the former controls the latter. How is it possible?

The secret is that the strong current is switched on when two ends of a switch are brought into contact with each other. The circuit with the weak current is wired around these two ends without being in contact with them. When current is flowing through the circuit with the weak current a magnetic field is created, the two ends in the switch are brought into contact with each other and the circuit with the strong current is switched on.

The teacher started the lessons revising the electronic devices used in the previous lessons. These included the symbol, abbreviation, function and structure of the Light-emitting diode (LED 發光二極管) and light – dependent resistors (LDR 光敏電阻). LED allows a current to flow through it in one direction only. When the resistance in a circuit increases, the current decreases. Current is greatest when the low-value resistor is used. The current flowing in the circuit is greater when light falls on the LDR because the resistance of the LDR is much lower in light than in the dark. The teacher gave an explanation of the structure of the Reed switch. (Figure 7.1). A current – carrying a coil produces a magnetic field. If we place the Reed switch inside the coil, we could operate it by passing a current through the coil. The teacher explained the coil was really wound around the Reed switch. However, in circuit diagrams, it is conventional to draw them alongside each other.

Figure 7.1
The Reed switch

The teacher asked the students to carry out the first experiment. The students were asked to connect two circuits. One circuit was controlled by the press switch (Figure 7.2). They pressed the press switch, the LED glowed. The other circuit was controlled by a Reed relay (Figure 7.3). If a current was set up in the coil of the Reed relay, the Reed switch closed and the LED glowed also. In the first experiment, the LED glowed in both circuits.

Figure 7.2

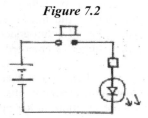

Figure 7.3

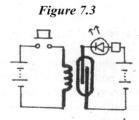

Afterwards, the teacher asked the students to carry out the second experiment. They were asked to connect another two circuits. One circuit was controlled by the LDR to make the motor rotate. However, this time the motor did not rotate. (Figure 7.4)

Figure 7.4

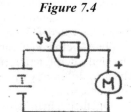

Figure 7.5

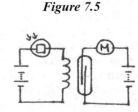

Students were asked to connect another circuit controlled by the LDR and the Reed relay to operate the motor. When a bright light shined on the LDR, resistance was small and the coil current was now large enough to operate the relay. The Reed switch contacts closed and this time the motor rotated (Figure 7.5).

Ammeters connected in series with the coil and motor were used to demonstrate that a motor required a relatively large current to make it rotate (at least 200 mA). It was impossible to control the motor without using the Reed relay. The concept of controlling a large current by a much smaller current is very important in electronics. During the whole class feedback, the teacher used a daily life example , starting motor of a car, to illustrate a large current being controlled by a much smaller current passing through the coil.

Finally, the teacher gave exercises and checked the answers.

All together there were nine transactions (T). The teaching sequences were identical in each medium.

The space of learning

Our theoretical inspiration guided us to look for aspects of the classroom interaction between the teacher and students that varied observably, or potentially – in the minds of the students. Furthermore, we were looking for aspects which we assumed to be critical in relation to the object of learning. We believed that we knew what *kind* of aspects we were looking for, but we did not know which specific aspects to consider. In that sense we have adopted a "grounded-theory approach" to the analysis of the data whereby the categories emerged through repeated readings and comparisons.

As we pointed out above, underlying our analysis of classroom data there is the assumption that the pattern of variation inherent in the classroom discourse is of critical importance to learning. In the teacher's presentation, in her questions, and in what the students say, certain aspects of the phenomenon dealt with may vary or may be pointed out without being varied or may be taken-for-granted and not mentioned at all. The aspects that vary are likely to capture the students' attention, they are likely to trigger off movement in their minds; variation opens up the students' (and the teacher's) awareness in the dimensions in which it located. So if the class is dealing with a particular way of solving a certain kind of problems in Mathematics , for instance, and the very same procedure is applied to structurally identical problems with different numbers, numbers constitute the dimension of variation. In such a case students will probably focus on the given numbers in different problems, while the structure and the meaning of the problem recede to the back-ground in their awareness. If they have to deal with structurally different problems instead, which have to be interpreted before they can be solved, the students will probably focus on the structure and interpretation (meaning of the problems). If the very same problem is solved in different ways instead, the method of solution will likely become the object of attention.

Dimensions of variation constitute a space together. There is one space of variation if the problems given differ as to structure and numbers and another space if they differ in wording and in numbers, but not in structure. If the problem is given but the ways of solving it, and perhaps also the ways of representing it differ, we have yet another space of variation.

In our own study, for instance, we might compare the case when the Reed relay is dealt with in the classroom context only and the context is thus taken-for-granted, with the case when the Reed relay is dealt with both in the classroom context and in the context of every day life. In the latter case the space of variation is widened as variation in the context is introduced. Students will, in this situation be likely to become conscious of the context of the phenomenon, and be reminded of the difference between classroom and every-day life. (And they are very likely to become conscious of the similarities pointed to as well). In this way, the context in which the Reed relay is dealt with varies and we can say that the context is a dimension of variation and a constituent part of the space of variation in the classroom.

The main finding of this study is that the space of learning is widened and transformed in very specific respects when the medium of instruction is Chinese as compared to when the medium of instruction is English. We are not saying that more variation necessarily implies a better learning environment, but in this case we have been carefully looking for aspects which we believe to be critical in relation to mastering the object of learning. We have also found differences in how the space of learning is constituted which have to do with what aspects of the object of learning are focused. These differences are differences in what dimensions of variation that are opened up, rather than differences in how much certain dimensions are opened up. These two questions are, of course, closely related empirically.

The object of learning was in this case the understanding of the Reed relay (see above). So in the first place we have looked at how the content of the lesson was dealt with, structured, handled, and lived. We found that all the aspects considered to be critical were handled by the teacher in both lessons in the same sequence and the same structural relationships between the constituent parts were brought out.

So to begin with we did not find any differences in respects that one would expect to be most critical from the point of view of the mastery of the object of learning. The same content was taught in the structurally same way in both lessons. But we found other differences, differences which may not be critical in relation to the technical description of the Reed relay, but which we assume to be critical in relation to how the students were thinking about it.

Due to limitation of space we will only illustrate this widening of the space of learning by means of examples of differences of three kinds. We have found that the teacher kept shifting between different contexts when talking about the same thing to a greater extent when she teaches in Chinese. She is thus widening the space of learning with respect to the context in which the object of learning is embedded. At the same time the different contexts get linked to each other.

The other example concerns something else. Here the teacher is not widening the space of learning by opening up dimensions through introducing variation in those respects. But she is opening up for (implicit) variation to be grabbed by the students for turning it into explicit variation. This is done by means of using open-ended questions that can have many answers. Corresponding dimensions of variation in possible answers are thus opened up for the students as compared to the case when closed questions are asked to which particular answer is expected. We found that the frequency of open-ended questions as compared to closed, "one answer" questions is greater when the teacher is teaching in Chinese.

Furthermore, we will illustrate how rather subtle differences in the linguistic exchange between the teacher and student have important implications for what critical aspects of the object of learning the focus of the students' awareness is directed to.

Contextual shifts

Variation between contexts can of course be found in many different respects (dimensions). In this study we found shifts above all between the object of learning dealt with by means of symbolic representation (yes, we call it a context here) on the one hand and the object of learning as a "real" (material thing) (again, we call it another context). Furthermore, we have found shifts between the context of the classroom and the context of the world outside.

Let us look at an extract from the transcript of each of the two lessons where the same part of the content is dealt with (the introduction of the Reed relay), as an example.

(1) [EMI T1][1]

[talking about the symbolic representation]

T: Now then this component that we will discuss today is called Reed relay.

T: But surely we won't use it as a symbol since this is so complicated in this way. Usually we want here and beside have this symbols so I'd rather like the coil and this switch written separately side by side over here.

T: I'll draw it once for you here. Now here coil first, it represents the coil all right while the Reed switch is drawn it here. It is clear and precise.

The discourse remains focused on the symbolic representations throughout.
In Chinese the corresponding part is much longer. As a matter of fact many more words are used in Chinese. Our interest is what the words are used for. In this special case they are used – it seems – for bringing about pedagogically relevant variation, shifts between dealing with the same phenomenon as a material object and by means of symbolic representation, and between dealing with the same phenomenon in the school context and in the context of daily life. In the lesson in English the discussion was limited to the symbolic representation and to the school context.

(2) [CMI T2]

CMI Translation	CMI
[talking about the real object]	
T: Yes, Reed switch.	T: 係，簧片開關。
T: Generally, when a Reed switch is switched on, the two ends will not touch each other. If we want the two ends to touch each other, close this switch, what should I do? Ng Yee Wah?	T: 係普通嘅情況之下呢，一個簧片開關呢係敞開嘅，呢兩個掂點互相唔接觸，如果希望接點接觸，關閉呢個開關，我應該點樣做呀？吳綺華？
T: I've got a glass shield, I can't make the two ends touch each other.	T: 我有個玻璃罩㗎，咁我唔可以令到佢接合。

---

[1] For the data from the EMI lesson, verbatim transcription is given. No attempt has been made to edit the language. For the data from the CMI lesson, we have tried to make the English translation as close to the Chinese original as possible. Semantic translation is used rather than literal translation.

Effects of the Medium of Instruction

S: Magnetic field.

T: Yes, use magnetic field. Then we'll put a magnet near the Reed switch, right?

[shift from school to everyday context]

T: So we seldom use a Reed switch in our daily lives. We can't use a Reed switch for the switches in the sitting room or switches for fans because we will have problems when we switch them on. Every time we want to turn on the light, turn on the fan, we have to put a magnet near the switch. That's why we don't use the (Reed) switch.

[shift back to school context]

T: We've talked about this last time. We'll try to use a magnet to control the Reed switch. This new equipment, we looked at it last time, what do we call it? Wong Choi Ping?

S: Reed relay.

T: Once again.

S: Reed relay.

T: Yes, OK, let's talk about the Reed relay today.

[shift from real object to symbolic representation]

T: OK, let's take a look at the Reed relay first. We'll take a photo. Actually, what does a Reed relay look like? It has the structure of an electro magnet, and also the structure of a Reed switch.

S: 磁場。

T: 係，利用磁場，咁我哋就會將一舊磁鐵靠近簧片開關，係咪？

T: 咁所以我哋平時生活裡面我哋好少用簧片開關㗎，即我哋唔可以將廳D 電制呀、風扇制呀整晒做簧片開關，因為咁嘅時候開關我哋就會有困難囉，每一次我哋想開燈、開風扇我哋要放個磁鐵靠近個開關，咁所以我哋唔用開關。

T: 我哋上次話啦，我哋呢就企圖利用電磁鐵嚟到操控呢一個簧片開關，呢一個新嘅儀器啦，我哋上次見過㗎啦，叫咩名？王彩平？

S: 簧片繼電器。

T: 再講一次。

S: 簧片繼電器。

T: 係，好，我哋今日講簧片繼電器。

T: 好啦，我哋睇番個簧片繼電器先，我幫佢影幅相，實際上一個簧片繼電器呢係點嘅樣呢？佢有一個電磁鐵嘅構造，亦都有一個簧片開關。

T:	Actually, it has a Reed switch which is placed inside a coil. If this coil has an electric current, we call this an electric coil. That means, we allow electricity to flow through the coil. If an electric current flows through the coil will change into an electromagnet, generating a magnetic the diagram, the Reed switch to close. Is that okay? Okay, good.	T:	真正嚟講呢，佢就係將個簧片開關放係一個線圈入面，當如果哩個線圈係帶電嘅時候呢，我哋叫哩個叫做再電線圈，意思即係話，我哋讓電流流經線圈，如果電流流經線圈佢就連綠色嘅部份，線圈嘅部份就形成一個電磁鐵啦，有磁場產生，咁就會令到圖上面紅色嘅部份，一個簧片開關呢係關閉，可唔可以？可以，好。

By introducing variation it is likely that the students are made aware both of context (school vs daily life) and of representation (real object vs symbolic representation). At the same time the different contexts and the different forms of representation are being linked to each other.

As should be obvious from the Table 7.1, we found these differences throughout the two lessons.

Table 7.1
Contextual shifts in Chinese and English medium classes

Contextual Shifts:	CMI	EMI
From classroom context to daily life example	2	1
From daily life example to classroom context	2	1
From symbolic rep. to real object	16	6
From real object to symbolic representation	12	5
Total:	32	13

Questioning

Questioning is perhaps the most distinctive feature of classroom discourse. Teachers ask questions for a number of reasons: for comprehension checking, for knowledge checking, for focusing attention, for classroom management purposes, and so on. In this study, we are only interested in the ways in which learning is mediated and created by the language used by the teacher, specifically the questions asked by the teacher.

In examining the questions in both lessons, we made a distinction between "closed" and "open" questions. By closed questions we mean questions where there is only one acceptable answer and by "open questions" we mean questions where there is a range of possible answers. By "acceptable" we do not mean right or wrong because in classroom situations, most of the questions do have a right or wrong answer. For example, "Why does this motor work?" is an open question whereas "What is the name given to this magnet?" is a closed question. When the teacher asks an open question, the space of learning is widened because the question challenges the students to consider a number of possibilities and to formulate an answer which makes sense not only to themselves but to the rest of the class. The formulation of an answer itself is a process in which the students clarify their thinking and understanding of the object of learning. The following example demonstrates how language and learning is intertwined.

(3) [CMI T8]

	CMI Translation	**CMI**
T:	… Why is it that it works in this circuit?	T: 咁點解呢個又得呀？呢個咁乖，呢個又著嘅，吓馮敏如？
	(pointing at the circuit with the LED) Why was it so well-behaved, it lit up? (nominate)	(point to circuit exp. I)
-> S:	Because the resistance that the LDR needs, no, the current that it needs is smaller than (that needed) by the motor.	S: 因為 LDR 需要嘅電阻係比電動機，唔係，需要嘅電流比摩打少。
T:	Say that once again, you are right, I understand you.	T: 你再講一次，你講得啱，我明白你。
S:	LDR needs	S: LDR 需要嘅。
T:	Which is the LDR? This one?	T: 邊個係 LDR，佢係呀？
-> S:	Because the electric that LED needs compared ….	S: 因為 LED 需要嘅電 流比…
T:	Electric what?	T: 電乜？
-> S:	Electric current is smaller compared with the motor.	S: 電流需要比摩打少。
T:	That's right. So if I press (cover) it (LDR) here, there will be enough current to make this LED glow. Okay? Now we found that if we don't use the Reed relay, that there are problems because some circuit must use a Reed relay to operate. Let me give you an example….	T: 冇錯啦，咁所以呢呢度如果我按制嘅時候呢，呢度有電流係足以推呢個 LED 發光，可唔可以呀？噚，咁我哋發現呢，唔用繼電器呢就唔係好妥當，因為有一 D 電路呢必定要用繼電器呢先至會有嘢睇，先至會做工㗎。咁，其實我舉個例俾你聽….

In (3) above, we can see that the formulation of the answer to the question was actually a process in which the student clarified her thinking, with skilful guidance from the teacher, about "resistance" and "electric current", about which is the LED and which the LDR, and about "electric" and "electric current". It is also a process in which she had to formulate the cause-and-effect relationship between the lighting up of the LED and the electric current needed.

On the other hand, closed questions narrow down the possibilities to only a limited number of choices and hence reduce the space of learning. In cases where the answer is reduced to an either-or choice, the cognitive challenge to the students is often minimal. The following is an example.

(4) [EMI T8]

-> T: =Oh, then, surely, now girls can you explain to me, why doesn't this motor work?

S: (no reply)

-> T: Why doesn't this motor work? Just because motor must use __?

S: (no reply)

-> T: The current that is __? Large or small?

S: Large.

T: Large.

In (4) above, as soon as the teacher posed the closed question "The current that is ____? Large or small?", in order to answer the teacher's question, the students' focal awareness would be shifted from thinking about the reasons to explain why the motor did not work to thinking about whether the current used by the motor was large or small. The latter is much less challenging than the former because it requires less work on the students' part to come up with the correct answer.

Research on classroom discourse has shown that teachers tend to modify their questions either in order to make it easier for students to understand the question or to respond to the question. Tsui (1995) refers to the former as "comprehension-oriented modification" and to the latter as "response-oriented modification". In classrooms where English is used as a medium of teaching and learning, both types of modifications are prevalent when the students' English is not proficient enough. The modification of wh-questions, from why questions to what questions, and from wh-questions to yes-no questions, is typically found. This is because responding to why questions are linguistically much more demanding than responding to what questions which often require only one or two words, or a phrase, and yes-no questions or alternative questions are least demanding because the possible answer is limited to "yes" or "no", or one of the alternatives provided. Also typically found are what we would call "blank-filling" questions where the teacher provides part of the sentence and blank out the key word(s) for the students to fill in so as to lessen the linguistic burden of the students (see (4) above).

In analyzing the two lessons, we excluded the last segment in which the teacher was going over the questions given in the worksheet with the students. Table 7.2 presents the number of different types of questions found in both lessons, and the number of questions which were not responded to.

Table 7.2
Question type and response by medium of instruction

Question Types					No response			
	EMI		CMI		EMI		CMI	
Closed Questions (blank filling)	20 (11)	(74%) (55%)	25 (6)	(60%) (24%)	4 (4)		2 (0)	
Open Questions	7	(26%)	16	(40%)	6	(85.7%)	4	(25%)
Total	27	(100%)	41	(100%)	10	(37%)	6	(14.6%)

From the above data, we can make the following observations:

1: In the EMI lesson, the percentage of "closed" questions is much higher than the percentage of "open" questions. In the CMI lesson, however, although the percentage of "closed" question is still higher than the percentage of "open" questions, the absolute number of "open" questions in the CMI lesson is more than doubled.

2. For the 7 "open" questions in the EMI lesson, 6 of them failed to elicit a response from the students. In other words, only one "open" question succeeded in eliciting a response from students without modification (85.7%). By contrast, in the CMI lesson, for the 16 "open" questions, only 4 failed to elicit a response (31.3%). In other words, in the EMI lesson, only one "open" question was responded to by the students whereas there were 12 "open" questions that were responded to in the CMI lesson. The difference of 11 "open" questions in a forty minute lesson could make a considerable difference in the quality of the interaction between the teacher and the students.

3. For the 20 "closed" questions in the EMI lesson, 11 of them (55%) were blank-filling questions whereas for the CMI lesson, only 6 out of 25 (24%) were blank-filling questions.

The above quantitative analysis suggests that in the CMI lesson, the space of learning is much wider than the EMI lesson because of the higher number of open questions asked which encouraged the students to consider a number of possibilities when answering these questions. The much higher number of responses to open questions that the CMI teacher was able to elicit suggests that the CMI students were much better able to take advantage of the widened space than the EMI students because they had the linguistic resources to do so. The much higher success rate for closed questions also suggests that the open questions had to be modified as a closed question before a response was forthcoming. Excerpt (3) below is a frequently found questioning sequence in the EMI lesson.

(5) [EMI T8]

The teacher asked the students to compare the current flowing through the LDR and that flowing through the motor.

> T: Now I want you to compare the two current(s). ... Current through the LDR and current through the motor. <u>What have you discovered?</u>
>
> (Teacher looks at the class and waits)
>
> S: (no reply)
>
> -> T: Now current flowing through the LDR is __?
>
> S: Smaller.
>
> -> T: Smaller, while the current through the motor is ____?
>
> S: ((inaudible))
>
> T: Okay, can you repeat your whole answer?
>
> S: Current flow through the LDR is smaller than the current flowing through the motor.

In the first question (arrowed), the teacher posed an "open" question. When the student had difficulties responding to the question, the teacher modified the question into a "closed" question, specifically a blank-filling question where the teacher provided the linguistic structure of the first part of the answer and required the students to fill in only the key word "smaller". The teacher then posed another blank-filling question which provided the linguistic structure of the second part of the answer. In other words, the answer to the teacher's initial "open" question was broken up into two blank-filling questions in order to lessen the linguistic burden of formulating the response for the students. (See also excerpt (4) above.)

The use of this type of questioning sequence has several adverse effects on students' learning. Firstly, it focuses the students' attention on how they can finish the sentence in a way which will fit into the syntax of the partial sentence provided and very often which will fit into what answer the teacher has in mind. Secondly, as we have already seen in (5), above it deprives the students the opportunity to formulate and make explicit their understanding of the object of learning.

When we examined closely sequences of this kind in the data, we observed that in trying to elicit a response from the students by posing closed questions, the focus of the students' awareness actually shifted. Let us compare the following two excerpts, one from the EMI lesson which is a continuation of (5) above and the other from the CMI lesson, in which the teacher is explaining the same phenomenon to the students.

Effects of the Medium of Instruction 149

(6) [EMI T8, continuation of Excerpt (5)]

-> T: =Oh, then, surely, now girls can you explain to me, why doesn't this motor work?

S: (no reply)

-> T: Why doesn't this motor work? Just because motor must use __?

S: (no reply)

-> T: The current that is __? Large or small?

S: Large.

T: Large, but unluckily, that LDR is just allow small current pass through it. Why? Because its resistance, it decrease, but it now not small enough, alright. I repeat it once. Now as light shines on the LDR, surely it's resistance decrease, but its still NOT small enough, NOT small enough, so, there it's still no large, very large current pass through the circuit and the motor does not work, understand? How about the LED here? It works, it works. Surely, there shouldn't be very large current flowing through the circuit. <u>Why does the LED work here,</u> (nominate)

S: (no reply)

T: The LED works, but it (refers to the motor) does not rotate. It's similar Construction. (nominate) Tell me, <u>how much current is needed to operate a motor</u>?

S: (no reply)

-> T: <u>How much current is needed</u>? It should be very __?

S: 200mA.

T: Ah, nearly 200mA, very good, very large current. But can you tell me <u>how much current is needed to operate a LED</u>?

S: Very small current.

-> T: Yes, very small current is enough all right. Then can you explain to me, <u>why does this LED light</u>?

S: (no reply)

T: It does not rotate, just because there's no large current. The LED works just because ___?

S: because the LED -

T: Use -

S: use small current and the motor use very large current.

T: All right, yes, your answer is so impressive. Would you please repeat it once. It's correct, repeat it once.

S: The LED used small current while the motor use very large current.

T: Yes, very good, the LED use small current while the motor used very large current, Alright, OK.

In (6) above, the teacher asked two open question: "Why doesn't this motor work?" and "Why does the LED light (up)?" They opened up a number of possible answers, as pointed out before. However, as the teacher used blank-filling questions to help the students to provide an answer to the open questions, the students' focus of awareness shifted from the reasons why the motor does not rotate and why the LED lights up to the amount of current needed by the motor and the LED. Yet, it was the former which was critical to the understanding of how a Reed relay operates, which is the object of learning of this lesson.

That the lack of linguistic competence was one of the major reasons for using these blank-filling questions can be best seen in the second part of the excerpt which dealt with the LED. When the teacher failed to elicit a response from the students after posing the question "Why does the LED light (up)?", she used closed questions to elicit from the students that the current flowing through the LED was very small. However, when she posed the initial open question again "Then can you explain to me, why does this LED light?", no response was forthcoming. It was only when she provided linguistic help that the student was able to complete the answer.

If we compare the explanation of why the motor does not work in the CMI lesson, we will see that the focus is a bit different.

(7) [CMI T8]

	CMI Translation	CMI
	T: We find that even though we use strong light to shine on the LDR, yes, its electric resistant value decreases. But in fact the electric current that will pass through is __ ? but then the electric current needed to by the motor is __ ?	T: 我哋發覺呢即使用強光照射LDR，冇錯，佢嘅電阻值下降，不過，其實佢可以引進嘅電流呢都係__，但係__
->	T: Do you know what I would like you to answer? (Nominate) you try, you try to explain why nothing happens here. Now I use strong light to shine on LDR, right? Its resistance is __?	T: 電機佢需要用嘅電流就，吓你知唔知我想你答乜嘢吖？楊素麗你試吓，你試吓解釋吓點解呢一度，冇嘢睇嘅，嗱我用強光照射LDR，right，佢嘅電阻值？
	S: Small.	S: 小。

-> T: Yes, small. So there will naturally be electric current coming in. <u>Can you guess what's the difference between this electric current and the electric current it actually needs</u>?	T: 係，小，咁自然會有電流流入嚟啦可，<u>你估呢個電流量同佢需要嘅電流量比較，有D咩分別吖</u>啦？
S: The resistor resistance's electric current is smaller than the motor.	S: 電阻所需要的電流比摩打小。
-> T: This means the motor, motor, needs electric current which is ___?	T: 意思即係摩打，電動機啦，需要嘅電流量係？
S: Large.	S: 大。
T: Not only large, but very large. Yes, and so – thank you, you have answered correctly. And so even though we use strong light to shine on LDR, its resistance value drops, and the so-called larger electric current flows through the current, the motor needs a very large electric current to rotate, then this is the difference between this circuit and the other circuit.	T: 唔單止大呀可，好大，係，咁所以呢，唔該晒，你答得啱啦。咁所以我哋縱使係用強光照射 LDR，佢嘅電阻值下降，而嗰個叫做大D嘅電流流經電路，但係電動機需要強嘅電流先可以推動，咁呢個電路呢就係同呢個電路嘅分別。

In the above excerpt, the teacher asked the students to explain why nothing happened even though they used strong light to shine on the LDR. She started off by providing a clue to the student in the form of a blank-filling question, "Its resistance is ---?". Having established that there would be current going into the motor, the teacher posed another "open" question which focused the students' awareness on the difference between the electric current that will reach the motor and the amount of current that is needed to rotate the motor. This question is critical to the understanding of why the motor does not rotate, which in turn is critical to the understanding of the operation of the Reed relay. As we can see from the transcript, the student had no problems answering the question.

In the above discussion, we have seen that the difficulty that students had in responding to open questions in EMI lessons led to the modification of these questions which shifted the focus of the students' awareness. Another possible consequence is that the teacher will adopt an avoidance strategy, by either taking over the part of the explanation which is complex by a monologue instead of a collaborative construction of the explanation in the form of question and answer, or by asking closed questions which the teacher is more sure of getting a response from the students.

The following are two parallel excerpts from the EMI and the CMI lessons where the teacher is explaining why the motor rotates in the complicated circuit.

(8) [CMI T8]

	CMI Translation	CMI
	T: OK. (pointing to the complicated circuit) We love using strong light to shine on the LDR. Now, here it comes, strong light shines on the LDR. (Teacher uses the torch to shine on the LDR) I'll ask you questions step by step. For the circuit in the left side, this circuit, the largest effect is the electric resistant value, right? Strong light shines on the LDR, I've asked you before, the electric resistant value	T: 好啦，係啦，我哋最鐘意用強光照射 LDR，嗱，嚟啦，強光照射 LDR，(Teacher uses the torch to shine on the LDR symbol) 逐部分問啦，對左近哩個電路，哩個電路吓，最大影響呢就係個電阻值，RIGHT，強光照射 LDR，我剛才問過㗎啦，電阻值下降，好，到哩一近電路裡面，電流有咩影響？徐詩蕾。
->	drops, okay, <u>what effect will it have on the electric current on this side of the circuit?</u> (nominate)	
	S: Electric resistance drops	S: 電阻減少
	Prompt T: Electric resistance drops, the electric current -?	T: 電阻減小，電流……
	S: Increases.	S: 增加
	T: Yes, electric current increases, the electric current becomes larger, right? When electric current flows through the circuit, this coil is no longer simply a coil, it becomes an	T: 係，電流增加，電流大咗啦，Right，當有電流經電路嘅時候呢，嗱，哩個線圈，就再唔係線圈咁簡單啦喎，佢會變成一個，電磁鐵，<u>電磁鐵能夠產生？</u>
->	electromagnet. <u>Electromagnet can produce -?</u>	
	S: Magnetic field.	S: 電磁場

Effects of the Medium of Instruction

T: Yes, it will produce magnetic field. When it produces an electromagnetic field, it will have a series of effect on this side (of OQ -> the circuit). Then what? (nominate), you try and continue. (Pointing to the complicated circuit)	T: 係，產生磁場，咁佢產生磁場啦，對哩一近有一連串嘅影響。如何呢？呂詩琪，係試吓繼續吖。(Point to the complicated circuit)
S: …(no reply)…	S: …(冇回答)…
T: Now, the coil has a magnetic field, CQ -> then the Reed switch -? The Reed switch?	T: 嗱，線圈帶有磁場，咁簧片開關。簧片開關？
S: … (no reply)…	S: …(冇回答)…
T: The Reed switch, the two ends do not touch each other originally, OQ -> now what happens to these two ends?	T: 簧片開關本來呢就不接觸㗎，哩兩個接點呵，咁而家呢兩個接點點呀？
S: Touch each other.	S: 接觸。
T: Yes, the two ends touch other. OQ -> If the two ends touch each other, how do we describe this switch?	T: 係㗎，接點接觸，如果接點接觸嘅時候我哋點樣描述呢個開關？
S: … (no reply)…	S: …(冇回答)…
T: The two ends touch each other, Repeat OQ -> how do I describe this switch?	T: 接點接觸，我點樣描述呢個開關呀？
S: Closed.	S: 關閉。
T: Closed, very good. Yes, thank you. CQ -> Now, if this switch closes, then the electric current can pass through this circuit. This motor - ?	T: 關閉，非常好，係，唔該。嗱，如果呢個開關係關閉嘅時候嘅話呢，咁電流就能夠流經呢個電路，呢個電動機 - ？
S: Rotates.	S: 轉動。
T: Rotates. Is that okay?	T: 轉動。可唔可以？

In excerpt (8), the teacher asked 4 "open" questions (OQ) plus one repetition of one of the questions, and three "closed" questions (CQ). If we examine the content of the questions, we can see that most of them focused on process. For example, the effect the drop in resistance had on the electric current, what happened when the electromagnet produced a magnetic field, what happened to the two ends of the Reed switch, and what happened to the motor when the electric current passed through the circuit. In other words, the understanding of the processes involved was co-constructed by the teacher and the students. Let us compare (8) with (9) below in which the teacher was explaining the same process.

(9) [EMI T8]

    T: How about this circuit? (Teacher goes the complicated circuit) Now once again light shines on the LDR, its resistance decrease. So, current flows through this circuit. Now it's not
CQ-> only a coil but a__? now this question again (nominate) now this time is not merely a coil but a __ ?
    S: (no reply)
CQ-> T: Artificial magnet, all right. <u>Do you still remember (the) name</u>?
    S: Electromagnet.
    T: Once again.
    S: Electromagnet.
    T: Electromagnet, thank you, it became a electromagnet, and it produce magnetic field. So the switch here will close and a current pass through this circuit, so the motor rotate. There is a sequence of process occurs here and it make the motor rotate.

In this excerpt, the teacher only asked two questions, both of which are closed questions. However, the foci of both questions were on labeling the electric carrying coil as an electromagnet. The processes which were co-constructed by the teacher and the student were constructed only by the teacher in the form of a monologue. On the basis of our observation that questions often result in focusing students' awareness on the aspect of the phenomenon which was questioned, we can reasonably conclude that the consequence of asking questions about the devices rather than the processes would result in the former coming to the fore of the students' awareness and the latter receding to the background. Yet, critical to the understanding of the operation of the Reed relay is the processes and not the devices.

Words and awareness

There is yet another way in which language plays a central role in mediating the space of learning. It is when the use of language by the teacher and the students are crucial to the understanding of the critical aspects of the object of learning. The following are some examples.

(10) [CMI T7: Group Experiment]

		CMI Translation		CMI
->	T:	What do you do if it doesn't move? Yes, why doesn't it rotate? You shine on it first, yes, it rotates. Now I want it to stop. <u>What did you do just now?</u>	T:	喂，唔轉咁點呀？係啦，點解佢會唔轉呀？吓，你照住佢先啦，係，佢轉啦喎，嗱我想佢唔轉，你頭先做過咩動作？
	S:	Press (cover) it.	S:	按住。
->	T:	Press (cover) it, <u>why didn't it move when you pressed it?</u>	T:	按住，<u>點解按住佢會唔轉呀？</u>
	S:	Electric resistance is larger.	S:	電阻大。
	T:	Which side has a larger electric resistance? The symbol, no magnetic field, then the switch will…	T:	邊面電阻大？符號，冇磁場，咁開關制就……
	S:	(It) stopped.	S:	停咗。
->	T:	<u>Why do you use "stopped" to describe the Reed switch?</u> [2]	T:	<u>開關叫做停咗咩？</u>
	S:	It's open.	S:	開咗。
	T:	Yes, it's open, right. Very good. That means the motor cannot rotate.	T:	係，敞開咗，right，非常好，咁即電動機冇機會轉動。

In the above excerpt, the teacher asked a student to explain why the motor did not move when she covered the LDR. The student said that the resistance became larger and when the teacher followed it up by asking her to describe what happened when there was no magnetic field, the latter said, "stopped". The teacher pointed out that it was the wrong word to describe what happened to the Reed switch. What the student probably meant was that the motor did not work. However, the teacher took it as a description of what happened to the Reed switch. The opening and closing of the two ends of the Reed switch is one of the critical features of the operation of the Reed relay. Therefore, by forcing the student to give a more precise description of the Reed switch, she was in fact focusing the students' awareness on the Reed switch and the change that took place in the Reed switch

---

[2] Literally, the teacher's question is "'open and close' is described as 'have stopped'?' The literal translation of Reed switch in Chinese is "open and closed switch".

when there was no magnetic field. Hence, what may appear to be a very trivial correction of the wrong use of word in fact plays an important part in focusing the students on the critical aspects of the object of learning.

In the above example, we have seen that what appears to be a linguistic correction had profound effect on the focus of awareness. In the following, we shall see how language is inextricably interwined with conceptual understanding. In both excerpts, the teacher was explaining what happened to the resistance of the LDR when strong light shines on it.

(11) [EMI T8]

>   T: Now as light shines on the LDR, what happen to its resistor, resistance?
>   What happen to it, Ah Leung, light shines on the LDR?
> -> S: Low.
>   T: <u>Thank you. It (the resistance) reduces, it becomes smaller.</u>

(12) [CMI T1]

	CMI Translation	CMI
	T: If we strong light to shine on the LDR, what will be the change in its resistance? (nominate) Strong light shines on the LDR. (Teacher uses a torch to shine on the LDR)	T: 如果而家呢我用強光照射 LDR，咁佢嘅電阻值有咩改變？馬麗儀，強光照射 LDR？ (Teacher use the torch to shine on the board)
->	S: Small.	S: 小。
	T: What is small?	T: 咩小呀？
	S: Electric resistance.	S: 電阻。
	T: Electric resistance is small. I give you another chance to answer this question. You think about this carefully. We use strong light to shine on the LDR.	T: 電阻小，我俾你再答多次，你諗清楚，用強光喎，照射 LDR 喎？ (Teacher use the torch to shine the bound)
	S: Electric resistance is small.	S: 電阻小。
->	T: Electric resistance decreases or increases?	T: 電阻下降定電阻提升？
	S: Decreases.	S: 下降。

T: Are you sure?	T: 你好肯定？
S: Yes.	S: 係。
T: Yes, you're right. Electric resistance decreases.	T: 啱，係，電阻下降。

In (11) and (12) above, the words "low" and "small" are adjectives which describe a static situation. In the EMI lesson the teacher simply accepted the answer as correct, and modified the student's answer by replacing "low" with the verbs "reduces" and "becomes smaller". These two verbs of action describe the change of state of the resistance. Notice that the teacher did not draw the student's attention to the difference between using an adjective and a verb to describe what happened to the resistance. By contrast, the teacher did not accept the adjective "small" as the correct answer. She challenged the student to think about the question again and provide another answer. When the student gave the same answer, the teacher posed an alternative question using verbs of action. The teacher's question focused the student's awareness on the change of state. Like (8) above, what appeared to be a mere linguistic correction was in fact a sharpening of the student's conceptual understanding.

Does Language Matter?

The extent to which language matters is in a very obvious sense a function of the students' mastery of the Medium of Instruction. If they do not understand what the teacher is saying in one language, but understand her in the other language, such a difference has reasonably very serious implications for their learning.

In the study reported here this does not seem to be the case. The students probably understood most of what the teacher said, regardless of whether she said it in Chinese or in English. Still we found some profound differences between the two cases. The teacher introduced variation in respects that can be deemed pedagogically critical when she taught in Chinese, while she introduced variation in the same respects to a lesser extent when she taught in English. This is true about shifts between different contexts, such as the school context and the context of everyday life and it is true about shifts between real objects and symbolic representation. Furthermore, she used more open-ended questions in Chinese than in English. There was thus a wider space left for the students' answers when the teaching was in Chinese. On the whole, the space of learning was wider when the lesson was in Chinese. The more frequent shifts there brought out aspects or dimensions which were brought out to a lesser extent when the medium of instruction was English. And the space left for the students' answers – the implicit variation constituted by means of the questions asked by the teacher was wider when she taught in Chinese. So why was that?

One way of understanding this difference may look like this.

As has been argued elsewhere (see, for instance, Marton & Booth, 1997), teaching is an object-mediated relation between the teacher and the students.

Teaching is always teaching about something. This "something" is the object of teaching. And the students are supposed to learn about this "something", hence it is the object of learning. There is thus a topic, that is made sense of and dealt with somehow by the teacher (the object of teaching) and made sense of and dealt with somehow by the students (the object of learning). The object of teaching and the object of learning are not identical, but closely related. They are two sides of the pedagogical object that the teacher and students have in common.

As far as they do have it as a shared object of attention, the work in the classroom proceeds smoothly. But when the object of attention is not shared by the teacher and the majority of the students, problems start. Students stop learning what they are supposed to learn and the teacher's grip on what is happening gets weakened. This is why maintaining the object-mediated contact with the students is most teachers' highest priority and very much of what they are doing in the classroom can be understood as the employment of strategies towards that end. No teachers can afford "losing" their students. Very much of the interaction between the teacher and the students has the form of the teacher telling about something for the students to grasp and the teacher asking questions, the students answering and the teacher following up on their answers. More variation means more things to understand, introducing variation in a new dimension means that a new aspect of the topic dealt with is added. If the teacher's perception is that the students are already having too much difficulties because of the medium of instruction, she is likely to refrain from introducing more variation (and hence more difficulties in her view). This is probably true whether it is explicit variation through contextual shifts, for instance, or implicit variation through open-ended questions. We have seen in our analysis of questioning in the previous section that when the teacher experienced difficulties in getting her students to respond to open questions, she reduced the implicit variation effected by a range of possible answers, by resorting to closed questions, or by resorting to monologue. By doing so, the teacher inadvertently narrows the space of learning and opportunities for learning are lessened.

We have also seen that in EMI lessons, in order to make it easier for students to formulate answers to the open questions, the teacher used closed questions and blank-filling questions which shifted the focus of awareness of the students. Consequently the students' object of attention became somewhat different from that of the teacher, probably without the teacher's being aware of this. For example, in helping students understand why the motor does not rotate, the object of attention for the students was the electromagnet because the questions asked when in fact the teacher's intended object of attention was the difference in the current passing through the LDR and the current needed by the motor.

While differences in how much space is opened for the students to use usually make differences in what aspects of the object of learning that the focus of the students' awareness is directed to, differences in the latter respect can also be brought about by subtle differences in the choice and acceptance of critical words in the communication between the teacher and the students. This was shown in the previous section.

We have thus pointed out some mechanisms in relation to which the classroom discourse in Chinese and in English differ. We believe that these differences are critical for the understanding developed by the students. Our point is that Chinese students in Hong Kong are handicapped as far as the mastery of the content of the lesson is concerned when they are taught in English. We have tried to show some of the ways in which their handicaps are linguistically constructed.

REFERENCES

Brimer, A., Cheng, W., Ip, B., Johnson, K., Lam, R., Lee, P., Leung, J., Sweeting, A. & Tong, S.M. (1985). *The Effects of the Medium of Instruction on the Achievement of Form 2 Students in Hong Kong Secondary Schools*. Hong Kong, Educational Research Establishment, Education Department, Hong Kong Government and Faculty of Education, Hong Kong University.

Cheng, N.L., Shek, K.C., Tse, K.K. & Wong, S.L. (1973). At What Cost?: *Instruction through the English Medium in HK schools*. Hong Kong: Shum Shing Printers.

Cummins, J. & Swain, M. (1986). *Bilingualism in Education*. London: Longman.

Education Department. (1997). *Medium of Instruction Guidance for Secondary Schools*. Hong Kong: Hong Kong Government Printer.

Johnson, K. & Swain, M. (1994). From Core to Content: Bridging the L2 Proficiency Gap in Late Immersion. *Language and Education*, 8(4), 211-229.

Marsh, H.W., Hau, K.T. & Kong, C.K. (in press). Late Immersion and Language Instruction (English vs Chinese) in Hong Kong High Schools: Achievement Growth in Language and Non-language Subjects. *Harvard Educational Review*.

Bowden J. & Marton, F. (1998). *The University of Learning*. London: Kogan Page.

Marton, F. & Booth S. (1997). *Learning and Awareness*. Mahwah, N.J.: Lawrence Erlbaum Associates.

Tsui, A.B.M. (1995). *Introducing Classroom Interaction*, London: Penguin.

Tung, P.C.S. (1990). Why Changing the Medium of Instruction in Hong Kong could be Difficulty. *Journal of Multilingual and Multicultural Development*, 10(4), 279-295.

8

Solving the Paradox of the Chinese Teacher?

Ida Mok, P.M. Chik, P.Y. Ko, Tammy Kwan, M.L. Lo, Ference Marton, Dorothy F.P. Ng, M.F. Pang, U. Runesson and L.H. Szeto

The Stereotype of Chinese Classrooms

In the eyes of many westerners, Chinese classrooms are usually seen as 'conservative' and 'traditional'. Such a perception is paralleled by a number of Chinese sayings. For instance, the metaphor 'cramming the duck' in Hong Kong or 'mantanguan' (literally, teacher-talk throughout the lesson) in mainland China suggests that teachers' talk is a dominant feature of the Chinese classroom. The common expression of 'teaching' in Chinese is 'the teaching of books' (jiao shu) which puts high values on textbooks. Among Chinese scholars, it is not uncommon for them to describe their own school learning experience as "teacher-dominated", "textbook oriented", or "focused on drills and practice". As a result, imitation and repetition are seen as the main features of the Chinese way of learning, and this is perhaps captured well in the famous Chinese saying, 'Read the book a hundred times and the meaning appears'.

Many studies conducted in mainland China suggest that rote learning is a popular model underpinning school learning tasks, for example, in mastering Chinese characters (Cleverly 1991, pp.236-237). Very often, the teacher plays a prominent role in delivering and supervising such tasks. Paine (1990, 1992), for example, based on her fieldwork conducted in 1986-87, put forward a 'virtuoso' model to describe Chinese teachers and their teaching methods. The model suggests that Chinese lessons are dominated by teacher-talk in an expository and explanatory format whilst students are the audience. In doing so, the teacher may use a precise and elegant language, and the entire teaching act may resemble an artistic performance. However, teaching and learning does not go beyond 'transmitting knowledge'. Paine's view is that such an orientation of teaching and learning is conservative in nature (Paine, 1992, p.193).

In sum, the Chinese classroom is described as under a high degree of teacher-control and having passive students. Usually, such descriptions are contrasted with portrayals of classrooms in Western countries such as Sweden, for instance, where typical classrooms are seen as exhibiting very little teacher-control but very active students (Carlgren & Marton, forthcoming).

A Paradox and Its Solution

Whilst a high-degree of teacher control and passive students are thought to be not very conducive to high quality learning, international comparisons of students' attainments revealed that students in Confucian-heritage cultures (CHC) outperformed students in Western countries. The Third International Mathematics and Science Study (TIMSS) showed that students in Asia (e.g. Singapore, Taiwan, Japan and Hong Kong) did much better in mathematics than their counterparts in North American countries (Law, 1996, 1997). Stevenson & Lee (1997) compared schools (year one to six) in Beijing and Chicago and found that there was a great difference in the mathematics achievements between Chinese and American students. Chinese students did better than the American students in the beginning years, and the gap widened in subsequent years. Ma (1999) found that Chinese elementary school teachers had more of what she called 'profound understanding of fundamental mathematics' than their American counterparts. An interesting question thus arises: how can classrooms which are ostensibly filled with teacher dominated features (and thus not conducive to learning) produce such good learning outcomes? This is what we call "the paradox of the Chinese teacher".

Recent studies suggest an alternative view of the Chinese classroom. Biggs (1996) points out that it is in fact a misconception to believe that learners from CHC are rote learners. He suggests that "CHC students may be repetitive learners but there is no evidence that they rote learn any more than their Western counterparts" (Biggs, 1996, p.63). As far as the role of repetition is concerned, Biggs' view concurs with that of Gardner – repetition skill development comes first, following by meaning and interpretation, with repetition being used as the tool for creating meaning (in Biggs, 1996, p.57).

Stevenson & Lee (1997) examined in great detail the mathematics classrooms in both China and Japan. They came to the conclusion that although the whole class instruction method is prevalent in both cultures, it gives children maximal opportunity to benefit from the teacher. They also found that Chinese teachers hold children's attention by varying the learning tasks. They expect students to respond to their questions in a rapid-fire manner but at the same time, they also emphasize conceptual understanding (p.47).

Cortazzi (1998) used the sequence "initiation (I), response (R) and follow-up (F)" to describe the lessons he observed in Chinese kindergartens and primary schools. The teachers engaged students by Socratic questions, in the form of cycles such as I-R-F-R-F-R-F. He believes that this model is particularly effective because while only one child is answering a teacher's question, the others participated through listening (see also Chapter 6).

Hong Kong, as a result of its geographical position and political background, has always been under the influence of both Chinese and Western cultures. The Hong Kong classrooms in the 80's were often portrayed as teacher-centred with passive students (Visiting Panel, 1982). Such environments have been seen as detrimental to learning, leading to arguments for curriculum reforms. One of the reforms, known as the Target Oriented Curriculum (TOC), was initiated by the Hong Kong Government in 1993. TOC was seen as an attempt to tackle these

Solving the Paradox of the Chinese Teacher? 163

problems and to improve the learning environment with a focus on the teaching of Chinese, English, and Mathematics. Paramount amongst these problems are teacher-centred instruction, norm-based examinations and rote oriented classrooms (Morris, et al., 1996).

Reforms such as the Activity Approach and the TOC have brought about some changes to the Hong Kong education scene. In the TOC evaluation project, nearly 200 Chinese lessons were observed for three academic years. It was found that as far as structure was concerned, a lesson usually consisted of a sequence of learning activities, which involved a teacher-led whole-class discussion with a focus on a specific theme, or completion of a learning task / worksheet by an individual student or a group. Thus, a lesson might consist of a flexible combination of whole-class, group work or individual learning activities. Nearly all lessons contained episodes of whole-class teaching and the majority of these episodes consisted of teacher-student or student-student interactions. Analysis of the nature of the interactions indicated that the teacher spent most of the lesson time in direct teaching and questioning. The high percentage of questioning showed that interaction was in general encouraged in the context of teacher-centred activities which were the major components of the observed lessons. However, this high proportion of teacher-centred activities did not necessarily mean that the students were learning passively. Results of the TOC evaluation project revealed that the proportion of time in which students were answering the teacher's questions, engaging in activities specified by the teacher and chanting out choral answers was consistently between 20% to 30%. Although there was evidence indicating that students were active in TOC classrooms, teacher-control remained a dominant feature (Mok & Ko, 2000).

The aforementioned provides a picture different from the stereotype described at the beginning of the chapter. A gradual recognition of the pluralistic style of teaching in Chinese classrooms can be observed while putting together the results of several studies. Many Chinese teachers (in both Hong Kong and mainland China) seem to manage to engage students to a high degree, to create a space for their active involvement and make it possible for them to learn not only from the teacher but also from each other (e.g. Mok & Ko, 2000; Ko, 1999). So what we have in many cases is highly active and attentive students learning within the framework of lessons carefully orchestrated by the teacher. Such a learning environment might not be that bad after all. And if it is not, then there is no paradox.

There are certainly differences among Chinese classrooms (including those in Hong Kong) as there are among Swedish classrooms, or among classrooms anywhere in the world. Judging from research carried out in Hong Kong such differences are not so much differences between arrangements for learning (or teaching methods) such as whole class, group work, individual work (students doing their own work in their seats during lessons). The important differences are to be found *within* different arrangements for learning. Exploring the nature of what, in our view, makes the difference is a major aim of this chapter. By doing so we hope to illustrate in depth an instance of "good practice" which follows the above mentioned pattern of high degree of teacher control combined with a careful constitution of space for the students' active contributions to the content of the lesson, found to be characteristic for Hong Kong classrooms (Mok & Ko, 2000).

Teaching as Seen From the Point of View of Learning

For a full understanding it is necessary that teaching should be studied with different purposes and foci. In the literature mentioned above, the lesson structure, the organization of the classroom work and the role of the teacher formed the focus of the investigation. Whilst classroom organisation is not an unimportant issue, there are in fact other aspects of the teaching-learning process which are critical, if we focus on *what* students could possibly learn. Such a focus is fully justified because a teacher must handle or present the object of learning (i.e., what is to be learned) in a certain way in order to achieve particular student understandings. Thus, attention must be paid to the ways by which the content is taught and communicated in the classroom.

This study investigates the way the teacher handles the content in a Chinese lesson. More specifically, we tried to analyze the content taught from a theoretical perspective which we argue, is capable of examining the learners' experience (Marton & Booth, 1997). The study has two aims. First, it tries to identify the features of a teacher-dominated lesson through the description of a certain Chin-ese lesson. The chosen lesson may be atypical in terms of the teaching strategy used. However, the lesson can be considered as exemplary in the sense that the teaching was conducted in a whole-class manner, and it was combined with intense student activities. Second, it provides a model for analysing teacher-student interactions. The model involves the use of a set of conceptual tools – variation, simultaneity, and discernment. These three concepts we argue are central in understanding and enhancing classroom learning.

However, before embarking on the analysis, it is essential that we first clarify and elaborate our perspective of learning.

Learning and experiencing

Imagine students studying the same text or struggling with a mathematical problem with the same aim: to understand or to learn something. Although they may spend the same amount of time trying to learn this and they may have similar educational background, it is a fact that some of the students will succeed better than others, and the outcome of the learning will be different. The reason for this could, of course, be studied from different points of view. For instance, the differences could be analyzed from a psychological perspective where the variation is related to motivation or intelligence. However, the same case could also be analyzed from quite a different point of view, that is, from the point of view of the learner.

Describing the world as it is seen from the point of view of the learner is the object of research in phenomenography (Marton, 1981, 1993, Marton & Booth, 1997; Bowden & Marton, 1998). Phenomenography is a research specialization that investigates learning in specific settings. It is a way of:

... identifying, formulating, and tackling certain sorts of research questions, a specialization that is particularly aimed at questions of relevance to learning and understanding in an educational setting. (Marton & Booth, 1997, p.111)

The object of phenomenographic research is the variation in the ways which people conceive of, understand or experience something. The outcome of phenomenographic research is thus a description of the variation in which a particular phenomenon is experienced. A number of phenomenographic studies have been carried out during the last twenty-eight years. These have revealed a variation in the way which various phenomena such as number (Neuman, 1987), Newtonian motion (Johansson, Marton & Svensson, 1985) or learning (Marton, Beaty, & Dall'Alba, 1993) are experienced by the learners. From all these studies it can be deduced that each phenomenon could be experienced in a limited number of different ways. This variation in experiencing is critical to learning, and we would argue also central to teaching.

Several phenomenographic studies have investigated the ways a text is experienced by the learner. Säljö (1982) for instance studied Swedish university students reading the same text about learning. In the text there were a number of perspectives on learning, different principles, research results, examples and application described. By asking the students (after reading the text) what the text was about, two qualitatively different ways in which the students comprehended the text could be identified. One way of comprehending the text was seeing it as being about forms of learning embracing different perspectives on learning and illustrated by different examples. Quite a different way of comprehending the text was experiencing it as being about different examples of learning. When the text was experienced in this way the students had difficulties in coming up with an answer when they were asked about the main theme of the text (Marton & Booth, 1997).

Referring to what was said previously about the variation in the outcome of learning about something (for instance learning about learning from a text or from a lecture) could be described as a variation in the ways the learners experience something. But what do we then mean by "experiencing something" and "experiencing something in a certain way"?

Firstly, "experiencing something" is related to the structure and organization of human awareness. To be aware of something means that some things are in focus and that our awareness is directed to these. Marton & Booth (1997) is following and elaborating the notion "field of consciousness" (Gurwitsch, 1964) when they apply awareness to learning. They argue that in any situation we are simultaneously aware of the here and now, of the past and of different aspects of the world, although we are not aware of them in the same way. What happens is that some aspects become figural in our awareness, they are discerned. When we experience an object, some aspects of the object are held in focal awareness at the same time. However we are not able to keep all aspects of the object in our awareness simultaneously, so some are left out. The discerned aspects are also related to each other in a specific way. From this it follows that the awareness has a structure. Marton & Booth (1997) use this notion of the nature of human awareness as an explanatory framework for understanding different ways of experiencing.

Secondly, "experiencing something" is related to experiencing something *as* something. That means the experienced object is assigned a meaning. But the meaning we assign to the object is related to the structure of our awareness. A certain meaning presupposes a certain structure. To experience an object *as* a small white cup, some aspects of the object, for example the size, the shape and the color, must be held in focal awareness, they must be discerned and related to each other and to the whole object at the same time. In addition to this the object must be discerned from the context in which it appears. The cup must be separated from other objects like the table on which it stands, and so on. So, to be able to experience an object – a physical object, a text or a theoretical concept – in a certain way, some aspects of the object must be discerned by the "experiencer" simultaneously. However, these simultaneously discerned aspects must be related to each other and to the whole in a certain way.

So, variation in ways of experiencing the same object is a function of differences in how the awareness is structured and organized at a certain moment. To conclude, those aspects of the object that are discerned and held in the individual's focal awareness simultaneously define a way of experiencing something. The difference in ways of experiencing the same thing is related to a difference in the structure of the awareness. Thus, a more complex way of experiencing implies that more or other aspects of the object are discerned simultaneously.

Studying teaching

Our awareness has a dynamic character. The structure and the organization of the awareness, and thereby the experience, can change and actually keeps changing all the time. This is actually what happens when we learn something. From the particular theoretical position taken here and from our line of reasoning it follows that learning can be seen as a change in the structure of our awareness (Marton & Booth, 1997). One learns to discern more or other aspects of an object of attention simultaneously and relates these to other aspects. But how does this change come about?

The concepts described above, i.e. discernment, simultaneity and variation, are grounded in empirical research on learning (Marton & Booth, 1997). Granted the assumption that these are highly significant in relation to certain outcomes of learning, it would make sense to look at teaching from the same point of view. This implies that the same theoretical concepts are used when analysing learning as well as teaching. According to Marton & Booth (1997), certain patterns of variation characterize certain ways of experiencing a phenomenon. In consequence, to bring about a particular way of experiencing a certain phenomenon, the presence of that very pattern of variation is necessary. When studying teaching from the point of view of learning it is thus critical to explore the extent to which teachers are contributing to constitute patterns of variation, necessary for learning.

Runesson (1999) used these concepts for analyzing audio recordings from mathematics lessons. The aim of her study was to investigate how teachers handle rational numbers as an object of teaching. She has shown that teachers, although

Solving the Paradox of the Chinese Teacher?

they teach the same topic and organize their teaching in a similar way, handle the content differently. She has also found that the teachers use variation – although in different ways – in order to enable students to discern critical aspects of the content. When the teacher focuses on some aspect of the content, she can open up a dimension of variation in respect to that particular aspect to the students.

For instance, in the case of rational numbers, in relation to the whole ¼ has always the same size (i.e. the relative size). But in absolute size ¼ could be different since the absolute size of ¼ is dependent on the size of the whole. So the absolute/relative size aspect is a critical feature of rational numbers. How could one learn to discern that? One of the teachers in Runesson's study used a rubberband divided into four parts. By stretching the rubberband alongside an object, a quarter, for instance, of the length of the object could easily be found. By "measuring" different objects of different length with the rubberband, the teacher varied the absolute size of the whole. Consequently, the absolute size of a quarter varied, whereas the relative size (¼) was kept constant. So in this case, the absolute size of the whole as well as a quarter (which both vary) made up a dimension of variation in the teaching process.

While stretching the rubberband alongside objects of different lengths, at the same time, the teacher represented ¼ by manipulative aids, she *talked* about "a quarter" and she *wrote* it on the blackboard with symbolic representations. That is, there was a variation in the way the rational number was represented. Or to put it differently, the teacher opened up a dimension of variation in the representation of ¼. Since the teacher also used different forms of representing a quarter in symbolic form: ¼ (fraction form) as well as 25% (percentage) the form of symbolic representation made up a dimension of variation. So what we find is that in this particular situation, there are simultaneously (at least) three dimensions of variation present in the teaching process. There is a variation in the representational mode, in symbolic form (mode) and a variation in the size of the whole that is partitioned. The dimensions of variation that are opened up are dynamic and sometimes overlap each other. A space of variation is thus constituted.

We want to stress that this variation is related to aspects of the content taught. The variation we have described so far is by no means simply alternative teaching methods. Our theoretical view of learning is grounded in a number of empirical studies of different subjects and different ages of the learners. These studies have supported the argument to see learning as a result of learners discerning the critical aspects of the object of learning. In order for discernment to happen, variation is essential. Runesson's study has applied the conceptual tools in this framework and successfully shown that teachers had used variation for directing students' awareness to a tacit dimension of their knowledge. Therefore, we find it reasonable to say that the way the space of variation is constituted in the teaching process is critical to students' learning.

Methodology

The lesson that we are going to examine in the current chapter was part of a school-based action research project initiated by the TOC Development Project of

Curriculum Development Institute of the Education Department of Hong Kong in 1997. The project was aimed at encouraging teachers to actively consider the improvement of Chinese Language teaching and its associated pedagogical change. In particular, the teacher in this lesson applied the ideas of a "reader theatre and creative drama" (Heinig, 1998) as the pedagogical basis of the lesson. In order to help students experience the meaning of the text, he invited students to come out and dramatize the meaning of the text with the intention of strengthening text comprehension and reinforcing sentence pattern learning.

The lesson was video-recorded. The video was transcribed verbatim[1] and subsequently translated into English. The analysis was carried out on the verbatim transcript and English translation in tandem and the video was referred to from time to time to ensure that the description represented the reality as closely as possible. Analysis was carried out by the researchers independently and also jointly in order to capture the different kinds of variation which were agreed to be relevant in the space of learning. All the identified variations were grounded in the empirical data. The methodology applied in the current chapter is an extension of that developed in Runesson's work (1999).

In the analysis of the lesson, we observed that the teacher directed the students' awareness on the text. When he focused on an object, which very often was a part of the text, he sometimes introduced a variation and the dimension of variation would become explicit. For example, when the teacher focused on the specific word "play", he introduced a variation so that the students could experience the different forms of the word (informal utterance and formal enunciation). Consequently, the word can be readily seen as a dimension of variation. In another example, when students were guided to understand a paragraph, they were given the opportunity to experience the meaning of the paragraph in different ways such as reading and enacting. Similar to the case of the word "play", the enactment was an instance of a variation of the meaning of the paragraph. Later in the lesson, the enactment itself constituted a dimension of variation, as there were variations in enacting the text as a result of different students enacting the same text. While going through these variations, we will see that the variations were embedded and happened simultaneously. In the aforementioned, words were embedded in a sentence and then within a paragraph, and also within an enactment. It is this simultaneity, which links the variations together, that helps students become aware of the space of learning as a coherent whole.

Besides identifying the different kinds of variation which are relevant to a specific content, related to the second aim of the chapter, we will put forward a model for describing the space of variation constituted in teaching. In this aspect, two facets are crucial. One is the scope of the space of variation: What dimensions vary? The other critical facet is whether the variation in these dimensions is simultaneous or non-overlapping. Are the dimensions embedded in each other or are they independent? In order to help readers to understand how dimensions were

---

[1] The Chinese lesson was in Cantonese. All the extracts in this chapter are translations of the verbatim transcripts.

found and how they varied in line with what happened in the lesson, we attempt, in the next section, to make the analysis explicit and allow the readers to revisit the lesson via the windows of the researchers.

Anatomy of a Chinese lesson

The lesson was a grade 2 lesson. The teacher had just marked an examination paper and returned it to the students. During the lesson, the teacher revised with the students the meaning of a text passage, which was included in the paper. The story of the text is translated below:

> A chick and a duckling went playing together. Feeling hungry, they came to muddy ground. The chick used its sharp-pointed mouth to pick up many little worms from the mud and invited the duckling to eat them together.
> They came to the riverside and the duckling said: 'Let me use my flat mouth to catch fish for you to eat.' It dived into the river and swam freely and comfortably. The chick also jumped into the river; but the chick did not know how to swim, therefore, in terror it cried for help. The duckling immediately let the chick sit on its back, and carried it back to the riverside.

Seeking the dimensions of variations. To begin with, the whole class read through the first paragraph silently. Then two students were called upon to role-play that paragraph in front of the whole class. While they were enacting, the teacher asked questions both at the word and sentence level.

At the word level, different words were focused on. For example, the Chinese word "playing" was read as "wan" (the informal utterance) in casual Cantonese conversation, and as "wun" (the formal enunciation) when it was read in the context of a written text.

(When the two students were enacting the first paragraph, the teacher asked the class whether their enactment was correct).

    T: Why do we say that they are correct? It is because our story is about …?
    S: <u>Playing</u>. ("wan", the informal utterance)
    T: Which word is playing?
    S: <u>Playing</u>. ("wun", the formal enunciation; the students were reading from the text.)
    T: Good, we speak this word together.
    S: A chick and a duckling went <u>playing</u> together. ("wun", the word was embedded in a sentence and being read aloud.)

There were occasionally variations between symbolic and enacted representation (e.g., saying "sharp-pointed mouth" and enacting the mouth by one's hands), and between symbolic, iconic and enactive representations (e.g., talking about picking worms, drawing worms on the blackboard and pretending to pick worms).

(While the two students were still enacting the text, the teacher drew the other students' attention to focus on the word "sharp-pointed").

> T: Not that quick. The end of last paragraph is not about catching fish. It is about a bird catching a fish. OK, Law XX, what does the mouth of the bird look like?
> S: (Law) It is very <u>sharp-pointed</u>. (Spoken form)
> T: Try to use your hand to make the shape. (The student performed the action, enacting the sharp-pointed mouth.)
> T: Close your fingers, try to mimic the action of picking. (The student performed the action.)
> T: OK, I put some worms here…. (Drawing some worms on the blackboard) you try to pick out the worms and give them to the duck, one, two, three. (The student performed the action of picking worms.)

So when the lesson had proceeded this far, there had been a variation between the paragraph, sentence and word level. In this phase of the lesson (when dealing with the first paragraph) the three levels were hierarchically organized, they were embedded in each other. This means that the sentences were focused within the paragraph and words were focused within the sentence. As a matter of fact the teacher had explained in the interview that he was consciously varying the level attended between text, paragraph, sentence, word and character.

'What else?' The attentive reader might ask. Of course, there are sentences within paragraphs and words within sentences. But paragraphs, sentences and words are in fact not necessarily dealt with only in this way in this educational context. Another possible way is, for instance, to focus on the whole text, paragraphs, sentences, or discrete words, either in sequence or on separate occasions.

Moreover, the paragraph level was seen as a dimension of variation itself in this lesson. Here, the same paragraph was first read, then enacted. As a result, there was a variation between reading and enacting the same paragraph.

What makes up a dimension of variation? There are three sentences within the paragraph and they are focused on one at a time. We would not call this variation according to our framework. Within the paragraph they form a sequence but they do not constitute different forms of the same thing or different instances of the same concept. Within each sentence one word is focused upon one at a time. That is, the word "playing" was focused in the first sentence, and similarly, "hungry" in the second and "sharp-pointed" in the third. Again these three words do not form a "variation" by themselves, nor do they form a sequence. However, each word constitutes a dimension of variation itself. For example, "playing" forms a dimension of variation between an informal utterance, a formal enunciation and a written form. Similarly, "hungry" varies between a spoken and a written form, whereas "sharp-pointed" is between spoken, written and enacted form.

Figure 8.1 shows a dynamic representation of the first paragraph which explains both the structure of variations and their temporal development.

Figure 8.1
A dynamic representation of the first part of the lesson

Reading Paragraph 1	Enacting Paragraph 1		
	First Sentence	Second Sentence	Third Sentence
	"Playing"	"Hungry"	"Sharp-pointed"
	(s[iu] / s[fe] / w)	(s / w)	(s / w / e)

We can thus conclude that as far as the first part of the lesson is concerned, there are variations between levels (paragraph, sentence, words), within paragraphs (reading, enacting) and within three different words: "playing" (informal utterance, formal enunciation, written), "hungry" (spoken, written) and "sharp-pointed" (spoken, written, enacted). There are thus altogether five variations. The first two variations occur simultaneously. The last three variations occurred in sequence but were also embedded in the first two simultaneously.

Variations and simultaneity. After this, the teacher and the class moved on to the second paragraph. Another two students were invited to enact the first sentence only[2]. This sentence then constituted a dimension of variation by itself. First it was enacted, then the moral aspect of the story was raised which actually corresponded to question 3 in the examination paper[3]. In order to answer the question why the duckling wanted to catch fish for the chick to eat, the teacher's questions probed into the analogy between the story and the meanings of "repay" and "friendship".

 T: OK, why does the duckie want to catch fish for the chickie?
 S_1: Because... (Students were very eager to be the first to give the answer.)
 T: Be quiet. Who wants to give the answer? (Some students raised up their hands eagerly.)
 T: Were you the chickie?
 S_2: I was the duckie.
 T: The chickie gave you worms, did you feel happy?
 S_2: Happy.
 T: Then what should you do to repay the duckie? It, the chickie not the duckie.
 S_2: I will catch fish for it.
 T: You will catch fish for it. Because friendship is that you treat your friend...
 S_3: (One student interrupted and answered.) You will treat him/her in return.

After that, the teacher focused on questions 1 and 2 ("What is the difference between the chick's mouth and the duckling's?" and "What is the difference

---

[2] They came to the riverside and the duckling said: 'Let me use my flat mouth to catch fish for you to eat.'
[3] Why does the duckling want to catch fish for the chick?

between the food caught by the chick and that by the duckling?"). Thus, there is a new type of variation which focuses on the different aspects (moral and explanatory) of the sentence. Embedded in the explanatory aspect, different words were focused upon: "sharp-pointed" and its opposite – "flat" (which was spoken, written, drawn and enacted), "worm" (spoken, drawn and written), and "fish" (spoken, written).

Another two students were invited to continue enacting the rest of the paragraph. Within this enactment, the second part of the sentence[4] was spoken and enacted. Both sentences were thus turned into dimensions of variation. Within this section a word was focused on and varied between spoken and written form. Also the last two sentences were spoken and enacted. In the second sentence, the word "diving" was varied between spoken and written form.

So far, we have identified variations between paragraph, sentence and word levels and these three levels are nested or hierarchically embedded. There is no variation on the paragraph level, but there is variation between the spoken and enacted form of word within each sentence. For sentence 1 within the enactment and discussion of meanings, there is a variation between the moral and the explanatory aspects. For question 1, there is a variation between the different forms (spoken, written, iconic and enacted) from the words "sharp-pointed" and "flat", and from "worm" and "fish" for question 2. In sentence 2, the word "diving" was varied between spoken and written form.

In addition to the variation between levels (paragraph, sentence, word), there is variation between spoken and enacted forms of each one of the four sentences; and between explanatory and moral aspects within one of the sentences. There is variation between spoken and written forms for five different words. Altogether, there are twelve variations in the second paragraph. Figure 8.2 shows a dynamic representation of how the second paragraph was dealt with.

The same two other students (the second pair) were then asked to read and enact the whole story. After they had finished, another pair of students (the third pair) was called upon to enact the whole story again. And after them, another two students (the fourth pair) were asked to do the same thing again. In this last round, the teacher read aloud the story sentence by sentence during which the students enacted the story simultaneously (see figure 8.3). A gradual enrichment of the students' enactment, in terms of what they had said, was observed. There is thus variation between the three pairs of students in their ways of enacting the very same story. Although the teacher's interference in the final round may make it somewhat difficult to compare, it seems that each enactment of the story was richer and more complete than the previous one.

For example,

"Thank you. Let me catch fish for you to eat."
"It [the worm] tastes good. Catch some more. Let me treat you back. I am jumping down into the river and catch fish."

---

[4] … the duckling said, 'Let me use my flat mouth to catch fish for you to eat.'

So far, we can observe the variation between spoken and enacted representations at the paragraph level for the first paragraph, at the sentence level for the second paragraph, and finally at the story level. The way that the teacher handled a part or the whole of the story can then be seen as another kind of variation (see figure 8.3).

To recapitulate, we have dealt with this lesson as being subdivided into different parts. The story was gone through four times. The first time was divided into two paragraphs and the paragraphs divided into sentences. The remaining three times dealt with the story as a whole. We thus have six different kinds of variation:

parts / wholes (of the entire story)
different pairs of students (enacting the whole story)
reading / enacting (the story, a paragraph or a sentence)
spoken / written (forms of words)
informal utterance / formal enunciation (versions of the spoken word)
moral / explanatory aspects (sentence 1 in the second paragraph)

Whilst the dimensions of variation are found, we notice that each variation focuses on a critical aspect of the objects of learning. There must always be something common running between levels. Moreover, the dimensions of variation could be embedded, partially overlapping, or sequential. The synthesis of the lesson thus became complex as there was more than one dimension varying simultaneously (see Figure 8.4).

Discussion

Asian classrooms have long been portrayed as teacher-centred with passive students. The features of high teacher control and passive learning have always been seen as detrimental to learning. However, results of recent comparison studies such as TIMSS (Law, 1996, 1997), studies conducted by Stevenson & Lee (1997) and Ma (1999) suggest a paradox. Despite the fact that Chinese classrooms have been seen as dominated by teacher control and student passivity (such features are seen as not very conducive to learning), there are indicators that students in Confucian-heritage countries outperform their counterparts in the Western world. More recent studies in Asian classrooms have shown that a high degree of teacher control does not necessarily imply passive students. Although these studies have identified some important features of these classrooms, they did not consider how the teacher handled the learning content in a lesson and how the space of learning was constituted.

In this chapter, we argue that in order to arrive at a more comprehensive picture, we should go beyond a mere description of the organization of the classrooms. The key must lie in the ways that the teacher deals with the content. Specifically, we study teaching from another perspective which theorizes on the relationship between student's experiences and the structures of their awareness. Learning depends on whether or not the learners are aware of the critical aspects of the learning objects. What is experienced depends on what the learners discern,

Figure 8.2
A dynamic representation of the second paragraph

First Sentence						**Second Sentence**	**Third Sentence**	**Fourth Sentence**
Reading	Enacting					e / s	e / s	e / s
	Question 3 Moral	Question 1 & 2 Explanatory						
	“Repay”	“Sharp-p ointed”	“Flat”	“Worms”	“Fish”	“Diving”		
	(s / e)	(s / w / e)	(s / w / e)	(s / w / i)	(s / w)	(s / e)		

Figure 8.3
Part/whole as a higher order of variation

Story	**Parts**				**whole (1)**		**whole (2)**		**whole (3)**	
Paragraph	par.1		Par.2							
Pairs of students	1st pair		2nd pair				3rd pair		4th pair	
Acts	reading	Enacting	reading	Enacting	reading	enacting	reading	enacting	reading	enacting

Figure 8.4: The six types of variation

Story (paragraph)	parts par.1									
Pairs of students	1st pair									
Acts	reading	enacting								
(sentence)		sen.1	sen.2	sen.3						
(words)		play	Hungry	sharp-pointed						
Forms of the word		s(iu/fe)/w	s/w	s/w/e						
Versions of the spoken		iu/fe								
Moral/explanatory										

Story (paragraph)	parts par.2									
Pairs of students	2nd pair									
Acts	reading	enacting			reading	enacting	reading	enacting	reading	enacting
(sentence)	sen.1				sen.2		sen.3		sen.4	
(words)		repay	sharp-pointed	flat	worms	fish	diving			
Forms of the word		s/e	s/w/e	s/w/e	s/i/w	s/w	s/e			whole (1)
Versions of the spoken		question 3	questions 1&2							
Moral/explanatory										

Story (paragraph)	whole (2)			whole (3)	
Pairs of students	3rd pair			4th pair	
Acts	reading	enacting		Reading	enacting
(sentence)					
(words)					
Forms of the word					
Versions of the spoken					
Moral/explanatory					

Keys:
s(iu/fe)/w: spoken (informal utterance / formal enunciation) / written
s/w/e: spoken / written / enactive   s/i/w: spoken / iconic / written

and this in turn depends on the variation they are responding to. As a result, the pattern of variation inherent in the learning environment is critical to what can possibly be learnt.

We applied this framework to our study of a Chinese lesson in detail. Whilst bringing the readers through the major events in the Chinese lesson via our windows, we attempted to reveal the dimensions of variation. Our analysis described how the variations were constituted in the space of learning. In the lesson we described, the teacher successfully engaged his students actively in enacting the story. He also probed into both the surface and deep meaning of the text, whilst maintaining a high degree of control. He determined when the students should read and enact the passage, and when the students should focus on words, sentences, paragraphs or the whole story. He asked questions which were prescribed in the examination paper. Although the lesson contained activities (enacting texts) which may not be commonly found in a Chinese lesson, it demonstrated the potential learning space in which the teacher takes a dominating role.

It is not our purpose to argue for a particular arrangement for learning in the classroom. However, with our framework, did enable us to observe how the teacher had created different dimensions of variation pertinent to the understanding of the meaning of the parts and the whole of the story, and those specific to the linguistic nature of the language. The teacher carried out the lesson as if he had an invisible script. He choreographed what the students were supposed to perform. In spite of the students acting spontaneously, the teacher constructed meanings upon their participation and managed to expose the students to the variations of the critical dimensions related to the objects of learning. In this way, the students' enactment of the story and their responses are seen to be an important part in the construction of the space of learning. The lesson is reminiscent of a "dance" in which the learners and objects of learning form a melody. As such, the communication itself shows evidence of this interactive dance (Fosnot, 1993). It is indeed fascinating to see that such an arrangement is possible and actually exists in a whole-class teaching environment. Although we have not looked into what the students actually learned in this lesson, there is evidence to refute the claim that teacher-centred whole class teaching must imply the transmission of knowledge and little student involvement. The potential of the space of learning created could be very powerful. The close relationship between the space of variation constituted in the classroom and what students learn has been demonstrated in other studies (e.g., Rovio-Johansson, 1999).

Now, we may have demonstrated that full teacher control is not irreconcilable with active students, but it is hardly a unique finding. And as we have not looked at learning outcomes, on what grounds could we possibly argue that what this particular teacher does really "makes a difference"? And on what grounds could we possibly argue that what this teacher does actually points to the solution of "the paradox of the Chinese teacher"?

Our line of argument has necessarily to be indirect and tentative, having a conjecture rather than a conclusion as its trajectory.

Using the TIMSS-video study (Stigler & Hiebert, 1999) and various reports on Chinese classrooms (Stevenson & Stigler, 1992; Cortazzi & Jin, this volume, etc.) Marton (2000) argues that the most important difference between Chinese and Japanese classes on the one hand and classes in the U.S., on the other hand, which gives rise to the dramatic differences in the students' achievements in mathematics, is the difference in the pattern of variation. The Chinese and Japanese mathematics classes are, as a rule, organized around one complex problem, or in other words, "the problem of the day". The students are trying to find solutions and they are doing it in different ways. Different methods for solution are subsequently compared and the students' attention is drawn to different aspects of the problem. In a typical American mathematics class the teacher frequently introduces a particular method for solving a particular kind of problem and the students have to practice that method on a substantial number of different but similar problems. Chinese and Japanese students learn to do *different things* (finding different solutions, focusing on different aspects) to *the same thing* ("the problem of the day") while American students learn to do *the same thing* (applying the same method of solution) to *different things* (the problems they keep practicing on). There is, of course, a higher degree of complexity, a more advanced mathematical content in the former case.

We can find similar patterns of variation in other disciplinary subjects too, when a lesson is organized around a coherent text, frequently a narrative, as was the case with the lesson analysed in this chapter. We can also see that the different levels of the text were dealt with simultaneously (they were embedded in each other and varied at the same time). The text, the paragraphs, the sentences, the words were dealt with differently. The object was the same and the acts (writing, saying, enacting) varied, instead of applying the same act to different objects. *Different things* were done to *the same thing*, instead of doing *the same thing* to *different things*.

Differences in the pattern of variation cannot only be found between different cultures, but also within the same culture. Lo and Chik (manuscript) have shown recently the extent to which different levels of the text are dealt with simultaneously, and the extent to which objects are superimposed acts ("doing different things with the same thing") in Chinese was closely related to the quality of what the students gained from the lessons.

We have tried to make a culturally characteristic and powerful pattern of teaching visible. And we have tried to exemplify a way of looking at teaching. The paradox of the Chinese teacher we may not have solved fully. Some, however, would argue that there was no paradox to begin with.

Acknowledgements

This research was funded by the Standing Committee on Language Education and Research (SCOLAR) whose support we gratefully acknowledge.

REFERENCES

Biggs, J.B. (1996). (Ed.) *Western Misperceptions of the Confucian-Heritage*

Learning Culture. In D.A. Watkins & J.B. Biggs (Eds.), *The Chinese Learner: Cultural, Psychological, and Contextual Influences.* Hong Kong / Melbourne: Comparative Education Research Centre, The University of Hong Kong / Australian Council for Educational Research, 45-67.

Carlgren, I. & Marton, F. (forthcoming). *Lärare av I morgon* (Teachers of tomorrow). Stockholm: Lära förlaget.

Cleverley, John (1991). *The Schooling of China.* Sydney: Allen & Unwin Pty Ltd.

Cortazzi, M. (1998). Learning from Asian Lessons: Cultural Experience and Classroom Talk. *Education 3 to 13,* 26(2), 42-49.

Fosnot, C.T. (1993). Rethinking Science Education: A Defense of Piagetian Constructivism. *Journal of Research in Science Teaching,* 30(9), 1189-1201.

Gardner, H. (1989). *To Open Minds.* New York: Basic Books.

Gurwitsch, A. (1964). *The Field of Consciousness.* Pittsburgh: Duquesne University Press.

Heinig, R.B. (1998). *Creative Drama for the Classroom Teacher.* (3rd edition). New Jersey: Prentice Hall.

Johansson, B., Marton, F. & Svensson, L. (1985). An Approach to Describing Learning as a Change between Qualitatively Different Conceptions. In A.L. Pines & T.H. West (Eds.), *Cognitive Structure and Conceptual Change.* New York: Academic Press, pp.233-257.

Ko, P.Y., (1999). The Professional Development of an Expert Teacher in China. Paper presented at the Comparative and International Development Education Center at OISE/UT, April.

Law, N. (Ed.) (1996). *Science and Mathematics Achievements at the Junior Secondary Level in Hong Kong. A Summary Report for Hong Kong in the Third International Mathematics and Science Study (TIMSS).* Hong Kong: TIMSS Hong Kong Study Centre, The University of Hong Kong.

Law, N. (Ed.) (1997). *Science and Mathematics Achievements at the Mid-primary level in Hong Kong. A summary Report for Hong Kong in the Third International Mathematics and Science Study (TIMSS).* Hong Kong: TIMSS Hong Kong Study Centre, The University of Hong Kong.

Ma, L. (1999). *Knowing and Teaching Elementary Mathematics: Teachers' Understanding of Fundamental Mathematics in China and the United States.* Mahwah, NJ: Lawrence Erlbaum Associates.

Marton, F. & Booth, S. (1997). *Learning and Awareness.* Mahwah, NJ: Lawrence Erlbaum Associates.

Marton, F. & Bowden, J. (1998). *The University of Learning.* London: Kogan Page.

Marton, F. (1981). Phenomenography – Describing Conceptions of the World Around Us. *Instructional Science,* 10, 177-200.

Marton, F. (1993). Phenomenogrpahy. In T. Husén & T.N. Postlethwaite (Eds.), *The International Encyclopedia of Education.* (2nd edition). Oxford: Pergamon Press, pp.4424-4429.

Marton, F. (2000). Some Critical Features of Learning Environments. Invited Keynote Address, The Bank of Sweden Tercentenary Symposium on Cognition, Education, and Communication Technology. Stockholm, Sweden.

March 30 - April 1.
Marton, F., Beaty, E. & Dall'Alba, G. (1993). Conceptions of Learning. *International Journal of Educational Research*, 19, 277-300.
Mok, I.A.C. & Ko, P.Y. (2000). Beyond Labels – Teacher-centred and Student Activities. In Adamson, B., Kwan, T. & Chan, K.K (Eds.), *Changing the Curriculum: The Impact of Reform on Primary Schooling in Hong Kong*. Hong Kong: Hong Kong University Press.
Morris, P., Adamson, R., Au, M.L., Chan, K.K., Chan, W.Y., Ko, P.K., Lai Au-yeung, W., Lo, M.L., Morrris, E., Ng, F.P., Ng, Y.Y., Wong, W.M. & Wong, P.H. (1996). *Target Oriented Curriculum Evaluation Project (Interim Report)*, Hong Kong: INSTEP, Faculty of Education, The University of Hong Kong.
Neuman, D. (1987). *The Origin of Arithmetic Skills: A Phenomenographic Approach*. Goteborg: Acta Universitatis Gothoburgensis.
Paine, L. (1992). Teaching and Modernization in Contemporary China, In R. Hayhoe (Ed.), *Education and Modernization, the Chinese Experience*. Oxford: Pergamon Press.
Paine, W.L. (1990). The Teacher as Virtuoso: A Chinese Model for Teaching. *Teachers College Record*, 92(1), 49-81.
Reynolds, D. & Farrell, S. (1996). Worlds Apart? *A Review of International Surveys of Educational Achievement Involving England*. London: Office for Standards in Education, HMSO.
Rovio-Johansson, A. (1999). *Being Good at Teaching. Exploring Different Ways of Handling the Same Subject in Higher Education*. Göteborg: Acta Universitatis Gothoburgensis.
Runesson, U. (1999). *The Pedagogy of Variation: Different Ways of Handling a Mathematical Topic*. Variationens pedagogik: Skilda sätt att behandla ett matematiskt innehåll. Göteborg: Acta Universitatis Gothoburgensis.
Säljö, R. (1982). *Learning and Understanding: A Study of Differences in Constructing Meaning from a Text*. Göteborg: Acta Universitatis Gothoburgensis.
Stevenson, H.W. & Stigler, J.W. (1992). *The Learning Gap*. New York: Summit Books.
Stevenson, W. & Lee, S. (1997) The East Asian Version of Whole-class Teaching, In W.K. Cumming & P.G. Altback (Eds.), *The Challenge of Eastern Asian Education*. Albany: State University of New York Press.
Stigler, J.W. & Hiebert, J. (1999). *The Teaching Gap*. New York: The Free Press.
Visiting Panel (1982). *A Perspective on Education in Hong Kong*. Hong Kong: Government Printer.

9

Promoting Learning and Understanding through Constructivist Approaches for Chinese Learners

Carol K.K. Chan

The idea that learning involves knowledge construction rather than knowledge reception has now been widely accepted (Greeno, Collins & Resnick, 1996; Bereiter & Scardamalia, 1989). Theoretical notions such as self-regulated learning (Schunk & Zimmermann, 1994); mindfulness (Salomon & Globerson, 1987); metacognition (Brown, Bransford, Ferrara & Campione, 1983); self-explanation (Chi, de Leeuw, Chiu & LaVancher, 1994); constructive activity (Chan, Burtis, Bereiter & Scardamalia, 1992) and knowledge building (Bereiter & Scardamalia, 1993; Chan, Burtis & Bereiter, 1997) have similarly indicated the importance of students' active roles in their own knowledge construction. The goal of this paper is to examine the effects of Western developed principles of constructivist instruction on the learning and understanding of Chinese students.

Parallel with cognitive research on student learning emphasizing learners' constructive roles (Biggs, 1993) is the gradual shift in paradigms of instruction (Greeno et al., 1996). Whereas the behaviorist approach was seen to be useful for building up sub-skills and basic knowledge, increased attention has now been given to constructivist and social-constructivist approaches emphasizing *teaching for understanding*. It needs to be noted that constructivism is more a meta-theory than a particular learning theory or a specific teaching method. Important variations also exist within constructivism. Some researchers have argued that cognition is socially situated and tied to contexts, whereas others see individual learning as paramount, and social process only as a contributing factor to individual learning. Some researchers have also extended the notion of community of practice (Lave & Wenger, 1991) to examining how knowledge is socially constructed in communities of learners (Brown, 1997; Collins, Brown & Newman, 1989).

Despite considerable differences, some central tenets of constructivist learning may be identified: Learning is not the accretion of bits of information; it involves meaning making and knowledge transformation as learners construct their new and revised understandings integrating new information with existing prior knowledge. Drawing on cognitive research on student learning, Resnick (1989) has identified three key principles bridging learning with instruction. These three principles of learning include: (a) Prior Knowledge – Learning is related to what students already know; (b) Strategy – Learning is related to learner strategy; and (c) Social Contexts – Learning is socially constructed. Rather than focusing on quantitative learning emphasizing isolated facts and skills, the goal of constructivist instruction is to develop meaning construction, understanding, and conceptual change. These theoretical notions parallel the constructivist principles advocated for promoting deep learning with additional emphasis given to motives and intentions (Biggs & Moore, 1993).

Different strands of research have provided evidence indicating how the principles of constructivist learning—prior knowledge, learner strategy, and collaboration – can promote meaningful understanding. Regarding the roles of *prior knowledge*, educational research in the past few decades has provided substantial evidence indicating the pervasive roles of prior or alternative conceptions in student learning (Alexander, 1996; Pfundt & Duit, 1991). Instructional research involves identifying students' prior conceptions and confronting them with scientific ones so students can experience cognitive conflict and conceptual change (Hewson & Thorley, 1989). Constructivist teaching emphasizing the understanding of students' prior conceptions and knowledge restructuring has become a major theme in science education (Fensham, 1994).

The important roles of *learner strategy* are well supported in the large body of instructional research on metacognition (Brown et al., 1983), self-explanation (Chi et al., 1994), and cognitive strategy instruction (Pressley, 1990) conducted in various domains. One exemplary instructional program for promoting literacy is called reciprocal teaching (Palincsar & Brown, 1984; Rosenshine & Meister, 1994) in which students take turns being teachers developing strategies employed by expert readers and taking increased responsibility over their own learning. Caution needs to be taken with respect to simplistic distinction between student-centred versus teacher-directed teaching. Cognitive strategy instruction such as reciprocal teaching is premised on principles of *direct instruction* according to which teachers demonstrate, model and provide scaffolding to help students construct their understanding. Another distinctive feature of constructivist-based instruction is that it goes beyond improving students' academic attainments as measured on achievement tests. It involves helping students to develop deep learning strategies for reading that could be transferred to other contexts together with some qualitative changes in conceptions about reading (Anderson, Chan & Henne, 1995).

Considerable research attention has been given to learning as *social construction of knowledge* (Brown, Collins & Duguid, 1989). There are different theoretical positions on social cognition, and this chapter takes a cognitive perspective emphasizing the roles of increased student interactions in promoting learning. As students interact, the collaborative processes of *articulation, conflict*, and *meaning negotiation* provide scaffolding effects to foster student understanding. Key research relevant to the present investigation includes cognitive apprenticeship (Collins, Brown & Newman, 1989), communities of learners (Brown, 1997), and collaborative knowledge building in computer-supported intentional learning environments (Scardamalia & Bereiter, 1994). As students work together, they acquire the practices of a learning community as they help each other pursue deeper understanding. Whereas the importance of peer learning has long been recognized, distinctive features of collaborative knowledge building pertain to the emphasis on the *process* of collaborative problem-centred inquiry and advances of *collective understanding* over and above individual learning outcomes.

The present research considers constructivist instruction as encompassing both constructivist and social-constructivist views of learning emphasizing both individual and collective knowledge construction. This chapter addresses the question of whether constructivist approaches are relevant for Chinese students and teachers. Three classroom studies were designed incorporating constructivist principles to investigate how student learning could be promoted in Hong Kong classrooms.

The Hong Kong Context

To date, the great majority of the research supporting constructivist approaches comes from research in Western classrooms. Do constructivist approaches work for Chinese students and teachers? Some researchers have cautioned that imported Western approaches need to be examined in relation to cultural contexts and characteristics of learners (Boekaerts, 1998). Traditionally, the Chinese teacher is viewed as a respected figure with all wisdom, and the idea that students should control their own learning might contradict such cultural beliefs. An effective Chinese teacher is often viewed as someone who provides clear guidance for students rather than letting them flounder when exploring for themselves. There is also the general belief that Chinese teachers brought up in a system emphasizing didactic teaching might not be accustomed to constructivist instruction. Some might even argue that the lack of success of the Target Oriented Curriculum (TOC) indicates that imported Western approaches just would not work in Chinese contexts.

Different views could be identified regarding the applicability of Western approaches for different cultural groups. One extreme is to endorse the Western approach indiscriminately and the other is to reject its relevance completely. Whereas there might be some general principles of how human learn, how social and cultural factors affect the teaching and learning processes need to be considered. As argued by Biggs (1999), principles of good teaching might exist across cultures although educators need to be sensitive to the teaching contexts and the characteristics of the learners involved.

Increased interest has now been given to examining teachers' conceptions and their relations with their practices in the classrooms. For centuries, the Western tradition has emphasized learning as an inquiry into the nature of phenomena. On the other hand, for Chinese thinkers and teachers, the moral and ethical dimensions have been emphasized. Specifically, learning is to contribute to the changing of persons and improvement of the collective welfare of society. Whereas Western thinkers explored the question of where knowledge comes from, Chinese philosophers examined the problem of how to become a better person. Research on Chinese teachers' conceptions of teaching has shown the moral and personal dimensions emphasizing the roles of teachers in guiding student development (see Chapters 2 and 6).

Despite such emphasis on moral and ethical aspects among the Chinese teachers, it does not follow that Chinese teachers do not embrace other views. Research on conceptions of teaching conducted among Mainland and Hong Kong teachers has both identified their views of teaching as facilitation of learning that parallel the constructivist views (see Chapters 2 and 11). There are also some preliminary findings indicating that Chinese teachers' conceptions of teaching can be changed from transmission to facilitation views (see Chapter 12). It is now recognized that conceptions are not fixed and they may vary across different contexts. Hence, the Chinese teachers' emphasis on moral and ethical dimensions does not necessarily contradict constructivist conceptions of learning. In other words, while emphasizing the importance of guidance or even character formation in the affective domain, Chinese teachers could also hold views of teaching as facilitating learning.

Although it is generally believed that Chinese teachers tend to use didactic approaches, it is argued that such approaches might stem from contextual constraints in Hong Kong classrooms where teachers and students need to cope with examination pressures. One might argue that the traditional Confucian teaching also encompasses aspects of thinking, understanding, reflection, and modeling (Lee, 1996). Interestingly, both the great teachers in the West and East, Socrates and Confucius, used questioning to probe and extend their students' understanding. There could be different manifestations of how student learning is taken into consideration by Western and Chinese teachers. Nevertheless, the transmission approach commonly observed in Hong Kong classrooms does not typify the teaching of great Chinese teachers.

Questions also have been raised regarding the characteristics of learners in relation to constructivist instruction. Some intriguing questions exist with respect to the performance of Chinese students, sometimes called the paradox of the Chinese learner (Watkins & Biggs, 1996). One question is how students perceived as using rote-memorization can perform so well. This problem is addressed by Marton, Dall'Alba & Tse (1996) who distinguished between rote memorization and deep memorization. The other question is how students can perform so well despite the unfavorable classroom environments (Biggs, 1996a). Explanations such as attribution patterns, parental expectations, cultural beliefs, and economic structures can certainly be invoked to explain the performance of Chinese students. What is relevant here is the idea that Chinese learners are not predisposed to be surface or deep learners but that their *approach to learning varies as a function of the learning environment.* Deep learning can be interpreted as how Chinese students seek cues, make meaning, and adapt their learning to succeed (Biggs, 1996a). For instance, the differences in writing systems might call for more emphasis on memorization at earlier years; and the emphasis on examinations might have led Chinese students to develop certain strategies such as 'deep-memorization' to deal with the perceived requirements of the curriculum. Models of classroom learning also suggest that interactions exist among student characteristics, processes of learning, and contextual factors influence learning outcomes (Biggs & Moore, 1993).

If it is argued that Chinese learners are not necessarily predisposed to specific kinds of learning approaches, and that learning approaches develop as responses to different environments, it would be important to investigate whether constructivist learning environments would affect student learning in Chinese contexts. When provided with constructivist learning environments, would Chinese students respond to such approaches? If students are indeed culturally predisposed to passive or rote learning, it is probable that constructivist-based instruction would not work. Conversely, if students' responses vary as a function of the learning contexts, constructivist approaches might similarly facilitate the development of deeper learning among Chinese students. Instructional studies would be important as they would provide ways to investigate the interactions among learning environments, approaches to learning, and learning performance.

Despite increased research interest given to issues related to Chinese learners, much less attention has been given to instructional approaches for promoting learning. Can Chinese learners benefit from constructivist instruction? Are they predisposed to certain learning approaches or do approaches vary as a function of the learning environments? The goal of this chapter was to investigate the effects of constructivist instruction on students' learning and understanding, and to consider the relevance of constructivist instruction for Chinese students and teachers.

Instructional Studies

Three instructional studies were designed based on constructivist principles of learning relating to prior knowledge, learner strategy, and student interactions. Each study focused on one of the three principles although all three were incorporated to different extents. These studies were also selected because participants were recruited from different levels of schooling including both student and teacher participants.

Study One – Cognitive Conflict and Conceptual Change

Background. Study One examined the roles of prior knowledge and cognitive conflict in promoting students' conceptual change. Research in science education has indicated the importance of examining students' prior conceptions (Fensham, 1994). This study extended research on cognitive conflict incorporating elements of metacognition to help students reflect on their understanding (Chong & Chan, 2000).

Participants. Eighty Form-Four students (equivalent to Grade 10), thirty-nine from experimental and forty-one from comparison classes participated in the study. Students were drawn from a secondary school with students of average ability (Band 2 and 3). Students from both science classes were of similar academic levels.

Instructional Program. The domain of investigation was particle theory in physics and the instructional program lasted for eight sessions. Instruction was designed using constructivist principles that capitalize on understanding students' prior conceptions and confronting their prior beliefs with new information. Students were also asked to engage in metacognitive activities. The model of instruction included several components:

Becoming aware of own conceptions. Students were presented with a problem pertaining to the scientific experiment (e.g. What would happen to the blade when you put it on the water?) and they were asked to predict and explain. Focus was placed on helping students identify and reflect on their own conceptions. They were then asked to share their predictions and compare alternative perspectives.

Confrontation of conceptions. Students conducted the science experiments and they were confronted with the experimental results. The focus of this component was to students with conceptual conflict to help them engage in deeper processing.

Co-construction of explanations. Students were provided with scaffolding support to help them construct explanations to account for the experimental results. Focus was placed on the "whys" underlying the observations. Students worked together to resolve conflicts and examined different explanations.

Fostering metacognition. Students reflected and inquired about their own learning as they extended their understanding to other contexts. They submitted learning journals that included the following: (i) identify what they think they have learned; (ii) formulate problems related to the topics; and (iii) construct examples to link what they have learned to new situations in everyday life. In addition to exposing students to cognitive conflict and different contexts, they were provided with opportunities to reflect on their own understanding; to make connections between scientific concepts and daily life; and to pursue additional problems and questions.

Measures. The study was conducted using a quasi-experimental pretest-posttest design with two intact classes. The comparison class learned the same topic using the regular classroom approach within the same time frame. Three key measures were included: (a) memory recall questions using multiple-choice formats; (b) examination-questions taken from The Hong Kong Certificate of Education Examination (HKCEE); and (c) conceptual-change problems designed to examine students' misconceptions and qualitative understanding. The first two were quantitative and the third qualitative measures. To examine learning strategies, students' learning journals were collected and analyzed qualitatively.

Findings. Table 9.1 shows the pretest and posttest scores of the experimental and comparison students on memory recall, HKCEE, and conceptual-change questions. Analyses of covariance showed significant differences on conceptual change questions, $F(1, 77) = 49.05$, $p<.001$ favoring the experimental students. Differences on both quantitative measures including recall and examination questions were not statistically significant. In addition to between group analyses, within-group analyses were conducted to examine whether student engagement in deep learning activities was related to subsequent gains. As expected, metacognitive scores was related to academic ability measured by first-term examination results ($r = .59$, $p<.01$). More importantly, metacognitive scores were also correlated with pre-posttest gain scores on conceptual-change measures ($r = .43$, $p<.01$) after partialling out the effects of ability. These results indicated that (a) Significant effects were obtained on qualitative, conceptual-change learning scores; (b) Experimental students were shown to engage in deep learning activities including construction of explanations and reflective understanding; and (c) Student engagement in metacognitive activities was related to gains in qualitative learning measures.

Table 9.1
Mean Pre- and Posttest Scores on Recall, School Certificate Examination, and Conceptual-Change Questions for Groups (standard deviations in brackets)

Question Types	Experimental		Comparison	
	Pretest	Posttest	Pretest	Posttest
Recall	42.56 (27.21)	52.82 (20.77)	43.90 (23.76)	54.15 (18.02)
Examination	28.85 (21.10)	37.82 (28.02)	29.88 (30.22)	42.68 (29.18)
Conceptual Change	22.19 (14.45)	55.52 (17.20)	22.80 (12.10)	35.10 (12.73)

In this study, care was taken to avoid teaching to the tests, and the pre-posttest instruments were carefully piloted. Comparison students obtained similar gains to those of experimental students on other measures suggesting they were not unmotivated in learning. Interestingly, whereas comparison students could answer the examination questions, they still held alternative conceptions. Experimental students made gains on both quantitative and qualitative measures. This conceptual-change study for Chinese secondary students parallels research using a conceptual-change approach on changing university teachers' conceptions (see Chapter 12).

Study Two – Learning Portfolio and Conceptions of Learning

Background. Whereas the Study One focused on examining students' prior conceptions, this study emphasized another key constructivist principle— maximizing learner activity. The effects of learner strategy on promoting student learning through portfolio assessment were investigated (Lee, 1998).

Participants. Twenty-nine Form Six students (Equivalent to Grade 12) in a high-banding school attending the Advanced Level geography course participated. As with most secondary schools in Hong Kong, there is only one class of students taking geography at Form Six level.

Instructional Program. The instructional approach of learning portfolio was conducted in a regular classroom from October to May. As an integral part of the school curriculum, a number of different geography topics were included in accordance with the Advanced Level examination syllabus. Students were asked to submit a learning portfolio as part of the assessment scheme. As well, learning portfolio was also the vehicle of instruction as classroom teaching often centred around students' learning experiences reflected in the learning entries. Because students were encouraged to take increased responsibility over their learning, the objectives of the portfolio assessment program were made explicit to the students. Key components of the program were described as follows:

Setting own learning goals. Students were asked to develop a learning portfolio consisting of items that documented what they had learned. They could submit learning items including learning diaries, concept maps, self-generated questions, newspaper cuttings, projects, self-designed experiments, and any items they considered relevant. Unlike traditional assessment that specified what student had to produce, the learning portfolio system aimed to help students take increased responsibility over their own learning. There were no specified number of assignments; quantity and quality varied as students determined how they would set their own learning goals and monitor their own learning.

Deep processing and knowledge organization. Different learning entries were designed to maximize deep processing. For example, when students wrote a learning diary on learning ideas and questions, they were provided with opportunities to reflect on what they knew, make connections between ideas, connect prior knowledge with new information, and inquire into knowledge problems. When students produced concept maps, they would maximize knowledge structure and make connections among isolated pieces of information. These student-generated concept maps also helped reveal students' alternative conceptions that formed the basis for discussion and inquiry. Newspaper cuttings with explanations helped students to examine how phenomena described in the texts actually looked like in different contexts.

Modeling, explanation, and scaffolding. Providing meaningful learning tasks is important but it is not sufficient. It would be wonderful if students could automatically produce deep ideas and questions; in fact, they need to be taught how to do so. In this program, the teacher modelled, explained, and demonstrated to students how to produce learning diaries and concept maps. Furthermore, a powerful notion of learning is to provide students with varied examples that extend their levels of understanding. Students were shown examples of portfolio entries produced by other students. They then discussed what they thought about these learning entries and how these examples demonstrated different levels of understanding. Exposure to varied examples and discussion was shown to provide powerful scaffolding effects as students readily shifted to produce deeper learning entries after the group discussion.

Measures. Participants were individually interviewed at the beginning and end of the instructional program on conceptions of learning and learning strategies.

During the course of instruction, students were asked to submit their portfolio once a month to monitor the progress of their learning. Students' learning entries were analyzed to examine strategies employed for integrating new materials. Other measures also included students' examination results. Because this project focused on qualitative learning, it was of interest to examine whether students would fall behind in examination questions as they had spent time working on portfolios instead of practicing model essays.

Findings. Qualitative analyses indicated that different kinds of conceptions about learning could be observed, and they seemed consistent with those reflecting quantitative, institutional, and qualitative views (Biggs & Moore, 1993). Some students believed that learning is a matter of knowing more and remembering information; others focused on obtaining good grades in examinations. Some students, however, observed learning as relating to thinking and understanding. Multiple conceptions were also observed among students who seemed to hold different conceptions as they responded to different contexts. Different levels of learning strategies were also identified ranging from surface to deeper approaches to processing information.

Students' conceptions of learning and learning strategies were given scores ranging from quantitative to qualitative understanding on a 3-point and 4-point scale respectively. The mean scores (standard deviations in brackets) increased from 1.67 (.44) to 2.41 (.46) for conceptions of learning, and 1.59 (.59) to 3.01 (.74) for learning strategies from October to May. Statistical analyses showed significant increases in qualitative conceptions, $t(27) = 7.83$, $p<.001$; and learning strategies, $t(27) = 12.27$, $p<.001$. Students' engagement in deep learning activities reflected in portfolio entries was significantly correlated with gains in learning strategies ($r = 0.36$, $p<.05$). In terms of quantitative measures, students' examination results were comparable to results obtained by students in past years. As the examination questions and the admission criteria of Form Six students based on HKCEE results were similar across years, the teacher noted that this cohort performed just as well as other cohorts.

Results of the portfolio study indicated the following: (a) Students could be taught to engage in deep processing activities reflected in portfolio entries; (b) Students made shifts towards more sophisticated conceptions of learning and learning strategies; and (c) Gains in learning strategies were related to depth of processing reflected in their learning portfolios. Increased interest has now been given to portfolio assessment in educational settings; this study provided some evidence suggesting that portfolio could help students develop different ways of thinking about learning.

Study Three – Computer-Supported Collaborative Learning

Background. This study on computer-supported learning was designed focusing on the principles of collaborative learning. Specifically, the notions of collaborative knowledge building were employed (Scardamalia & Bereiter, 1994). With the advent of the knowledge-based era, new goals of schooling would include helping students work as knowledge building communities posing problems, seeking out information, constructing explanations, and solving problems collaboratively (Bereiter & Scardamalia, 1996). Whereas notions of constructivist views are often espoused in university courses, there have been few efforts in developing constructivist instruction for teachers. This study sought to examine collaborative learning among teacher participants and to investigate relations between collaborative learning and qualitative understanding (Chan, 1999).

Participants. Twenty-three experienced teachers attending a graduate level course in educational psychology participated in the study. There were 8 male and 15 female teachers. Their teaching experience ranged from 4 to 16 years.

Instructional Program. The context of the study was a twelve-week graduate course in educational psychology. Key components of the program are outlined as follows:

Deep processing. Computer supported collaborative learning was integrated with regular teaching. Each week, participants produced computer-based learning notes based on course readings and discussions. There was no specific number of notes they needed to write; students determined how often they produced learning entries. Similar to the program with learning portfolio described earlier, participants were encouraged to process the materials more deeply and reflect on their understanding.

Models of understanding. Whereas learning entries in the portfolio study were primarily read by the teacher, the computer network provided opportunities for participants to find out what others thought about the course materials. Students were asked to post their learning notes on the computer network for others to browse and comment on. The computer learning environments made it possible for students to have access to different models of understanding. Exposure to varied conceptions and perspectives helped students to broaden their scope of reflection. Examining more sophisticated views also provided scaffolding effects to enrich their understanding.

Collaborative inquiry. As participants represent and communicate their ideas on the computer network, they have to articulate what they believe. Writing out what they believe helps students to clarify their ideas, and help them become more aware of their own conceptions. As well, as different ideas are now being represented on the computer network, students could comment on these ideas elaborating, refuting, extending, or refining them. They could also query and challenge certain ideas or take them up for further inquiry. Knowledge was now represented as an object of inquiry in this knowledge building community.

Metacognitive prompts and scaffolding. Although other computer-mediated communication networks also encourage increased student interactions, this program was distinctive because it was designed to maximize metacognition and knowledge building. The teacher-researcher provided scaffolding prompts to help participants engage in knowledge building. Some examples are given as follows: Is there anything interesting or useful you have learned? What are some things you find difficult to understand? Would you agree or disagree with these ideas? How did reading these notes help you think about X and Y? How have you changed your ideas about them? What similar or different views could you identify? What are some key themes in the discussion? These scaffolding prompts were provided, but they were not given as assignment labels so students would not turn knowledge building into assignments. These prompts also provided the contexts promoting collaborative problem-centred inquiry.

Measures. Participants were asked to write what they thought about teaching and learning at the beginning and end of the course. As part of the assignments, they were asked to produce a summary statement to explain what they had learned. These summary statements provided further information about their conceptual understanding. Students' learning processes and strategies were examined by analyzing their computer notes. As well, qualitative analyses were undertaken to identify collaborative knowledge building episodes on the computer network.

Findings. Quantitative analyses. Participants' responses to the open-ended questions and summary statements were examined for transmission versus constructivist views of teaching and learning. Protocols were blind rated and participants were classified into three groups: There were 7 in high, 8 in medium, and 8 in low conceptual-growth groups. Computer notes were divided into those reflecting individual versus collaborative learning; and they were all scored using a 5-point scale reflecting surface to deep meaning-making activities (Chan et al., 1992).

Table 9.2 shows student engagement in learning on the computer network for the high-gain, medium-gain, and low-gain groups. Analyses were conducted to examine whether students who made different conceptual gains differed in their learning activities. For the total number of computer notes, there were no significant group differences. Two kinds of computer notes were included: (a) individual notes, and (b) collaborative notes that built on or extended others' computer notes. There were no differences in the number of individual notes among groups. However, multiple comparison indicated that significant differences were obtained in the number of collaborative notes favoring high-gain over low-gain groups ($p<.001$), and medium-gain over low-gain groups ($p<.013$).

As noted before, all computer notes were scored using a 5-point scale and they were then categorized into high (4-5) and low quality (1-3) notes. Significant differences were obtained on the number of high-quality collaborative notes favoring high-gain over medium-gain groups ($p<.002$) and high-gain over low-gain groups ($p<.001$). Finally, significant differences were obtained on quality rating favoring high-gain over medium-gain groups ($p<.015$), and high-gain over low-gain groups ($p<.003$). These results indicated that students with different conceptual gains did not differ in the total number of computer notes or the number of individual notes. However, differences were obtained on the number of collaborative notes and the overall quality of computer notes. Taken together, these findings suggest that participants with more conceptual growth were more engaged in deep collaborative learning on the computer network.

Table 9.2
Mean Frequency and Quality of Computer Notes ratings for High, Medium, and Low-Gain Groups (standard deviations in parentheses)

	High-Gain Group	Medium-Gain Group	Low-Gain Group
<u>Frequencies</u>			
Computer Notes	13.0 (5.2)	14.1 (9.2)	6.0 (5.6)
Individual Notes (Low-Level)	3.4 (2.2)	7.2 (6.0)	5.6 (5.3)
Individual Notes (High-Level)	1.3 (1.7)	1.7 (2.0)	0.0 (0.0)
Collaborative Notes (Low-Level)	3.2 (3.0)	4.0 (1.7)	0.4 (0.7)
Collaborative Notes (High-Level)	5.1 (2.0)	1.2 (2.0)	0.0 (0.0)
<u>Quality Rating</u>			
Computer Notes	3.6 (0.5)	2.9 (0.4)	2.6 (0.4)

Qualitative analyses. The quantitative findings indicate that students who made more conceptual gains were more involved in collaborative learning. Qualitative analyses were conducted to examine how computer-based discussion might help students to develop deeper understanding. The following example illustrates how students worked together to co-construct deep understanding.

The first computer note was initiated by a teacher as she related to some personal readings and pondered the relations between philosophers and schoolteachers. In her note entitled "Constructivism: schoolteachers vs. philosophers", the teacher wrote:

> *In the book Sophie's World, the 14-year-old Norwegian schoolgirl Sophie says, "We don't learn anything there (school). The difference between schoolteachers and philosophers is that schoolteachers think they know a lot of stuff [that] they try to force down the throats [of pupils]. Philosophers try to figure things out together with the pupils."* ... [Student #12]

This is quite an interesting note as she presented a provocative situation. This initial question then elicited a query from another teacher whose note helped steer the discourse into a deeper direction. This teacher seemed to be pondering the relations between teachers and philosophers further and contributed her piece of knowledge:

> *As to my knowledge, most of the recent education and learning theories had their origin in ancient great philosophers, like Socrates and Aristotle...and of course the more recent one Dewey.* [Student #19]

This comment was built on or extended by another student who contributed his idea. Instead of merely adding a piece of information, he attempted to construct and deepen his understanding of constructivism as he posed some rather intriguing questions:

> *Out of the Socratic dialogue, contradictions were identified and [need] to be resolved. In this process, students came to a deeper understanding. I think Socrates was a constructivist teacher. Do you agree with me?* Then he went on and wrote:

> *How about the great Eastern philosophers/teachers: Confucius and Lao Tse? Were they constructivist teachers? And what about him who is considered the greatest teacher by Christians, Jesus Christ? I thought he taught using parables, and is this a constructivist approach?* [Student #6]

The inquiry about philosophy and constructivism was continued and collective knowledge was improved as other ideas were brought into the discourse. The inquiry questions led to the following response:

> *You asked, "How about the Eastern philosophers/teachers: Confucius and Lao Tse?" Well, to me as a Chinese teacher, it is a lovely question to explore....*

> *In Analects II.15, [Confucius] said, "Seeking knowledge without thinking is labor lost; thinking without seeking knowledge is perilous." I think he believed in deep learning... and reflective thinking which requires a spirit of inquiry and open-minded[ness], was his usual practice in the process of learning...The way he learned directly influenced how he taught....*

> *While I attempt to answer your question, I suddenly think of another question. It seems to me that Eastern and Western philosophers think differently. For example, the western philosophers like to ask questions such as where does knowledge come from? But Eastern philosophers such as Lao Tse and Confucius do not ask such questions. Is this kind of thinking less common in Chinese society? So do we need to change our thinking patterns so we can be more alert in self-monitoring our understanding?* [Student #12]

In discussing what she thought about the Eastern philosophers, this teacher went beyond answering the question to conjecturing about Eastern and Western thinking as she continued to inquire into implications for thinking and learning. In engaging in computer-based discussion, these teachers were pursuing deep learning that went well beyond the contexts of the reading materials as they helped each other extend their scope of understanding.

As shown in the above example, the discourse advanced as participants engaged in inquiry, conjecture, explanation, and more questioning as they pursued for deeper understanding. Whereas there might be some misperceptions that Chinese students do not disagree with others, these participants were well able to agree and disagree; to question and to challenge; thus helping the discourse to advance. The following excerpt from a student's summary statement provided further glimpses of how computer-supported collaborative learning might work to scaffold metacognition and understanding.

> *Like my students, there had been times when I was not clear how to make the most of the course. At the beginning, I put most effort in understanding the readings assigned and my questions generated were aimed at seeking clarification of concepts; mostly unistructural and multistructural in Biggs' terms. Later, as I had a chance to browse through my classmates' [computer] notes, impacted by their abstract thoughts, my scope of thoughts began to extend beyond the assigned readings. This extension enriches my picture of what teaching and learning is [about]. I think this is an example of collaborative learning.* [Student #18]

To summarize, this study suggests the roles of computer-supported learning in enhancing quality learning: (a) Students involved in more collaborative learning activities on computer networks had more conceptual understanding; and (b) Episodes of knowledge building on computer networks could be identified that characterized how knowledge is socially constructed. Whereas there is a great deal of enthusiasm about information technology in university teaching, it needs to be informed by theories of learning. For example, storing information on the web for student access might reflect a transmission mode of teaching if the emphasis is merely placed on delivery of information. This study provides an example of how computer-based teaching designed with constructivist principles might promote quality learning. Such programs might be of particular benefit for teacher education courses as they provide the contexts for teachers to work as members of knowledge building communities seeking to make meanings about teaching and learning as they integrate theory with practice.

Discussion

This chapter examined the effects of constructivist instruction on promoting student learning and understanding. Three instructional programs were designed and their effects on student learning were investigated. These studies are now examined in relation to effects on student learning; principles of effective instruction; and relevance of constructivist instruction for Chinese students.

Effects of Instruction on Student Learning

It is generally recognized that a student's approach to learning is related to learning outcomes (Biggs, 1993; Watkins & Biggs, 1996). Questions arise as to how students can be taught to engage in a deeper approach to learning and understanding. Results of the studies provided some evidence suggesting that constructivist instruction was effective in fostering deep learning with concomitant changes in qualitative understanding. Study One, on cognitive conflict for Form Four students, showed that students in the experimental group outperformed comparison students on qualitative understanding. As well, student engagement in metacognitive activities was correlated with gains in their qualitative understanding, controlling for ability effects. Study Two, on portfolio assessment for Advanced Level students, showed that students moved from quantitative towards qualitative conceptions; they also reported use of deeper strategies. Students' gains in learning strategy were related to their engagement in writing portfolio items. Study Three, on computer-supported learning for teacher participants, indicated that participants who obtained more conceptual understanding outperformed others both on quantity and quality of collaborative learning. Qualitative analyses also provided examples suggesting how deep learning was manifested and enhanced in computer learning environments. Whereas some were engaged in superficial exchange of information, collective knowledge advances were made when participants generated problems of inquiry, formulated conjectures; and constructed explanations. It is important to note that these qualitative gains were not made at the expense of conventional test scores.

The positive effects of these studies are consistent with instructional research promoting conceptual understanding (Greeno et al., 1996). What is important about these instructional studies is that focus was placed on process not products of learning—conceptual change and learning to learn strategies were emphasized. Learning performance was measured in terms of both quantitative and qualitative outcomes. As well, process analyses helped to characterize different kinds of deep processing activities such as constructing explanations in science; maximizing knowledge structure in geography; and examining multiple perspectives in psychology. These learning strategies provided examples of how deep learning was manifested in different contexts; and possibly how these strategies could be taught to students.

Results of these studies are also consistent with research on student approach to learning (Biggs, 1993; Marton & Booth, 1997; Watkins & Biggs, 1996): These students were shown to employ different approaches and strategies when they learned; and such differences were significantly related to learning outcomes. Current research on student approach to learning has shown positive correlations between deep approach and learning outcomes (Watkins, 1996). The present intervention studies provided evidence of possible causal relations between deep approach and qualitative learning outcomes.

Some concerns may be raised because self-report measures of learning approaches were not included. Increased attention has now been given to the importance of examining student learning in specific domains and contexts. We took the view that learning is situated in contexts and it needs to be examined in relation to specific domains. Our emphasis has been placed on how deep learning is manifested in different domains and contexts rather than focusing on general dispositions. With the short duration of the projects, it might also be unrealistic to expect changes to take place in students' general approach to learning. Nevertheless, the complex relations between specific and global approaches to learning should be further investigated.

Bridging Learning with Instruction

This section addressed the question of why these instructional programs might be effective in promoting student learning. Cognitive research has shown substantial evidence indicating that learning is related to students' prior knowledge, strategy, and interactions (Resnick, 1989). The present instructional studies were designed using these constructivist principles of *how people learn*. Although each study focused specifically on one of the principles, different principles were all incorporated.

Study One focused on the importance of learners' prior conceptions: Different models and conceptions were identified and information was presented to confront such conceptions. The notion of cognitive conflict was extended to incorporate metacognitive activities helping students to reflect on their understanding. Study Two emphasized learners' self-directed strategy and deep processing activities: Instead of passively receiving information, students elaborated, questioned, and constructed meanings as they took increased responsibility over what they had to learn. Both Study One and Two also incorporated the component of group learning; and student interactions were used in ways to scaffold deeper understanding. Study Three on computer learning was designed to capitalize on prior understanding, articulation of ideas, metacognition, and collaborative inquiry. As participants represented and communicated their ideas, they became more metacognitive about what they believed; these knowledge ideas could then become objects of collaborative inquiry. Exposure to these different ideas could help students construct meaning as they reflected on their understanding in the contexts of other views and perspectives.

The positive effects of these studies provide some support to the position that constructivist principles of knowledge, strategy, and collaboration are involved in student learning (Resnick, 1989). They also suggest that instruction that aims to promote deep learning should take into consideration these related principles. Constructivist instruction emphasizing meaning making would seem particularly important for promoting deep learning and conceptual understanding. These instructional programs were designed taking into consideration students' differing ways of understanding, and different models and perspectives were shown to scaffold student understanding. Furthermore, students were provided with opportunities to construct meaning as well as to work with others as members of a knowledge building community. Simply put, students were provided with the varied learning contexts that encouraged them to focus on meaning signified by the tasks, rather than merely remembering the sign or the materials themselves.

These instructional programs could also draw support from research on student learning from other theoretical perspectives. Despite some fundamental ontological differences, both constructivist and phenomenographic traditions are premised on the belief that learning is not created by the accretion of information. Instead, learning is viewed as complex, involving qualitative changes in students' understanding. As well, both theoretical perspectives focus on students' learning experiences, on how they make meaning, rather than emphasizing environmental manipulation. In the present studies, emphasis was given to examining qualitative understanding and students' active roles in their own learning. Varied perspectives were emphasized as students were exposed to different contexts and asked to reflect on the differences to help them develop new understanding.

This chapter employs an instructional paradigm to examine the roles of constructivist instruction on student learning. A few notes on methodological background are in order. Some researchers might object to the apparent "technification" of learning, whereas others might have concerns about the roles of teacher-researchers and the lack of control groups. It is argued that intervention studies are useful because they help to examine whether constructivist principles of learning are psychologically valid and educationally relevant. Caution was taken not to focus on the technical aspects of boosting performance; rather, attention was given to investigating how learning takes place. From a broader perspective, cognitive research on classroom learning has moved towards using research-design experiments that deviate from classical experimental-control designs in order to capture the complexity of learning process (Brown, 1992). These studies did not merely answer the questions of whether the instructional programs work but how they might work. For example, Study Three did not focus on investigating whether computer-based discussion was effective; rather, it examined how deep learning was possible using computer networks. Such methodology based on cognitive research is evidently useful to address the problem of understanding learning in complex classroom settings.

Relevance for Chinese Learners and Teachers

This section considers the relevance of constructivist approaches for Chinese students and teachers in Hong Kong classrooms. Results indicated that constructivist instruction was generally effective for enhancing student learning. The present findings are consistent with research on problem-based learning (Chapter 10); conceptual change in staff development (Chapter 12); constructive alignment (Biggs, 1996b); and action learning (Chapter 13); they also extend research to Chinese secondary students. In addition to these intervention studies, other emerging evidence on constructivist instruction has been obtained: Some examples included conceptual change through self-questioning and self-explanation for secondary school students (Chui & Chan, 1999) and problem-centred learning for pre-service mathematics teachers (Taplin & Chan, 1998).

Closer examination of the results also indicated some interesting patterns. Whereas there were few differences between traditional and constructivist instruction on examination questions, differences were obtained in qualitative measures. Although comparison students were able to perform just as well on the HKCEE questions, they continued to hold misconceptions reflected in the qualitative measures. These findings were remarkably similar to those of action research indicating that experimental students performed significantly better than comparison students on problem-based questions but there were no differences on examination questions (Gow, Kember & McKay, 1996). There was also some evidence indicating that Hong Kong students performed better on multiple-choice questions on The International Mathematics and Science Study (TIMSS) but they did more poorly on open-ended questions that require problem solving (Law, 1996). As the TIMSS questions are presented in bilingual versions and Hong Kong students can use either English or Chinese to write the answers, it does not seem to be merely a language issue. Whereas Chinese students performed well on academic attainments, what they have actually learned or understood needs to be examined further. These findings point to the importance of including different measures for examining both quantitative and qualitative learning for Chinese learners.

Results of the studies provided some empirical evidence supporting the notion that learning approach is not inherent within Chinese students; they develop specific approaches in response to the learning environments (Biggs, 1996a & b). Chinese students are often assumed to be passive. However, as shown in these instructional studies, when given the opportunities to engage in deep learning, they responded readily. These findings are consistent with the idea that Chinese students are highly adaptive and attuned to the contexts. When exposed to traditional classroom teaching, Chinese students develop certain approaches to cope with examination demands. When the teaching contexts require qualitative understanding, Chinese students adapt their approach to learning accordingly. One major implication is that changing the learning environments would be important to help students develop different ways of thinking and approaching learning.

To tackle the problem of cultural relevance, it is useful to consider how Chinese teachers implemented constructivist instruction in the Chinese contexts. The present findings provided some evidence indicating that constructivist approaches were effective with Chinese students and teachers. There are certainly examples when researchers have failed to import Western instructional approaches into the Chinese contexts. It is argued that for whatever instructional innovations, teachers play a pivotal role in the instructional process. If the approach were implemented without teachers' understanding, it would not work whether it is based on the Eastern or Western traditions.

How did these Chinese teachers respond to constructivist approaches and what made them succeed in the implementation? Primarily, although constructivist instruction seems to be 'invented' in the Western contexts, there are certain principles of effective teaching that might apply in different cultural contexts. For example, the analysis of mathematics lessons in Japanese schools indicated that the teachers had incorporated some effective principles of teaching and learning similar to those advocated by constructivist teachers in the Western contexts (Stigler & Hiebert, 1999). These Chinese teachers also understood that focus needs to be placed on student learning. A common problem with the implementation of Western approaches is focusing on the "form" rather than the "substance" of instruction. For example, students in some Target-Oriented classrooms could be seen as engaging in group work because they were seated in groups but in reality, they were each doing their own exercises. Indeed, merely focusing on the form of constructivist instruction such as cognitive conflict or portfolio assessment would not work for Chinese or any students. Similar to good teachers from any culture, they understood that the most important thing is not how they teach but how students learn. Good teaching, constructivist or other approaches need to take into consideration students' ways of thinking and experiencing as teachers extend their understanding.

Apparently, teachers' beliefs and practices are influenced by the broader socio-cultural contexts. Similar to Chinese learners who developed specific approaches to cope with the task demands, these Chinese teachers also developed interesting ways to adapt constructivist approaches in relation to the educational contexts. As discussed earlier, some might argue that, unlike Western teachers, Chinese teachers tend to give more emphasis to students' moral and personal development. Therefore, constructivist approaches often viewed as 'cold' cognition might be incompatible with the cultural beliefs of the teachers. It is interesting to observe how these Chinese teachers adapted their beliefs and developed some rather interesting ways of thinking about constructivist instruction. One of the teachers remarked that he never thought constructivist instruction could be valuable in helping him develop good teacher-student relationships. He noted he had become much closer to his students because he now strove to understand how they think. His students seemed more motivated because the teacher was learning with them and showed so much interest in their ideas even though these ideas were incorrect. The idea that constructivist instruction would bring about better teacher-student relationships is primarily unexplored in Western research and it remains to be examined in the Chinese classrooms. This example, however, illustrates how these Chinese teachers developed some ways of thinking about the constructivist approach that were congruent with the cultural beliefs in the Chinese contexts.

Other questions about the relevance of constructivist approaches in Chinese contexts pertain to the limitations imposed by an education system that focuses so much on public examinations. As with any good teachers, these successful Chinese teachers were well able to adapt to the different constraints imposed by the educational contexts. Specifically, they related constructivist instruction to the school curriculum rather than teaching some decontextualized higher cognitive skills. As well, they were cautious to check out and make provision to ensure that their students would perform well on examination questions when instructional time had been given to teaching for understanding rather than just drilling on test papers. The Chinese teachers involved in constructivist instruction all indicated they need to include some measures to examine how students performed on conventional examination questions. Interestingly, even though constructivist instruction did not boost conventional test scores, these teachers gradually shifted from a quantitative towards a more qualitative view of teaching and learning. One teacher said that as long as his students did not fall behind in the examination results, he thought he had succeeded because students had made gains both in qualitative understanding and intrinsic interests in the subject.

There were some other ways that the Chinese teachers adapted constructivist instruction and developed ways to think about teaching and learning that work in Chinese contexts. Whereas portfolio assessment might be seen as complicated, the teacher believed it was useful for examination. The teacher explained that students' deep processing activities in producing their learning portfolios would help them understand and learn the materials more thoroughly. When the time came when students need to memorize the materials to prepare for the Advanced Level Examination, it would be much easier for them because they did not need to rote learn as they had now understood the materials. Interestingly, some of the suggested portfolio items included answers to examination questions and analyses of own performance.

These examples suggest that constructivist approach is effective only when teachers attempted to make sense of what it means to their students. In some ways, these teachers were also engaged in some meaning-making process using their experiences and beliefs as related to the cultural and educational contexts. As well, these examples also show how Chinese teachers adapted to the contexts as they themselves developed some deeper conceptions of teaching and learning. Such teacher conceptions would certainly affect the degree to which teachers could implement constructivist instruction successfully. How Chinese teachers' conceptions change when implementing instructional innovations and how such conceptions are related to socio-cultural factors and student learning remain to be investigated.

Finally, questions might be raised as to why it is even necessary to consider constructivist instruction when Chinese students have performed better than their Western counterparts. It depends very much on the goals of schooling in the 21st century. If our focus continues to be placed on examination results, there would perhaps be incongruence between constructivist instruction and the cultural and educational contexts. With the advent of the knowledge-based era, educational reforms globally as well as locally have called for an emphasis on life-long learning (Review of Education System, 1999). An important educational goal is the development of educated citizens capable of learning independently; transferring their learning across contexts; and working with the production of knowledge. There needs to be changes in instructional approaches concomitant with changes in social-cultural and educational contexts. Hence, the notion of students taking on constructive roles in pursuit of learning would have increased significance in the research and educational agendas.

Conclusion

This chapter examined the effects of constructivist instruction on Chinese students' learning and understanding. Three key themes were identified. First, the findings indicated that constructivist instruction could be implemented successfully in Hong Kong classrooms for promoting students learning. There was some evidence suggesting positive relationships between student engagement in a deep approach to learning and qualitative understanding. Second, the effectiveness of these programs were examined in relation to constructivist principles of learning involving prior knowledge, learner strategy and student interactions. The importance of bridging learning with instruction is highlighted. Third, the positive effects of constructivist instruction with Chinese students suggest that learning approaches are not inherent in the learners; they could vary as a function of the learning contexts. Effective Chinese teachers developed different ways of adapting constructivist approaches in relation to contextual constraints as they themselves deepened their understanding about teaching and learning. Further investigations of how learning and understanding could be promoted would help provide different perspectives about learning in Chinese classrooms.

REFERENCES

Alexander, P. (1996). The Past, Present, and Future of Knowledge Research: A Reexamination of the Role of Knowledge in Learning and Instruction. *Educational Psychologist*, 31(2), 89-92.

Anderson, V., Chan, C.K.K. & Henne, R. (1995). The Effects of Strategy Instruction on the Literacy Models and Performance of Reading and Writing Delayed Middle School Students. In K.A. Hinchman, D.J. Leu & C.K. Kinzer (Eds.), *Perspectives on Literacy Research and Practice. Forty-forth Yearbook of the National Reading Conference*, 180-189.

Bereiter, C. & Scardamalia, M. (1989). (Ed.) Intentional Learning As A Goal of Instruction. In L.B. Resnick (Ed.) *Knowing, Learning and Instruction: Essays in Honor of Robert Glaser*. Hillsdale, NJ: Erlbaum, 361-392.

Bereiter, C. & Scardamalia, M. (1992). Cognition and Curriculum. In J.W. Jackson (Ed.), *Handbook of Research on Curriculum*. New York: Macmillan, 517-542.

Bereiter, C. & Scardamalia, M. (1993). *Surpassing Ourselves: An Inquiry into the Nature and Implications of Expertise*. La Salle, IL: Open Court.

Bereiter, C. & Scardamalia, M. (1996). Rethinking Learning. In D.R. Olson & N. Torrance (Eds.), *The Handbook of Education and Human Development*. Blackwell Publishers, 485-513.

Biggs, J.B. (1996a). Western Misperceptions of the Confucian-heritage Learning Culture. In D.A. Watkins & J.B. Biggs (Eds.), *The Chinese Learner: Cultural, Psychological, and Contextual Influences*. Hong Kong / Melbourne: Comparative Education Research Centre, The University of Hong Kong / Australian Council for Educational Research, 45-67.

Biggs, J.B. (1996b). Enhancing Learning Through Constructive Alignment. *Higher Education*, 32(3), 347-364.

Biggs, J.B. (1999). *Teaching for Quality Learning at University: What the Student Does*. Buckingham. Open University Press.

Biggs, J.B. & Moore, P. (1993). *The Process of Learning*. New York: Prentice-Hall.

Boekaerts, M. (1998). Do Culturally rooted Self-construals affect Student' Concept of Control over Learning? *Educational Psychologist*, 33(2-3), 87-108.

Brown, A.L. (1992). Design Experiments: Theoretical and Methodological Challenges in Creating Complex Interventions in Classroom Settings. *The Journal of Learning Sciences*, 92(2), 141-178.

Brown, A.L. (1997). Transforming Schools into Communities of Thinking and Learning about Serious Matters. *American Psychologist*, 52, 399-413.

Brown, A.L., Bransford, J.D., Ferrara, R.A. & Campione, J.C. (1983). Learning, Remembering, and Understanding. In J.H. Flavell & E.M. Markman (Eds),

Handbook of Child Psychology, Vol. 3. Cognitive Development (4th edition). New York: John Wiley & Sons, 77-166.

Brown, J.S., Collins, A. & Duguid, P. (1989). Situated Cognition and the Culture of Learning. *Educational Researcher*, 18, 32-48.

Chan, C.K.K. (1999). *Teachers' Belief Change and Knowledge Building in Computer-supported Collaborative Learning.* Paper presented at the 8th Biennial Meeting of the European Association for Research in Learning and Instruction. Gothenborg, Sweden

Chan, C.K.K., Burtis, P.J., Scardamalia, M. & Bereiter, C. (1992). Constructive Activity in Learning from Text. *American Educational Research Journal*, 29(1), 97-118.

Chan, C.K.K., Burtis, J. & Bereiter, C. (1997). Knowledge-building Approach as a Mediator of Conflict in Conceptual Change. *Cognition and Instruction*, 15(1), 1-40.

Chi, M.T.H., de Leeuw, N., Chiu, M.H. & LaVancher, C. (1994). Eliciting Self-Explanations Improves Understanding. *Cognitive Science*, 18(3), 439-477.

Chong, Y.L. & Chan, C.K.K. (2000). *The Effects of Cognitive Conflict and Metacognition on Conceptual Change*. Paper presented at the annual meeting of the American Educational Research Association, New Orleans.

Chui, H.W. & Chan, C.K.K. (1999). *Fostering Conceptual Change in Ecology through Self-questioning and Self-explanation*. Paper presented at the annual meeting of the American Educational Research Association. Montreal.

Collins, A., Brown, J.S. & Newman, S.E. (1989). Cognitive Apprenticeship: Teaching the Crafts of Reading, Writing and Mathematics. In L.B. Resnick (Ed.), *Knowing, Learning and Instruction: Essays in Honor of Robert Glaser*. Hillsdale, NJ: Lawrence Erlbaum Associates, 453-494.

Fensham, P. (1994). *The Content of Science: A Constructivist Approach to its Teaching and Learning*. Falmer Press, Taylor and Francis, Inc.

Gow, L., Kember, D. & McKay, J. (1996). Improving Student Learning through Action Research into Teaching. In D.A. Watkins & J.B. Biggs (Eds.), *The Chinese Learner: Cultural, Psychological, and Contextual Influences*. Hong Kong / Melbourne: Comparative Education Research Centre, The University of Hong Kong / Australian Council for Educational Research, 243-265.

Greeno, J., Collins, A. & Resnick, L. (1996). (Eds.) Cognition and Learning. In D.C. Berliner & R. Calfee (Eds.), *Handbook of Educational Psychology*. New York: NY, USA: Macmillan, 15-46.

Hewson, P. & Thorley, R. (1989). The Conditions of Conceptual Change in the Classroom. *International Journal of Science Education*, 11(5), 541-553.

Law, N.W.Y. (1996). (Ed.) *Science and Mathematics Achievements at the Junior Secondary Level in Hong Kong: A Summary Report for Hong Kong in the Third International Mathematics and Science Study (TIMSS)*. Hong Kong: Faculty of Education, The University of Hong Kong.

Lave, J. & Wenger, E. (1991). *Situated Learning: Legitimate Peripheral Participation. Learning in Doing: Social, Cognitive and Computational Perspectives*. Cambridge: Cambridge University Press.

Lee, E.Y.C. (1998). *Assessing and Fostering Senior Secondary School Students'*

Conceptions of Learning through Authentic Assessment. M.Ed. Dissertation. The University of Hong Kong.

Lee, W.O. (1996). The Cultural Context for Chinese Learners: Conceptions of Learning in the Confucian Tradition. In D.A. Watkins & J.B. Biggs (Eds.), *The Chinese Learner: Cultural, Psychological, and Contextual Influences.* Hong Kong / Melbourne: Comparative Education Research Centre, The University of Hong Kong / Australian Council for Educational Research, 25-41.

Marton, F. & Booth, S. (1997). *Learning and Awareness.* Mahwah, N.J.: L. Erlbaum Associates.

Palincsar, A.S. & Brown, A.L. (1984). Reciprocal Teaching of Reading Comprehension-fostering and Comprehension-monitoring Activities. *Cognition and Instruction*, 1, 117-175.

Pfundt, H. & Duit, R. (1991). *Bibliography: Students' Alternative Frameworks and Science Education.* (3rd edition). Stafford: University of Kiel.

Pressley, M. (1990). *Cognitive Strategy Instruction that Really Improves Children's Academic Performance.* Cambridge MA: Brookline Books.

Review of Education System: Framework for Education Reform. Learning for life (1999). Hong Kong: Education Commission.

Rosenshine, B. & Meister, C. (1994). Reciprocal Teaching: A Review of the Research. *Review of Educational Research*, 64(4), 479-530.

Salomon, G. & Globerson, T. (1987). Skill is Not Enough: The Role of Mindfulness in Learning and Transfer. *International Journal of Research in Education*, 11, 623-638.

Scardamalia, M. & Bereiter, C. (1994). Computer Support for Knowledge Building Communities. Special Issue: Computer Support for Collaborative Learning. *The Journal of the Learning Sciences*, 3(3), 265-283.

Schunk, D.H. & Zimmermann, B.J. (1994). *Self-regulated Learning and Performance: Issues and Educational Applications.* Hillsdale, N.J.: Lawrence Erlbaum Associates.

Stigler, J. & Hiebert, J. (1999). *The Teaching Gap.* New York: The Free Press.

Taplin, M. & Chan, C.K.K. (1998). *Teaching and Learning as Problem Solving for Preservice Mathematics Teachers.* Paper presented at the annual meeting of the American Educational Research Association, San Diego.

Watkins, D.A. (1996). Learning Theories and Approaches to Research: A Cross-cultural Perspective. In D.A. Watkins & J.B. Biggs (Eds.), *The Chinese Learner: Cultural, Psychological, and Contextual Influences.* Hong Kong / Melbourne: Comparative Education Research Centre, The University of Hong Kong / Australian Council for Educational Research, 3-24.

Watkins, D.A. & Biggs, J.B. (1996). (Eds.) *The Chinese Learner: Cultural, Psychological, and Contextual Influences.* Hong Kong / Melbourne: Comparative Education Research Centre, The University of Hong Kong / Australian Council for Educational Research.

10

Problem-Based Learning in a Chinese Context: Faculty Perceptions

Stephanie F. Stokes

Since its inception as a method of learning for the McMaster University (Hamilton, Canada) post-graduate medical programme, Problem-based Learning (PBL) has attracted considerable interested as an alternative teaching/learning paradigm. Alternative, that is, to a conventional teacher-centred approach of lecturing, or other student-centred approaches such as cooperative learning. PBL is now practiced worldwide in various academic contexts, in a variety of disciplines. Generally, PBL is comprised of several components: a) small-group work, b) a tutor, and c) resources and a study/work programme to aid self-directed/independent learning. In most implementations, PBL has been attempted in post-graduate courses. This implies that students come to the programme with already well-established study methods and skills. In recent years PBL has been adopted in undergraduate programmes. It remains to be seen whether or not this paradigm is successful with undergraduate students, and indeed, how teachers on such a programme react to the need to engender independent-learning behaviours in first-year university students.

Problem-based learning was introduced to the BSc (Speech and Hearing Sciences - S&HS) at the University of Hong Kong in the 1995/96 academic year as an embedded unit in the first year of a traditional university course. The success of this implementation resulted in two subsequent trials of PBL, in the same format, for the 1996/97 and 1997/98 academic years, again only in the first year of the course. Student responses to this embedded programme were carefully monitored, and have been reported in three publications. The first (MacKinnon, 1999) identified elements of motivation that seem to be important for students engaged in a PBL context, claiming that the social context of learning was of utmost importance (called 'community'), along with 'ownership' (control of their own learning), followed by professional 'relevance' and 'empowerment'. MacKinnon identified these four elements as the 'CORE' factors for success in a PBL course, and was careful to point out that synergy of these CORE factors contributed to high student motivation in an independent, learning context.

The second publication (Stokes, MacKinnon, & Whitehill, 1997) reported quantitative (student ratings of course and teachers) and qualitative (a questionnaire on learning preferences) data collected from students which illustrated that a PBL course was rated more highly than traditional pedagogical teaching and that students preferred a student-centred, independent learning environment once they had had the opportunity to experience it. The third report (Whitehill, Stokes, &

MacKinnon, 1997) described student characteristics that seemed to be particularly germane to Chinese students, for example, the need to maintain harmony while resolving conflicts about information or process, the preference for working collectively, the importance of academic staff as a source of information (or a confirmation that the students were 'on the right track'), and an intrinsic desire to learn.

These reports of intrinsic motivation, collective learning, respect for teachers and maintenance of harmony all concur with previous reports of what has been coined the Confucian-Heritage Culture (CHC, Ho, 1986) which is mooted to include valuing group cooperation; a high regard for education in Confucian society; the predominance of effort over ability; and a drive for deep learning (and hence an intrinsic motivation to learn). Authors have suggested that the CHC and the way that Asian students rapidly adjust to the demands of any learning context contribute to students' academic performance, regardless of the pedagogy (e.g., Biggs & Watkins, 1996; Gow, Balla, Kember, & Hau, 1996) and others have claimed that these very factors ensure that a student-centred, independent learning context such as PBL is very suited to Chinese learners. Given these findings, the department of S&HS implemented a total PBL curriculum for the first three years of the four year degree programme in the 1998/99 academic year (the fourth year remained a clinical internship and dissertation year). Subsequently, student questionnaires and journals were collected in order to determine student satisfaction with a purely PBL teaching/learning context. These findings will be reported elsewhere. Aside from student perspectives of the learning context, an intriguing question is 'what do teachers make of a new pedagogy?' How do faculty, teaching within a CHC context, respond to a PBL curriculum? Some background information about the new course is provided before exploring the question of staff perceptions.

The Course

Unlike the pilot studies of 1995/96, 1996/97 and 1997/98, the wholesale implementation of PBL was not as an imbedded PBL programme, but as a total PBL course (see Figure 10.1). As shown in Figure 10.1, there are, broadly speaking, three main models of PBL implementation, the imbedded, the hybrid and the total. The imbedded model allows for a gradual shift to PBL, or a piloting of PBL within a continuing traditional curriculum. The second sees the adoption of a learning block around a particular aspect of the curriculum (voice and voice pathology in the example), and a hybrid of lectures and PBL tutorials as the teaching mechanism. The third model, total PBL, sees the elimination of lectures and a totally student-centred learning context of only PBL tutorials and the use of skills laboratories ('skills labs') to learn professionally-relevant psycho-motor skills.

In the imbedded approach a PBL unit/course is run along side all other conventional courses (see Figure 10.1a).

Figure 10.1a
An example of imbedded courses

Monday	Tuesday	Wednesday	Thursday	Friday
Lecture: Anatomy	Lecture: Acoustics	Lab: Anatomy	Lecture: Phonetics	
Lecture: Psychology		Lab: Anatomy		
Lecture: Syntax	Lecture: Phonetics	Lecture: Life-span Development	PBL course: Introduction to Communication Disorders	Lecture: Psychology

In the hybrid approach the entire curriculum is converted, but conventional teaching methods are used along side PBL tutorials (see Figure 10.1b). Semesters may be separated into learning blocks (topic areas).

Figure 10.1b
An example of hybrid courses

Monday	Tuesday	Wednesday	Thursday	Friday
Lecture: A & P Larynx	Lecture : Normal Voice	Lecture : Voice Pathology	Lecture : Voice Assessment	Lecture: Voice Treatment
	PBL tutorial	Voice: Laboratory		PBL tutorial

Where total PBL is adopted, the entire curriculum is converted, and PBL tutorials and skills labs/workshops are scheduled (see Figure 10.1c). There are no lectures. Problems act as a catalyst for learning.

Figure 10.1c
An example of total PBL

Monday	Tuesday	Wednesday	Thursday	Friday
PBL Tutorial				PBL tutorial
	Skills Lab			Seminar on request

A problem ran across three tutorials for the first year students and across two tutorials for second and third year students. At the commencement of the programme, we adopted a 'pure' PBL approach: students were given problems and a grid of learning objectives within a student handbook that included other information such as the role of the tutor and the role of students. The skills labs complemented the tutorials in that skills relevant to a particular problem were addressed in the relevant week of the semester.

In designing and implementing a new curriculum two concerns were uppermost in our minds: to facilitate a deep approach to learning in students and to successfully engage all staff in the adoption of a new teaching/learning paradigm. The first concern, to facilitate deep learning by students and an integration across subject disciplines, saw the development of a PBL curriculum. This was believed to offer a way of adhering to the principles of good teaching believed to engender good learning (Biggs, 1999; p.73):

1. A well structured knowledge base.
2. An appropriate motivational context.
3. Learner activity.
4. Interaction with others.

The second concern, to positively engage all staff, was an attempt to engender a shift in conceptions of teaching and foster a belief in PBL. We were attempting to cause a change in university teaching. In hindsight, we were perhaps attending to two factors which Biggs (1999) identified as essential components in the successful facilitation of changing university teaching. These were that staff developers (or, in our case, curriculum managers or change agents) needed to "consult individuals" and "to consult on a departmental basis, to get the whole teaching context and departmental policy and procedures right" (p.5). Every faculty member had a specialist area, and therefore everyone was consulted for input on curriculum planning specific to their expertise. Also, in order to engage every individual in the process, planning was done en masse; all staff were actively engaged in writing the new curriculum. As a large group, and in small groups where required, we wrote the outcome objectives, problems, predicted learning issues, identified learning resources and constructed protocols for assessing a) student learning, b) student tutorial performance and c) tutor performance. At the same time, we also undertook workshops as tutors under expert guidance. Then, in the semester immediately prior to wholesale implementation, all staff experienced the process as a tutor, before performing as a tutor as their sole role in the new pedagogical model. Each staff member acted as a tutor on the imbedded unit in the 1997/98 first year course. At that time, we had 11 tutors, ten of whom had taught for at least six years, with a range of experience from one to 25 years. With the total conversion in 1998/99, we employed three part-time staff for a total of 14 tutors.

In summary, the shift from an imbedded PBL model to a total PBL model necessarily required not only a new curriculum including the structure, content and assessment of student learning, but also a shift in conceptions of teaching. The new curriculum is not discussed here, rather the focus is on teachers' responses to the new curriculum.

Thinking about Teaching

Biggs, (1999) described three 'levels of thinking about teaching'. These are

1. Learning is a function of individual differences between students.
2. Learning is a function of teaching.
3. Learning is the result of students' learning-focused activities, which are engaged by students as a result of both their own perceptions and inputs, and of the total teaching context (p.21).

It is not difficult to see that the third level needs to be adopted as a way of thinking about teaching if a teacher is to whole-heartedly adopt PBL. As Biggs points out, the development of level three thinking is part of a developmental process that occurs over time. How was this developmental process considered during the implementation of total PBL? We attempted to allow for a gradual shift in conceptions of teaching by having all academic staff act as tutors in the third year of the pilot and to engage all staff members in curriculum planning. Although we have no pre-PBL data, we can report the (anonymous) comments of tutors after the first year of the total PBL implementation. Subscription to different levels of thinking about teaching is seen in the following comments[1]. These are examples of level two thinking:

1. 'The most difficult is if it's an area that I'm familiar with. I get 'itchy' and succumb to speaking more. I know it means they don't think but it's difficult.'
2. 'I'm quite interventionist. I give early feedback and I'm participatory. If someone says something unreasonable, I say 'that's not reasonable.' Some students told me I shouldn't say that, but others like it.'

---

[1] All quotes in this chapter were sourced from a survey of staff and student perceptions of the new PBL course. The survey was conducted by an independent agent.

3. 'Occasionally I step in and I say 'I hope you realise that I shouldn't do this.' The students laugh and look visibly relieved. So I can't do it often. But it's my responsibility not to leave them with incorrect information.'
4. 'I felt sorry for the students. I knew in my brain what I should do, but my heart makes me step in and provide information. And the students were thankful. It's three hours wasted if they go round in circles and you don't tell them.'

In these comments, it is apparent that the faculty members feel that learning can be achieved by 'teaching'. Tutors felt compelled to rescue students from circuitous discussion and point them in the right direction (5), or provide 'answers' or information (1, 3, 6). Other tutors took a less direct approach, but nonetheless still reflect a belief in needing to keep the information correct (2, 4). Level three thinking is seen in these comments:

5. 'I let them discuss until they get stuck and then I reflect on what they've said and ask them if they can see any contradictions. I try not to say, you're wrong.'
6. 'You can reassure them that you'll step in if they don't cover enough or if they go off-track. That means if I say nothing, assume everything is OK... I don't give information or mini-lectures, just challenge, question, request clarification, expansion, etc.'
7. 'Guidance doesn't mean pointing to what knowledge to learn, but what are ways of thinking.'
8. 'Tutors are meant to guide but not give knowledge. You should encourage, question or challenge.'

The implementation experience is still raw, and it remains to be seen if all tutors develop along the continuum to level three thinking.

The Implementation

Although all of the full-time academic staff had participated as tutors in the 1997/98 pilot, this occurred in only one 'unit', once per week for students and staff. Thus, faculty still taught in their main content area, their area of specialisation, within the BSc. Once the total PBL model was adopted, this expert teaching ceased. All tutors essentially performed as non-expert tutors as only a minority of problems would match any tutors expertise at any given time. Thus, tutors forfeited the role of an expert – thus losing their place as an essential provider of knowledge, which is highly respected and desired in a CHC. While this may have caused some dissonance for ethnic Chinese colleagues, who supposedly held similar CHC views as the students, it resulted in similar reactions from Western colleagues. Several academics commented on how they missed teaching; the 'performance' and display of knowledge. Although the source is not known, (that is, Chinese or Western) this quote from a staff survey/interview captures the feeling: 'we used to do expert teaching but now anyone can do it.' Despite this loss of control, three of the tutors were very happy with the conversion, eight were pleased but saw major problems with implementation, and two tutors were not convinced that PBL was a suitable pedagogical approach. Reflecting on the total implementation, the above views are expressed in the following comments:

9. '(*PBL is*) less rigid and boring, more enjoyable.'
10. 'It challenges me more. I'm less stale.'
11. 'There's more interaction with students and more teamwork with other tutors.'
12. 'I really enjoy seeing the progress of students at close hand.' Some reservation about a total conversion is seen in this comment:
13. 'They need a combination (*of lectures and PBL tutorials*), especially initially. The transition from school is very difficult, especially for the more passive ones.'

The Role of Tutors

One of the major areas of concern, from the staff perspective, was their role as tutors. Almost all comments about the tutoring aspect of PBL reflected insecurity and uncertainty. Most commented on the need for more information or more training on how to be a tutor:

14. 'How to be a tutor is an area on which we need more information.'
15. 'I need to have more concrete operational definitions of optimal standards and good practice. At the moment it's very relative. I find it very difficult to give specific feedback because it's only based on my impression.'
16. 'Students want feedback on whether they've learned enough. I've struggled as I don't want to say 'that's correct.' They should judge from the objectives. But it's also the tutor's job to make sure they cover the objectives. We should give more feedback on the appropriateness of their learning in terms of breadth and depth.'
17. 'I'm unclear on my role. It's a bit like a seminar, but I can't teach anything.'
18. 'I think the majority of tutors were not giving enough guidance at first.... Some intuitively improved over the year.'
19. 'Currently, it's not clear how much freedom (*in the tutor role*) is allowed. The students told me their previous tutor answered all their questions.'

This feeling of not knowing enough about the process carried over, for some tutors, into not knowing enough about the course content, or the course objectives:

20. 'Planners may have the 'big picture' of learning objectives, but other tutors only know them on a problem by problem basis.'

The lack of comment about not seeing 'the big picture' is a positive outcome of the conversion; given that the conversion was achieved by all, but driven by a few members of staff, it is surprising that, given the opportunity, there were not more complaints about not having a clear overview of the entire curriculum.

Conduct of Tutorials

It became clear that one of the major problems in implementation (voiced by both students and staff) was in the inconsistency, real or perceived, of tutorial format. This was not so much as to who was or wasn't a 'good' or 'bad' tutor, but rather variations in how tutorials were conducted. At the beginning of the year, students generated learning issues in the first session, assigned issues to particular students, dispersed to research the topics (step 5 in Figure 10.2), and reconvened in the second (and third, for year 1 students) tutorial to discuss new information.

Figure 10.2
The processes of the tutorial

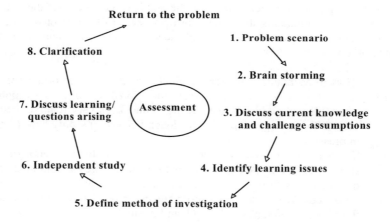

This process is widely accepted as the 'model' for PBL. However, this model, designed for post-graduate students in a medical curriculum, may not be the most appropriate method for implementing PBL with undergraduate students. Undergraduate students (in Hong Kong at least) come to university from a traditional teaching/learning paradigm, where teachers train students for examinations. The demands of a new PBL curriculum are many and taxing. Students need to learn how to a) become a team member, b) critique, discuss and challenge information, c) define problems and areas of learning, d) set boundaries on information searches, e) locate appropriate literature, f) read for meaning, g) summarise and synthesise information, h) construct an argument based on literature, i) present their learning, either orally or verbally, and j) recognise and discuss further learning needs relevant to the problem at hand. (Some of these are of course also requirements of a conventional teaching/learning environment.) Our implementtation of PBL was a first run with an undergraduate course. If the process is found to be wanting, should tutors continue nonetheless, or seek a different, possibly better method of implementing PBL? Are there some parts of the process which can be manipulated, and what may they be?

Mid-way through the second semester, one tutor of a second year group was dissatisfied with the given format as students were not engaging in true reflective discussion (step 7 of Figure 10.2), but were simply providing mini-lectures to their group as they had researched one learning issue each. In order to facilitate real discussion, the tutor suggested that all students address all issues, but they be provided with one key reading for each issue selected for follow-up investigation. This effectively meant that each student did not spend time in searching for references and collating information for each member of the group, but rather read key readings for each learning issue and prepared a written summary of how this information related to the problem, highlighting remaining questions. This proved to be a very effective strategy for facilitating good-quality discussion as all students came to the tutorial with a shared knowledge-base, from which they could resolve misunderstandings or questions. However, the change in format was met with mixed reactions among the tutors and the students. Leaving the students aside, tutor reactions fell into four broad categories:

a) some objected to the way in which the change had been made (21, 22 and 23):

21. 'It felt like the decision had been made. The decision was not made in a meeting. One tutor did it so the others felt they should too. It wouldn't be nice if we didn't. We weren't forced to but we'd feel bad because the students feel bad if you don't do the same.'
22. 'Dr X (*one of the instigators of PBL*) instigated it and there's a feeling that, especially if she did it, it must be better. Students think this too. So everyone adopted it.'
23. 'I don't mind if we give references or not, but we have to be consistent. So far, some have and some haven't and the students are upset about this;'

b) some objected only to the provision of references, ignoring the benefits of increasing the quality of discussion (24, 25, 26, 27, 28).

24. 'Giving references would erode the principles of PBL, even if it is of practical benefit in the short term.'
25. 'Giving references is a crime against PBL…It's a let-down that some have done this, but I'm not surprised.'
26. 'I wouldn't give all the references as they would never learn to find information for themselves.'
27. 'I prefer to share out the issues. Some students bring better references than those recommended anyway.'
28. 'I don't know if Y1 students could cope with having to do so much

reading.'

On the other hand, c) other tutors agreed that the change had benefits (29, 30, 31):

29. 'The way we structure the workshare makes for very efficient information search but it results in limited knowledge per student. Also, some students do misleading presentations of their topic, so it can result in that topic not being understood properly at all.'
30. 'We need to make the sessions more efficient so that there's time for synthesis of information.'
31. 'I see improvements. Previously, 40% of references found were wrong or the wrong level, and only one student had the information for each area. Better students would read for themselves but others were left in the dark;'

while others d) rejected it outright (32):

32. 'I'm surprised Dr X has made this change. It's not PBL.'

The issue of which aspects of the PBL tutorial can be modified to suit local needs and contexts requires further investigation and only widespread publication and discussion of such modifications will lead us to a clearer understanding of how PBL implementation varies world-wide. Such investigations should include reflective evaluation of modifications to the process. Whatever modifications are attempted, it is clear, from our experience, that modifications require discussion before implementation to ensure that everyone with an investment in the process is privy to the modifications.

Assessment of Student Learning

A crucial component of any curriculum is the method and content of assessment. Biggs (1999) clearly outlines the need for alignment of learning objectives and assessment practices. In order to map assessment onto the PBL model of teaching/learning, we assessed both process and content in our assessment of student learning/performance. The process (student performance in tutorials and reflections on learning) was assessed by a) tutor assessment of student tutorial performance, peer assessment and self assessment of the same, b) the submission of a reflective journal, and c) a single component of the end-of-semester examination, in which the student was required to reflect on what they had learned during examination, and how he/she had learned it. Content (knowledge) was assessed by two written assignments and an end-of-semester examination.

The end-of-semester examination was in written form consisting of three parts. In part I, students read a new problem, defined four learning issues, selected two for investigation, and justified their choice of issues for investigation by outlining their existing knowledge on all issues and where they saw a need for further development of their learning. In part II, students dispersed for four hours to collect information and prepare a written response for part III. During this time they were free to consult any source for information. In part III, students wrote what they had learned about their two selected issues, discussed how these issues were relevant to the problem, outlined what else they would need to investigate and reflected on their learning.

Staff had mixed reactions to this assessment, and their comments reflected long discussions at the end-of-year staff retreat to review the programme, where discussion on assessment weighed heavily towards the issue of open book assessment and students' use of the investigative phase (part II) to construct 'group' written responses:

33. 'I think this is great. If the problems are written well, it should tap into the broad areas they've already covered and into new areas. The negatives are only in the wording of the problems.'

Clearly this responder felt that the examination served its purpose, providing the problem statement was well-written.

34. 'I'm not worried that it's open book or that they can discuss. But I'm not sure if they really can.'
35. 'Why shouldn't they discuss? It's a paradox if the whole pedagogical approach is based on teamwork but the assessment is individual.'

Responses 34 and 35 highlight the sentiment that the examination should be aligned with the teaching/learning paradigm: if students have open access to information and their peers during learning, then they should have the same access during assessment.

Yet other staff felt that the examination did not tap into skills which he/she considered central to the course, research and knowledge; and that while consultation may be part of a professional's daily work, it should not be part of students' assessment (36), or that the examination really tapped just accessing information and writing skills (37):

36. 'This is worrying. I fear the PBL exam is weak in assessing real research skills and knowledge. There's lots of getting together to help. This is okay in a professional setting, but less satisfactory for assessing individual students.'
37. 'It's a good idea in theory, but in reality it tests their speed at getting and rewriting information. It doesn't test their knowledge or any other ability.'

One responder focussed on the whole framework of assessment, suggesting an addition to the existing assessment protocol:

38. 'I would like more on knowledge assessment. In fact I would like to do this on a continuous basis – a product for every problem, even if it's

only one page. Students complain about leaving a problem and not knowing what they've learned. With this, they could compile a portfolio of what they've learned and get feedback on it. Currently, they also don't get enough feedback on what they've learned and done.'

Lessons Learned and Changes to the Curriculum

Some key points for facilitating the implemention of PBL are outlined here. In order to have a successful conversion, it is very clear that all staff must be 'on side'. This is not easy to achieve. As Abrahamson (1991) stated 'good planning is not enough' (p.59). It is apparent from the quotes above that some members of staff were not happy with the conversion, or parts of its implementation, which is to be expected for a new curriculum. However it is also apparent that not all staff may have been convinced that converting to PBL was the right choice. It is likely that in any academic setting these concerns would not be expressed openly. An independent survey provided information that would not have been forthcoming otherwise.

Revision of Our Curriculum

An outcome of the survey of staff and student perceptions has been a systematic revision of the curriculum. The tutorial format has changed. All tutorials now adopt the new approach (all students addressing all learning issues), with consideration for the year of the course. For example, all students address all learning issues in all years. First-year students are provided with all references, and in the first semester they carry out extension reading for one problem only. In the second semester, they take turns to find a resource for one faculty-determined learning issue for each problem. Likewise, in second year, resources (references or key readings) are provided for all of the learning issues, and all of the students source an extra reference for a faculty-determined learning issue for each problem. In third year, references are given for all of the learning issues, and in addition students search for extra information on a learning issue of their choice. The objective is to facilitate high-quality discussion, while building on research skills. In defense of this approach, the students in the BSc are undergraduates, most of whom come directly from secondary school. They need time to adjust to the new process of reading references in English, formulating understanding of the issues, outlining arguments and identifying remaining issues and questions. At the same time, they need to develop skills in team work and group dynamics, learning skills in challenging, questioning and extending lines of thought to get the most out of PBL tutorials. The step-wise introduction of the hunt for resources frees up some cognitive space and time for the students to develop skills which are needed immediately, or very early in a PBL course. Research skills can be developed over time.

Tutor training sessions are ongoing, with input from different experts in an effort to build our own conception of the role of the tutor. With more tutor training and a change in the tutorial format, tutors may see and recognise better student learning, demonstrated in higher level discussions among students during tutorials. It is hoped that tutors will develop along the continuum of thinking about teaching to level three. It may be possible to facilitate these development through more discussions about the nature of teaching and learning, but a more productive method may be the use of reflective diaries for tutors to help them reflect on their perceptions of teaching and learning.

Assessment of student learning, while undergoing significant changes (for example, it is no longer an 'open book' examination) is still, like most of the course, under review in order to achieve continual improvement.

Conclusions

A survey of staff perceptions of a new PBL curriculum in a Health Science curriculum in Hong Kong revealed that three main areas were of concern to tutors at the end of the first year of the new programme: a) the role of tutors, b) consistency across tutors, and c) assessment of student learning. The first reflects a concern shared by most academics who are interested in being effective teachers: am I doing a good job and how can I do it better? As this is a new teaching context for all staff, the uncertainty and insecurity are expected. The second concern reflects the need for cohesion in such a massive conversion: All staff should be doing the same thing at the same time. Implementing a new process is difficult, and inserting variation in that process is painful. Ad hoc changes should be avoided. The last concern is an ongoing one. We have yet to find the best method for assessing all of the desired outcomes of a PBL curriculum: from research skills, content knowledge, clinical competence, communication skills to team work. Much remains to be done but it seems clear that the PBL approach can work well with Hong Kong students.

REFERENCES

Abrahamson, S. (1991). Good Planning is Not Enough. In D. Boud & G. Feletti, (Eds.), *The Challenge of Problem Based Learning*. London: Kogan Page, 59-64.

Biggs, J.B. & Watkins, D.A. (1996). The Chinese Learner in Retrospect. In D.A Watkins & J.B. Biggs (Eds.), *The Chinese Learner: Cultural, Psychological, and Contextual Influences*. Hong Kong / Melbourne: Comparative Education Research Centre, The University of Hong Kong / Australian Council for Educational Research, 269-285.

Gow, L., Balla, J., Kember, D. & Hau, K.T. (1996). The Learning Approaches of Chinese People: A Function of Socialization Process and the Context of Learning? In M.H. Bond (Ed.), *The Handbook of Chinese Psychology*. Hong Kong: Oxford University Press, 109-123.

Ho, D.Y.F. (1986). Chinese Patterns of Socialization: A Critical Review. In M.H. Bond (Ed.), *The Psychology of the Chinese People*. Hong Kong: Oxford University Press.

MacKinnon, M.M. (1999). *CORE Elements of Student Motivation in Problem-based Learning*. Research Report. Hong Kong: Centre for the Advancement of University Teaching, The University of Hong Kong.

Stokes, S.F., MacKinnon, M.M. & Whitehill, T.L. (1997). Students' Experiences of PBL: Journal and Questionnaire Analysis. *Austria Journal for Higher Education*, 27(1), 161-179.

Whitehill, T.L., Stokes, S.F. & MacKinnon, M.M. Problem-based Learning and the Chinese Learner. In R. Murray-Harvey & H.C. Silins (Eds.), *Learning and Teaching in Higher Education: Advancing International Perspectives*. Adelaide: Flinders Press, 129-146.

CHANGING TEACHERS

11

The Influence of Teacher Education on Conceptions of Teaching and Learning

Thomas K.W. Tang

A number of studies have demonstrated that students' approaches to learning are influenced by their teachers' approaches to teaching, which are in turn regulated by the conceptions of teaching held by these teachers (e.g. Gow & Kember, 1993; Ho, 1998; Tang, 1993; Trigwell, Prosser & Waterhouse, 1999) (see also Chapter 1). As teachers are known to hold different conceptions of teaching, they must have developed these conceptions through a certain process. Teacher education is often cited as the root of these conceptions of teaching (e.g. Mellado, 1998; Scott & Rodger, 1995). This chapter examines the relationship between the learning process that teachers go through and the conceptions of teaching that they hold. In this research the participants are simultaneously teachers in their schools and students in some in-service courses.

In this chapter, the results of a quantitative survey which investigates the relationship between conceptions of learning and teaching are first reported. The impact of these courses can be inferred from how these conceptions change from the beginning to the end of the courses. Then an interview study using a phenomenographic approach provides a more in-depth delineation of the relationship between conceptions of learning and teaching, and how these change over the course of study. In the discussion that follows, the quantitative and qualitative studies are integrated, the reasons for conceptual changes are explained, and the findings are compared with similar studies to shed light on the effect of culture and other circumstantial factors. Finally, the implications of the research, especially with respect to teaching in a Chinese cultural context are considered.

The Questionnaire Survey

Participants

The participants of the study were teachers in primary and secondary schools in Hong Kong – all of them being ethnically Chinese. They were concurrently students in the Open University of Hong Kong enrolled in in-service degree programmes: the BEd (Hons) in Primary Education, the BEd (Hons) in Secondary Education and the MEd. All were studying a course in educational psychology appropriate to their degree programmes.

It is worth noting that, in the Hong Kong school education context, most primary school teachers and some secondary school teachers graduated with sub-degree qualifications from the Colleges of Education or the Institute of Education. The BEd (Hons) being offered by the Open University of Hong Kong is one of the ways by which they may up-grade their qualifications to a graduate-teacher status, and subsequently, they may reap some financial benefits on the condition that they actually get such a post. The MEd is an academic qualification for teachers who are already graduates, and bears no direct linkage to any immediate salary gains.

Material and procedures

The survey questionnaire consisted of two parts. The first involved an adapted version of the Study Process Questionnaire (SPQ; Biggs, 1992) plus some items measuring directly conceptions of learning. The second part was based on the Orientation to Teaching Questionnaire (Kember & Gow, 1994) and an earlier version of the Approaches to Teaching Questionnaire (Prosser & Trigwell, 1993; 1999). As the two questionnaires on teaching were originally designed for academics in university settings, items were selected and modified to suit the needs of the current study. Responses to all the main scales were found to be fairly reliable (all Cronbach alphas > 0.65 and the mean alpha was 0.75).

The questionnaires were mailed to all participants (457) one month into their course of study. A total of 316 (69.1%) returned questionnaires were received. Questionnaires, which were basically the same as the first one, were sent to those 291 students returning their first questionnaires and remaining in the courses. A total of 220 (75.6%) were returned. The return rate was considered as high for a mail survey.

Results

Structural equation modeling was the main analytical tool for exploring the relationships among the conception of learning, the approach to learning, the conception of teaching and the course results of the students. The method was used partly to include latent variables in the analysis and partly to counteract the response set observed in the way that the students filled in the answer sheet (cf. Gu, Wen & Wu, 1995). A 'nested model' procedure (Maruyama, 1997) was used with the AMOS package (Arbuckle, 1997). The model that fitted the observed data best was a four-correlated-factor model (χ^2=171.06, df=169, p=0.441). 'Learning' and 'teaching' were two of the four latent variables accounting for the main variations of the scales. While space here does not allow a detailed description of the path model here, the factor analysis using structural equation modelling, supported the existence of the conception of learning and the conception of teaching as two latent variables (see Tang, 1999a, for details).

Table 11.1 shows the respondent's change of questionnaire scores over the year studying the course. Two scales showed a significant change. The respondents scored lower on 'achieving approach' and 'surface approach' scales. The changes in the 'deep approach' score and the 'learning as an increase in knowledge' were not statistically significant. The results suggested that through the year of studying, students moved towards a more meaning-focused conception of learning. However, none of the change in scores concerning the teaching approaches and orientations reached a statistically significant level.

Table 11.1
Questionnaire scores at the early and final stages of teacher education courses

Scales	Early stage		Final stage	
	Mean	SD	Mean	SD
Achieving Approach*	40.61	7.68	39.54	7.92
Deep Approach	45.11	7.64	45.66	7.13
Surface Approach*	43.47	8.52	42.59	8.01
Learning as gaining more knowledge	18.12	3.23	18.38	2.86
Learning as understanding	15.99	2.49	15.90	2.28
Teaching: transferring knowledge	21.62	2.79	21.53	2.83
Teaching: examinations	20.47	3.36	20.84	3.23
Teaching: problem solving	22.83	3.22	22.66	2.93
Teaching: understanding	21.85	2.91	21.55	2.59

* $p < .05$, 2-tailed (paired t-test)

Partial correlations, with control of the response set, were used to study the changes in questionnaire scores between the early and final stages of the course (see Table 11.2). The results indicated that those who increased the use of a deep approach would likely decrease the use of a surface approach. Over the same period, the same group would be less likely to consider teaching as preparing students for examination or as transmitting knowledge. This indicated that a change in the orientation towards learning would likely be accompanied by a change in the same direction in their orientations towards teaching. It was found that the examination scores of those teachers studying part-time degrees correlated negatively with an increase in the surface approach and also negatively with 'teaching as transmitting knowledge'.

The Phenomenographic Study

The interviewees were a subset of the participants in the questionnaire survey. Twenty-nine of them were interviewed in the first phase of the study 3-4 months after they had begun the course of study about educational psychology. Twenty-five of the 29 were interviewed for a second time after they finished their final examination but before the release of their final results.

As the interview study was for a more in-depth understanding of relationships between studying a course of educational psychology and the conception of teaching, it would be appropriate to describe the background of these courses here. To complete the course, a student needed to submit five assignments, which were argumentative essays related to issues in the area of educational psychology. Within the postgraduate level course, one of the assignments was a small-scale research project, which was given double weighting with respect to the other assignments. The content of the two undergraduate courses covered both develop-

Table 11.2
Partial correlation coefficients between changes in learning process and conception and teaching conception scores and examination scores (expressed as Z scores)

	CHANGES IN THE SCORES DURING THE COURSE								
CHANGES IN SCORES	Achieving approach	Deep approach	Surface approach	Learning – as more knowledge	Learning – understanding	Teaching – preparing for examination	Teaching – solving problems	Teaching – transmitting knowledge	Teaching – developing understanding
Exam results	.03	-.01	-.15*	-.09	-.01	-.06	-.05	-.16*	.09
Assignments	-.05	-.10	.00	.05	.04	-.01	-.01	-.14	.05
Achieving approach	—	.16*	.03	-.04	-.11	-.23**	-.12	-.24**	-.12
Deep approach		—	-.38**	-.13	.10	-.31**	-.05	-.23**	-.08
Surface approach			—	-.05	-.24**	.07	-.11	.15	-.12
Learning as more knowledge				—	.40**	.12	-.05	-.06	.18*
Learning as understanding					—	-.01	.04	.01	.15*
Teaching – preparing for examination						—	.02	.39**	.14
Teaching – solving problems							—	.14	.32**
Teaching – transmitting knowledge								—	-.30**

* p<0.05 ** p<0.01   2-tailed

mental theories and theories of learning with many examples drawing the implication of these theories in the school context. The master's level course was narrower but more in-depth being based on the socio-cultural perspectives of Vygotsky and Bruner. It also included critical evaluations of attachment theory, Piagetian developmental stages and literature on cognitive and social development in schools.

The interviews were conducted in Chinese – the mother tongue of these students. During the early part of the course, the participants were asked questions such as:

- How did you work on your assignment?
- How do you conduct your day-to-day study?
- What do you mean by learning?
- Could you give an example and a counter-example of learning?
- How do you prepare for your lessons and teach in class?
- What do you mean by teaching?
- Could you give an example and a counter-example of teaching?

The questions for the second round covered more or less the same ground, but with some questions about the preparation for examination replacing those about doing the assignments. In addition, the participants were asked whether their conceptions and approaches had changed over the period of time and whether the course of educational psychology had any impact on them.

Analysis. The interviews were tape-recorded and transcribed into English. The translation was checked by at least one other person besides the translator to ensure accuracy in meaning. The first interview of one participant was dropped due to recording problems. The interview protocols were analysed using a phenomenographic approach with the help of the NUD*IST software.

Phenomenography, according to Marton (1994), involves rigorous empirical investigation of the qualitatively different ways in which people experience and conceptualize various phenomena, and is a way of describing the variations in a finite set of categories of description. In the language of phenomenography, 'conception' refers to a category of description of the generalized way of experiencing something. Within each conception, the phenomenon is experienced as having a 'referential' aspect focusing on the meaning of the experience and a structural aspect. Within the structural aspect, there is a 'what' facet referring to the content of learning and teaching, and a 'how' facet referring to the acts and outcomes of learning and teaching. The conceptions can be put into a hierarchical structure according to their respective inclusiveness and complexity, in as much as each conception is depicting a part or parts of the same whole phenomenon. (For further details on phenomenography, see Bowden, 1996 and Marton & Booth, 1997)

Results

Conceptions of learning and teaching

The phenomenographic analysis of the interviews during the early part of the course yielded six conceptions of learning and six corresponding conceptions of teaching. The categorization of these conceptions together with illustrative quotations are reported elsewhere (Tang, 1999b). Tables 11.3 and 11.4 present the conceptions of learning and those of teaching identified here.

Table 11.3
Six conceptions of learning

Learning	The meaning of learning (referential aspect)	The object of learning ('what' aspect)	The act of learning ('how' aspect)
L-A	Acquiring knowledge – gaining more knowledge (quantitative)	Knowledge within books or course materials – as facts or statements of truth	Putting in effort – reading everything and studying hard
L-B	Preparing for examinations or completing assignments – fulfilling the requirements of the course (externally controlled).	Relevant points and theories for answering questions – knowledge as facts or correct answers	Picking up the key points (like a treasure hunter)
L-C	Applying – direct use of theories or methodologies in real life situations (job skills orientated)	Theories and methods that can be used in real life or classroom contexts – a testing ground for whether the knowledge is truth	Picking up theories and methods and applying them in real-life situations
L-D	Explaining and relating phenomena – using theories and perspectives to make sense of the world	Theories and perspectives of others for analyzing and explaining phenomena – modifying theories where necessary	Picking up theories and perspectives and using them to explain and relate phenomena
L-E	Changing one's own perspectives or attitudes – comparing alternative perspectives	Theories and perspectives of others as alternative frameworks of seeing the world – knowledge as changeable	Gathering new perspectives and recognising the inadequacy of one's own perspective.
L-F	Personal development – becoming a different person	Personal perspectives, value system, moral beliefs and attitudes reconsidered in the light of theories and perspectives	Reflecting with an emphasis on the moral and belief aspects.

Table 11.4
Six conceptions of teaching

Teaching	The meaning of teaching (referential aspect)	The object of teaching ('what' aspect)	The act of teaching ('how' aspect)
T-A	Transmitting knowledge – teachers giving what they know to learners	Knowledge and moral behaviour – as facts or statements of truth	Mostly, teachers tell the learners or give them some tasks to do.
T-B	Preparing learners for assessment – teachers passing on skills and ability to learners.	Relevant points and theories for answering questions – knowledge as facts or correct answers.	Teachers tell learners and give them tasks, learners are expected to become able to do the required tasks.
T-C	Demonstrating applications – teachers showing learners how to apply	Theories, methods and attitudes that can be used in real life or classroom contexts – a test for how well learners are learning.	Teachers show learners by examples. Learners observe examples and build up right methods or attitudes.
T-D	Helping learners' understanding – providing stimulation to make learners think about phenomena	Theories and perspectives of others for analyzing and explaining phenomena – modifying theories where necessary	Teachers provide suitable environment. Learners make sense of the world with teachers' help.
T-E	Facilitating changes in perspectives or attitudes – providing stimulation to challenge and change beliefs.	Theories and perspectives of others as alternative frameworks of seeing the world – knowledge as changeable	Those mentioned in the above category (T-D) and teachers treating the learners with sincerity and a caring attitude.
T-F	Supporting learners' development – helping learners to grow up and become a better person	Personal perspectives, value system, moral beliefs and attitudes related to life.	Teachers interact with learners trying to think through the perspectives of each other.

Relationship between conceptions

The interviewees were classified by the categories of description for the purpose of checking the relationship between the two sets of conceptions. As many interviewees showed more than one conception of learning and that of teaching, the highest conception reached in the above-mentioned hierarchical structure was selected for the analysis (see Marton, Dall'Alba & Beaty, 1993 for justification of this decision).

It was important for this research to probe the relationship between the conceptions of learning and teaching. The interviewees in this study were asked to describe their learning process of studying a part-time degree in the Open University of Hong Kong and their work as full-time teachers in the school system. The two experiences were not necessarily logically related (cf. Trigwell & Prosser, 1996). A teacher who, in his professional capacity, helps students develop personally may engage in learning, solely to collect some information. This was illustrated by two teachers who reported they perceived their own learning as explaining and relating phenomena while they considered their teaching only as preparing students for taking examinations. Second, scrutinizing the fine structures of the two sets of categories of description, the linkages between them were incidental rather than logical. In several cases, some elements of the conceptions of teaching were absent in the corresponding conceptions of learning, and vice versa. Hence, any observed relations were probably not artifacts of the interview or the analysis procedures, but something in the experienced world of the interviewees.

Table 11.5
Cross-tabulation of the conceptions of learning and teaching

LEARNING		Teaching						Total
		T-A	T-B	T-C	T-D	T-E	T-F	
	L-A	1						1
	L-B							0
	L-C	3	2	4				9
	L-D		2	6	2			10
	L-E				4	2		6
	L-F					1	1	2
Total		4	4	10	6	3	1	28

As shown in Table 11.5, conceptions of learning and teaching were highly correlated (Spearman's rho = .84). Perhaps the conceptions of learning affect conceptions of teaching, or vice versa, or perhaps a third factor impacts on both conceptions. Such a third factor is epistemology or the ways of experiencing knowledge.

Closer examination of the pattern in Table 11.5 suggests another plausible explanation for the correlation. In that table a person's conception of teaching is never higher than the corresponding conception of learning. Perhaps the conception of learning is a limiting factor on the conception of teaching. A teacher without the experience of deep learning is unlikely to structure teaching at that level for their students.

Table 11.6
Changes in the conceptions of learning and teaching

S	Degree	F/M	Early		Remark	Post-exam	
1	BEd(P)	F	L-E	T-E		L-E	T-E
2	BEd(P)	F	L-D	T-C	L↑T↑	**L-F**	**T-E**
3	M.Ed.	M	L-C	T-A		L-C	T-A
4	BEd(P)	F	L-D	T-B		L-D	T-B
5	BEd(S)	F	L-C	T-A	L↑T↑	**L-E**	**T-D**
6	BEd(S)	F	L-D	T-C		L-D	T-C
7	BEd(S)	F	L-C	T-C		L-C	T-C
8	M.Ed.	F	L-C	T-B	L↑	**L-E**	T-B
9	BEd(P)	F	L-D	T-C			
10	BEd(S)	M	L-F	T-F		L-F	T-F
11	M.Ed.	M	L-C	T-C	L↑	**L-E**	T-C
12	BEd(P)	F	L-E	T-D		L-E	T-D
13	BEd(P)	F	L-E	T-E		L-E	T-E
14	M.Ed.	F	L-C	T-B		L-C	T-B
15	BEd(P)	F	L-E	T-D	L↑	**L-F**	T-D
16	M.Ed.	F	L-E	T-D		L-E	T-D
17	BEd(S)	F	L-D	T-D	L↑	**L-F**	T-D
18	BEd(S)	M	L-F	T-E	T↑	L-F	**T-F**
19	M.Ed.	M	L-C	T-C	L↑T↑	**L-D**	**T-D**
20	BEd(P)	F	L-C	T-C			
21	M.Ed.	M	L-D	T-C	T↑	L-D	**T-D**
22	M.Ed.	M	L-D	T-C		L-D	T-C
23	BEd(S)	F	L-C	T-A		L-C	T-A
24	M.Ed.	M	L-D	T-D			
25	BEd(P)	F	L-A	T-A	L↑T↑	**L-D**	**T-C**
26	M.Ed.	M	L-E	T-D	L↑T↑	**L-F**	**T-F**
27	BEd(S)	F	L-D	T-C		L-D	T-C
28	BEd(S)	M	L-D	T-C			

Note: L↑ and T↑ indicate that respondents reported a change to a higher order conception of learning and teaching, respectively.

Moreover, scrutinizing Table 11.6 shows that the high correlation between the conceptions of teaching and learning remained unchanged in the interviews later in course. The limiting effects of the conception of learning on that of the conception of teaching also remained intact.

Changes after studying the course

When the highest levels reached for the conceptions of learning and teaching were used as the basis for comparing the data from the first and the second interviews, half of the students did not demonstrate any change over the year of study. Nine students (37.5%) were found to have reached some higher levels in their conceptions of learning while seven (29.2%) demonstrated the same advancement in their conceptions of teaching. Out of these, five (20.8%) showed concurrent changes in the conceptions of teaching and learning. One student had a change in the conceptions of teaching in the opposite direction, from a T-B conception to a T-A one. At the end of the course, none of those students held a conception of learning below the L-C level.

There was no pattern relating gender or the course to those students who demonstrated changes in their conceptions of learning. All these students reached at least a L-D level, indicating that they more or less encompassed the meaning focus of learning and no longer saw knowledge as something-out-there and transmittable.

As there was not any clear external factor which explained the changes, the students' own accounts for the changes in the interviews formed the basis to further understand the contributing factors. Of the nine students, only six were aware of their changes in the conception of learning. Of those so aware, some explained their changes in the following manner:

> The more I learn, the more I find myself inadequate. ...Sometimes, when I think of my childhood, I would find the same factors (influencing me). ... Would it relate to my upbringing – influencing me? ... I did not have such thoughts before taking the course. (S2: L-D to L-F)

> The most direct impact was from reading the notes and books. Moreover, after reading, I thought about it myself and found that it was really different. ... Observing the reality and my life, I became aware that I had changed in thinking and behaviour. Then I think that I have learned something. (S17: L-D to L-F)

Two other interviewees (S5: L-C to L-E and S15: L-E to L-F) also explained their changes in similar ways. For all four, there was a clear linkage of their changes in the conceptions to their own personal experiences. While none of them was very clear about how the course of study had impact on them, one student (S19) had more difficulties in relating the change to the course of study but considered the course helped him to think more:

> I have not thought about what learning is, well, because learning is very abstract. ... But after taking the course, I would think about what learning is. I have thought about it, thinking about it. I have learned something, anyway. (S19: L-C to L-D)

A similar viewpoint was observed in one of those who indicated no change in his conception of learning but described the general impact of studying the course as

> Knowing more... My perspectives have become more in-depth and wider in scope. I think that it is a change, a difference, I can feel it. (S26: L-E to L-F)

For the above students, in trying to see one's own experience through the study material or in thinking more as stimulated by the material, they increased their personal involvement in learning. Such an increase in involvement might bring about learning being more focused on something meaningful to the learners. In short, such personal involvement, in term of self-reflection or in-depth thinking, was the reason behind the changes in the conceptions of learning.

One of those recognizing the change in the conception of learning (S8: L-C to L-E) did not account for the change but indicated that the study of some research has altered her awareness about Piagetain stage theory. The remaining two who did not recognize their change in conceptions of learning also reported that they were influenced by some theories in the course material, including Vygotskian (S11: L-C to L-E) and the 'self-fulfilling prophecy effect' (S25: L-A to L-D). They seemed to be suggesting that the cause of the changes was the direct impact of some theoretical views that allowed them now to see some phenomenon from a new perspective. However, the relationship between these theories and the understanding of the nature of learning was far from clear. We will return to this issue later in the chapter.

Of those identified as changing their conception of learning, five also showed an increase in the highest level of the conceptions of teaching expressed. Two others were considered to have higher conceptions of teaching but without a corresponding change in the conception of learning. One (S18) was classified as having the highest level of the conception of learning in both occasions of the interview study, so there would not be any possible room of improvement in that aspect.

One student (S21: T-C to T-D) reached a higher level in the conceptions of teaching but remained unchanged in the conception of learning while there was still room for improvement. He explained the change in his conception of teaching in terms of the impact from the theory of scaffolding. Another student (S19: T-C to T-D) ascribed the change to the theory of 'zone of proximal development'. In both cases, the Vygotskian theory made teachers recognize the auxiliary or the assistance nature of the teacher role.

Two of the other five with an enhanced conception of teaching explained their changes in terms of the impact of learning in general.

> That is my feeling. I am teaching and learning at the same time. I have changed my view. (S2: T-C to T-E)

Mainly, it (the course in educational psychology) enabled me to stimulate more students to learn by themselves, i.e. more self-learning. Not done by teachers ... As I have mentioned, I now think more about the students. (S5: T-A to T-D)

The three others were not aware of their own changes in the conceptions of teaching but admitted the course had made them think more about teaching or about student learning.

Similar to the explanation about changes in the conceptions of learning, the changes in the conceptions of teaching might be explained in two ways. One was that the change was a result of the direct impact of some theories concerning teaching – in this particular case, the Vygotskian perspective about the nature of teaching. On the other hand, a change in the conception of teaching could be a result of the experience of learning. Only five of the nine with a change in the conception of learning changed their conceptions of teaching and only one with a change in the conception of teaching did not also manifest a change in their conception of learning. That particular one explained the change in conception, not in terms of the general experience of learning but using rather of Vygotskian theory. It is reasonable to speculate that in the case where certain experiences of learning caused a change in the conception of teaching, it would be preceded by a change in conception of learning.

Discussion

Integrating the quantitative and qualitative studies

The results from the quantitative and the qualitative studies here are complimentary and provide a consistent picture. The phenomenographic analysis of the interview data suggests that teachers doing in-service courses hold qualitatively different conceptions of learning and teaching and such conceptions are identifiable in the exploratory factor analysis. While the qualitative data show more details about the variation of such conceptions with six categories in each conception, the statistical data confirm two general bipolar conceptions of 'learning as meaning focused' to 'learning as text focused' and that of 'teaching as helping student development' to 'teaching as content based'.

The statistical data show that, after studying the course, the students were more likely to report focusing on meaning in their learning. However, the quantitative data failed to show a clear pattern of change about the orientation of teaching. This is consistent with the interview data, in which nine of the twenty-two cases that had room for improvement (that is they had not reached L-F at the beginning of the course) are actually observed to have changed their conceptions. This represents a 40.9% rate of change. On the other hand, only seven of the twenty-three teachers (30.4%) with the potential for change actually changed their conceptions of teaching and improvements in the conceptions of teaching noted are generally smaller than that of the conceptions of learning.

The partial correlation analysis shows concurrent changes in the conceptions of learning and teaching. This pattern is also supported by the interview data in that five out of the nine with a change in the conceptions of learning are also observed as having a change in the conceptions of teaching.

In brief, the quantitative data and the qualitative data are in agreement with each other. They both detect the existence of variation in the conceptions of learning and teaching, the movement over the year of study towards a meaning-focused learning and the likelihood of concurrent improvement in the conceptions of learning and teaching.

Accounting for the changes in conceptions over the course

While the statistical data provide grounds for generalizing the findings, they shed very little light on the reasons for, and the mechanisms of, the changes in conceptions. Focusing on the interview data, two pathways of change have been identified and are worthy of further discussion.

The first pathway of change is the consequence of coming across some theories or pieces of information which bring new light into the understanding of some current phenomena. This pathway is quite common in the description about conceptual change in a science education context (e.g. Guzzetti & Hynd, 1998). In the case where a teacher, who has considered teaching as transmitting knowledge to students by demonstrating the correct ways (a Bandura social learning theory conception) reads about the Vygotskian theory of scaffolding, he or she may change and adopt the conception of teaching as a partnership between students and teachers mediated through social interactions. The change is logical and consistent with the change in the theoretical frameworks.

On the other hand, it is much more difficult to see the logic in how the work of Donaldson (1978) in refuting the Piagetian theory of development stages and that of egocentrism changes a person's conception of learning from learning as an application to learning as a change in perspectives. A logical explanation of how the theory of 'self-fulfilling prophecy in classrooms' can change one's conception of learning from 'learning as an increase in knowledge' (L-A) to 'learning as relating and explaining phenomena' (L-D) is even more far-fetched. Between the impact of the courses as seen by the three students (S8, S11 & S25) and the changes in conceptions, there seem to be some missing links. These cases argue for the need of some alternative explanations.

The second mechanism for a change in the conceptions may hold the key to the alternative explanations. The majority of the interviewees alluded their changes in conceptions to an increase in self-reflection or in thinking about some phenomena. However, it is important to note that these students did not explain their changes in conceptions as a result of specific insights reached in these self-reflections or thinking processes. Instead, they saw those changes as a general consequence of increased reflections and thinking. Probably, when they reflected on some issues, they experienced that the same phenomenon could be seen from different angles – with a shift of foreground and background, or the boundaries between the objects. It was not one or more of these different angles that impressed them, but the general experience of seeing things from many perspectives.

As they experienced this, they felt that maybe this was learning. The argument here is that their changes in conceptions are experiential rather than cognitive – they have experienced learning differently rather than directly seeing learning as defined differently. For those who become aware of their own changes in conceptions (e.g. S15 & S17), they may experience learning as a change as a person (L-F).

Returning to the three cases where the students have shown some changes in the conceptions and experienced the impact of some specific theories, it is more convincing to explain these changes in the conceptions as a result of their experience in studying the theories. For example, the student studying the 'self-fulfilling prophecy' theory found that there were other plausible explanations for some classroom events. In the process, the student experienced that learning brought about a way of explaining and relating phenomena. In a nutshell, the change in the conceptions of learning is brought about through the experience rather than as a direct consequence of the theoretical positions.

Reviewing the sixteen cases where a change in the conceptions of learning or teaching has been identified, only two cases of the change in the conception of teaching can be accounted for by the impact of some theories or insight. The majority are explicable in experiential rather than cognitive or content-specific terms. It can be argued that the main road to conceptual change, at least in relation to the conceptions of learning and teaching, is in experiencing learning differently. Moreover, the experiential mechanism of conceptual change is also consistent with the explanation of why the conception of learning may be a limiting factor for the conception of teaching. Unfortunately, current research into change in conceptions of learning and teaching is limited. So, it is not yet possible to make a more definitive statement about the role of learning experience in such conceptual change.

Last but not least, the explanation in which the experience and conception of learning is a limiting factor of the conception of teaching, though tentative, will have significant implications for teacher education practice. If a teacher's conception of learning entails a ceiling effect on his conception of teaching – and if we aim at enhancing the teachers' quality of teaching – the potential of in-service teachers should be developed to reach the highest level in experiencing learning. The content, assessment structures and pedagogy of teacher education programmes have to be orchestrated towards this goal.

Comparisons with other studies

The comparison drawn here is based on several phenomenographic studies in Hong Kong and elsewhere. The contexts of the studies and the conceptions identified are summarized in Tables 11.7 and 11.8, with similar conceptions shown as horizontal rows in the tables.

Table 11.7
Comparing three studies on the conceptions of learning

Study		Current	Marton, Dall'Alba & Beaty, 1993	Marton, Watkins & Tang, 1997
Culture		Hong Kong: Chinese	United Kingdom: English	Hong Kong: Chinese
Institutional		Open University	Open University	Secondary school
C O N C E P T I O N S	Text Focused	Acquiring knowledge (L-A)	Increasing one's knowledge (A)	Committing to memory – words (A) – meaning (B)
		Preparing exam or completing assignments (L-B)	Memorizing and reproducing (B)	
		Applying (L-C)	Applying (C)	
	Meaning Focused	Explaining and relating phenomena (L-D)	Understanding (D)	Understanding – Meaning (C) – Phenomenon (D)
		Changing perspectives or attitudes (L-E)	Seeing something in a different way (E)	
		Personal development (L-F)	Changing as a person (F)	

Table 11.8
Comparing three studies on the conceptions of teaching

Study		Current	Pratt, 1992	Prosser, Trigwell & Taylor, 1994
Culture		Hong Kong: Chinese	Cross cultural	Australian
Participants		School teachers	Adult educators	University teachers
C O N C E P T I O N S	Teacher Focused	Transmitting knowledge (T-A)	Engineering: delivering content (A)	Transmitting syllabus (A) Transmitting knowledge (B)
		Preparing students for assessment (T-B)		Helping student to acquire the syllabus (C)
		Demonstrating applications (T-C)	Apprenticeship: modeling (B)	Helping students to acquire teachers' knowledge (D)
	Student Focused	Helping learners' understanding (T-D)	Developmental: cultivating the intellect (C)	Helping students to develop conceptions (E)
		Facilitating change in perspectives or attitudes (T-E)		Helping students to change conceptions (F)
		Supporting learners' development (L-F)	Nurturing: facilitating personal agency (D)	
			Social reform: a better society (E)	

Pratt's (1992) five conceptions of teaching closely resemble those identified in the current study. Conception T-B is missing in his study, probably because examinations are not a crucial part of many adult education courses. Pratt's conception E, which is more socially orientated, is missing in the current study, probably because equality and open access are more an issue in adult education than in school education. However, as many of Pratt's adult educators are working on basic literacy for adults, it is not surprising that his conceptions A to D closely resemble the conceptions of teaching observed in this study. Moreover, contrary to the claim of Pratt's (1998) conceptions A, B, C and D are quite clearly hierarchical.

In comparison to the results of Prosser et al. (1994), there are some differences in the ways the conceptions are categorized and the personal change in perspectives is missing in their categories. The differences between Prosser et al.'s research and this study may be discussed in terms of the totality of the conception of teaching. In their context, teaching was about students having conceptions and worldviews within undergraduate physical science courses. Yet in the context of the current research, teaching is about helping students develop into mature persons in school education. Nevertheless, the current findings do not rule out the possibility of the effect of cultural differences – Hong Kong versus Australian. Whether the distinct institutional contexts or the contrasting cultures have sown the seeds of difference between the two studies needs further research to determine.

The conceptions of learning identified in this research closely resemble those in Marton et al. (1993). The similarities are the results of the analytic process rather than a planned objective of this research. It is interesting to find differences between the current research and that of Marton et al. (1997) in terms of the categories of description generated, even though the subjects in both studies have shared the same cultural background. Regarding the institutional context, the Marton et al.'s (1997) participants are secondary school, Hong Kong Chinese students whereas those interviewees in the current research are Hong Kong Chinese teachers taking part-time degree course. Memorization, a central issue in the Hong Kong secondary school study, was seldom mentioned spontaneously by the subjects of the current investigation. In addition, the category D of Marton et al. (1997) can barely embrace the idea of changing perspectives (L-E) in this research. The idea of relating different knowledge in this category D is more likely to be mainly in the conception of learning as explaining and relating phenomena (L-D).

Here, the idea of the totality of the conceptions may be helpful in making sense of the situation. For the learners of Marton et al.'s (1997) secondary school research, the totality of the conception of learning lies in synthesizing knowledge, often from a school curriculum to make sense of the phenomena, again probably in a classroom setting. However, for the teachers undertaking a part-time degree in the current research, the totality of the conception of learning is in developing the person and his knowledge system to deal effectively with the demands of life and professional practices. In the light of this, the absence of the two highest categories among the high school students is not unexpected. Also, teachers are much more likely to be aware that solely committing things to memory seldom works in an everyday context. Hence, memorization is comparatively a less significant part in the totality of the teachers' conception of learning than in that of the high school students.

Integrating the comparison of the current research findings with the two studies in somewhat similar contexts – the distance education context of learners in the United Kingdom Open University (Marton et al., 1993) and the socio-cultural context of high school students in Hong Kong (Marton et al., 1997), the current outcome space is more similar to that of the United Kingdom Open University research (particularly as much of the UK Open University material is used in the Hong Kong Open University courses also). This probably points to the greater significance of the institutional context (see Eklund-Myrskog, 1998) over the cultural one. Nevertheless, caution should be exercised in putting too much confidence in the inferences from a single study.

Conclusion

It is appropriate in this book about the Chinese teachers to discuss, as a conclusion, the impact of culture on the conceptions of learning and teaching. The current findings seem to indicate a significant correlation between the two sets of conceptions. The correlation probably results from the strong influence of the experience of learning on both the conceptions of learning and teaching and the effect of institutional contexts on such conceptions. However, after scrutinizing the results of this study, the comparison with those from other cultures and the cross cultural research by Pratt (1992), there is no indication of a strong impact of Chinese culture on the conceptions of learning and teaching among the Hong Kong school teachers.

The study has pointed to the possibilities that the conception of learning as a limiting factor on the conception of teaching and that the experience of learning as the main pathway through which the conceptions of learning and teaching may be changed. More research is needed to ascertain these suggestions, especially whether such explanations are only valid within a certain cultural context.

REFERENCES

Arbuckle, J.L. (1997). *Amos User Guide Version 3.6.* Chicago, IL: SmallWaters Corp.

Biggs, J.B. (1992). *Why and how do Hong Kong Students Learn? Using the Learning and Study Processes Questionnaires.* Education Paper 14. Hong Kong: Faculty of Education, The University of Hong Kong.

Bowden, J.A. (1996). Phenomenographic Research – Some Methodological Issues. *Göteborg Studies in Educational Sciences*, 109, 49-66.

Donaldson, M. (1978). *Children's Minds.* Glasgow, UK: Fortana.

Eklund-Myrskog, G. (1998). Students' Conceptions of Learning in Different Educational Contexts. *Higher Education*, 35, 299-316.

Gow, L & Kember, D (1993). Conceptions of Teaching and Their Relationship to Student Learning. *British Journal of Education Psychology*, 63, 20-22.

Gu, Y., Wen, Q. & Wu, D. (1995). How Often is Often: Reference Ambiguities of the Likert-scale in Language Learning Strategy Research. *Occasional Papers in English Language Teaching*, 5, 19-35.

Guzzetti, B. & Hynd, C. (Eds.) (1998). *Perspectives on Conceptual Change.* Mahwah, NJ: Lawrence Erlbaum Associates.

Ho, S.-P.A. (1998). *Changing Teachers' Conceptions of Teaching as an Approach to Enhancing Teaching and Learning in Tertiary Education.* Unpublished Ph.D. Thesis, Hong Kong: The University of Hong Kong.

Kember, D. & Gow, L. (1994). Orientations to Teaching and Their Effect on the Quality of Student Learning. *Journal of Higher Education*, 65(1), 58–74.

Marton, F. & Booth, S. (1997). *Learning and Awareness.* Mahwah, NJ: Lawrence Erlbaum Associates.

Marton, F., Dall'Alba, G. & Beaty, E. (1993). Conceptions of Learning. *International Journal of Educational Research*, 19, 277-300.

Marton, F., Watkins, D.A. & Tang, C. (1997). Discontinuities and Continuities in the Experience of Learning: An Interview Study of High-school Students in Hong Kong. *Learning and Instruction*, 7(1), 21-48.

Maruyame, G.M. (1998). *Basics of Structural Equation Modeling.* Thousand Oaks, CA: Sage.

Mellado, V. (1998). The Classroom Practice of Preservice Teachers and their Conceptions of Teaching and Learning Science. *Science Education*, 82, 197-202.

Pratt, D. (1992). Conceptions of Teaching. *Adult Education Quarterly*, 42(4), 203-220.

Pratt, D.D. & Associates. (1998). *Five Perspectives on Teaching in Adult and Higher Education.* Malabar, FL: Krieger.

Prosser, M. & Trigwell, K. (1993). Development of an Approaches to Teaching Questionnaire. *Research and Development in Higher Education*, 15, 468-473.

Prosser, M. & Trigwell, K. (1999). *Understanding Learning and Teaching*, Buckingham, UK: Open University Press.

Prosser, M., Trigwell, K. & Taylor, P. (1994). A Phenomenographic Study of Academics' Conceptions of Science Learning and Teaching. *Learning and Instruction*, 4(3), 217-231.

Scott, R. & Rodger, B. (1995). Changing Teachers' Conceptions of Teaching Writing: A Collaborative Study. *Foreign Language Annuals*, 28(2), 234-247.

Tang, T.K.W. (1993). Do Teachers' Belief Influence Student Learning. In J.B. Biggs & D.A. Watkins (Eds.), *Learning and Teaching in Hong Kong: What is and What Might Be.* Hong Kong: The University of Hong Kong, 53-66.

Tang, T.K.W. (1999a). Approaches to Learning of School Teachers Studying Distance Education Courses in Educational Psychology. In R. Carr, O.J. Jegede, T.-M. Wong & K.-S. Yuen (Eds.), *The Asian Distance Learner.* Hong Kong: Open University of Hong Kong Press, 100-115.

Tang, T.K.W. (1999b). *Conceptions of Learning and Teaching: A Phenomenographic Study of Teachers Working for In-service Degrees.* Paper presented at the 8th European Conference for Research on Learning and Instruction, Göteborg, Sweden.

Trigwell, K. & Prosser, M. (1996). Changing Approaches to Teaching: A Relational Perspective. *Studies in Higher Education*, 21, 275-284.

12

A Conceptual Change Approach to University Staff Development

Angela S.P. Ho

It is widely recognised in the literature that teachers at all levels hold personal conceptions of teaching which have developed from their long years of classroom experiences as a student and subsequently as a teacher and that such conceptions fundamentally influence their teaching practices. Thus in a major review of research into teachers' thought processes, Clark & Peterson (1986, p.287) concluded that:

> They [researchers] hold in common the idea that teacher's cognitive and other behaviours are guided by and make sense in relation to a personally held system of beliefs, values, and principles.

Ramsden (1993) observed that all teachers hold their own *vernacular* (or *informal*) theories of teaching and learning. He pointed out that in higher education lecturers and administrators alike generally make decisions concerning teaching and learning based on their 'amateur' informal theories which unfortunately are insufficient for promoting quality teaching and learning in many cases. Accordingly, Ramsden argued that improving teaching and learning in higher education requires improving lecturers' personal theories of teaching and learning.

Research into tertiary teachers' conceptual frameworks of teaching and learning is able to provide staff developers with the necessary understanding about lecturers' informal theories or, in other words, their conceptions of teaching. This branch of research has prospered in the last decade or so, initially in the Western world (Dall'Alba, 1991; Dunkin & Precians, 1992; Fox, 1983; Martin & Balla, 1991; Martin & Ramsden, 1992; Pratt, 1992; Prosser et al., 1994; Samuelowicz & Bain, 1992; Trigwell et al., 1994), and recently this momentum has spread to Hong Kong (Gow & Kember, 1993; Kember & Kwan, 1999; see also Chapters 1, 2, and 11). Published empirical studies have shown that only a limited number of conceptions of teaching are common among lecturers. While the number of categories differentiated in individual studies varies, conceptions of teaching proposed generally range from those that strongly adhere to transmission of information from the teacher to the students to those that value facilitation of understanding in students. This spectrum emerges similarly in both Western and Chinese studies.

Conceptions of teaching and teaching practice

Research has produced evidence that the teacher's conceptions of teaching are fundamental to the quality of teaching and learning. Trigwell, Prosser & Taylor (1994) and Trigwell & Prosser (1996a) interviewed first year physical science lecturers about their approaches to teaching. In their analysis, an approach to teaching was described in terms of the teaching strategies adopted and the intention expressed for those strategies. They found that a logical relationship existed between teaching strategies and intentions. For example, those lecturers who intended to transmit information only adopted a teacher-focused strategy while those intending to facilitate student development adopted a student-focused strategy. Trigwell & Prosser (1996b) further showed a logical relationship between lecturers' conceptions and approaches to teaching.

Studies conducted in Hong Kong produced results comparable to those obtained in the Western community. Kember & Kwan (1999) interviewed lecturers in a university in Hong Kong to characterize both their conceptions of and approaches to teaching. They arrived at two broad categories of conceptions: transmission and facilitative teaching. Whereas for approaches to teaching, they found lecturers to vary in a continuum between content-centred and learning-centred approaches. They found a strong relationship between these variables. Lecturers who conceived of teaching as transmitting knowledge were more likely to adopt content-centred approaches to teaching while those who espoused a facilitative conception tended to use learning-centred approaches.

Conceptions of teaching and student learning

Gow & Kember (1993) reported that the predominant view of teaching within a department of a Hong Kong university was related to the approaches to studying adopted by students in that department. A view of teaching as transmission of knowledge appeared to discourage students from adopting deep approaches while a belief in teaching as the facilitation of learning was less likely to induce surface approaches. From this the researchers argued that if it is considered desirable that students adopt meaningful approaches to learning, it is important to direct staff development efforts towards changing teachers' conceptions of teaching to the facilitation of student learning. Another study by Sheppard & Gilbert (1991) carried out in-depth qualitative studies on 40 students and their lecturers in two arts and two science university departments and found that lecturers' theories of teaching was one of the factors that influenced the development of student epistemology.

Changing conceptions of teaching and staff development

The empirical evidence reviewed above show that teachers' conceptions of teaching are related to their teaching practices and consequentially to student learning approaches; with conceptions of teaching as transmission of knowledge being more commonly associated with a surface approach to learning while conceptions of facilitating learning appearing to be more conducive to deep learning. Such relationships indicate that conceptions of teaching should be the starting point for staff development.

The notion that effective learning involves conceptual change has already gained acceptance in the context of the teaching of students (Ramsden, 1988; Searle & Gunstone, 1990; Svensson & Högfors, 1988; Thijs, 1992). It has also been established in teacher education in the secondary and elementary sectors (Kennedy, 1991). However, in the field of staff development in higher education, it is only very recently that this idea has been taken up with some degree of seriousness. The few cases reported in the literature are from English speaking countries, mainly Australia. There was a one-day workshop by Bowden (1989) which focused on helping teachers to bring their teaching practices to match with their intended learning outcomes for students; another one-off workshop by Trigwell (1995) attempted to change participants' conceptions of teaching by increasing their awareness of the existence of other conceptions more conducive to better student learning; and a more formal one-year course was described by Ramsden (1992). However, evidence of the effectiveness or otherwise of these workshops is minimal.

This study attempted to implement the conceptual change approach to staff development in a university in Hong Kong. It began by synthesizing a model for such a programme from change theories. This served as a basis for developing a conceptual change programme which was then implemented and evaluated.

Developing a model for the conceptual change approach

It is well known in the literature that changing teachers' conceptions is a difficult task (Holt-Reynolds, 1991; Kennedy, 1991; Simon & Schifter, 1991; Taylor, 1990). Staff developers are in need of strategies which specifically tackle the changing of conceptions and which are potentially effective. Four change theories seem to provide a comprehensive theoretical foundation for a model for conceptual change programmes.

According to Argyris & Schön (1974) the process of increasing professional effectiveness involves the building and rebuilding of one's theories-of-action which are the rationale that someone holds for one's action. Learning can take place at two different levels. At the lower level, single-loop learning is limited to the linear increase of new micro-theories that conform to the basic principles of already held theories such that professionals learn about new skills and strategies to achieve existing goals and beliefs. A professional, on the other hand, grows and develops with double-loop learning which entails theory transition or in other words a fundamental change in terms of goals and beliefs. According to Argyris and Schön, transitions between theories-of-action are usually initiated by dilemmas associated with existing theories-of-action, for example, an inconsistency between espoused theory-of-action and theory-in-use, or an incompatibility of coexisting theories, or difficulties in achieving intended goals. When such dilemmas surface, the confrontation experienced by the professional will create tension to resolve the dilemmas, thus leading to changes in the espoused theory or theory-in-use.

However, people's existing theories-in-use tend to be self-maintaining and may blind them from perceiving dilemmas or may even result in them adopting a defensive attitude. Therefore in the process of theory transition, the professional needs to become aware of one's own theories-of-action, to admit the sources of dilemmas and to value the confrontation.

Lewin (1947) considered social groups as functioning at specific levels of social force fields and hypothesized that at any time a social group is at a quasi-stationary equilibrium of a particular force field level. Changing from the present level to a higher level of group performance requires added forces to act on the original level to change it. However, within the group there are inner resistances to change, mainly coming from the well established social habits which are grounded in the social values of the individuals in the group. Therefore additional forces are necessary to 'unfreeze' the original values and habits, that is to challenge and diminish their influence. A successful change will need to go through a three-stage process. The first stage is unfreezing of the present level, a process of clearing up the preexisting prejudices which would involve 'emotional stir-up' to 'break open the shell' (p.229). The second stage is the moving stage when new beliefs, attitudes, values and habits are built. And the third stage is freezing again at the new level.

The conceptual change theory proposed by Posner, Strike, Hewson & Gertzog (1982) has been very influential in conceptual change Science teaching for over a decade. These authors specified that the kind of conceptual change with which their theory is concerned is one which encompasses central and organising thoughts, analogous to Kuhn's notion of a paradigm shift (Kuhn, 1970). The central idea of Posner et al.'s theory rests with the learner being confronted with a conceptual conflict: for instance, the inability of existing conceptions about a scientific concept to explain observed phenomena. According to Posner et al. dissatisfaction with the misfunction of existing conceptions is the first and fundamental requirement to initiate a conceptual change. This dissatisfaction will initiate a learning process which involves the replacing of the original conception with a scientifically accepted one, provided that the new conception satisfies the conditions of being intelligible, initially plausible, and fruitful.

Shaw et al. (1990) considered that for change to actually occur a person has to be perturbed by an unsatisfying current situation and thus becomes aware of the need to change. It is also necessary for the person to build up a commitment to change, a vision of what the changes will bring about, and a projection into the vision.

Synthesizing the above theories, a model for a conceptual change programme is proposed which contains the following four potent elements:

The confrontation process. There is a striking commonality amongst these four theories of change. All pose 'confrontation' as essential for change to occur. Lewin visualised the necessity to unfreeze individuals from the quasi-stationary equilibrium which may cause 'emotional stir-up'. Argyris and Schön perceived the tension created by dilemmas would provide the momentum for transition between theories-of-action. Both Posner et al. and Shaw et al. posit the psychological state of being 'dissatisfied' with the existing conceptions or situation of matters as the first condition for change.

The self-awareness process. Argyris and Schön pointed out that the tendency towards consonance would blind professionals from seeing the mismatch between their ideal and their actual practice or any other inadequacies in their existing conceptions. They stressed the importance of self-realisation and self-analysis so the professional becomes aware of and admits existing dilemmas. Shaw et al. included awareness of the need to change as the second requisite for change. Although Posner at el. have not categorically isolated self-awareness in their theory, it is clear that they assume that when they talk about the feeling of dissatisfaction arising from a perception of the inadequacies of the current conceptions.

The availability of better alternative conceptions. Argyris & Schön (1974) diagnosed that the theories-in-use held by professionals are in general limiting and they labeled these "Model I" theories. They developed a "Model II" theory-of-action which could allow professionals to function more effectively and spend a lot of effort in facilitating people to change their theories-in-use from one which resembled "Model I" to that of "Model II". Posner et al. devoted their attention to the quality of the new conception that is introduced to the students for a replacement of the old conceptions. Their work suggests that in order for the old conceptions to be abandoned, there have to be better alternative(s) available for the learners to aspire to, to experiment with, and to model on.

The commitment building and refreezing process. The availability of better alternative conceptions opens up a direction of conceptual change yet it does not guarantee that a change would take place. Change will be able to consolidate if a mechanism for refreezing is included (Lewin, 1947). Nevertheless, whether the change will be successful essentially depends on the psychological disposition of the teachers (Shaw et al., 1990).

To conclude, for a conceptual change programme to be most effective it is desirable to include four elements which are, in logical order of occurrence, the self-awareness process; the confrontation process; exposure to better, alternative conceptions; and the commitment building and refreezing process. It is anticipated that these processes will be to a large extent intertwined. For example, it is natural to expect that in the process of diagnosing one's own conceptions, a lecturer will be confronted by the deeply embedded weaknesses which have now become plain to them. Also encouraging the development of a sense of commitment and vision should permeate throughout all the activities in a programme, although some stand-alone activities may still be designed for refreezing the new conceptions at the final stage.

The Conceptual Change Staff Development Programme

Based on the above model for conceptual change programmes, a four-session staff development short-course was designed which aimed to produce changes in the conceptions of teaching of participants towards one which is more conducive to quality student learning. In April 1995, the Programme was offered to academic staff of the Hong Kong Polytechnic University (PolyU) as an activity of the Educational Development Unit (EDU), under the title of 'Developing Your Personal Theory of Teaching'. Table 12.1 outlines the activities in the four sessions and their respective objectives.

Table 12.1
Outline of the conceptual change staff development programme

Activity	Objectives
Session 1	
Participants filling out a Self-Reflection Document which contained two parts: Part A tapped their espoused conceptions of teaching and Part B asked about their teaching practices.	- Self-awareness process - Building up data base for self-analysis
Presentation on conceptions of teaching research. In particular the work of Samuelowicz & Bain (1992) was discussed in detail because it was chosen as a reference framework for analysing one's conception of teaching.	- Promoting awareness of alternate conceptions - Providing a theoretical framework for self analysis
Session 2	
Participants analysed their espoused conception and teaching practices based on their answers to Part I and Part II in the Self-Reflection Document.	- Self-awareness process - Confrontation process
Participants discussed in groups to prioritise the five conceptions of teaching identified by Samuelowicz and Bain.	- Exploring alternative conceptions
Participants individually elected a conception of teaching which they would aspire to for improvement.	- Building a desire for change - Building commitment to change
Participants individually compared their aspirations with their current teaching practices.	- Confrontation process
Participants reflected upon and then discussed in groups the possible reasons for any inconsistencies between espoused conceptions and actual teaching practices and how could such inconsistencies be overcome.	- Envisioning changes
Session 3	
Presentation/discussion on learning approaches theories.	- Exposure to alternatives
Group discussion on case studies of "good teaching".	
Session 4	
Redesigning teaching (take home exercise).	- Building commitment to change
Sharing new teaching designs.	

Impact of the Programme

The hypothesis behind the conceptual change staff development Programme was that changing teachers' conceptions of teaching towards more elaborated levels would bring about improvement in their teaching practices and that their students' learning would be enhanced subsequently as a result. Accordingly a comprehensive evaluation was carried out to examine the impact of the Programme at these three levels: conceptual change of participants, subsequent impact on their teaching practice and eventual effect on student learning.

Twelve PolyU teachers who finished the entire four-session Programme completed all the data collection in the evaluation. Among these twelve three were found to hold high level conceptions of teaching before the Programme, thus leaving nine effective subjects, of whom seven were Chinese. Another four Chinese teachers who had initially agreed to take part in the study but eventually failed to attend the Programme were used as controls. The Control Group went through the same data collection processes as the Experimental Group. This allowed contemporaneous factors such as changes in institutional/departmental policies, differences in student in-take in the pre- and post-Programme years which may have caused changes in the teaching of the teachers or the learning of their students to be controlled.

The effect of the Programme on the participants' teaching conceptions was assessed by identifying and comparing the conceptions of teaching of the participants before and after the Programme. Three semi-structured interviews were used to solicit conceptions of teaching espoused by the participants: the *Pre-Programme Interview* recorded the initial conceptions of teaching of the participants before they attended the Programme; the *Immediate Post-Programme Interview* solicited the immediate impact of the Programme; while a third *Delayed Post-Programme Interview* conducted one year after the Programme allowed more lasting changes to be differentiated. The interview data were analysed with reference to a framework for delineating conceptions of teaching identified from empirical research (Samuelowicz, 1997; Samuelowicz & Bain, 1992). The analysis results were shown to a panel of nine professional educational developers who made a judgement on the degree of changes in teaching conceptions of the teachers. Highly consistent results were obtained from the nine panel members. Two teachers (one being Chinese) in the Experimental Group were classified as having big changes in their conceptions of teaching while another four (all Chinese) showed moderate changes. All the changes were judged to be in a positive direction. The other four teachers in the Experimental Group and all those in the Control Group showed no difference in their conceptions over the pre- and post-Programme time frame.

The resultant impact of the Programme on teaching practices was judged by comparing students' perceptions of their experience in the courses taught by the participants in the pre- and post-Programme years using Ramsden's 1991 Course Experience Questionnaire (CEQ) which involves scales of Good Teaching, Clear Goals, Appropriate Workload, Appropriate Assessment and Emphasis on Independence. Multivariate analyse of variance was carried out for each teacher. The model used was two-way 2x2 MANOVA on CEQ scale scores with group (teacher vs Control group) and student cohort (pre-Programme year cohort vs post-Programme year cohort) as between-subject variables. Significant multivariate effects were found for six teachers. In order of magnitude of effect they are: Brian $F(5, 512) = 20.05$, $p < .001$; Gloria $F(5, 543) = 9.79$, $p < .001$; Quentin $F(5, 479) = 7.12$, $p < .001$; Oscar $F(5, 620) = 6.47$, $p < .001$; and Tracy $F(5, 481) = 4.03$, $p = .001$. Scale means showed that all the significant results found in the Experimental Group were positive changes. It is interesting to note that for three of the four teachers in the Control Group there was a significant deterioration in their CEQ scale scores in the post-Programme year.

Finally the effect of the Programme on student learning was assessed by comparing the impact of the participants' teaching on their students' studying approaches in the pre- and post-Programme years using Entwistle's 1992 revised version of the Approaches to Studying Inventory (ASI). A pre- and post-test design was used to capture the change within each cohort of students. Accordingly, in each of the pre- and post-Programme years the ASI was administered first at the beginning and then again at the end of the course. Repeated measure MANOVA analyses involved teachers and student cohorts (pre-Programme year cohort vs post-Programme year cohort) as between-subject factors; time (pre-test and post-test) was the within-subject factor; while the five ASI scale scores were the dependent variables. In this analysis significant multivariate effects were found for three teachers: Brian $F(5, 390) = 8.47$, $p < .001$; Gloria $F(5, 419) = 5.13$, $p < .001$; Oscar $F(5, 458) = 4.34$, $p = .001$; while Quentin though did not produced a significant multivariate effect, had one significant univariate difference for the scale of Academic Aptitude $F(1, 369) = 12.55$, $p < .001$.

Table 12.2 summarises the changes across the pre- and post-Programme years in the three levels of conceptions of teaching, teaching practices and student approaches to studying for the nine effective subjects in the Experimental Group and also for the four teachers in the Control Group. The teachers are represented by false names.

To sum up, of the nine teachers who started with a relatively low level conception of teaching six (66%) showed positive change in conceptions of teaching after the programme. All six teachers whose conceptions changed demonstrated a significant improvement in their teaching practices. However, only three (50%) of the teachers who demonstrated a change in their conceptions of teaching instituted a change in their teaching practices to the extent of inducing a positive change in their students' studying approaches. Comparing the effect of the Programme on students' learning to that on students' perception of teaching practices, the former is obviously of lesser impact. Such a result can be interpreted as follows: If a lecturer tries out new methods to improve his/her teaching, it is easy for the students to detect a difference in their learning experience. But whether a change would achieve as much as to induce improvements in students' studying approaches would depend on how successful the new practices were and how resistant the students were to change.

Table 12.2
Changes across the pre-Programme year and the post-Programme year

Teacher	Changes in conceptions of teaching	Changes in teaching practices	Changes in student learning approaches
Experimental Group			
Brian*	Big (+)	Big (+)	Big (+)
Gloria	Big (+)	Big (+)	Big (+)
Oscar	Moderate (+)	Moderate (+)	Moderate (+)
Quentin	Moderate (+)	Moderate (+)	Marginal (+)
Raymond	Moderate (+)	Moderate (+)	No
Tracy	Moderate (+)	Moderate (+)	No
Nicholas*	Little/No	No	No
Philip	Little/No	No	No
Walter	Little/No	No	No
Control Group			
Eric	No	Significant (-)	No
Kelvin	No	Significant (-)	No
Leo	No	Significant (-)	No
Martin	No	No	No

Note 1: The two non-Chinese teachers are indicated by asterisk '*'.
Note 2: A (+) represents positive changes while a (-) represents negative changes.

Thus it can be concluded that the conceptual change staff development model and the Programme which was designed on the basis of this model was fairly effective in bringing about both changes in teachers' conceptions initially and also improvements in teaching and learning as an ultimate result.

Implications of the Results

This study involved the development and evaluation of methodology for the conceptual change approach to staff development. While the model for conceptual change programmes is synthesized from four theories about change which all have their origins in the Western cultures, the conceptual change staff development programme thus developed was implemented in a university in Hong Kong in which around 85% of the academic staff and a higher percentage of students were of Chinese origin. The implication of the encouraging evaluation results described in the above section is therefore two-fold: one is that the model and the programme of conceptual change staff development developed in this study is effective; and the other is that such a model based on Western change theories can be applied successfully in a Chinese community of university academics. Moreover, the results may also provide support to several important hypotheses concerning the teacher change process and a conceptual change approach to staff development:

It is feasible to bring about conceptual change by means of a staff development short-course with appropriate programme design.

The literature has recognised the difficulties of changing people's existing conceptions, both in the case of academic concepts (Champagne et al., 1984; Dahlgren, 1984; Dreyfus et al., 1990; Feltovich, et al., 1994; Thijs, 1992) and in the case of conceptions of teaching in particular (Holt-Reynolds, 1991; Kennedy, 1991; Simon & Schifter, 1991; Taylor, 1990). Success rates of conceptual change teacher education programmes or staff development programmes reported in the literature are generally low. Most studies reported only limited or no change in conception after the programme (Bird et al., 1992; Calderhead & Robson, 1991; Gore & Zeichner, 1991; Herrmann et al., 1993; McLaughlin, 1991; Tillema & Knol, 1997). Cases where obvious positive changes in conceptions were recorded in some of the participants were comparatively few (Feiman-Nemser et al., 1989; Florio-Ruane & Lensmire, 1990; Richardson, 1990). Therefore the 66% success rate obtained with this conceptual change programme is an encouraging result.

A change in conceptions of teaching is likely to lead to rapid improvement in teaching practice.

A very encouraging finding of this study was that *all* those who espoused more advanced conceptions of teaching after attending the Programme were perceived as providing significantly better teaching by their students in the year after the Programme. This implies that a change in conceptions does not only remain at the espoused level, there is a high probability that it will bring about changes in practice. In the case of this study, consequential change in teaching practices occurred for all those who changed their conceptions. Furthermore consequential changes in teaching practices can happen within a short time frame: in this study, it happened in the semester following the Programme. This finding offers empirical support for the fundamental belief underlying a conceptual change approach to educational development that a change in conceptions of teaching will indeed bring about changes in teaching practice.

In educational development the ultimate goal is improvement of teaching and learning. Educational developers who advocate a conceptual change approach have grounded their arguments largely in theoretical predictions that if teachers' conceptions of teaching are developed to a higher level, their teaching practices should accordingly be improved (Bowden, 1989; Gibbs, 1995; Gow & Kember, 1993; Ramsden, 1992; Trigwell, 1995). The research evidence that is drawn upon to underpin this contention is that teachers' existing conceptions of teaching are related to their teaching practices such that a facilitative conception of teaching is more likely to be associated with student-centred approaches to teaching and a transmissive conception with more teacher-centred approaches (Bennett et al., 1996; Kember & Kwan, 1997; Trigwell & Prosser, 1996a, 1996b). However, the literature lacks empirical evidence that *development* in conceptions of teaching will accordingly and promptly bring about improvement in teaching practice. The issue of *transition* between a change in conceptions of teaching to a change in

A Conceptual Change

teaching practices has not been studied in a systematic way previously. On the other hand, there are research findings which suggest that discrepancies between espoused ideals and actual practices are common (Argyris & Schön, 1974; Gow et al., 1992; Samuelowicz & Bain, 1992). It is therefore probable that newly developed conceptions will exist as espoused conceptions, or that it will take some time before new conceptions are put into operation in actual practice. Contemporary research only informs us of the static relationship between existing conceptions and teaching practice, but lacks findings relating to the dynamics of the way changes in teaching conceptions are transferred to changes in teaching practices and at what rate.

The findings of this study undoubtedly present a very promising picture that a development in teaching conceptions very likely will lead to improvements in teaching practices and this can happen within a short period of time. However, since this study was not originally designed for the investigation of the transfer from conceptual change to practice change and since there were only a small number of six cases, we have to be cautious in drawing any definite conclusions.

Advancement in conceptions of teaching is a basis for improvement in teaching practices; lack of change in conceptions results in no change in practices.

Another noteworthy result of this study is that none of those who showed no change in their original teaching conceptions exhibited any progress in their teaching practices after the Programme, while all those who developed their teaching conceptions did. Among those who have improved in their teaching, a variation in the extent of improvement was also observed. The two teachers who showed most changes in their conceptions both demonstrated big and fundamental changes in teaching practices, while all the other four teachers who modified their conceptions in milder ways were found to have produced moderate yet significant changes in their teaching.

This result can be interpreted as that a change in conceptions of teaching is a basis for change in teaching practices to occur. Without a change in conceptions, no change in practice is likely. The finding that the deeper the conceptual change, the bigger the change in practice which followed accordingly provides further support for a causal relationship that changes in teaching conception precedes changes in teaching practice in the context of this study.

In the literature, there exist different schools of thought concerning the causal order relating changes in beliefs and changes in practices. The fundamental assumption of the conceptual change approach to staff development is that conceptual change precedes practice change in the teacher change process. Therefore efforts have to be directed to reconstructing conceptions of teaching in order to bring about desirable changes in teaching practices. This has become the basic premise of many models, theories and recommended agenda of teacher development (Diamond, 1991; Handal & Lauvås, 1987; Kennedy, 1991; Nias, 1987). The ideas are recommended by a number of staff developers in higher education (Gow & Kember, 1993; Gibbs, 1995; Ramsden, 1992; Trigwell, 1995) and now this study provides empirical support.

On the other hand, Guskey (1986), also acknowledges change in teachers' beliefs and attitudes as an important outcome for staff development, but argues for a different ordering: starting with changes in practices, leading to changes in student learning outcomes, and ending in changes in teachers' attitudes and conceptions. It has to be noted that Guskey's model of teacher change is proposed with reference to staff development provided for the purpose of introducing innovations to secondary or elementary classrooms. On such occasions, implementation of new practices is being imposed on the teachers by external educational authorities. In the tertiary sector, however, where lecturers have autonomy in deciding the teaching approach, it would be difficult for imposed practice changes to be accepted.

This study, though supporting a change process which proceeded in the opposite direction, did not produce findings which can reject Guskey's model. However, there is abundant research evidence that teachers adapt and modify innovations which have goals and principles that deviate from their own conceptions (Richardson, 1990; Taylor, 1990). Peterman (1991) reviewed many reports of imposed educational reforms and found little evidence that actual changes in practice had occurred. All these suggest that Guskey's assumption about the effect of an imposed practice would fail in many cases.

In support of the conceptual change approach to teacher development

It is the hope of this author that the outcomes of this study can be used in informing professional development and teacher education: in particular, in fostering the development of a conceptual change approach in staff development.

Despite the growing call for a conceptual change approach to staff development in higher education, actual attempts to implement the approach in workshops and courses are still limited, though there has been considerable effort to use action research as a means to promote conceptual change (Gibbs, 1992; Kember et al., 1997; Zuber-Skerritt, 1993). An extensive interest in the approach among the general community of educational developers has not yet been established. The approach is still at an early developmental stage. That we have not seen a conference theme or a special issue of journal on the conceptual change approach to professional development is illustrative of this fact.

There are probably many reasons for the limited influence of the innovation. One possibility is the existence of fundamental doubts about the casual relationship that changes in conception would lead to changes in practice (e.g. Guskey, 1986). Second, the well-known difficulties of changing teachers' conceptions and attitudes residing in teachers' defensiveness for their entrenched existing conceptions (Kennedy, 1991) is presumably another significant inhibiting factor. A third probably is the lack of knowledge and experience of programme design and methods appropriate for conceptual change. These obstacles together make a conceptual change approach something which few staff developers would feel comfortable with, and feel confident in launching.

The results of this study are useful for informing the community of staff development practitioners about the potential of a conceptual change approach.

The encouraging results relating to the three levels of educational change: conceptual change in teachers, subsequent development in teaching practices and resultant improvement in student learning approaches supports the view that the conceptual change approach is a promising alternative to existing practices. More importantly, this study provides a design model and field experiences which can be shared by educational developers and can become a point of departure where further development and improvement in terms of programme design and methodology can be discussed.

REFERENCES

Argyris, C. & Schön, D.A. (1974). *Theory in Practice: Increasing Professional Effectiveness*. San Francisco: Jossey-Bass publishers.
Au, K.H. (1990). Changes in a Teacher's Views of Interactive Comprehensive Instruction. In L.C. Moll (Ed.), *Vygotsky and Education: Instructional Implications and Applications of Sociohistorical Psychology*. Cambridge: Cambridge University Press.
Bennett, N., Wood, E. & Rogers, S. (1996). Teachers' Theories and Classroom Practice: Teaching through Play. Seminar paper presented at the Faculty Seminar, University of Hong Kong.
Bird, T., Anderson, L.M., Sullivan, B.A. & Swidler, S.A. (1992). *Pedagogical Balancing Acts: A Teacher Educator Encounters Problems in an Attempt to Influence Prospective Teachers' Beliefs*. East Lansing, MI: National Center for Research on Teacher Education.
Bowden, J.A. (1989). *Curriculum Development for Conceptual Change Learning: A Phenomenographic Pedagogy*. Paper presented to the Sixth Annual (International) Conference of the Hong Kong Educational Research Association, Hong Kong.
Calderhead, J. & Robson, M. (1991). Images of Teaching: Student Teachers' Early Conceptions of Classroom Practice. *Teaching and Teacher Education*, 7, 1-8.
Champagne, A.B., Gunstone, R.F. & Klopfer, L.E. (1984). Instructional Consequences of Students' Knowledge about Physical Phenomena. In L.H.T. West & A.L. Pines (Eds.), *Cognitive Structure and Conceptual Change*. Orlando: Academic Press.
Clark, C.M. & Peterson, P.L. (1986). Teachers' thought Process. In W.C. Wittrock (Ed.), *Handbook of Research on Teaching*. New York: Macmillan.
Dahlgren, L.O. (1984). Outcomes of Learning. In F. Marton et al. (Eds.), *The Experience of Learning*. Edinburgh: Scottish Academic Press.
Dall'Alba, G. (1991). Foreshadowing Conceptions of Learning. *Research and Development in Higher Education*, 13, 293-297.
Diamond, C.T.P. (1991). *Teacher Education as Transformation*. Milton Keynes: Open University Press.
Dreyfus, A., Jungwirth, E. & Eliovotch, R. (1990). Applying the "Cognitive Conflict" Strategy for Conceptual Change – Some Implications, Difficulties, and Problems. *Science Education*, 74(5), 555-569.

Dunkin, M.J. & Precians, R.P. (1992). Award-winning University Teachers' Concepts of Teaching. *Higher Education*, 24, 483-502.

Entwistle, N.J. (1992). *Scales and Items for Revised Approaches to Studying Inventory (revised August 1992)*. Personal communication.

Feiman-Nemser, S., McDiarmid, G.W., Melnick, S.L. & Parker, M. (1989). *Changing Beginning Teachers' Conceptions: A Description of an Introductory Teacher Education Course. Research Report 89-1*. East Lansing, MI: National Center for Research on Teacher Education.

Feltovich, P.J., Coulson, R.L., Spiro, R.J. & Adami, J.F.A. (1994). *Conceptual Understanding and Stability, and Knowledge Shields for Fending off Conceptual Change. Technical Report No. 7*. Springfield: Southern Illinois University, Springfield, School of Medicine.

Florio-Ruane, S. & Lensmire, T.J. (1990). Transforming Future Teachers' Ideas about Writing Instruction. *Journal of Curriculum Studies*, 22, 277-289.

Fox, D. (1983). Personal Theories of Teaching. *Studies in Higher Education*, 8(2), 151-163.

Gibbs, G. (1992). *Improving the Quality of Student Learning*. Bristol: Technical and Educational Services Ltd.

Gibbs, G. (1995). Changing Lecturers' Conceptions of Teaching and Learning through Action Research. In A. Brew (Ed.), *Directions in Staff Development*. Buckingham: SRHE and Open University Press.

Gore, J.M. & Zeichner, K.M. (1991). Action Research and Reflective Teaching in Preservice Teacher Education: A Case Study from the United States. *Teaching and Teacher Education*, 7, 119-136.

Gow, L. & Kember, D. (1993). Conceptions of Teaching and Their Relationship to Student Learning. *British Journal of Educational Psychology*, 63(1), 20-33.

Gow, L., Kember, D. & Sivan, A. (1992). Lecturers' Views of Their Teaching Practices: Implications for Staff Development Needs. *Higher Education Research and Development*, 11(2), 135-149.

Guskey, T.R. (1986). Staff Development and the Process of Teacher Change. *Educational Researcher*, 5-12.

Handal, G. & Lauvås, P. (1987). *Promoting Reflective Teaching: Supervision in Action*. Milton Keynes: Open University Press.

Herrmann, B.A. et al. (1993). *Building Professional Contexts for Learning for Preservice and Inservice Teachers and Teacher Educators: Reflections, Issues and Questions*. Paper presented at the 43rd Annual Meeting of the National Reading Conference, Charleston, SC.

Holt-Reynolds, D. (1991). *Practicing What We Teach. Research Report 91-5*. East Lansing, MI: National Center for Research on Teacher Learning, Michigan State University. ERIC document: ED 337460.

Kember, D. with Ha, T.S., Lam, B.H., Lee, A., Ng, S., Yan, L. & Yum, J.C.K. (1997). *Action Learning Project. Final Evaluation Report*. Hong Kong: Action Learning Project Management Committee.

Kember, D. & Kwan, K.P. (1999). Lecturers' Approaches to Teaching and Their Relationship to Conceptions of Teaching. In N. Hativa & P. Goodyear (Eds.), *Teacher Thinking, Beliefs, and Knowledge in Higher Education*. Dordrecht:

Kluwer.
Kennedy, M.M. (1991). *An Agenda for Research on Teacher Learning*. Texas University, Austin: Center for Foreign Language Studies.
Kuhn, T.S. (1970). *The Structure of Scientific Revolution*. (2nd Edition). Chicago: University of Chicago Press.
Lewin, K. (1947). Frontiers in Group Dynamics. In D. Cartwright (1976), *Field Theory in Social Science: Selected Theoretical Papers by Kurt Lewin*. Chicago: University of Chicago Press.
Martin, E. & Balla, M. (1991). Conceptions of Teaching and Implications for Learning. *Research and Development in Higher Education*, 13, 298-304.
Martin, E. & Ramsden, P. (1992). An Expanding Awareness: How Lecturers Change their Understanding of Teaching. In M.S. Parer (Ed.), *Academic under Pressure: Theory and Practice for the 21st Century*. Churchill, Vic: HERSDA.
McLaughlin, H.J. (1991). The Reflection on the Blackboard: Student Teacher Self-evaluation. *Alberta Journal of Educational Research*, 37, 141-159.
Nias, J. (1987). *Seeing Anew: Teachers' Theories of Action*. Victoria: Deakin University Press.
Nicol, D.J. (1997). *Research on Learning and Higher Education Teaching. UCoSDA Briefing Paper Forty-Five*. Sheffield: UCoSDA.
Peterman, F.P. (1991). *An Experienced Teacher's Emerging Constructivist Beliefs about Teaching and Learning*. Paper presented at the Annual Meeting of the American Educational Research Association, Chicago, IL.
Posner, G.J., Strike, K.A., Hewson, P.W. & Gertzog, W.A. (1982). Accommodation of a Scientific Conception: Toward a Theory of Conceptual Change. *Science Education*, 66(2), 211-227.
Pratt, D.D. (1992). Conceptions of Teaching. *Adult Education Quarterly*, 42(4), 203-220.
Prosser, M., Trigwell, K. & Taylor, P. (1994). A Phenomenographic Study of Academics' Conceptions of Science Learning and Teaching. *Learning and Instruction*, 4, 217-231.
Ramsden, P. (1988). Studying Learning: Improving Teaching. In P. Ramsden (Ed.), *Improving Learning: New perspectives*. London: Kogan Page.
Ramsden, P. (1991). A Performance Indicator of Teaching Quality in Higher Education: The Course Experience Questionnaire. *Studies in Higher Education*, 16(2), 129-150.
Ramsden, P. (1992). *Learning to Teach in Higher Education*. London: Routledge.
Ramsden, P. (1993). Theories of Learning and Teaching and the Practice of Excellence in Higher Education. *Higher Education Research and Development*, 12(1), 87-97.
Richardson, V. (1990). Significant and Worthwhile Change in Teaching Practice. *Educational Researcher*, October 10-18.
Samuelowicz, K. (1997). *Revised Dimensions for Establishing Conceptions of Teaching II*. Personal correspondence.
Samuelowicz, K. & Bain, J.D. (1992). Conceptions of Teaching held by Academic Teachers. *Higher Education*, 24, 93-111.

Searle, P. & Gunstone, R.F. (1990). *Conceptual Change and Physics Instruction: A longitudinal Study*. Paper presented at the Annual Meeting of the American Educational Research Association, Boston.

Shaw, K.L., Davis, N.T., Sidani-Tabbaa, A. & McCarty, B.J. (1990). *A Model of Teacher Change*. Paper presented at the annual meeting of the International Psychology of Mathematics Education Conference, Oaxtepec, Mexico.

Sheppard, C. & Gilbert, J. (1991). Course Design, Teaching Method and Student Epistemology. *Higher Education*, 22, 229-249.

Simon, M.A. & Schifter, D. (1991). Towards a Constructivist Perspective: An Intervention Study of Mathematics Teacher Development. *Educational Studies in Mathematics*, 22, 309-331.

Svensson, L. & Högfors, C. (1988). Conceptions as the Content of Teaching: Improving Education in Mechanics. In P. Ramsden (Ed.), *Improving Learning: New Perspectives*. London: Kogan Page.

Taylor, P.C.S. (1990). *The Influence of Teacher Beliefs on Constructivist Teaching Practices*. Paper presented at the Annual Meeting of the American Educational Research Association, Boston.

Thijs, G.D. (1992). Evaluation of an Introductory Course on "force" Considering Students' Preconceptions. *Science Education*, 76(2), 155-174.

Tillema, H.H. & Knol, W.E. (1997). Promoting Student Teacher Learning through Conceptual Change or Direct Instruction. *Teaching and Teacher Education*, 13(6), 579-595.

Trigwell, K. (1995). Increasing Faculty Understanding of Teaching. In W.A. Wright (Ed.), *Teaching Improvement Practices: Successful Faculty Development Strategies*. New York: Anker.

Trigwell, K. & Prosser, M. (1996a). Congruence between Intention and Strategy in University Science Teachers' Approaches to Teaching. *Higher Education*, 32, 77-87.

Trigwell, K. & Prosser, M. (1996b). Changing Approaches to Teaching: A Relational Perspective. *Studies in Higher Education*, 21(3), 275-284.

Trigwell, K., Prosser, M. & Taylor, P. (1994). Qualitative Differences in Approaches to Teaching First Year University Science. *Higher Education*, 27, 85-93.

Zuber-Skerritt, O. (1993). *Department Excellence in University Education (DEUE) Programme 1992, Final Report*. Brisbane Australia, University of Queensland.

13

Transforming Teaching through Action Research

David Kember

The findings discussed in this Chapter followed from one of the collaborative projects which led to this book's companion volume, *The Chinese Learner*. The earlier stages of educational development through action research at the Polytechnic University were described in Chapter 13 of that book.

Initial examinations of student approaches to learning had convinced the research team that Hong Kong students were no more inclined to use a surface approach than those elsewhere (Gow & Kember, 1990; Kember & Gow, 1990; 1991). In many cases observations of rote learning could be attributed more to the teaching environment and the nature of the curriculum than inherent characteristics of the students.

This conclusion led to attempts to do something about the issues. Our value judgement was that higher education should be promoting qualities, like critical and creative thinking, consistent with a deep approach. If this was not happening then a way was needed to address the contextual problems.

The student approaches to learning (SAL) research tradition had been instrumental in diagnosing the situation, but appeared unlikely to be applicable to tackling the problems. The SAL tradition is part of the interpretive paradigm which seeks understanding. It is not inherently concerned with bringing about change or transforming attitudes.

A mode of research which does embrace change is action research. There are several types or schools of action research. These range on a spectrum from quite pragmatic procedures for dealing with ill-defined problems to approaches derived from critical theory, with associated political overtones. There are, though, characteristics common to action research which collectively distinguish it from research conducted under positivist or interpretative paradigms. A definition of the essential components of action research by Carr & Kemmis would be widely accepted.

> It can be argued that three conditions are individually necessary and jointly sufficient for action research to be said to exist: firstly, a project takes as its subject-matter a social practice, regarding it as a form of strategic action susceptible of improvement; secondly, the project proceeds through a spiral of cycles of planning, acting, observing and reflecting, with each of these activities being systematically and self-critically implemented and interrelated; thirdly, the project involves those responsible for the practice in each of the moments of the activity, widening participation in the project

gradually to include others affected by the practice, and maintaining collaborative control of the process. (Carr & Kemmis, 1986, pp.165-166).

When I first proposed trying action research projects to transform teaching and learning in some courses, there were a number of sceptics who thought it might not work in Hong Kong. This quotation, which is taken from the minutes of a course meeting in one of the universities in Hong Kong, is typical of attitudes held by many at the time.

> Students in Hong Kong ... expect lecturers to teach them everything that they are expected to know. They have little desire to discover for themselves or avail themselves of the facilities which are available to them within the teaching institution. They wish to be spoon fed and in turn they are spoon fed. Lecturers are under pressure to feed the student with a certain amount of academic and community needs information and the simplest way to do it, given the programme does not confer a degree and the student wishes to be fed in the traditional manner, is to adopt the old and traditional approaches to teaching. The result of this is that the student is not encouraged to think for himself and rarely goes beyond the level of understanding principles. In other words the student is stuck at a stage where he finds it difficult to apply those fundamental principles to situations outside the norm. The responsibility for learning remains with the teacher, rather than the student. (Minutes of the [...] Course Planning Committee, 1989, p.13)

The first component of the sceptical attitude was a belief in the conservatism of Hong Kong students. The above statement was recorded, unchallenged, in the minutes of an official university committee. This is indicative of how widespread at the time was the conviction that the students would resist any form of teaching and learning other than didactic lecturing to a passive audience.

The lecturer who provided this quotation clearly attributes the nature of the prevailing teaching and learning environment to the students. It is also, though, quite clear that he himself holds beliefs about teaching which are highly teacher-centred. A review of thirteen studies of teachers' conceptions of teaching in higher education (Kember, 1997) synthesised the outcomes into a two level category-sation scheme. At the higher level were two broad orientations. The first was teacher-centred with an orientation towards content. The other was student-centred and had a focus towards students' learning.

It is quite clear that the above quotation was made by someone whose beliefs would belong in the teacher-centred orientation. Persuading such a person to introduce more innovative forms of teaching could only happen if these beliefs about teaching were first changed. As it appeared that such teacher-centred beliefs were widespread this might be expected to constitute a major impediment to change.

The final argument of the sceptics related to the position of reflection within the action research cycle. In most of the variants of action research reflection is seen as a communal process involving all participants in a particular project. The aim of the reflection is for the participants to consider their observations and actions and together to reach a perspective to carry forward to the next cycle. The process inevitably involves exposing personal beliefs and the critical discourse must involve trying to resolve positions where there are initially discrepancies. Perspective transformation through critical dialogue is often seen as an outcome of this facet of action research.

It did seem to some that this process of critical reflection would be in conflict with the traditional Chinese concept of 'face'. If this were the case it would be a significant issue because face is important in Chinese society. Redding and Ng (1982), for example, asked a sample of 102 Hong Kong business managers whether face was important in daily transaction and all said it was. Ting-Toomey (1988) argued that saving face would mean that conflicts were less likely to be resolved. Gao, Ting-Toomey & Gudykunst (1996) observed that the Chinese practised implicit communication in which everything was not spelt out so that individuals were left with room to manoeuvre.

The other conceptual hurdle to proceding with action research projects came, not from individual sceptical academics, but from prevailing attitudes to ensuring teaching quality. At that time my own institution was a Polytechnic and had instituted a teaching quality control system modelled on that imposed upon the British polytechnics by the Council for National Academic Accreditation. It was by no means unusual in this respect. World-wide, of the resources devoted to promoting or ensuring teaching quality, the majority were, and indeed still are, allocated to quality assurance, control or inspection measures.

The predominant approach, by far, to quality enhancement was through workshop-type activities (Moses, 1985). To show that action research was not an established approach to enhancing learning and teaching quality it is sufficient to note that the initial proponents of the approach in higher education were able to publish accounts of their initial trials in which they found it necessary to explain the basis for the approach and show how the theoretical framework was appropriate (Kember & Gow, 1992; Kember & Kelly, 1993; Schratz, 1992; Zuber-Skerrit, 1992).

Quality enhancement through action research was, therefore, both a new approach and one which did not fit within the prevailing paradigms of quality control/ assurance or quality enhancement through workshop-type activities. Its most radical distinction from these approaches was the assumption it makes of academic staff. Both of the other broad approaches make something of a deficit assumption of academics. Quality control assumes there are teachers or courses which are not up to standard so reviews have to identify these and ensure that remedial action is taken. Workshop activities assume that there are academics whose teaching ability could be improved through being taught better teaching skills.

Action research takes a more positive view of academics. It assumes that there exists a body of academics who are sufficiently committed to their students' learning and interested in their own teaching to commit themselves to engaging in a project to improve some aspect of learning and teaching in one of their courses. Further it assumes that they are capable of taking this on, though it does recognise that they may need some support in doing so. In forging ahead with action research, assumptions about academics were also to be put to the test.

In spite of these reservations educational development through action research was tried out. The initial trials within one university (Kember & Gow, 1992) spread to a second university (Kember & Kelly, 1983) and eventually encompassed all tertiary institutions in Hong Kong through the Action Learning Project. This initiative has supported 50 projects in its first phase and 40 in the second, thanks to funding from the University Grants Committee of Hong Kong.

This mushrooming of involvement in action research itself suggests that the sceptics were wrong. The process of supporting over a hundred action research projects and organising the Action Learning Project has resulted in a great deal more evidence to confront the sceptics' negative stereotype of Hong Kong teachers and their students. It has also resulted in a valuable body of knowledge about action research as a means of enhancing the quality of teaching and learning. It is the purpose of this Chapter to paint a more positive picture of the attitude to innovation of both teachers and students in Hong Kong. At the same time some of the lessons learnt about educational action research will be passed on, but the full picture is a book in its own right (Kember, 2000).

Evaluation Design

The first round of the Action Learning Project employed a three level multiple voice and multiple method evaluation design. The project teams were responsible for evaluating their own projects and used a wide variety of methods to do this. Assistance and advice was available from the coordinating team on the design, collection, and analysis of evaluation data.

The coordinating team contributed to the evaluation of the overall project through reflections upon their involvement with the initiative. They conducted a survey of participants in the projects using open- and closed-response questions. A randomly selected sample of eight project teams were also interviewed.

A panel made an independent evaluation of the overall project. They had access to the reports of the individual projects and the survey and interview data. They also conducted interviews with the coordinating team and some participants in projects.

For the second round the evaluation design was similar except there was no independent evaluation panel. It became clear that the initiative would not continue for a third round so independent judgement was less necessary. Many lessons about the overall organisation of the mode of educational development had been clearly established from the first evaluation so it seemed prudent to dedicate a lower level of resources to evaluating the second round.

The surveys contained both open- and closed-response questions. The large majority of the questions were the same for both rounds of the project so that comparisons could be made. The small number of alterations to questions were due to differences in the way the project operated between the two rounds. Percentage responses to the survey questions are used to substantiate points in the remainder of the Chapter. The typical quotations given come from either the open-ended questions or the interviews conducted with first round participants.

The response to the surveys was 72 from the first round and 57 for the second. This represents response rates of about 65% and 60% respectively. The figures are approximate because of uncertainty over exactly how many participants there were in some project teams. Quite a few projects had a core of committed workers and others with more peripheral involvement. Some project proposals contained lists of participants, not all of whom subsequently appeared to be actively involved in a significant way. The response rates given are based upon the coordinating teams' perception of active participants.

Conservatism of Teachers

The Action Learning Project was funded by the University Grants Committee of Hong Kong. A large proportion of the funds received were in turn used to fund action research projects by academics into some aspect of teaching and learning in courses they taught. The method of selecting projects to fund was the conventional approach of calling for proposals and selecting the best applications.

The inter-institutional management committee, which ran the project, was not drawn from the sceptics. However, even members of the committee wondered how much of a response there would be to the call for proposals. Five of the seven institutions involved in the first round had no history of involvement in such action research projects.

In spite of newness of the concept a total of 109 applications were received for first round funding; 80 in response to an initial call and 29 for a second supplementary one. For the second round of the project a total of 104 grant applications were received, requesting a total sum nearly six times that available.

Not only were the applicants requesting funding to introduce an innovative form of teaching, those applying for first round funding were committing themselves to a mode of educational development which, at the time, was in its infancy in higher education. There had been some initial projects in the Polytechnic University to try out the approach (Kember & Gow, 1992; Kember & Kelly, 1993). There had also been a small number of projects at City University, mostly within one department (Kember & Kelly, 1993). In the rest of the world there had been a small number of initiatives (e.g. Zuber-Skerrit, 1992; Weeks & Scott, 1992) but other methods of educational development still predominated.

The type of initiatives put forward in the proposals and carried out in the projects were very diverse. To give some idea of the range of initiatives the figure below is an attempt to classify the projects carried out in the first round by the type of educational change attempted.

Figure 13.1
Types of projects in round 1

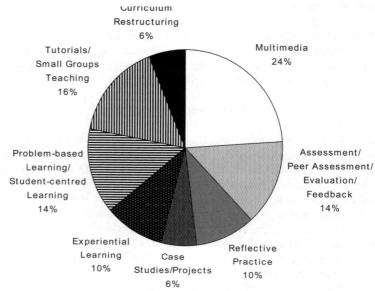

The level of teachers willing to write proposals for innovative teaching projects and the number involved in successful projects suggests that Hong Kong academics are far from conservative in their attitude to teaching. The diversity of the innovations attempted shows a rich vein of imaginative thinking about how to transform student learning for the better.

Resistance of Students

If there was any reluctance to utilise innovative forms of teaching, there would be two most likely explanations. The first of these would be that the teachers held teacher-centred content–oriented beliefs about teaching (Kember, 1997). Those holding such beliefs tend to stick with didactic forms of teaching simply because other forms are incompatible with their belief of what teaching is. Even when a class is designated as a tutorial, those with such beliefs often talk for most of the session (Kember, 1997).

The other likely cause for reluctance to engage in non-didactic forms of teaching is a perception that students will resist or show displeasure if any alternative is tried. Conservatism and negative reactions from students to educational innovation is a common item of anecdotal wisdom. It has perhaps been particularly prevalent with respect to Asian students particularly if the innovation involves a shift from didactic teaching to more interactive forms (Gow, Kember & Sivan, 1992).

If this were a real phenomenon it would have a marked effect on the numbers of teachers willing to try anything innovative. Those who did would experience negative reactions which might cause then to abandon the innovation and would almost certainly deter them from other experiments with their teaching. Most would, no doubt, relate these experiences to their colleagues so they in turn would be deterred from trying anything different.

The results from the two surveys are pertinent to determining whether student resistance is a significant phenomenon and hence a real blockage to innovation. The questionnaire to participants asked them to agree or disagree with statements that they had received support from their departmental head, colleagues and students in participating in the project. The results from the answers about students in the two rounds are shown below.

Combining the agree and strongly agree responses results in very high levels of agreement that the students did support the projects in the two rounds. This was higher than that from either the department heads or departmental colleagues. Such high levels of support are hardly indicative of student resistance.

The written comments substantiate this point by showing that the Asian students, who are often described as passive, are perfectly able to participate actively if the teaching encourages active learning.

Figure 13.2
Level of support from students

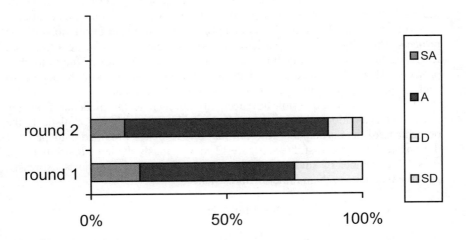

The PBL approach engaged students far more actively and sustained their involvement far more than any other courses within the Department.

- students more active in learning
- students contribute more in discussion

> The project was really quite successful in giving students an alternative learning experience.

The large majority of participants felt that students supported their initiatives rather than resisting them. Comments saying that students preferred more active participation strongly out-weighed the remainder, which were limited to a small number of students.

> Some prefer the traditional one [teaching method] more .... For example, some say that 'I am conservative in thinking, so I like the traditional one.'

The participants were also pleased with the impact of the projects on the students attitudes towards teaching and learning and teacher/student relationships.

> As far as learning is concerned, I feel that students are gaining – their attendance and participation is good, skills are developing and their performance is improving.

> one of the classes invited me to be in their class photo, it did not happen before, and I was delighted.

The results of the survey show clearly that the attitude that students resist academic innovation is a myth which needs debunking. If Asian students are truly more conservative, their Western counterparts must positively relish innovation.

Yet further evidence of this contention comes from the evaluations of the projects. Virtually all of the participants judged their projects to be successful. Evidence for successful outcomes comes from the evaluations of the individual projects. All of these incorporated feedback from students through techniques such as questionnaires, interviews and classroom observation.

It is obviously impossible to succinctly summarise the evidence from the individual evaluation of 90 projects. Perhaps the most relevant statistic is the percentage of the participants who felt that this feedback provided evidence that their project was successful (see Figure 13.3). Obviously the large majority of the very large number of students involved in these innovative projects expressed positive reactions to them rather than resistance.

Need for Adaptation

A possible explanation for the widespread perception of the conservative nature of Asian students lies in the need to allow them to adapt to new forms of teaching and learning. In a number of the Action Learning Project initiatives, students initially found the new course formats taxing, but eventually came to appreciate them.

It should be appreciated that just about all of the students would have passed through the Hong Kong school system and would therefore have a long history of exposure to didactic forms of teaching. They would have been used to a system geared to learning material for frequent external examinations which have a major

Figure 13.3
Percentage of participants who thought their project was successful

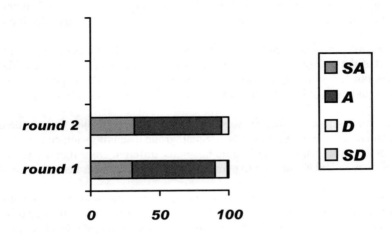

impact upon their future in a system which is still highly selective.

Such exposure to this didactic teaching and learning environment inevitably leaves its mark. It results in new cohorts of students with beliefs that the normal way of teaching is transmissive and they conceive learning as a passive activity in which their aim is to absorb as much as possible for the examinations. They would also see both knowledge and what had to be learnt as something which was defined by the curriculum set by the education department and then passed on by their teacher.

It is not easy to change any long established beliefs or practices, and indeed it can be quite a traumatic experience if the activity is a central one. The process of learning and teaching is obviously pivotal to students so it is only to be expected that initial experiences of new approaches to teaching could take some getting used to. It is, therefore, important for teaching innovations to incorporate measures to help students adjust and to allow time for them to do so.

An example comes from a project which focussed upon students reflecting upon their own experience through reflective writing and small group discussion (Kember et al., in press, ch. 10). The students initially found the approach difficult as it was expected that much of the content would come from the students' own experience of working in the field. Having to take greater responsibility for their own learning, was a quantum leap for many of the students. They also found reflective writing difficult as personal reflection is a very different form of writing to normal academic essays in which the content is drawn from external sources.

> In the past I was quite inflexible in my method of study. I only revised what the teachers said was important. Now I have to read books and find (relevant)

> material for myself. Of course they are different... very different, so I am not able to cope with this (learning approach). ... I could not decide what was right or wrong, the feeling was so insecure. Through journal writing and sharing in the learning process, I found that writing papers is very difficult. Maybe I am still not familiar with the learning approach in tertiary education.

The above quotation was taken from an interview in the early stages of the course. By the end of the course most of the students had not only overcome these initial difficulties but had come to see the value of learning from the experiences of themselves and their fellow students, as shown by the typical quotation below.

> When we discussed it further, some of them even agreed with me, so there was an integration of our thoughts .... Small group discussion helped me a lot. The other students are from different hospitals, different clinical units. Sometimes, they talked about their experiences which I have never heard before.

Those who formed the impression that Asian students resist innovation may not have allowed the students time to adapt. They also might not have taken steps to ease the transition process. In the project used as an example, the teachers provided a structured introduction to reflective writing and students making the transition received support from tutors and fellow students (Kember et. al, in press, ch. 10). Most people find change of any sort can be difficult to adapt to, so when new forms of teaching are introduced it is important to address the issue of implementing the change and allow the students time to make the transition.

It seems possible to generalise this explanation for perceptions of resistance to innovation to a wider context. Most people find it difficult to adapt from well established practices and beliefs. It is common for any form of major change to meet initial resistance. Successful integration of an innovation requires strategies to deal with the initial resistance.

Fine Tuning

An additional factor in recognising the students' need for adaptation to an innovation, is that the innovation itself will inevitably need some adaptation or fine-tuning. Action research recognises that the first time something new is tried everything will not be perfect, however careful the planning. The observation and reflection phases of the action research cycle are for the participants to determine what might be improved and how to do so. The next cycle can then incorporate the necessary modifications.

Evidence of this happening is found in many of the project's final reports (Kember, Lam, et al. 1997) and in the interviews with the project teams. It was clear that the teams recognised the importance of reflecting upon their observations and evaluation data and using it to re-plan for the next cycle.

> You know that we have to redesign the cycle as the research goes along. That is the characteristic of action learning. It is required to redesign and make

amendment to the action. When you have new data and you need to decide how to use the data. These are important and we need to discuss it together.

In some cases the observations revealed that quite radical departures for the original design would be needed.

> In our forum, we found that the students had great anxiety. This really surprised us. We found out about their responses to the field work. They become sick and cannot sleep.

Whether the iterations were major or minor, the fact that they were necessary adds confirmation to recognising the need for students to adapt to the changes. If the innovation itself needs adaptation it is hardly surprising that those involved need time to adjust to it.

Cultural Incompatibility of Reflection

To counter the sceptics view that reflection was incompatible with Chinese culture, there was considerable evidence of reflection taking place and it being in itself a valuable outcome of the projects. The participants saw action research as an appropriate framework for work of this type and none expressed any difficulties with the position of reflection as an integral component of the action research cycle.

To the contrary, there were a significant number of comments from both the open-ended questions and interviews suggesting the value of the reflective process. The following response talked about the experience of self-reflection.

> It has helped me to reflect on my own teaching as well as trying to understand how the students learn.

More significantly there was a greater emphasis from respondents upon reflection as a group activity. From the perspective of the sceptics it would be communal reflection rather than self-reflection which might be alien to Chinese culture. The majority of the teams noted the importance of reflection-in-action in fine-tuning their teaching practices. They expressed the need to discuss and listen to others experiences in the action process, because this helped them to step back from the action and reach new perspectives.

> The most useful was the team meeting in reflecting the results and the experience.

> That is important because we would like to know how to adjust our own teaching by knowing the effect of other classes.

Evidence of Changing Perspectives

It was also clear that in many cases the meetings engaged in what Dewey (1933) called "critical reflection" or Mezirow labelled perspective transformation (1991). The participants were seriously re-appraising existing beliefs and assumptions and were prepared to alter their practices in the light of these reflections.

> By involving a group of colleagues in active regular discussions of teaching styles and learning needs, it has raised questions about what we are trying to do and how best we should go about this.

> To implement action research in teaching and learning, we need to change to adjust our method of teaching to accommodate the need of students.

This is incidentally an illustration of the example of the process of engaging in these action research projects being an outcome in itself. Firstly the process of reflection leads to insights into better approaches to teaching and a greater understanding of student learning. Secondly, and perhaps more importantly, by engaging in this collective refection the participants realise the importance of reflecting on their teaching and hopefully should adopt a reflective stance in the future.

Development of a Team

There is then considerable evidence that the teams of participants did reflect together upon the observations and experiences arising from their projects. What is more, in many cases there was evidence of this reflection resulting in reconsideration of existing positions. It is clear that the sceptical view that reflection would not be compatible with Chinese culture had not transpired. It is worth examining why this apparently plausible expectation had not been upheld.

The reason advanced for reflection perhaps not being appropriate in Hong Kong was that re-consideration of existing positions and resolution of discrepancies would lead to an unacceptable loss of face. This hypothesis, though, assumes a hierarchical structure within the participant teams. It assumes that there will be an authority figure and subordinates.

Traditional Chinese beliefs do stress respect for authorities (Wu, 1996). The notion of face has most commonly been invoked in terms of the need for authority figures to avoid or not be exposed to loss of face (Ting-Toomey, 1988). It implies that subordinates should avoid situations or confrontations which might make their head have to back track on a decision. There is also a tendency for those authority figures who see face as important to adopt authoritative rather than consultative management styles to minimise the chance of any discord.

The reason that such concerns did not deter the Action Learning Project teams from engaging in reflection is that they did not adopt authority-subordinate relationships. Even though the formal positions of the participants within a team might have been radically different, their relationships within the team could be quite democratic. The teams could have participants who were deans or heads of department at one end of the spectrum and research assistants at the other. When engaged on the project, though, it seemed possible for those involved to set aside these formal differences in status and function as a genuine team.

The participants usually ranged in status from full Professor to research assistants. They seemed to be quite happy to be learning together. I remember one workshop on NUD•IST where the (full) Professor was getting a lot of help in the exercises in using the program from his research assistant.

Many projects attributed their success to the existence among the participants of a willingness to put effort into their project and collaborate with others in a united front. This sense of ownership of some common goals led to a commitment to persevere towards the outcome.

I think the most important factor (that makes our project so successful) is the commitment of people. Although there were problems in coordination at the beginning and technical difficulties, all of us are very committed. We are determined to complete the project. Otherwise, we could not have done the evaluation. So although there were some delays, it's because everyone of us wanted to give our best. We all put in great effort to make it work.

I agree with [...] point of view. If there had not been such great commitment, it would have been difficult to complete this project. At first, we got many problems and quite often had to work overnight. Without that commitment, we just couldn't do it. Besides, the animation was very creative. I didn't expect it would be so interesting. I don't think I can make it myself.

The reason for this commitment was that they had been able to forge themselves into a coherent team. These were teams in which everyone was valued and all opinions were accepted. Criticism was acceptable if it could help enhance the project's effectiveness. A problem solving norm was upheld. People became confident to speak out and open-minded about taking initiatives to evaluate their work for further improvement.

Here, the culture is, as it has been said earlier, more open. We can discuss our problems openly. We don't need to hide anything. That should be better. I have learnt how to cooperate with other people and give suggestions to one another for improvement. This is what I've gained apart from the technical side.

Besides, everyone is willing to speak out. If there's a problem, it would be known. Everyone is willing to make suggestions and accept the need for changes when necessary. All of us are willing to be open. So if there is any problem that needs to be solved, it will be solved first. We are not afraid of criticising our own systems. This is also very important.

The reason they were able to develop open teams of this nature may be because of another characteristic of Chinese society. Salili (1996) has argued that Chinese culture is marked by collectivism. Traditionally the primary group has been the family but loyalty to other social groupings has been recognised. Wu (1996) argues that achievement motivation in Chinese society has a social or collective orientation whereas Western measures of achievement motivation have stressed individual achievement. The evidence of strong affiliation within the project teams may, therefore be seen as a manifestation of this traditional recognition of collective goals.

Indeed it is possible to go further than this and argue that reflection itself has long had a place in Chinese culture. Lee (1996) argues that the Confucian tradition has stressed reflective thinking. He provides a quotation from Confucius himself to substantiate the point.

> While there is anything that he has not reflected on, or anything which he has reflected on which he does not apprehend, he will not intermit his labour. While there is anything which he has not discriminated, or his discrimination is not clear, he will not intermit his labour. If there be anything which he has not practised, or his practice fails in earnestness, he will not intermit his labour. (*The Mean*, XX.20)

It is true that these admonishments were directed largely to the individual scholar, and do not deal with perspective transformation through collective discourse. It does show clearly, though, that reflective thinking is hardly an alien concept to Chinese culture. Those who have quoted Dewey (1933) to show that reflective thinking is not a new concept might recognise that it has older origins than they first thought and that the roots were planted in a different part of the world.

Effectiveness of Action Research

The other issue to deal with is that, at the time these ventures into action research started, the prevailing mode of attempting to achieve quality in teaching and learning was through quality control measures. In most parts of the world it still is. Indeed in Britain, for example, the screws have been tightened and both universities and schools face regular and rigorous external inspections which are meant to ensure that the teaching is of an acceptable standard.

Whether such quality control measures are effective in ensuring a high standard of education is a hard question to answer. The greatest barrier to finding an answer is that the schemes have themselves rarely been evaluated – even though they require schools and universities to be evaluated.

I have argued at length elsewhere (Kember, 2000) that the law of diminishing marginal returns applies to approaches to ensuring and enhancing quality in education. This is particularly pertinent to quality assurance schemes as ever increasing levels of time and resources have been devoted to them.

There is growing evidence, for a number of reasons, of unintended outcomes of quality assurance measures. Quality control procedures can easily become a game played to a set of formal and informal rules. As the systems become more developed the informal rules become more widely known. Academics learn how to play the system and pass the test rather than use the procedures to improve teaching (Kember, 1991).

This issue is compounded by the fact that reviews examine documentation about teaching rather than teaching itself. If the expectations of panels become well known, documentation can be tailored to fit. In the case of program approval, the documentation may bear little relationship to what is taught and how it is taught. The practice of what happens in the privacy of the classroom may be quite different to the rhetoric of the accepted proposal (Bowden, 1988).

Quality control processes tend to operate on a pass/fail basis with very few failures. It may be possible to identify courses and teaching which would benefit from improvement, but there may be no binding mechanism for remediation. Even if requirements are made for revisions to proposals, the alterations may be incorporated into a revised proposal but not put into effect. Peer panels are often transient bodies formed specifically for a particular review. Once that is over they cease to exist and certainly have neither responsibility nor any mechanism for ensuring that changes or improvements they suggested are implemented. Even if course leaders or department heads embrace any recommendations, they too may find them difficult to implement. Argyris & Schön's (1978) distinction between *espoused theory* and *theory in use* is often well illustrated by the gap between accepted course proposals and what is taught.

Quality control measures frequently have negative impacts on morale by taking responsibility for quality out of the hands of the teacher. Even with 'peer review' processes within an institution the panel will be made up of those not teaching the course and normally from outside the responsible department. More inquisitive or adversarial regulatory systems imply a deficit model so create an atmosphere of distrust which results in conservatism and saps enthusiasm for innovation (Ramsden, 1992).

Whatever the quality of the control system itself, compliance with monitoring procedures takes time, which otherwise could have been spent on teaching or research. The imposition of the quality control measures, therefore, diverts effort and energy away from the very acts which the procedures are supposed to encourage (Woodhouse, 1995).

Once quality assurance procedures exceed simple minimal systems it may be more cost-effective to shift resources and effort to quality enhancement schemes like the Action Learning Project. In most countries the opposite has happened and quality assurance measures have become more elaborate, more expensive and many would say more intrusive. I have argued that as a result they have become less cost-effective (Kember, 2000).

Hong Kong is one of the few places where there has been any shift towards quality enhancement. The UGC has carried out a teaching review of each university. Part of this process was to ensure that the universities had their own internal quality assurance schemes. In this respect Hong Kong is not dissimilar to other educational systems: any differences are essentially of degree.

Where there is a distinction is that substantial resources have also been allocated to quality enhancement measures through Teaching Development Grants, which have been in two forms. Part have been passed directly to the universities for internal priorities and part of the funding has been allocated competitively with priority being give to collaborative proposals. The Action Learning Project is the largest scheme funded under the latter measure.

There is an enormous volume of data attesting to the success of the first round of the project (Kember, 2000; Kember, Lam, et al., 1997). Preliminary data for the second round suggests that it was more effective still. This is probably partly because lessons were learnt from the first round which enabled the organisation and framework to be more efficient in supporting the projects. It was also clear that there was a learning effect on the Hong Kong academic community as the quality of the submissions improved and the teams awards grants seemed better equipped to carry them out.

Rather than trying to drastically condense the large volume of evaluation data into the remainder of this Chapter it would seem more fruitful to highlight some of the more important conclusions from the overall initiative. This will mean though that these conclusions will be presented here with little supporting evidence.

Academic Empowerment

In contrast to the deficit assumptions of quality control schemes, the Action Learning Project made the assumption that there would be academics who were both keen and able to engage in projects aimed at improving their teaching and their students' learning. Essentially the aim was to shift responsibility for quality from university and system managers and hand it back to the academics themselves.

The evidence above shows that there were more than enough academics who did wish to participate in this venture and turned out to be capable of doing so. What is more, showing faith in their ability to monitor quality themselves turned out to have a very powerful motivating and empowering impact. The following quotation is typical of the attitudes engendered.

> I think this was a far-sighted initiative. It was able to support such a variety of different projects generated bottom-up, from the delivery point of instruction. It had more impact on the quality of learning than any of the top-down quality initiatives I've encountered!

A further important factor in motivating participants was that the initiative was formulated as a scholarly academic activity. The Action Learning Project followed the processes and structure of research grant awarding bodies. Firstly these are accepted approaches for equitably judging and managing grants and the ensuing projects. Secondly the aim was to enhance the status of teaching as a valued scholarly activity.

The Importance of Dissemination Activities

The academic status of the initiative was further enhanced through the contribution of the project teams to a range of dissemination activities. During the course of the projects teams were brought together in Interest Group Meetings in which those in similar disciplines or carrying out related types of projects could discuss progress and outcomes. At the end of each round participants were expected to write final reports for presentation at a conference. After the conference these papers were refereed, edited and collated into a case-book (Kember, Lam, et al., 1997).

The meetings and conference were open to all academics in Hong Kong and the case-book was widely distributed. The main aim was to pass on lessons learnt from the projects so that others might also incorporate them within their teaching. The side benefit was a reinforcement of the message that teaching too is a scholarly activity.

The Process as an Outcome

In many ways engagement in the process of conducting an action research project is as much a part of the outcomes as any changes made or products developed. In fact the development of the practitioner through the engagement can be seen as more important than project outcomes because they can have a lasting effect.

Firstly, the action research cycle contains the step of reflecting upon the observation of the action cycle. This helps practitioners to develop the ability to monitor, observe and evaluate their own teaching – they become reflective practitioners capable of self-monitoring.

Being forced to confront evidence of the outcomes of their projects led to at least some of the participants re-appraising their approach to teaching. Interestingly this seemed to happen more often in projects where the progress was not as smooth as anticipated. Meeting a rocky path made the participants consider more carefully where they were heading towards, which showed again that the journey could be as or more important than the destination.

Need for Support

Support for the participants in their projects was provided by a small coordinating team. The orientation of this support was that of the *critical friend* (Kember, Ha, et al. 1997). The coordinators had an initial meeting with each project team at which the level and nature of support needed was negotiated. The types of support provided was, therefore, multi-faceted with no less than twelve facets being identified in Kember, Ha, et al. (1997).

In the evaluation of the project the questionnaire asked whether the various facets of the support were necessary. In the first round evaluation the majority of respondents agreed that all but one of the facets of support were necessary. The second round evaluation data still showed the need for support, particularly for: arranging contact with teams doing similar projects, advice on evaluating the project and on methodology. The proportion of teams expressing a need for support fell for each of the support facets compared to the first round. This outcome should be seen in a positive light as indicating that the academic community in Hong Kong had learnt better how to apply action research themselves, which was one of the overall aims of the initiative.

Action Research as a Quality Enhancement Mechanism

At the time of writing the Action Learning Project is drawing to a close. This does not mean though that project-type initiatives will no longer be a feature of the Hong Kong university education system. Under various banners and in various guises projects operate within each of the institutions. Funding comes either from the UGC, for some large projects, or from internal funds.

The Hong Kong university sector is, therefore, one of very few in the world where the level of activity in quality enhancement approaches that in quality assurance. It is certainly not a time for complacency, but the prevailing attitudes have changed markedly in the ten years since the quote at the start of the Chapter.

It is perhaps time to see whether the same mechanism might be beneficial in other educational sectors. The Education Commission is currently reviewing education in Hong Kong and has produced a very adventurous blueprint for reform known as 'Learning for Life' (Education Commission, 1999). Looking back over the previous Education Commission Reports, though, it is possible to find many fine sounding proposals. The speed of implementation of these proposals can only be described as slow and the fact that the same issues keep recurring shows that many proposed reforms are not effectively implemented at all.

The top-down approach to change of the Education Department has clearly not been a dynamic force for innovation and reform. Perhaps it is time to learn from the university sector and shift towards a bottom-up style of implementing innovation through action research. It may be felt that school teachers would be less able to participate in action research projects than their university counterparts, but then there were sceptics who thought Hong Kong academics would not take to action research. They were wrong!

Acknowledgements

This Action Learning Project was generously supported by grants from the University Grants Committee of Hong Kong and the Hong Kong Polytechnic University.

REFERENCES

Argyris, C. & Schön, D. (1978). *Organisational Learning: A Theory-of-action Perspective*. Reading, MA: Addison-Wesley.

Bowden, J. (1988). Achieving Change in Teaching Practices. In P. Ramsden (Ed.), *Improving Learning*. London: Kogan Page.

Carr, W. & Kemmis, S. (1986). *Becoming Critical: Education, Knowledge and Action Research*. Brighton, Sussex: Falmer Press.

Dewey, J. (1933). *How We Think: A Restatement of the Relation of Reflective Thinking to the Educative Process*. Boston: D.C. Heath.

Gao, G. Ting-Toomey, S. & Gudykunst, W. (1996). Chinese Communication Processes. In M.H. Bond (Ed.), *The Handbook of Chinese Psychology*.

Oxford: Oxford University Press.
Gow, L. & Kember, D. (1990). Does Higher Education Promote Independent Learning? *Higher Education*, 19, 307-322.
Gow, L., Kember, D. & Sivan, A. (1992). Lecturers' Views of Their Teaching Practices: Implications for Staff Development Needs. *Higher Education Research and Development*, 11(2), 135-149.
Education Commission (1999). *Learning for Life*. Hong Kong: Hong Kong Special Administrative Region Education Commission.
Kember, D. (1991). A Curriculum Development Model based on Deforestation and the Work of Kafka. *Higher Education Review*, 24(1), 7-13.
Kember, D. (1997). A Reconcepualisation of the Research into University Academics' Conceptions of Teaching. *Learning and Instruction*, 7(3), 255-275.
Kember, D. (2000). *Action Learning and Action Research: Improving the Quality of Teaching and Learning*. London: Kogan Page.
Kember, D. & Gow, L. (1990). Cultural Specificity of Approaches to Study. *British Journal of Educational Psychology*, 60, 356-363.
Kember, D. & Gow, L. (1991). A Challenge to the Anecdotal Stereotype of the Asian Student. *Studies in Higher Education*, 16(2), 117-128.
Kember, D. & Gow, L. (1992). Action Research as a Form of Staff Development in Higher Education. *Higher Education*, 23(3), 297-310.
Kember, D. & Kelly, M. (1993). *Improving Teaching Through Action Research*. N.S.W.: HERDSA Green Guide No. 14.
Kember, D., Ha, T.S., Lam, B.H., Lee, A., Ng, S., Yan, L. & Yum, J.C.K. (1997). The Diverse Role of the Critical Friend in Supporting Educational Action Research Projects. *Educational Action Research*, 5(3), 463-481.
Kember, D. with Jones, A., Loke, A.Y., McKay, J., Sinclair, K., Tse, H., Webb, C., Wong, F.K.Y., Wong, M.W.L. & Yeung, E. (in press). *Reflective Teaching and Learning in the Health Professions*. Oxford: Blackwell Science.
Kember, D., Lam, B.H., Yan, L., Yum, J.C.K. & Liu, S.B. (1997). *Case Studies of Improving Teaching and Learning from the Action Learning Project*. Hong Kong: Action Learning Project.
Lee, W.O. (1996). The Cultural Context for Chinese Learners: Conceptions of Learning in the Confucian Tradition. In D.A. Watkins & J.B. Biggs (Eds.), *The Chinese Learner: Cultural, Psychological, and Contextual Influences*. Hong Kong / Melbourne: Comparative Education Research Centre, The University of Hong Kong / Australian Council for Educational Research, 25-41.
Mezirow, J. (1991). *Transformative Dimensions of Adult Learning*. San Francisco: Jossey-Bass.
Moses, I. (1985). Academic Development Units and the Improvement of Teaching. *Higher Education*, 14, 75-100.
Ramsden, P. (1992). *Learning to Teach in Higher Education*. London: Kogan Page.
Redding, S.G. & Ng, M. (1982). The Role of Face in the Organizational Perceptions of Chinese Managers. *Organization Studies*, 3, 201-219.
Salili, F. (1996). Accepting Personal Responsibility for Learning. In D.A. Watkins & J.B. Biggs (Eds.), *The Chinese Learner: Cultural, Psychological, and*

Contextual Influences. Hong Kong / Melbourne: Comparative Education Research Centre, The University of Hong Kong / Australian Council for Educational Research, 85-105.

Schratz, M. (1992). Researching While Teaching: An Action Research Approach in Higher Education. *Studies in Higher Education,* 17(1), 81-95.

Ting-Toomey, S. (1988). Intercultural Conflict Styles: A Face-negotiation Theory. In Y.Y. Kim & W.B. Gudykunst (Eds.), *Theories in Intercultural Communication*. Beverly Hills, CA: Sage, 213-235.

Weeks, P. & Scott, D. (Eds.) (1992). *Exploring Tertiary Teaching: Papers from the TRAC (Teaching, Reflection and Collaboration) Project*. Armidale: University of New England.

Woodhouse, D. (1995). Efficient Quality Systems. *Assessment and Evaluation in Higher education*. 20(1), 15-24.

Wu, D.Y.H. (1996). Chinese Childhood Socialisation. In M.H. Bond (Ed.), *The Handbook of Chinese Psychology*. Hong Kong: Oxford University Press.

Zuber-Skerrit, O. (1992). *Action Research in Higher Education: Examples and Reflections*. London: Kogan Page.

OVERVIEW AND CONCLUSIONS

14

Insights into Teaching the Chinese Learner

John B. Biggs and David A. Watkins

This book started with what we called the paradox of the Chinese teacher. This is that teachers in Chinese classrooms produce positive learning outcome under conditions that Western researchers would regard as most unpromising. This paradox led contributors variously to reveal through their investigations what some of the secrets for success in teaching Chinese learners might be. They focused on what teachers thought, how they interacted with their students, how well certain Western innovations worked in Chinese classrooms, and how change might be brought about in teacher thinking and practice.

Some rich themes emerged, each of which could be developed at length. Methodological issues would include the use of longitudinal research methods in the study of conceptual change and its outcomes, as in Chapters 12 and 13; and how quantitative and qualitative methods could be used to complement each other, as in Chapters 6, 7, 11 and 12. We shall have to leave these, and theoretical issues relating to the operation of attribution theory and motivational theory in different cultural contexts, for individuals to follow through according to their interest.

Instead, we shall in this final chapter retain a more practical focus, on the question we started with: How teachers of Chinese students produce the results they do. Then there is the related question of what, if anything, Western teachers can learn from that. Finally, there are the implications locally for the Hong Kong system in particular, which is at the time of writing undergoing a drastic review and transition.

Let us start at the beginning.

Teachers or Teaching?

The original working title of this book was *The Chinese Teacher*, an elegant juxtapositioning we thought to its predecessor, *The Chinese Learner*. However, the more we looked at that, the less satisfactory it became. Many of the teachers researched in the Hong Kong studies were not in fact Chinese, although the great majority of their students were. Perhaps more importantly, we came to realize that we were talking not about teachers but *teaching*. In retrospect, we see how Western we were being in our first choice of title; the difference is instructive.

A pedagogical flow

In their preliminary report of the IEA Third Mathematics and Science Study

(TIMSS), Schmidt et al. (1996) refer to "a pedagogical flow" that is characteristic of the teaching in each country. The nature of any particular flow springs from socialisation practices, values about education, and so on, in the culture concerned. Teaching practices thus acquire a contextual validity deriving from the culture itself. While CHC systems have large classes, seem highly authoritarian, and are examination oriented, it may well be that the expectations and perceptions held by those students would create a different effect from that which those same characteristics would have on students in a Western system with different expectations. Indeed, the high performance of CHC students indicates precisely this.

A classroom is an ecosystem, in which all the components have a mutual effect on each other (Biggs, 1993). If any one component is changed, the system changes. But the class is also a component of a larger system, the school, which itself is a component in a wider system still, the community, which with other communities comprises the system of the culture itself. Thus, a very complex, multi-layered equilibrium is set up, with the culture over-riding. Thus is established the pedagogical flow that is characteristic of a country's schools and classrooms.

This flow, based on mutual interaction between all components, means that one factor, such as class size or teaching method, cannot be isolated from the other components and be expected to work in a different system the same way as it works in its own. Thus, achievement differences found in TIMSS cannot be attributed "*solely* to school factors or to a *single* organizational or instructional factor" (Stedman, 1997: 9, emphases in original). The key to the paradox of the Chinese teacher must surely reside in the flow typical of the educational ecosystem, not in any one factor. In that case, any "paradox" gives way to a reasonable explanation.

Stigler & Hiebert (1999) tried to characterise the pedagogical flow of different systems by video-taping classrooms in three countries, Japan, USA and Germany. When they analysed the tapes they "were amazed at how much teaching varied across cultures, and how little it varied within cultures." (p.11). Each culture had developed its own "script" for teaching, and what determined high level learning outcomes was the script, not the particular actor delivering it. The Japanese teaching script was not only more student centred and focused on high level outcomes than the others, but had its own built in quality enhancement mechanism. Learning outcomes in Japan were superior to those attained in Germany, and far superior to those in the US.

What Stigler and Hiebert mean by a script is illustrated in the following response to their findings from a maths education professor:

> I believe I can summarize the main differences between the teaching styles of the three countries ... In Japanese lessons, there is the mathematics on the one hand, and the students on the other. The students engage with the mathematics and the teacher mediates the relationship between the two. In Germany, ... the teacher owns the mathematics and parcels it out to students as he sees fit, giving facts and explanations at just the right time. In US

lesson, there are the students and there is the teacher. I have trouble finding the mathematics..." (Stigler & Hiebert, 1999: 26).

In the US, teaching was algorithmic: the teacher demonstrated a procedure, and the students worked through many similar examples of the procedure. The cognitive level was low, the content level nearly two grades behind that of other countries. A Japanese teacher who was watching the tapes was amazed when the PA system interrupted a US maths lesson with an announcement reminding students that Bus 31 was now rescheduled. This would never happen, he said, in a Japanese class. And it didn't. Analysis showed that 30% of US lessons were interrupted by routine management business, 10% of German lessons, none in Japan.

It is not difficult to see why Japan performed so well, and the US so poorly. The US scriptwriters, not to mention the production team, had got it wrong. This is not to say that there aren't excellent teachers in the US, but they are excellent in the norm-referenced sense that they enact the same script more effectively than do other teachers. Stigler and Hiebert concluded that within a culture, all teachers have essentially the same script, so that the singer matters, not the song. However, when comparing across cultures, the singer is unimportant; what matters is the song, or in their terms, the script not the actor: teaching not the teacher. It is only when we see different scripts being enacted that the possibility dawns that there may in fact be other and better ways of doing what we have been doing until now.

Further, in the TIMSS countries surveyed, Japan was the only one where it was generally believed that effective teaching was a continuing exploration of how to achieve improved student learning outcomes. Japanese schools have an in-built quality enhancement mechanism, *kounaikenshuu*, which is essentially like a continuing group action research (see Chapter 13). All teachers believe that they can teach better than they are currently doing, and the object of *kounaikenshuu* is to explore how, lesson by lesson. Japanese teachers are reflective practitioners, and it shows in the high academic achievement of Japanese students.[1]

We saw how in Chapter 6 Cortazzi and Jin described a similar system in Mainland China (without the *gakkyu hokai*). In China, teachers have light teaching loads in order to enhance lesson preparation, and to allow more out of

---

[1] Not that Japanese schools are all a bed of roses. A recent article in *The South China Morning Post* (22 June, 2000) reported an increasingly common phenomenon in Japan: *gakkyu hokai*, "a situation in which classes become completely uncontrollable, with students fighting, talking or wandering about." As one student wrote to a Japanese newspaper: "Why do we do it? Because it's fun. Daily life is so boring!" Another wrote: "I hate school. I hate the way teachers teach ... the way everything is so tightly controlled." It seems that the *kounaikenshuu* might focus on the management and affective domains as well as on the instructional.

class contact with students. They structure lessons with impeccable sequence and timing, and use the "learner-trained learning" tactics described in Chapter 6, whereby the performances that enable learning to take place are choreographed and rehearsed with the children. Even in Hong Kong, where teachers are greatly overloaded with teaching hours, Mok and colleagues refer in Chapter 8 to the carefully planned "dance" movements between teacher and learners. In Mainland China, but not yet in Hong Kong, excellent teachers give demonstration lessons, not to show off how good they are, as Level 2 individualists, but as Level 3 collectivists, *so that their colleagues may learn effective teaching strategies*. Scripts are reviewed, and teachers generally are eager for new ideas, new scripts. So, despite what to Western teachers would be crippling class sizes and inadequate resources, teaching in China is continually under reflective review, at least in those schools Cortazzi and Jin studied, and there must be many others.

These Chinese and Japanese in-service activities reflect quite a different conception of excellent teaching from the Western one, which is the Level 2 conception that excellent teaching is doing what an excellent teacher does. They strut their stuff and get Distinguished Teacher Awards for it. The message here is not the collectivist "here is something from which we can all learn", but the individualist "distinguished teachers are a rare and gifted species, against whom you ordinary teachers cannot be expected to compete." In that case, we lesser beings cannot be blamed if we teach on in our own undistinguished way.

In many Western universities, and in the University Grants Committee guidelines in Hong Kong, an institutional performance indicator of good teaching is whether or not a distinguished teacher award system is in place. If it is, the institution may be seen to be doing its bit for good teaching. This is missing the point, because other teachers are then free to continue doing what they have always been doing. Unless there are good and well-resourced staff development facilities also in place, and the distinguished teachers are required to share their expertise in general staff development exercises, as in the Chinese and Japanese examples, the message of such award systems can be quite counterproductive. What is left is a conception of the excellent teacher as the Oscar winning performer, not the constructivist – and Confucian – view of the teacher as a facilitator of learning. This is precisely the difference between the proposed titles of this book we referred to at the beginning of this Chapter. We are not interested in the characteristics of Chinese teachers, so much as in the process of teaching Chinese learners.

Part of this East-West difference is the old polarity between analytic and holistic thinking. The positivist tradition in the West has encouraged researchers and educators to think in terms of an additive model: you isolate those independent variables you want to examine and vary them systematically, hold constant those factors that you are not currently interested in, and then observe what the effects are on one or more dependent variables. The thinking is in terms of particular independent or presage factors. What characteristics do expert teachers have that nonexperts do not: How much experience, what sort of training, what teaching competencies, do they possess? Likewise, from the side of the teaching context: What is the optimum class size? What are effective teaching methods? What resources are available? Some common assumptions based on additive thinking would include: good teaching costs more than poor teaching; using IT means good teaching; research can provide us with cross-contextual answers.

This positivistic view of education is giving way amongst most researchers and some educators to a more general holistic view. As Salomon (1991) says, in education we are more often dealing with "clouds of correlated events... (which) mutually define each other" (p.13). That is, events in education form an interactive system, rather than a linear sequence (Biggs, 1993, see also Chapter 6), so that Stedman (1997) is quite correct in saying that the differences TIMSS picked up between the performances of countries cannot be attributed to any one factor.

Unfortunately, however, the old positivistic way of thinking is still common amongst teachers, and is particularly congenial to the economic rationalist mind, which has taken over the educational agenda in most Western countries. Administrators and politicians of this bent think quantitatively, using positivistic, additive models. Thus, if the Chinese can get such good results with very large classes, then we in the West should be able to save a lot of money by increasing class sizes without any loss in teaching effectiveness (see Biggs, 1998). You don't have to be much of a systems thinker to see that Chinese teachers achieve the results they do in such large classes because they live in a different culture, where the pedagogical flow is different. We can all learn from each other, but it is not a simple transfer of techniques. Blowing one trumpet the Chinese way will not produce the *Yellow River Symphony*.

In short, we need to think in terms of the whole system, not of isolated components; in terms of teaching, not of teachers.

The Thinking of Chinese Teachers

Thus, Chinese teachers conceive their role in terms of teaching in the ongoing system more than Western teachers do. In Chapter 5, we saw that Ho's Australian teachers had a compartmentalised view of their responsibilities, while her Hong Kong teachers saw their role as extending well beyond the classroom itself. Inside the classroom the Australian teachers taught the curriculum, outside the classroom they got on with their personal lives. Students' personal or family problems were not perceived as their responsibility, even unfinished homework was the student's problem, not the teacher's. Hong Kong teachers saw this very differently, taking a pastoral as well as an instructional view of teaching.

This difference came up time and time again. Gao and Watkins in Chapter 2 refer to the role of teachers "cultivating" not only cognitive development but promoting positive attitudes to society and responsible moral behaviour. Teachers are expected to set themselves up as models both in the academic and nonacademic spheres. Thus, Cortazzi and Jin in Chapter 6 refer to education as "books and society", the teacher as friend and parent (see also Chapter 2). This reflects the Chinese holistic view of teaching, in which teaching refers not only to educating the whole person, affective and moral as well as cognitive, but also to teaching a person their role in society, with collectivist obligations to behave within that role in socially acceptable ways. This is the "moral" dimension so important in Chinese teaching.

One of the authors was recently on a panel for a distinguished teacher's award in a Hong Kong university. Teachers were nominated for the award by students, by peers, or by head of department. Most teachers were Chinese, as were most panel members. The pastoral role came out very strongly in many of the teachers who had been nominated by students. The following are some of the quotes these teachers made in the interview:

- "I teach from the heart. My students can feel that."
- "I love my students and they love me."
- "I know all my students by name. I have lunch with them, and they tell me their problems. I often ask them home, and I cook for them."
- "I am a committed Christian. I know God loves me, and I too love my students, through the love of God."

Such comments would not be expected from a similar exercise in the West. Westerners might well agree that mutual positive regard is a necessary if not sufficient condition for good teaching, but many would balk at the use of the word "love" to describe their relationship to their students, which apart from the intensity of the word, implies an ongoing, extra-curricular involvement. As we saw in Chapter 5, Western teachers tend to see their professional responsibility as ending after hours.

It is hard for non-Chinese to comprehend the seemingly contradictory ways in which this friend-and-parent dimension are manifested. On the one hand, there is the strong positive involvement exemplified by the award teachers mentioned above. On the other hand, there is the harshness referred to by I. Ho and Salili, whereby praise is withheld, and criticism is frequent. Whether Chinese teachers choose to emphasise the positive or the negative affective aspects seem largely to be contextual. One aspect of context refers to the sector one is teaching in, primary, secondary or tertiary, and this probably operates much as it would in the West. Another aspect is whether the teacher-student interaction takes place within or outside formal classes, and here there are clearer East-West differences. Whereas Western teachers focus on formal classroom interaction and little if at all on interactions outside, a Chinese teacher sees each context as requiring a different responsibility, with a different style of interaction.

Another angle to this is that criticism and punishment are, as one of Ho's teachers said, "declaring the system". Strictness in a collectivistic society means that one is conveying an appropriate moral message; there is not necessarily any personal animus involved. If Australian teachers are strict, it is because that is their personal way of operating, and if they are very strict, one could reasonably conclude that they enjoy bullying kids. Strictness thus conveys very different messages to students in Chinese and Western societies. In the latter, strictness is more likely to be seen as personal and spleen-driven, but in the former as instructionally related and less emotionally charged.

Other aspects of teacher thinking focus on the instructional roles. Here again it is a question more of both-and, rather than of either-or. The Guangdong teachers' conceptions investigated by Gao and Watkins did not split into the transmission *versus* supporting learning division noted by Kember (1997). Rather, the ideas of transmission and supporting learning were both present, in the "moulding" and "cultivating" conceptions, and the Chinese teachers saw their role as variously including both, depending on circumstances. For example, when examinations were imminent, "stuffing the duck" over-rode all other conceptions. Indeed, some schools openly recognise the different teaching styles needed to fulfil conflicting moulding and cultivating conceptions by having two teams of teachers, "one for exam-driven education and one for quality education" (Wu Qi, Principal of Guangzhou Peizheng Middle School, reported in *South China Morning Post,* 15 July, 2000).

The "cultivating" conception is far wider than cultivating cognitive learning. Cultivating referred to other aspects of individual potential, including morals and correct attitudes as befit a Chinese citizen. This concept of education is very old, going back to Confucianism (Lee, 1996), and to the idea of filial piety. In this, the son's filial duty (if not the daughter's) is to care for and nurture his physical, mental, and moral virtues and qualities, to be as perfect as possible, in order to pay due honour to his father (Ho, 1998).

Finally, let us look specifically at conceptions of assessment, which as we have noted many times is a highly salient feature not only of Chinese education, but also of Japanese, Korean, and Taiwanese education (Zeng, 1999). Intense norm-referenced assessment has been a feature of Chinese education since the Han Dynasty in 320 BC (Siu, 1999), originating from Confucius' meritocratic belief that "those who excel in their study should become officials" (quoted in Zeng, 1999: 21). Examinations measure "not only intelligence, but also character, determination, and the will to succeed" (op. cit.: iv), and send the symbolic message that "learning is a long journey of ordeal. Without pain, one can hardly attain (success), and there is no shortcut" (op. cit.: v). Whereas earlier it was used in an extraordinarily rigorous way to select mandarins and high civil servants, more recently it is to select students for the Key Schools in China, and for the Band 1 schools in Hong Kong.

In Hong Kong at school level conceptions of teaching and assessment are separate, both conceptually and functionally. The role of teaching is to convey content, the role of assessment is to determine who learns better than who. These conceptions are deeply ingrained and underlie the strictures of present day vernacular Confucianism that played no small part in the failure of Target Oriented Curriculum in Hong Kong, as we discuss below. This split between teaching and assessment is represented by the fact that two independent bodies look after each function: the Government Education Department is responsible for curriculum and teaching, while the autonomous and financially independent Hong Kong Examinations Authority is in charge of all public examinations. This means in practice that the content and style of the examinations dictate the content of the functioning curriculum and the way it is taught. The negative consequences for school learning have been well documented (see Salili above, Chapter 4; see also Johnson & Yau, 1996; Morris, 1985; Tang & Biggs, 1996).

At university level, these conceptions may not be so strong, possibly because both Westernisation and a professional/vocational thrust are more clearly pronounced than at school level, both in China and in Hong Kong. Thus, dynamics are different from those in the school system. In Chapter 3, Dahlin, Watkins and Ekholm investigated university teachers in Hong Kong and Sweden and found they seemed to have similar conceptions of the role of assessment. However, despite fewer constraints and more independence than their school peers, few university teachers in either country seemed to use assessment to try to improve learning outcomes. There seems to be a clear need for staff development in both countries.

Classroom Practice in Hong Kong and Mainland China

As Cortazzi and Jin point out, China is a huge country with enormous variations regionally and socio-economically, so giving an account of the "typical" classroom would be as meaningless as it would be glib. We can only go on what has been reported here, in Cortazzi and Jin's Chapter 6, and in Gao and Watkins' research reported in Chapter 2. Basically the picture is optimistic, despite or perhaps because of the large class sizes and the poor resourcing (see below).

Conveying a picture of Hong Kong classrooms is rather easier, as it is a compact system, and relatively well researched. We gave a brief overview of the system in Chapter 1, and essentially saw that it is a system of extremes. For the successful students who make it into Band 1 schools, it is tough, but those who survive are set for life. For those in lower band schools, life is cruel and hard. These students are faced with an academic curriculum, when they have already been labelled "nonacademic", and with totally unrealistic exam requirements.

What have the chapters here added to this picture? In the affective domain, there is an added understanding of why the system seems so harsh to an outsider, however it may seem to the students themselves (Chapters 4 by Salili, and 5 by Ho). Two chapters address teaching. Chapter 7 by Ng et al. draws a stark contrast between the kind of learning that goes on in mother tongue instruction, and in English, while Chapter 8 by Mok et al. addresses teaching in a primary school, which illustrates sensitive and interactive teaching of high quality. So here again there are contrasts, and it is difficult to generalise, even within as self-contained a system as is that of Hong Kong.

Given all that, it may seem foolish to ask the next question, but let us try.

How "Chinese" are Hong Kong classrooms?

Given that the main structural influence on Hong Kong's educational system for well over a century has been that of the British, we might expect the teaching in the classrooms of Hong Kong and of Mainland China to be very different. There are both similarities and differences.

Similarities. Many of the similarities may be traced to a common cultural heritage.

1. Good learning occurs when to a Western eye there is a repetitive, teacher-dominated script. Closer scrutiny, however, reveals that much more is going on than appears to be the case:

    - *concentrated listening.* Students as a matter of course listen intently, when teachers present or interact with a few other students in a way that few Western students do. Chinese students in the West resent being accused of passivity, when they are in fact participating actively, if covertly (Chapter 6).
    - *vicarious learning.* In large classes, the teacher needs to interact only with a few, for the lesson to be experienced by all.
    - *careful planning, timed questioning, and associated activity.* The terms "choreography" and "dance" were suggested in Chapter 8 to describe this feature. However, it must be said that this was found to be true in Hong Kong only in a class conducted in mother tongue (Chapter 7).
    - *learner-trained learning.* Students learn stage-setting routines that enable the teacher to switch activities smoothly and without disruption. Although this feature might have been described as "robotic" (see Chapter 6), it is possibly one feature that is most lacking in Western classrooms, where even small classes spend a considerable amount of time in moving from one activity to another, and not infrequently descend into chaos, because this simple tactic is not implemented.

2. Both systems are *exam-dominated* and, in Hong Kong especially, *norm-referencing* remains the top priority in assessment The effects of this legacy from the ancient system of selecting mandarins for the Imperial Court seem more salient in Hong Kong than in China. A possible clue to this is the disruption caused by the Cultural Revolution (see footnote 2), which paradoxically allowed a "softer" version of Confucianism to prevail, and in fact, educational reforms in Guangdong Province are well ahead of those in Hong Kong (see below). Thus, while the pressure from exams might be intense in Guangdong, it is compartmentalised, so that after teachers have done their best in that area, there is still the "cultivating" to be done; sometimes specialist teams of teachers might attend to these different tasks.

Differences. However, there were several differences between Mainland and HKSAR classrooms, some quite unexpected:

1. The *classroom climate* seemed to be much more comfortable in China. Cortazzi and Jin note that one demonstration teacher took pains to publicly

praise students: "You all write very well." Then I. Ho mentions O'Connor's (1991) study, who found that Mainland teachers in discussing vignettes of students misconduct showed a great deal of concern for giving students face in dealing with their misbehaviour. Gary Cheung writes in an article comparing Hong Kong's educational system with that in neighbouring Guangdong:

> Guangdong is years ahead of Hong Kong in introducing education reforms that reduce pressure on students.
>
> (*South China Morning Post*, 15 July, 2000)

Hong Kong teachers, on the other hand, are reported as using praise very sparingly, and as deliberately using shaming or loss of face as a punishment (Chapters 4, 5), and as taking care to *increase* pressure on students, particularly perhaps in Band 1 schools (see Chapter 1). How does this seeming difference between Hong Kong and Mainland Chinese schools arise? The fact that the Guangdong Province is "years ahead" suggests that the Mainland Chinese teachers studied by Cortazzi and Jin, and by O'Connor, were not necessarily exceptional. It even begins to appear that Mainland teachers are more "Western" than Hong Kong teachers in their beliefs and practices.²

2. It thus seems that at least the better Mainland schools are more *student-centred* than Hong Kong schools, but whether it is helpful to call them more "Westernised" is another matter. As Chan mentions in Chapter 9, "the transmission approach commonly observed in Hong Kong classrooms does not typify the teaching of great Chinese teachers." (p.184). Suffice it to say that for various historical reasons, schools in Mainland China and Hong Kong have developed in different ways, as no doubt have those in Taiwan and Singapore, but all historically derive from the Confucian heritage at some point. Indeed, this is totally in keeping with the idea of "vernacular" Confucianism (Chang, 2000), a vernacular being precisely a local version of a major language or thought system. The interesting point for us is that:

> The SAR has been learning from the mainland for some time. Secretary for Education and Manpower, Fanny Law Fan Chiu-fan, visited Guangzhou in May last year, when she was Director of Education. She was impressed by the sweeping reforms that had been initiated.
>
> (*South China Morning Post*, 15 July, 2000)

---

² Professor Daniel Shek (private communication) agrees that the phenomenon is real, and that it is probably due to the Cultural Revolution, which in so assiduously banishing the various "Olds", took many aspects of vernacular Confucianism with it, including many traditional beliefs about praise and blame. These beliefs however continue to exist in other Chinese communities.

3. The extent to which *mother-tongue instruction* is given in China is not known. Officially, the language medium of instruction is Putonghua, which may or may not be mother tongue. In the case of Cortazzi and Jin's demonstration schools in or near Beijing it probably was mother tongue, but in Guangzhou it could have been either Cantonese (mother tongue) or Putonghua. In Hong Kong, we had examples of both mother tongue and English medium, and the results were striking in terms of richness of interchange, and level of learning and understanding displayed by the students. Together with the massive quantitative evidence of Marsh, Hau, & Kong (in press) the benefits of mother tongue teaching are all too clear. Given that, the statement by a well known Hong Kong educator, Professor Cheng Kai Ming, that "teaching in Cantonese is killing (*sic*) Hong Kong students" (quoted in *South China Morning Post*, 9 April, 2000), adds a novel dimension to the debate. It seems likely that the intended audience for that comment did not comprise educators, nor do they reside in Hong Kong. For our part, and for our audience, we have no difficulty in concluding that teaching in mother tongue is more effective than teaching in a second language. It may well be that part of the reason is that in mother tongue it is easier to introduce variation in dealing with the content, as claimed in Chapter 7, but it is not clear what the limits may be to such variation. Too much variation would surely become confusing, the wood invisible with all those trees. Further, if this explanation is to "solve the paradox" it would surely be necessary to show that Western teachers typically use less variation than Chinese teachers. Further research is clearly necessary on these points.

4. The provision, and indeed the tradition, for *in-service education* of teachers is completely different. In-service in Hong Kong is formalised, and decontextualised. The in-service training for Target Oriented Curriculum, for example, was carried out in crash-courses run centrally and very top-down, with a teacher representing a school. It is rare for the general run of teachers to obtain further qualifications, and when they do it is most frequently by virtue of their own individual choice and at their own expense. In China on the other hand, in-service staff development is *in situ*, run by the teachers themselves, and it is generally expected that all teachers would join in.

5. Differences in *teachers' pay* and *work load* are enormous, on both counts. Together, they may account for the differences in in-service training. Possibly because Hong Kong teachers are so well paid compared to their compatriots across the border, every hour of their expensive time is extracted, both in school hours and after. Free periods are few, and at night homework marking is prodigious. Most are too exhausted to even think of in-service training or reflective practice. In the Mainland, as in Japan, teachers may teach only half the time-tabled hours, the rest of the time is for lesson planning, student interaction, for improving their teaching through interaction and discussion with colleagues, and for attending demonstration lessons and

reflection sessions.

6. *Class sizes* are much larger in China than in Hong Kong, although the latter sizes, say 40 in primary, 30 and less in higher secondary, are still rather larger than in the West (Biggs, 1998). Thus, when comparing across cultures, we see a *negative* correlation between the quality of teaching and class size: the better teaching is in larger classes, which is not what one might expect. It might even be thought that the larger class sizes force teachers to teach and to manage better in order to cope at all, but there are of course many cultural and socialisation factors that make that adaptation so much more likely to be successful. Within Western cultures, that lack those cultural and socialisation factors, better teaching is more typically to be found in smaller classes (Bourke, 1986).

Teaching thinking, teacher practice, and the prospect of change

Cross cultural issues

We conclude then that the Hong Kong educational system is in values and traditions very "Chinese", despite the overlay of British superstructures, the Western rhetoric and initiatives in the many reforms sought by Education Commission reports over recent years, and the Western content and methods of teacher education. Given that, and given that the concepts of teacher- and student-centredness do not apply to Chinese teachers and their teaching philosophies in the same way as they apply in the West, I. Ho asks in Chapter 5: How relevant can Western classroom management models be to Chinese systems? She concludes that student-centred approaches are relevant in the Chinese school context but "may be operationalized in different ways", for example by developing personal relationships with students outside the classroom.

We needn't restrict the question to management. The same principles apply to more general concepts such as criterion-referenced assessment, to meta-theories such as constructivism, and to such "Western" methods as problem-based learning. Chan demonstrated in Chapter 9 how ordinary classroom teachers can utilise Western constructivist learning strategies effectively in Hong Kong classrooms, and Stokes in Chapter 10 showed that problem-based learning could be applied at undergraduate level. Some teachers had difficulties in adapting to the new roles demanded of them when implementing problem based learning, but those difficulties were created by their conception of teaching rather than by their ethnicity: teacher as dispenser of knowledge as opposed to teacher as facilitator of learning.

The initial point of inflection in initiating change thus seems to be the way teachers think about their job. When their thinking has been changed, then it would seem more likely that they would be prepared to change what they do. This is entirely in keeping with the model outlined in Chapter 1 (Figure 1.2), which posits a causal chain from conceptions of teaching, which determine what teaching procedures are used, and which in turn affect students' approaches to learning and through these, the learning outcomes. Thus, to improve student learning requires *inter alia* that teachers rethink what they have been doing. This apparently was the sticking point with some of Stokes's teachers.

That teachers can be induced to rethink is demonstrated in teacher education in Chapter 11 and in staff development in Chapter 12. Tang shows that a teacher education course can provide different kinds of learning experiences which can change conceptions of learning and in some cases conceptions of teaching. Ho demonstrates in staff development workshops that by changing teachers' views away from the transmission model, they will review their practices in a more effective way, and then the rest of the chain will be set to unroll. Requiring teachers to change their current practice will thus only be effective to the extent that the new practice fits their existing beliefs about what constitutes good teaching. The implications of this for the proposed reforms in Hong Kong are considered below.

Kember remarks several times in Chapter 13 that the very success of the Action Learning Project, which included one hundred odd projects representing all Hong Kong's tertiary institutions, must lay to rest any shibboleths about Western innovations not "taking" in Hong Kong or Chinese culture. Of course, there are modifications to be made, but the point to be stressed is not so much that you take a Western model and "adapt" it by strapping on a bunch of Chinese characteristics, but that you rethink from within the Chinese or local context. That is what action learning is about, and reflective practice, which is the engine-room of action learning, already exists in Chinese education.

However, you also have to have the appropriate context, and the techniques for making it work. This is strikingly illustrated by Linn, Lewis, Tsuchida, & Songer (2000), who report on practices in Japanese science teaching, which rely on carefully selected and orchestrated "activity structures", each of which is designed to illustrate a particular concept. Elementary students in classes of 30 and 40 surprised Western observers with their ability to "work collaboratively and responsibly in small groups" (p.9), often dealing with fragile and even dangerous equipment. They couldn't have done this unless responsible and cooperative work patterns had been part of the classroom culture from early days. This is very reminiscent of Cortazzi and Jin's description of "learner-trained learning" in Chinese schools. But, despite this crucial dependence on a "cultural" feature.

> Japanese elementary teachers expressed surprise that we were so interested in their science instruction, which they saw as heavily influenced by Western approaches, including the work of John Dewey and Jerome Bruner, discovery learning, inquiry based approaches, and various Sputnik-inspired reforms. (Linn, Lewis, Tsuchida, & Songer, 2000: 12)

Ironically, the Japanese, with their learner-trained learning activities were much better able to implement Western curriculum and teaching methods than Westerners were. There are good reasons for that, which have less to do with teaching than with extra-curricular priorities, as we see below.

The Paradox revisited

Let us return to the conceptions of teaching described in Chapter 1. Western research draws a sharp distinction between teaching conceived as teacher-centred and content oriented, and teaching conceived as student-centred and learning oriented. Western teachers tended to line up as emphasizing one or the other, whereas Chinese teachers were found here to be more situational, emphasizing one or the other at different times, and also with another conception of teaching as being concerned with affective and moral outcomes.

The Levels in teacher thinking outlined in Chapter 1 help clarify matters, by incorporating into the conceptions what teachers see as the important causes of learning. This helps to clarify the issue of what the teacher's responsibility is:

> *Level 1: What students are.* Learning occurs to the extent that students put in effort, are bright, are motivated, have the background, and so on. Teaching is exposition, and is as it were held constant. Differences occur because students differ, so the teacher has little responsibility for the outcomes.
> *Level 2: What teachers do.* Learning depends on the teacher's presentation skills. The teacher here has rather more responsibility, but what is salient is the teacher's performance, not the end-goal of teaching, which is student learning.
> *Level 3: How teachers can encourage students to engage in appropriate learning activities.* Learning depends on what student do, and the teacher needs to structure all aspects of the teaching/learning context, including the design, delivery and assessment of learning, so that students are most likely to behave appropriately. Here the teachers have a high responsibility, but the focus is not just teacher-centred, but on the whole system.

We have seen here that Chinese teachers tend to hold Level 3 conceptions of teaching at some point in their teaching. Teaching is more student-centred, and not only focused on cognitive aspects. Thus, in the demonstration lessons that Cortazzi and Jin reported, there was a continuing desire to engage students more effectively, achieved through a collective reflective practice. In other words, the skills of teaching were not seen in a Level 2 way as good or bad in themselves, but as a means for reaching the higher end of changing students. These skills evolved and cohered to form a powerful script.

Here then is the answer to what was posed as a paradox. It is not a paradox, of course. Any paradox would exist only if Chinese learners had been badly taught, and as far as the teaching we have visited on Mainland and some Hong Kong classrooms is concerned, that is simply not true.

It is interesting to see why this mistake has been made. The assumption of poor teaching is based on a Western perception focusing on Level 1 type secondary characteristics, such as large class sizes, teacher led classes, and authoritarian teachers, and poor resourcing. But these are only the phenotypes of poor teaching, conceived in a Western frame of reference. They do not look at the teaching itself, in a Level 2 framework, still less at how well the students are actually learning. These instances of the learning desert that the West has been trying to escape from are the teaching equivalent of the "blame the student" model that Level 1 teachers use. Focusing on large classes, say, as an index of poor teaching fails to take into account that Chinese students come to class eager and trained to learn (see Chapters 6 and 8, and *The Chinese Learner*), and who are trained to engage in "active listening" to the teacher and to other students. Whatever the appearance, they are in fact likely to be learning actively. They expect the teacher to be strict inside the classroom but caring outside (see Chapters 2 and 4). Western notions that a controlling teacher cannot be a nurturing teacher, and that teacher-centred teaching cannot lead to actively involved students, do not apply.

Any paradox is rather that Western teachers, with their small classes, knowledge banks on the scholarship of teaching accumulated from years of dedicated research, and relatively large budgets, get such poor results. Now that is an interesting paradox that needs to be addressed.

Adopting Chinese teaching tactics will not solve this one. Rather, Western educators need to develop their own script, using things that work in Western culture, and that will engage students socialised the Western way in productive learning. Just precisely how that is going to take place is not for us to say. Currently, there is an ongoing debate between the proponents of situative and cognitive research approaches (e.g. Anderson, Greeno, Lynn, & Simon, 2000) in the American Educational Research Association journal *Educational Researcher* on precisely this matter. European researchers, for their part, tend to see more value in the student learning paradigm, at least at the tertiary level (Biggs, 1999; Prosser & Trigwell, 1998). All these are attempts to engage at Level 3, to conceptualise and to put into operation ways in which student learning can be enhanced.

A more general comment is that administrators and educators in CHC cultures seem to have a "purer" agenda than Westerners. For example, we might recall that Japanese classes were not interrupted by trivial business announcements, while 30 per cent of American classes were. The design of many Western curricula – "a mile wide and an inch deep", as Stedman (1997: 10) quotes – favours coverage, not understanding. Teaching is dominated by "tell and show", which encourages rote learning (Stedman, 1997). Mathematics in the US is "taught by exposure" (Porter, 1989), which means that topics are "brushed past" the student, but as the assessment is frequently in terms of recognition only, the illusion is created that something has been taught and duly learned. "Quick and snappy" methods of questioning preclude students from giving reflective answers (Hess & Azuma, 1991). The result, as we saw in the case of the script for math teaching, was low level learning of procedures (Stigler & Hiebert, 1999). While the above applies specifically to the USA, similar situations exist on other Western countries. The cognitive content of public examinations in New South Wales,

Australia, for example, is lower than that in corresponding examinations in Thailand or Japan (Baumgart & Halse, 1999).

In Western universities, administrative considerations consistently over-ride educational ones. Clerically convenient quantitative assessments create "backwash" from assessment that debilitates learning, grading on the curve is used to conceal poorly performing departments, out-dated teaching and assessment methods are retained, staff development in teaching is downsized at the same time as small group teaching is condemned in an Australian Government report as "a poor use of resources" (Biggs, 1999; Dawkins, 1987). As one of the authors wrote recently:

> ....teaching in the Hong Kong tertiary sector is in terms of class size, resourcing, and innovative practice, currently of a high standard. In most Australian universities, it is mediocre and getting worse.
> (J.B. Biggs, in *Sunday Morning Post*, February 13, 2000)

Ironically, many of the mechanisms of quality assurance actually degrade educational quality (Bowden & Marton, 1998). Unfortunately, all the signs are that Hong Kong's tertiary sector will be "restructured" along the lines that have so badly impaired the quality of teaching and scholarship in so many Western countries, but that raises other issues we cannot do justice to here.

Without labouring the point further, in the West educational institutions seem more frequently to serve other ends than educational, a process that is rapidly getting worse rather than better with the corporatisation of education. To be blunt, quality education is in the West not a top priority. Extraneous factors usually prevent Western educators from practising what they preach. This is the other side of the "teaching paradox" coin; while Chinese educators get on with teaching as best they can with their resources, Western educators are floundering.

Here then is another condition of good teaching and the successful implementation of change, which is quite a separate dimension to teacher thinking, but which is vital if teaching is to work. It is a matter of meaning what you say, or putting your money where your mouth is. A more technical way of describing this is *alignment*, where teaching and assessment methods are aligned to the teaching objectives. A good Level 3 way of doing this is by endeavouring to build into the teaching methods and assessment tasks those learning activities that are likely to produce the desired outcomes (Biggs, 1999).

Some conditions of quality reform: Implications for Hong Kong's educational reforms

Let us put all this together. There are several components involved, and Figure 14.1 shows the relationships between them that have emerged here. The central component is the basic model outlined in Chapter 1 and developed throughout (solid lines) while the components etched in dashed lines provide the context for the model. First is the optimal design of the system itself, and for that to work, obviously it must be accepted into teachers' thinking, which may then lead to practices that maximise appropriate learning outcomes. Then the practical functioning system evolves, from the ideal, to how teachers have conceived it and put it into practice. However, as the work in Chinese and Japanese schools show, and as is part of action research, any evolving system needs quality enhancement mechanisms. We do not mean quality assurance, which so easily becomes a retrospective accountability exercise, but a system that looks ahead to how things can be carried out more effectively yet (Biggs, in press). In implementing new reforms and innovations there are bound to be initial mistakes. It is self-evident that these should be monitored and corrected as local wisdom accumulates. This is not something that a centrally administered quality assurance mechanism can do. The local teachers need to be involved in the fine-tuning of teaching and assessment techniques and procedures.

Figure 14.1
Some essential components in a reformed educational system

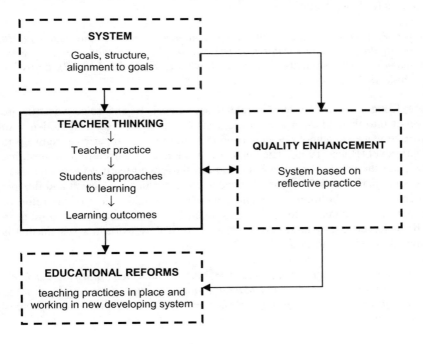

At the risk of appearing parochial, let us use the Hong Kong reforms of the school system by way of example (the tertiary sector reforms raise quite different issues to do with the financing and delivery of education, discussion of which would take us too far afield). A useful counter-example of how *not* implement a reform is the case of Target Oriented Curriculum (TOC) (see Carless, 1998; Morris, Chan & Lo, 1998).

Essentially, the proposed reforms for Hong Kong schools are intended to "depressure" the system, in the same way as did the Guangdong procedures some years earlier, in particular by mitigating the relentless norm-referenced testing. This is to be done by having only one public examination, at the end of schooling, and a "through train" for the first nine years of compulsory schooling. That is, no banding, no selection at the end of primary, and a much broader, less academic curriculum. The rhetoric refers to "student-focused", "no-loser", "all citizens …to realise their potentials", "all sectors of the community … contribute to the reform." The precise details have yet to be worked out, and until 2005 at least, banding will be retained, but reduced to three, and there is strong pressure to retain the elite, Band 1, schools.

All these factors are to replace those that we have seen here to be damaging: a selective system requiring relentless testing and exam-dominated teaching, and a single inflexible academic curriculum independently of a student's ability or life plans.

The major findings presented in this volume are relevant to the current proposals for Hong Kong.

1. *Good teaching begins with the way teachers think about teaching. In particular, it matters what teachers see as the important causes of good learning:* what students are *(Level 1),* what teachers do *(Level 2), and* what students do *(Level 3).*

Hong Kong's current system is relentlessly Level 1. The selective structure forces it into that. The purpose of the system is to selectively cull students, so that each stage of school depends on norm-referenced comparisons right up to tertiary level (Biggs, 1996). The content is academic, and irrelevant to most, but that is not the point. The point is to find out those who learn it faster and more accurately than others. Thus, any change to more personally relevant and flexible content, and the abolition of selection, which is the major goal of the reforms, can only be welcomed. However, the crunch is that if teachers are to think in terms of Level 3, they are likely to do so only if they work in a system that is designed for educating students, not for selecting them.

2. *The focus in improving practice thus is directed first at teacher's conceptions of learning and teaching, not on getting them simply to adopt new practices. Focusing only on what teachers do is a Level 2 conception of teaching.*

Here's the rub. So many reforms require teachers to change what they *do*, while ignoring what they *think* they should be doing. In the TOC initiative, for example, selected teachers attended "how-to" workshops. But since most did not see that there was a problem, they did not see the need to change what they were already doing. Thus, being asked to teach differently, without understanding why they should, sends a very demoralising message: "Everything you are now doing is wrong!" (Morris, Chan & Lo, 1998). But the message they got from parents was very different: "Continue with what you are doing now, only more so!" As long as selectivity is built into the system, most parents will want their children to go to the "best" schools, and as we saw in Chapter 1, will put pressure on teachers to prepare them for that with relentless drilling and testing. As one head-teacher remarked on the TOC steering Committee in 1995 (at which JB was present): "My teachers will go along with this, as long as they can have their weekly test. Otherwise, they will not participate." TOC was however designed precisely to *replace* the weekly test.

Parents and teachers will continue to behave the way they do as long as the system supports that behaviour. Vernacular Confucianism is at best a lubricant in a selective system, and cannot in itself be blamed for the problems in Hong Kong. Thus, nothing will change until selectivity is no longer an issue, and indeed the Education Commission has identified this as the main problem. However, the present proposal is only to reduce the bands from five to three, until 2005 at least, and it is likely that elite schools will remain, or what amounts to much the same thing, schools will have the power to select a proportion of their intake. However, as long as the system requires *any* selection amongst students, norm-referenced testing and the beliefs of vernacular Confucianism, that effort and pain are the defining attributes of learning, will endure.

3. *The shift to Level 3 thinking involves focusing on what can best be done to promote appropriate learning activities. This requires an approach to teaching that will work in the culture concerned.*

The schools described by Cortazzi and Jin, and the *kounaikenshuu* in Japan, have got this right. This is also the way action research works, and it can work well in Hong Kong tertiary institutions (Chapter 13). But it is not the way the Hong Kong school system works, not yet anyway. As we saw, reforms were imposed top-down, with inadequate conceptual preparation, doubly necessary for a conceptual background described as "a bizarre amalgam of disconnected ideas which are not linked to the local context" (Morris, 1998: 130-1). This difficulty was compounded by the political blunder that all of the design team were expatriates. In brief, the techniques and procedures needed to implement TOC were not understood and were therefore not carried out.

In the present reforms, IT is offered as the major technology to improve teaching and learning in school and tertiary systems, and both sectors are equipped with hardware and software and the instructions: "Use it!" Again, this is an atheoretical Level 2 approach. Unless teachers have a strong theory of teaching, putting lecture notes on the Web is operationalising a transmission model of teaching, except this is easier to plagiarise than conventional lecturing, while the bells and whistles of a full-blown PowerPoint presentation encourage maximal passivity in students. IT works only as well as its theory of implementation. Teachers need to be involved in developing and adapting in context the technology that will operationalise their theory of teaching. As

Stigler & Hiebert (1999) put it, teachers are the gatekeepers of the classrooms in which teaching and learning take place: "Teaching is unlikely to improve through researchers developing innovations in one place and prescribing them for everyone." (op. cit.: 134).

4. *The system has to be aligned. That is, the rhetoric and the design of the system, and the component parts, must have an overall integrity.*

This is the key to it all. It is where many Western systems have got it wrong, in that the rhetoric in the aims and objectives of systems and of institutions say one thing, while the administrative procedures and the approaches to teaching and assessment thus encouraged achieve something quite different. In Hong Kong, TOC could not have worked in the then existing selective system because the two are completely out of alignment. In the end, an "administrator's alignment" was obtained by simply declaring that the innovation was in place, as schools were told: "Oh, working out the detail is up to the teachers and the school!" (Morris, Chan, & Lo, 1998). This sounds very flexible and bottom-up, but in reality it is telling teachers that they have a licence to do what they always did, which was not TOC, just call it that. The real goal of innovation is improved student learning, not implementation *per se* (Stigler & Hiebert, 1999). However, governments tend to see it differently, which is to be able to say that the initiative has been adopted, whether or not student learning is improved. TOC is a classic case of pseudo-implementation.

Thus, in the case of the new reforms, even allowing only a little bit of selection may well be all that will be required to stall the reforms, given the history of the Hong Kong system.

5. *A quality enhancement system should be in place to check how the innovation is working, and to fine tune the details as experience is gained as to what works and what doesn't work in context.*

This is probably the most important feature of an innovation because it provides the acid test as to whether it is genuinely in place and working, or not. A retrospective quality assurance mechanism, requiring accountability data, performance indices, forms to fill in, quality control measures, and so on, is by definition one step too late. It has no necessary connection with tuning and testing, and improving while the system is operating. Figure 14.1 outlines where it fits in: it takes the rhetoric and aims, checks against the new system as it is working, and by interacting with the teachers and practitioners, identifies where problems might be and corrects them. The mechanism is reflective practice by the participants.

Quality enhancement was never mentioned in the case of TOC, and as a result anything went – as long as it was called "TOC". No governmental body or professional educator should ever give assent to such a subterfuge, nor should the public tolerate it. It is to be hoped that this will not happen with the new reforms.

Conclusions

Let us quickly conclude a long chapter with some observations based on these studies of what teachers of Chinese learners think and do.

The major point to be made is that, as we reported in *The Chinese Learner*, when outsiders look across cultures, perceptions are likely to be coloured by presuppositions formed from their own culture. That seems obvious enough, but when you apply it to teaching, it is extraordinarily difficult for many Westerners to accept. They see large classes, strict, expository teaching, and apparently passive learners, all hallmarks of poor teaching. So it is a paradox if those learners perform better than Western students! It ceases to be when we accept that if good learning is taking place, then what has been going on cannot be poor teaching. One of our aims in this book has been to demystify Chinese teaching, and the contributors to this book have been successful in achieving that.

The key is that there are universal principles of good teaching, which involve getting the students to engage the learning tasks at an appropriate cognitive level. How that is done depends on the approach to teaching that is appropriate to the culture, by virtue of socialisation practices, educational values, attributions for success and failure, and the like. Whereas *The Chinese Learner* looked at these latter macro-cultural features, in this book we have looked at the former: the approaches to teaching that worked. In this, it must be said that the approaches current in several Confucian heritage cultures seem to be working better than those in many Western countries.

Another lesson to be learned is that rectifying Western teaching cannot be achieved by mimicking what the Chinese and Japanese are doing. Ironically, in science teaching, if anyone has been mimicking anybody, the East has been copying the West – but with rather more success than the West had managed to achieve. Rather, the West needs not perhaps so much to develop ways of teaching that work, but to create a climate wherein the espoused aims of the system are given a higher priority than other priorities, such as administrative, managerial or commercial ones.

However, the "Confucian heritage" is not a monoculture. While there are some common features, Chang's (2000) term "vernacular Confucianism", which suggests the parallel between a local dialect and the parent language, captures this point very well. Thus, while there are some similarities between the classrooms in Mainland China and in Hong Kong, there are differences, and so the pedagogical flow in their classrooms is different. Hong Kong's system is in fact in trouble, as is officially recognized, and reform is proceeding.

One of the central conclusions in this book is that good practice is not just a matter of enacting a particular approach to teaching, but by focusing on enhancing student learning. This is a matter of choosing a teaching practice that is culturally appropriate and that is driven by a student-centred theory of teaching and learning. If reforms are to work, both these points need to be recognised and put into practice, along with a means of monitoring and improving teaching. One universal lesson that does come out of Mainland China and to an extent from Japan is that quality enhancement has to focus on teaching, not on teachers.

REFERENCES

Anderson, J.R., Greeno, J., Reder, L. & Simon, H.A. (2000). Perspectives on Learning, Thinking, and Activity. *Educational researcher*, 29(4), 11-13.

Baumgart, N. & Halse, C. (1999). Globalisation vs Cultural Diversity. *Assessment in Education*, 6, 321-339.

Biggs, J.B. (1993). From Theory to Practice: A Cognitive Systems Approach. *Higher Education Research and Development*, 12, 73-86.

Biggs, J.B. (Ed.) (1996). *Testing: To Educate or To Select? Education in Hong Kong at the Crossroads*. Hong Kong: Hong Kong Educational Publishing Co.

Biggs, J.B. (1998). Learning from the Confucian Heritage: So Size Doesn't Matter. *International Journal of Educational Research*, 29, 723-738.

Biggs, J.B. (1999). *Teaching for Quality Learning at University*. Buckingham: Open University Press.

Biggs, J.B. (in press). The Reflective Institution: Assuring and Enhancing the Quality of Teaching and Learning. *Higher Education*

Bourke, S. (1986). How Smaller is Better: Some Relationships between Class Size, Teaching Practices, and Student Achievement. *American Educational Research Journal*, 23, 558-571.

Bowden, J. & Marton, F. (1998). *The University of Learning: Beyond Quality and Competence in Higher Education*. London: Kogan Page.

Carless, D. (1998). Managing Systematic Curriculum Change: A Critical Analysis of Hong Kong's Target Oriented Curriculum Initiative. In P. Stimpson & P. Morris (Eds.), *Curriculum and Assessment for Hong Kong: Two Components, One System*. Hong Kong: Open University of Hong Kong Press, 223-242.

Chang, W.C. (2000). In Search of the Chinese in all the Wrong Places! *Journal of Psychology in Chinese Societies*, 1(1), 125-142.

Dawkins, J. (1987). *Higher Education: A Policy Discussion Paper*. (Green Paper), Canberra: Government Printing Office.

Hess, R.D. & Azuma, M. (1991). Cultural Support for Schooling: Contrasts between Japan and the United States. *Educational Researcher*, 20 (9), 2-8.

Ho, D.Y.F. (1998). Filial Piety and Filicide in Chinese Family Relationships: The Legend of Shun and Other Stories. In M.P. Gielen & A.L. Comunian (Eds.), *The Family and Family Therapy in an International Perspective*. Trieste: Edizione LINT.

Johnson, K. & Yau, A.S.N. (1996). Coping with Second Language Texts: The Development of Lexically-based Reading Strategies. In D.A. Watkins & J.B. Biggs (Eds.), *The Chinese Learner: Cultural, Psychological, and Contextual Influences*. Hong Kong / Melbourne: Comparative Education Research Centre, The University of Hong Kong / Australian Council for Educational

Research., 123-141.

Kember, D. (1997). A Reconceptualisation of the Research into University Academics' Conceptions of Teaching. *Learning and Instruction*, 7(3), 255-275.

Lee, W.O. (1996). The Cultural Context of Chinese Learners: Conceptions of Learning in the Confucian Tradition. In D.A. Watkins & J.B. Biggs (Eds.), *The Chinese Learner: Cultural, Psychological, and Contextual Influences*. Hong Kong / Melbourne: Comparative Education Research Centre, The University of Hong Kong / Australian Council for Educational Research, 25-41.

Linn, M., Lewis, C., Tsuchida, I. & Songer, N.B. (2000). Beyond Fourth Grade Science: Why do US and Japanese Students Diverge? *Educational Researcher*, 29 (3), 4-14.

Marsh, H.W., Hau, K.T. & Kong, C.K. (2000). Late Immersion and Language Instruction (English vs Chinese) in Hong Kong High Schools: Achievement Growth in Language and Non-language Subjects. *Harvard Educational Review*, 70 (3), 302-346.

Morris, P. (1985). Teachers' Perceptions of the Barriers to the Implementation of a Pedagogic Innovation: A South East Asian Case Study. *International Review of Education*, 31, 3-18.

Morris, P. (1998). *The Hong Kong School Curriculum: Development, Issues and Policies*. Hong Kong: Hong Kong University Press.

Morris, P., Chan, K.K. & Lo, M.L. (1998). Changing Primary schools in Hong Kong: Perspectives on Policy and its Impact. In P. Stimpson & P. Morris (Eds.), *Curriculum and Assessment in Hong Kong: Two components, one system*. Hong Kong: The Open University of Hong Kong Press, 201-222.

Porter, A. (1989). A Curriculum Out of Balance: The Case of Elementary School Mathematics. *Educational Researcher*, 18(5), 9-15.

Prosser, M. & Trigwell, K. (1998). *Understanding Learning and Teaching: The Experience in Higher Education*. Milton Keynes: Open University Press.

O'Connor, J.E. (1991). A Descriptive Analysis of Chinese Teachers' Thought Processes. Paper presented at the Conference on Chinese Education for the 21st. Century, Honolulu, November 21.

Salomon, G. (1991). Transcending the Qualitative-quantitative Debate: The Analytic and Systemic Approaches to Educational Research. *Educational Researcher*, 20 (6), 10-18.

Schmidt, W., & et al. (1996). *A Summary of Characterizing Pedagogical Flow: An Investigation of Mathematics and Science Teaching in Six Countries*. London : Kluwer.

Siu, M.K. (1999). How did Candidates Pass the State Examination in Mathematics in the Tang Dynasty? Myth of the Confucian Heritage Culture Classroom. Troisième Université d'été Européene sur l'histoire et l'épistemologie dans l'éducation mathématique, Leuven, Belgium, July.

Stedman, L.C. (1997). International Achievement Differences: An Assessment of a New Perspective. *Educational Researcher*, 26(3), 4-15.

Stigler, J. & Hiebert, J. (1999). *The Teaching Gap*. New York: The Free Press.

Tang, C. & Biggs, J.B. (1996). How Hong Kong Students cope with Assessment. In D.A. Watkins & J.B. Biggs (Eds.), *The Chinese Learner: Cultural, Psychological, and Contextual Influences*. Hong Kong / Melbourne: Comparative Education Research Centre, The University of Hong Kong / Australian Council for Educational Research,159-182.

Zeng, K. (1999). *Dragon Gate: Competitive Examinations and their Consequences*. London: Cassell.

About the Authors

John BIGGS retired as Professor of Education at the University of Hong Kong in 1995, and is now an educational consultant based in Australia. He is interested in the conditions for effective learning, particularly in Confucian heritage cultures, teaching, and the assessment of learning.

Carol CHAN is an Associate Professor at the University of Hong Kong. Her research areas are learning and instruction, and design of learning environments to foster deep understanding. Currently, she is working with an Ontario Institute for Studies in Education/University of Toronto team in developing knowledge-building communities mediated by computer supported collaborative environments in Hong Kong classrooms.

CHIK Pui Man is a Senior Research Assistant in the Department of Curriculum Studies at the University of Hong Kong. Since 1995, she has worked on a number of projects related to critical issues in Hong Kong Education such as the evaluation and assessment of the Target Oriented Curriculum, language learning, and catering for individual differences. Her current research focus is on relationships between qualitative differences in teaching and learning.

Martin CORTAZZI is Professor of Language Education at Brunel University, UK. He has taught and trained teachers in Iran, China, Turkey, Lebanon and elsewhere. He has published books and articles on primary education and narrative analysis. His other research publications are in language and culture, literacy, vocabulary learning, discourse analysis, and cultures of learning.

Bo DAHLIN is an Associate Professor in Education at Karlstad University, Sweden. He has a special interest in philosophy and qualitative methodology. His empirical research consists of phenomenographic studies of conceptions in various fields, such as morality and religion and cross-cultural comparisons of notions of learning, knowledge and understanding.

Mats EKHOLM is Professor in Education at Karlstad University, Sweden. His research area has for many years been school effectiveness and school development. At present he is General Director of the Swedish National Agency for Education.

GAO Lingbiao is a senior science teacher educator at the Institute of Curriculum Study and Teaching Material Development at South China Normal University in Guangzhou, China.

Angela S.P. Ho is Senior Educational Development Officer at the Educational Development Centre, Hong Kong Polytechnic University. Her research interests include professional development of academic staff, student learning, and conceptual change teaching. She is course leader of the PgC/PgD/MEd in Teaching in Professional, Vocational and Higher Education offered by the Hong Kong Polytechnic University and is project director of a University Grants Committee funded project entitled: 'Learning to learn: Developing students' cognitive, motivational and interpersonal strategies for learning'.

Irene Ho is an Assistant Professor in Educational Psychology at the University of Hong Kong. As a professional educational psychologist, she has extensive experience working with children with special educational needs. Her research interests include behaviour management and motivation in educational contexts.

Jin Lixian is Senior Lecturer in Linguistics at De Montfort University, UK, where she teaches general linguistics, sociolinguistics, syntax and clinical linguistics. She has taught TESOL/linguistics courses and trained teachers at universities in China, Turkey and Britain. Her publications and research interests are in intercultural communication, academic cultures, cultures of learning, second language development, and narrative analysis.

David Kember is Deputy Director of the Educational Development Unit at Hong Kong Polytechnic University, and was formerly the Director of the Action Learning Research Project based in that Unit.

Ko Po Yuk is a Teaching Consultant in the Department of Curriculum Studies at the University of Hong Kong. Since 1994, she has worked in teacher education, specializing in Chinese education. Her research interests include expert teachers in China, computer-assisted language learning and school curriculum development in Hong Kong.

Tammy Kwan is an Associate Professor in the Department of Curriculum Studies at the University of Hong Kong. She graduated first from the University of Hong Kong and then from the University of Oxford and Queensland University of Technology. Her academic areas of interests are Social, Geographical and Environmental Education with particular emphasis on teaching and learning processes.

Lo Mun Ling is an Associate Professor in the Department of Curriculum Studies at the University of Hong Kong, where she has been a teacher educator since 1994. She has over 15 years' teaching experience in secondary schools in Hong Kong and Australia. Her research interests include chemistry teacher education, curriculum reform and teachers' professional development.

About the authors

Ference MARTON was for three years a Distinguished Visiting Professor in the Department of Curriculum Studies at the University of Hong Kong. He has now returned to Gothenburg University, Sweden.

Ida MOK is an Assistant Professor in the Department of Curriculum Studies at the University of Hong Kong. Since 1990, she has worked in teacher education, with specialization in mathematics education. She has been active in research on students' mathematics learning.

Dorothy F.P. NG has been a teaching fellow in the Department of Curriculum Studies of the University of Hong Kong since 1995. She has over 15 years of experience in teacher education. Her research interests include Chinese language education, linguistics analysis, classroom language, and medium of instruction.

PANG Ming Fai is a Teaching Consultant in the Department of Curriculum Studies of the University of Hong Kong. His research interests include learning and instruction, curriculum evaluation, and economics education.

Ulla RUNESSON is Senior Lecturer at the Department of Education, Gothenburg University, Sweden. Her research interests include learning and teaching process with a particular interest in mathematics education.

Farideh SALILI is a Professor in Psychology at the University of Hong Kong. She obtained her PhD from the University of Illinois, USA. Her research interest is in the area of student motivation and attribution theory. She has published extensively on student motivation and achievement across different cultures and contexts of learning.

Stephanie STOKES is an Associate Dean of the Faculty of Education, and Associate Professor in the Department of Speech and Hearing Sciences at the University of Hong Kong. With a colleague she piloted the implementation of Problem Based Learning in the department's BSc programme between 1995 and 1997, and was a principal architect in the conversion of the entire BSc degree from lecture-based to problem-based learning, which commenced in 1998. She has published research on the design, implementation and evaluation of Problem-Based learning.

Sandy Lin Hei SZETO is a research assistant at the University of Hong Kong. Since 1998, she has participated in a range of research projects involving provision for less able primary pupils, and the qualitative difference between language teaching and learning in classrooms. She specialises in teaching English as a second language. Her research interests include the matching of teacher-student beliefs in classrooms, and students' perceptions of learning English as a second language.

David WATKINS is a Professor in the Department of Education at the University of Hong Kong. His research interests are in cross-cultural aspects of teaching, learning, and self-concept.

Index

ability grouping 14-15; 135; 282; 292; 294
action research 19; 195; Ch 13; 277; 287; 291
approaches to learning/learning strategies 7-10; 12; 17; 45; 55-60; 67; 78; 179-180; 185-188; 192; 206; 219-222; 238-239; 244; 253; 261; 287; 291; 294
assessment
    backwash effects 17; Ch 3; 281-282; 290
    methods 3; Ch 3; 212-215; 283; 289-290; 292
attributions 6-7; 16; 80-86; 91-93; 275
authoritarian teaching 3-4; 13; 77; Ch 5; 275-276; 280; 284

Chinese values 3-4; 16; 18; 31; 37-38; 40-41; 64; 77; 89; 91; 97-99; 104; 110; 121; 181; 191; 204; 234-235; 263; 266; 278; 281; 283-286; 289; 293; 295
class size 3; 13-14; 62; Ch 6; 276; 279; 282-283; 286; 289-290; 295
collaborative/group learning 161; 179-181; 187-194; 203-204; 277; 288
conceptions in general 9; 45; 60; 223
    of learning 8-12; 17-18; 215; 219-222; 224-235; 237-238; 261; 287; 292
    of teaching 8; 10-13; 16-18; 25-27; 45; 60; 68; 114-119; 127; 181; 185; 187; 193; 198; 207; 215; 219-222; 224-239; 243; 248; 254; 258; 278-279; 288; 292
conceptual change 17; 183-185; 193; 195; 206-209; 219-221; 227-235; Ch 12; 263-264; 275
constructivist teaching 18; 179-183; 192-198; 278; 286

individualism-collectivism 8; 16; 98; 109; 204; 265; 278; 280
information technology/computer-assisted learning 188-192; 194; 258; 293

language of instruction 14; 63; Ch 7; 282-283; 285
learner-trained learning 122; 126-127; 278; 283; 287; 289

memorisation/rote learning 3; 5; 50; 78; 159-160; 182-184; 234; 253
moral view of teaching 30-33; 38; 40; 77; 98-99; 116; 122; 181-182; 197; 279-280
motivation 7; 30; 51; 66; 75; 78; 123; 204; 206; 265

paradox
    of the Chinese learner 3; 5; 6; 182
    of the Chinese teacher 3; 13; 160-161; 171; 174-175; 275; 285; 288; 290
phenomenography 9-10; 12; 45-49; 162-163; 221; 223-224; 230
problem-based learning 18; 58; 62; 181; 195; Ch 10; 258
punishment 75-77; 79; 87-90; 92; 101-106; 109-110; 280; 284

reform implementation 16; 18-19; 130; 160; 196; 198; 248-249; 270; 286; 290-292; 294

staff development 18; Ch 12; 206; 253; 267; 278; 285; 292; 294
student centred/teacher-centred teaching 12; 18; 26; 32-33; 76; 81; 108; 110; 115; 159; 162; 171; 174; 238; 254; 258; 276; 284; 288-289; 295

student/teacher relationship and interactions 18; 29; 31-32; Ch 4; 104; 106-107; 110; 121; 161; 197; 279-280
systems approach to understanding education 69-70; 276; 291; 294

Target Oriented Curriculum 15-16; 76-79; 160-61; 181; 196; 281; 285; 291-294
teaching strategies 1; 11; 13; 15; 17-18; 25; 29; 31; 68; 75; 117; 122; 124-130; 142-144; 219; 292; 295

variation and the learning space 138-139; 155-156; 162-175; 285

CERC Publications

Series: CERC Studies in Comparative Education

25. Carol K.K. Chan & Nirmala Rao (eds.) (2009): *Revisiting the Chinese Learner: Changing Contexts, Changing Education.* ISBN 978-962-8093-16-8. 360pp. HK$250/US$38.

24. Donald B. Holsinger & W. James Jacob (eds.) (2008): *Inequality in Education: Comparative and International Perspectives.* ISBN 978-962-8093-14-4. 584pp. HK$300/US$45.

23. Nancy Law, Willem J Pelgrum & Tjeerd Plomp (eds.) (2008): *Pedagogy and ICT Use in Schools around the World: Findings from the IEA SITES 2006 Study.* ISBN 978-962-8093-65-6. 296pp. HK$250/US$38.

22. David L. Grossman, Wing On Lee & Kerry J. Kennedy (eds.) (2008): *Citizenship Curriculum in Asia and the Pacific.* ISBN 978-962-8093-69-4. 268pp. HK$200/US$32.

21. Vandra Masemann, Mark Bray & Maria Manzon (eds.) (2007): *Common Interests, Uncommon Goals: Histories of the World Council of Comparative Education Societies and its Members.* ISBN 978-962-8093-10-6. 384pp. HK$250/US$38.

20. Peter D. Hershock, Mark Mason & John N. Hawkins (eds.) (2007): *Changing Education: Leadership, Innovation and Development in a Globalizing Asia Pacific.* ISBN 978-962-8093-54-0. 348pp. HK$200/US$32.

19. Mark Bray, Bob Adamson & Mark Mason (eds.) (2007): *Comparative Education Research: Approaches and Methods.* ISBN 978-962-8093-53-3. 444pp. HK$250/US$38.

18. Aaron Benavot & Cecilia Braslavsky (eds.) (2006): *School Knowledge in Comparative and Historical Perspective: Changing Curricula in Primary and Secondary Education.* ISBN 978-962-8093-52-6. 315pp. HK$200/US$32.

17. Ruth Hayhoe (2006): *Portraits of Influential Chinese Educators.* ISBN 978-962-8093-40-3. 398pp. HK$250/US$38.

16. Peter Ninnes & Meeri Hellstén (eds.) (2005): *Internationalizing Higher Education: Critical Explorations of Pedagogy and Policy.* ISBN 978-962-8093-37-3. 231pp. HK$200/US$32.

15. Alan Rogers (2004): *Non-Formal Education: Flexible Schooling or Participatory Education?* ISBN 978-962-8093-30-4. 316pp. HK$200/US$32.

14. W.O. Lee, David L. Grossman, Kerry J. Kennedy & Gregory P. Fairbrother (eds.) (2004): *Citizenship Education in Asia and the Pacific: Concepts and Issues.* ISBN 978-962-8093-59-5. 313pp. HK$200/US$32.

13. Mok Ka-Ho (ed.) (2003): *Centralization and Decentralization: Educational Reforms and Changing Governance in Chinese Societies*. ISBN 978-962-8093-58-8. 230pp. HK$200/US$32.

12. Robert A. LeVine (2003): *Childhood Socialization: Comparative Studies of Parenting, Learning and Educational Change*. ISBN 978-962-8093-61-8. 299pp. HK$200/US$32. [Out of print]

11. Ruth Hayhoe & Julia Pan (eds.) (2001): *Knowledge Across Cultures: A Contribution to Dialogue Among Civilizations*. ISBN 978-962-8093-73-1. 391pp. HK$250/US$38. [Out of print]

10. William K. Cummings, Maria Teresa Tatto & John Hawkins (eds.) (2001): *Values Education for Dynamic Societies: Individualism or Collectivism*. ISBN 978-962-8093-71-7. 312pp. HK$200/US$32.

9. Gu Mingyuan (2001): *Education in China and Abroad: Perspectives from a Lifetime in Comparative Education*. ISBN 978-962-8093-70-0. 252pp. HK$200/US$32.

8. Thomas Clayton (2000): *Education and the Politics of Language: Hegemony and Pragmatism in Cambodia, 1979-1989*. ISBN 978-962-8093-83-0. 243pp. HK$200/US$32.

7. Mark Bray & Ramsey Koo (eds.) (2004): *Education and Society in Hong Kong and Macao: Comparative Perspectives on Continuity and Change*. Second edition. ISBN 978-962-8093-34-2. 323pp. HK$200/US$32.

6. T. Neville Postlethwaite (1999): *International Studies of Educational Achievement: Methodological Issues*. ISBN 978-962-8093-86-1. 86pp. HK$100/US$20.

5. Harold Noah & Max A. Eckstein (1998): *Doing Comparative Education: Three Decades of Collaboration*. ISBN 978-962-8093-87-8. 356pp. HK$250/US$38.

4. Zhang Weiyuan (1998): *Young People and Careers: A Comparative Study of Careers Guidance in Hong Kong, Shanghai and Edinburgh*. ISBN 978-962-8093-89-2. 160pp. HK$180/US$30.

3. Philip G. Altbach (1998): *Comparative Higher Education: Knowledge, the University, and Development*. ISBN 978-962-8093-88-5. 312pp. HK$180/US$30.

2. Mark Bray & W.O. Lee (eds.) (1997): *Education and Political Transition: Implications of Hong Kong's Change of Sovereignty*. ISBN 978-962-8093-90-8. 169pp. [Out of print]

1. Mark Bray & W.O. Lee (eds.) (2001): *Education and Political Transition: Themes and Experiences in East Asia*. Second edition. ISBN 978-962-8093-84-7. 228pp. HK$200/US$32.

Series: CERC Monographs Series in Comparative and International Education and Development

6. Eduardo Andere (2008): *The Lending Power of PISA: League Tables and Best Practice in International Education.* ISBN 978-988-17852-1-3. 138pp. HK$100/US$16.

5. Linda Chisholm, Graeme Bloch & Brahm Fleisch (eds.) (2008): *Education, Growth, Aid and Development: Towards Education For All.* ISBN 978-962-8093-99-1. 116pp. HK$100/US$16.

4. Mark Bray & Seng Bunly (2005): *Balancing the Books: Household Financing of Basic Education in Cambodia.* ISBN 978-962-8093-39-7. 113pp. HK$100/US$16.

3. Maria Manzon (2004): *Building Alliances: Schools, Parents and Communities in Hong Kong and Singapore.* ISBN 978-962-8093-36-3. 117pp. HK$100/US$16.

2. Mark Bray, Ding Xiaohao & Huang Ping (2004): *Reducing the Burden on the Poor: Household Costs of Basic Education in Gansu, China.* ISBN 978-962-8093-32-8. 67pp. HK$50/US$10. [Also available in Chinese]

1. Yoko Yamato (2003): *Education in the Market Place: Hong Kong's International Schools and their Mode of Operation.* ISBN 978-962-8093-57-1. 117pp. HK$100/US$16.

Series: Education in Developing Asia

1. Don Adams (2004): *Education and National Development: Priorities, Policies, and Planning.* ISBN 978-971-561-529-7. 81pp. HK$100/US$12 each or HK$400/US$50 for set of five.

2. David Chapman (2004): *Management and Efficiency in Education: Goals and Strategies.* ISBN 978-971-561-530-3. 85pp. HK$100/US$12 each or HK$400/US$50 for set of five.

3. Mark Bray (2004): *The Costs and Financing of Education: Trends and Policy Implications.* ISBN 978-971-561-531-0. 78pp. HK$100/US$12 each or HK$400/US$50 for set of five.

4. W.O. Lee (2004): *Equity and Access to Education: Themes, Tensions, and Policies.* ISBN 978-971-561-532-7. 101pp. HK$100/US$12 each or HK$400/US$50 for set of five.

5. David Chapman & Don Adams (2004): *The Quality of Education: Dimensions and Strategies.* ISBN 978-971-561-533-4. 72pp. HK$100/US$12 each or HK$400/US$50 for set of five.

Other books published by CERC

- 貝磊、古鼎儀編 (第二版) (2006)。《香港與澳門的教育與社會：從比較角度看延續與變化》。ISBN 978-7-107-19379-8. 361pp. HK$60/US$10. [簡體版]

- 貝磊、丁小浩、黃平 (2004):《減輕貧困家庭的負擔: 中國甘肅基礎教育的家庭成本》。ISBN 978-962-8093-33-5。53pp。HK$50/US$10. [Also available in English]

- Ruth Hayhoe (2004): *Full Circle: A Life with Hong Kong and China*. ISBN 978-962-8093-31-1. 261pp. HK$200/US$32.

- Yoko Yamato & Sally Course (2002): *Guide to International Schools in Hong Kong*. ISBN 978-962-8093-62-5. 82pp. HK$72/US$12.

- Mark Bray with Roy Butler, Philip Hui, Ora Kwo & Emily Mang (2002): *Higher Education in Macau: Growth and Strategic Development*. ISBN 978-962-8093-60-1. 127pp. HK$150/US$24.

- 貝磊、古鼎儀編 (第二版) (2005):《香港與澳門的教育與社會：從比較角度看延續與變化》。ISBN 978-957-496-478-9。318pp。HK$200/US$32. [繁體版]

- David A. Watkins & John B. Biggs (eds.) (2001, first reprinted 2009): *Teaching the Chinese Learner: Psychological and Pedagogical Perspectives*. ISBN 978-962-8093-72-4. 306pp. HK$200/US$32.

- Ruth Hayhoe (1999): *China's Universities 1895-1995: A Century of Cultural Conflict*. ISBN 978-962-8093-81-6. 299pp. HK$200/US$32. [Out of print]

- David A. Watkins & John B. Biggs (eds.) (1996, first reprinted 1999, second reprinted 2005): *The Chinese Learner: Cultural, Psychological and Contextual Influences*. ISBN 978-0-86431-182-5. 285pp. HK$200/ US$32.

- Mark Bray & R. Murray Thomas (eds.) (1998): *Financing of Education in Indonesia*. ISBN 978-971-561-172-5. 133pp. HK$140/US$20. [Out of print]

Order through bookstores or from:

Comparative Education Research Centre
Faculty of Education
The University of Hong Kong
Pokfulam Road, Hong Kong, China.

Fax: (852) 2517 4737
E-mail: cerc@hkusub.hku.hk
Website: www.hku.hk/cerc

The list prices above are applicable for order from CERC, and include sea mail postage. Please refer to the website for postage by air mail.

CERC Studies in Comparative Education 25

Revisiting The Chinese Learner
Changing Contexts, Changing Education

Edited by
Carol K.K. Chan & Nirmala Rao

This book, which extends pioneering work on Chinese learners in two previous volumes, examines teaching and learning in Chinese societies and advances understanding of 'the Chinese learner' in changing global contexts. Given the burgeoning research in this area, pedagogical shifts from knowledge transmission to knowledge construction to knowledge creation, wide-ranging social, economic and technological advances, and changes in educational policy, *Revisiting The Chinese Learner* is a timely endeavor.

The book revisits the paradox of the Chinese learner against the background of these educational changes; considers how Chinese cultural beliefs and contemporary change influence learning; and examines how Chinese teachers and learners respond to new educational goals, interweaving new and old beliefs and practices. Contributors focus on both continuity and change in analyzing student learning, pedagogical practice, teacher learning and professional development in Chinese societies. Key emerging themes emphasize transcending dichotomies and transforming pedagogy in understanding and teaching Chinese learners. The book has implications for theories of learning, development and educational innovation and will therefore be of interest to scholars and educators around the world who are changing education in their changing contexts.

Carol K.K. Chan is an Associate Professor in the Faculty of Education at The University of Hong Kong. Her research areas include learning, cognition and instruction, computer-supported knowledge building and teacher communities for classroom innovation. She is currently Co-Director of a Strategic Research Theme on Sciences of Learning at The University of Hong Kong.

Nirmala Rao is a Professor in the Faculty of Education at The University of Hong Kong. She is a Developmental and Educational Psychologist whose research focuses on early childhood development and education. She has also been actively involved, at the international level, in several professional organizations concerned both with the well-being of young children and research on early child development.

Publisher:
Comparative Education Research Centre (CERC) and Springer
June 2009; 360 pages; ISBN 978 962 8093 16 8; HK$250/US$38

CERC Studies in Comparative Education 24

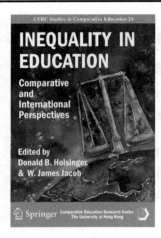

INEQUALITY IN EDUCATION

Comparative and International Perspectives

Edited by

Donald B. Holsinger & W. James Jacob

Inequality in Education: Comparative and International Perspectives is a compilation of conceptual chapters and national case studies that includes a series of methods for measuring education inequalities. The book provides up-to-date scholarly research on global trends in the distribution of formal schooling in national populations. It also offers a strategic comparative and international education policy statement on recent shifts in education inequality, and new approaches to explore, develop and improve comparative education and policy research globally. Contributing authors examine how education as a process interacts with government finance policy to form patterns of access to education services. In addition to case perspectives from 18 countries across six geographic regions, the volume includes six conceptual chapters on topics that influence education inequality, such as gender, disability, language and economics, and a summary chapter that presents new evidence on the pernicious consequences of inequality in the distribution of education. The book offers (1) a better and more holistic understanding of ways to measure education inequalities; and (2) strategies for facing the challenge of inequality in education in the processes of policy formation, planning and implementation at the local, regional, national and global levels.

Donald B. Holsinger is Professor Emeritus in Education and Development Studies at Brigham Young University, and has held academic appointments at the University of Chicago, the University of Arizona, and the State University of New York (Albany). He is a former President of the Comparative and International Education Society and Senior Education Specialist at the World Bank.

W. James Jacob is Director of the Institute for International Studies in Education at the University of Pittsburgh's School of Education, and is the former Assistant Director of the Center for International and Development Education at the University of California (Los Angeles).

Publisher:
Comparative Education Research Centre (CERC) and Springer
December 2008; 584 pages; ISBN 978 962 8093 14 4; HK$300/US$45